VICEREGAL ADMINISTRATION
IN THE
SPANISH-AMERICAN COLONIES

VICEREGAL ADMINISTRATION

IN THE

SPANISH-AMERICAN COLONIES

BY

LILLIAN ESTELLE FISHER

NEW YORK / RUSSELL & RUSSELL

UNIVERSITY OF CALIFORNIA PUBLICATIONS IN HISTORY

Volume 15, 1926

REISSUED, 1967, BY RUSSELL & RUSSELL

A DIVISION OF ATHENEUM HOUSE, INC.

BY ARRANGEMENT WITH THE UNIVERSITY OF CALIFORNIA PRESS

L.C. CATALOG CARD NO: 66−27069

PRINTED IN THE UNITED STATES OF AMERICA

TO MY MOTHER

ERRATA

Page 13, line 9. *For* Santa *read* Santo.

Page 71, line 1. *For* Santa *read* Santo.

Page 88, line 16. *For* Aviles *read* Avilas.

Page 212, line 7. *For* Marcillo *read* Morcillo.

Page 261, line 5 from bottom. *For* Carillo *read* Carrillo.

Page 344, line 6 from bottom. *For* Manual *read* Manuel.

Page 345, line 11. *For* Gasco *read* Gasca.

Page 346, line 20. *For* Morcello *read* Morcillo.

CONTENTS

CHAPTER V

The Vice-Patron: Religious Organizations

CHAPTER VI

The Vice-Patron: Education, Hospitals and Charity

CHAPTER VII

The Viceroy as Captain-General

CHAPTER VIII

The Viceroy and the People

PREFACE

A comprehensive study of viceregal administration in the Spanish-American colonies has long been needed. Donald E. Smith paved the way in *The Viceroy of New Spain,* but that book treats only the viceroys of Mexico for the latter part of the eighteenth century, a period of decreased powers for the viceroy and therefore not typical for the colonial executive. The administrative functions of the viceroy are here presented as they existed in New Spain and South America during the whole colonial period. To do this it has been necessary to cover a wide field in order to examine all phases of the gubernatorial duties of the viceroy under varying conditions and in different centuries.

Very little has been written on this subject, hence many of the materials are here used for this purpose for the first time. The most valuable of these have been the instructions which the viceroys left to their successors, the memorias of the viceroys, their royal instructions, their correspondence, the laws of the Indies, and many royal cédulas. The monumental *Recopilación de leyes de los reynos de las Indias* alone, if not supplemented by the instructions of the viceroys in order to see which laws were actually put into practice in the viceroyalties, would not be a true guide for a study of this nature. Used with the other materials referred to above, it is most valuable. The *Política indiana,* written by Solórzano y Pereyra (1629–1639) and edited by Francisco Ramiro Valenzuela (1776), which is an exposition and defense of the whole Spanish colonial system, has been very helpful. Many other works relating to colonial institutions in general, which have a bearing on the subject of viceregal administration, were used; however no attempt has been made to exhaust them, since this would take a lifetime. The spelling of the documents is kept in the footnotes and bibliography. The abbreviation AGI is used frequently for Archivo General de Indias.

Acknowledgment is gladly made of the helpful instruction of Professor Priestley during the years 1922, 1923, and 1924. To him and to Professor Chapman I owe my interest in Spanish-American history. The friendly interest of Professor Bolton has been much appreciated. I am especially grateful to Professor Priestley for his valuable advice and kindness.

LILLIAN ESTELLE FISHER.

CHAPTER I

THE VICEROY: HIS POWERS AND LIMITATIONS

The era of the viceroyalties was the most significant period in Spanish-American history. It was then that the foundation was laid for the language, religion, culture, and traditions of the modern Latin-American republics. In the present survey of the four viceroyalties and the causes for their establishment it will be shown that there was need of one man, untrammeled by the turmoils of the conquest, to rule over these great divisions. We must pass in review some of the men chosen for the high position of viceroy, and make a study of the powers of the viceroys and the limitations imposed upon them by the sovereign to keep them faithful to duty in dependencies so far distant from the mother country.

1. THE ESTABLISHMENT OF THE VICEROYALTIES

Viceroyalties were established by the Spanish monarch in his American possessions after the rule of the audiencias had proved to be a failure. Since the institution of the office of viceroy had been successful in Sardinia, Sicily, Naples, Aragon, Valencia, and had also been employed by Venice and Portugal in the Orient, it was thought to be particularly suitable for the distant colonies in America. The good results from the founding of the viceroyalties which held for one nation such a vast extent of territory for almost three centuries, more than justified the venture.

One man was needed—a powerful personage—to govern kingdoms so far.from Spain, one to whom the vassals in those remote provinces might go for assistance and from whom they could ask all that ought to be hoped for from a king.[1] A man of great prestige who was higher than the audiencia—one worthy indeed, to represent the monarch himself—must be chosen viceroy. Accordingly, it became customary to appoint the viceroy from among the distinguished nobles of the royal court. At first appointment to the new office of viceroy in America was not eagerly sought. Three names had been proposed for royal confirmation by the Council of the Indies for the position of viceroy of Mexico before Antonio de Mendoza, the fourth choice, was finally persuaded, in 1528, to accept the office.[2]

The authority of the viceroy was almost supreme during the first half of the sixteenth century, but time slightly modified the extent of this power. He was the highest official in the New World; in the provinces under his control he might do and order all that the king would be able to perform if he resided in them except in expressly stated prohibitions. All the ceremonies provided for kings in the royal chapel were to be observed in the case of the viceroys.[3] As the king's chief representatives, they were to administer justice equally to all subjects, take charge of everything conducive to the peace and welfare of the provinces, provide what was fitting for them, reward the descendants of the conquerors, and collect money for the treasury. With the royal assent they could make ordinances, put them into effect, revoke those not approved by the king, grant Indians under the encomienda system, remove governors, corregidores, and lesser officials, appoint judges of residencia for minor functionaries, dispatch fleets and armadas, protect the Indians, prevent disorders, keep the Catholic religion pure, preside over the audi-

---

[1] Solórzano y Pereyra, Juan de, *Política indiana* (Madrid, 1776), II, lib. 5, cap. 12–13, pp. 366–367, 376.

[2] Priestley, H. I., *The Mexican Nation, A History* (New York, 1923), 54.

[3] Croix, *Instrucción que . . . . dejó*, AGI, 85–5–13; Montesclaros to his successor, 1615, *Documentos inéditos . . . . de Indias* (*Madrid*, 1864–84), VI, 189; Antequera, José María, *Historia de la legislación española* (ed. 2, Madrid, 1884), 484.

encia, and perform innumerable other duties, the most important of which will be discussed in the proper place.[4]

The viceregal functions as they developed until the establishment of the intendancies in 1786 may be grouped generally under four divisions. The first included the civil, political, and economic administration, the second the supervision of the royal treasury and its branches, the third the use and conservation of the royal patronage, and the fouth the duties of the office of captain-general.[5] For a short time, the viceroy was relieved of the tasks connected with the second division by the intendants, but he performed all the other duties until the era of Spanish-American independence.

The first and by far the most important viceroyalties were New Spain, established in 1535, and Peru, in 1542. The viceroyalty of New Spain stretched northward from the isthmus of Tehuantepec on the south, including Guatemala or Central America, and the present republic of Venezuela. The most northerly boundary of Mexico in 1670 was the Savannah River. The provinces of the Californias, Texas, New Mexico, the lands between Louisiana and the Pacific, Louisiana from 1762 to 1801, the West Indies, Florida, and the Philippines from 1565 to 1584, formed part of it.[6] Louisiana and the two Floridas, however, were never governed directly by the viceroy, since they belonged to the captaincy-general of Havana. During the greater part of the history of the Philippines, the governor was independent

---

[4] *Recopilación de leyes de los reynos de las Indias* (ed. 4, Madrid, 1791), leyes 1, 2 tit. 3, lib. 3; Esquilache to Guadalcázar, 1621, *Memorias de los vireyes que han gobernado Perú* (Lima, 1859), I, 101–102; Palafox to his successor, 1642, *Documentos inéditos o muy raros para la historia de México* (Mexico, 1905–11), VII, 27; Branciforte to Azanza, 1797, *Instrucciones que los vireyes de Nueva España dejaron a sus sucesores* (Mexico, 1867), art. 6, p. 129.

[5] Croix, *Instrucción que . . . . dejó*, AGI, 88–5–13; Revillagigedo to Amarillas, 1754, *Instrucciones que los vireyes . . . .* art. 26, p. 10.

[6] *Recopilación*, leyes 1–14, tit. 15, lib. 2; Riva Palacio, Vicente, *México á través de los siglos* (Barcelona, 1888–89), II, 227–228, 462, 661–664; Rivera, Agustín, *Principios críticos sobre el vireinato de la Nueva España sobre la revolución de independencia* (San Juan de Lagos, 1884–88), I, 66.

of the administration in New Spain and directly responsible to the Council of the Indies.[7] The early viceroyalty of Peru extended from the borders of New Spain to Patagonia and included all the lands except Brazil.[8]

Two other viceroyalties were organized in South America when the population increased and it became felt that the seat of government was so far away that it was almost inaccessible and authority so weak that smuggling could not be prevented. The viceroyalty of Nueva Granada was established in 1718 to guard against the aggressions of the English; it was suppressed in 1724 because of its great cost, but was reëstablished in 1740. The jurisdiction of this viceroyalty extended over the northwestern part of the continent, including the isthmus of Panamá, Darien, the province of Veragua, and Quito.[9] In 1776 the fourth viceroyalty, Rio de la Plata, was organized as a barrier against the illicit commerce which the Portuguese carried on with Buenos Aires, but it was not until 1777 that the king declared it permanent.[10]

2. THE VICEROYS

The viceroys for the most part were efficient men who tried to perform faithfully the trust that was placed in them. A few were great men, others had only medium capabilities, and some were weak or corrupt. The first viceroy of New Spain, Antonio de Mendoza, could hardly be surpassed, and won the title of "father of the poor." The elder Velasco was called the "father of the country," and his able son was also a strong viceroy. The austere archbishop viceroy, Moya de Contreras, of Mexico and

---

[7] Cunningham, Charles H., *The Audiencia in the Spanish Colonies* (Berkeley, 1919), 39, 194.

[8] Montesclaros to his successor, 1615, *Memorias de los vireyes . . . .*, I, 4.

[9] Pinkerton, John, *Modern Geography* (London, 1807), III, 614, 618; Caroleu, José, *América historia de su colonización dominación é independencia* (Barcelona, 1894–95), I, 310.

[10] Pinkerton, *op. cit*, III, 529–530; Moses, Bernard, *Spain's Declining Power in South America*, 1730–1806 (Berkeley, 1919), 154, 159–160, 168.

the second Velasco, who served in Mexico and Peru, were highly honored by being made presidents of the Council of the Indies. Monterey was so incorruptible that at his death he left nothing and the audiencia had to pay for his burial. Montesclaros was a wise administrator of New Spain and Peru, who added luster to the name of viceroy. The first Alburquerque was an uncompromising executive who strictly carried out the duties of his office. The second Revillagigedo and Bucareli, perhaps, stand out as the most active and statesmanlike viceroys in the history of New Spain. In Peru, the first Marquis of Cañete was a cultured gentleman celebrated for his military, political, and administrative experience. Francisco de Toledo had remarkable executive ability and was noted for his judicious ordinances, which were observed for many years. He was called the Peruvian Solon. Teodoro de Croix, a good administrator, was one of the greatest military viceroys of Peru. Palata was zealous and intelligent, and Lemos ranks as a reformer, prudent ruler, and lover of literature. Solís, Guirior, Góngora, and Espeleta of Nueva Granada were eager patrons of culture and science.

On the other hand, several viceroys used their position to enrich themselves or to gain more power. Escalona and Baños became extremely unpopular because of their arbitrary acts. The first Revillagigedo acquired a huge fortune by speculating in the tobacco trade of Havana.[11] Branciforte did not live up to the beneficial and honest administration of the second Revillagigedo, for he increased his wealth by the sale of military offices. Iturrigaray made enormous profits from the illicit sale of merchandise and offices, from a levy on quicksilver, the acceptance of forbidden gifts, and by other fraudulent means.[12]

During the sixteenth century the viceroys were, as a rule, carefully chosen, experienced men who had already won dis-

---

[11] Bancroft, Hubert H., *History of Mexico* (San Francisco, 1883–87), III, 358–359; Priestley, *The Mexican Nation*, 185.

[12] Rivera Cambas, Manuel, *Los gobernantes de México* (Mexico, 1872–73), I, 488–489; Bancroft, *History of Mexico*, III, 487–490; *ibid.*, IV, 23–25.

tinction in the royal service. In the seventeenth century military viceroys were preferred for both Mexico and Peru.[13] In the latter part of the eighteenth century especially, and in the early nineteenth century, the kings grew careless in their choice. Some men were already hoary with age when they began to serve in the office. Those of the more aggressive type, like Toledo, the second Velasco during his second term in Mexico, Montañez, and O'Higgins may be numbered among the best colonial executives, but others, like Peralta, Coruña, Salvatierra, Pedro Melo de Portugal, and Garibay, were too lenient and lacking in energy to deal with corrupt officials. The Duke of Veragua was so feeble that he died after governing in Mexico for six days.[14] Of the later viceroys, Villarroel said that almost all of them returned to Spain with a very superficial knowledge of their viceroyalties; many of them were more interested in other matters than the obligations of their office.[15]

Several Spanish grandees received the viceregal appointment, but only the names of the first Alburquerque of Mexico and Esquilache of Peru stand out among them as competent executives. Escalona, the first grandee viceroy, was a failure; Veragua died in six days after his arrival in New Spain; Fuenclara was a very ordinary viceroy; no praises were sung in Peru concerning the Prince of Santa Bono; and Branciforte was one of the most corrupt and unpopular viceroys.

There were but four American-born viceroys, Moctezuma, Casafuerte, and Figueroa of Mexico, and O'Higgins of Peru. Casafuerte and O'Higgins both won fame as viceroys. The former, born in Lima, was remembered as the "great governor"

---

[13] The most noted military viceroys of New Spain and Peru in the seventeenth and eighteenth centuries were: Gelves, Mancera, Monclova, Casafuerte, Villagarcía, the first Revillagigedo, Amarillas, Cruíllas, Amat, the Marquis of Croix, Bucareli, Mayorga, Matías de Gálvez, Bernardo de Gálvez, Teodoro de Croix, and Avilés.

[14] Bancroft, *History of Mexico*, II, 738–739; *ibid.*, III, 268, 277; Moses, *Spain's Declining Power*, 382–383; Rivera Cambas, I, 87, 237, 461.

[15] Villarroel, Hipólito, *Enfermedades políticas que padece la capital de esta Nueva España* . . . . MS., I, pt. II, pp. 9–10, 23–24.

of New Spain—a worthy representative, indeed, of the creole class. He abolished the practice of selling offices to the highest bidder, would not receive gifts or favors, did not allow his household to intermeddle with appointments, which he based entirely upon merit, and was a great promoter of public improvements.[16] Moctezuma and Figueroa were as good as the average executive. The example of these four viceroys clearly shows that creoles were capable of filling successfully even the highest office.

The policy of advancing deserving governors or captains-general to the position of viceroy was followed during the latter part of the eighteenth century. The first Revillagigedo, Cagigal, Bucareli, Espeleta of Nueva Granada, and Apodaca had served in Cuba, either as captains-general or governors, before being promoted to the office.[17] Matias de Gálvez had been president, governor, and captain-general of Guatemala, Teodoro de Croix had seen long years of successful military service in Mexico; Marquina was governor of the Philippines, where he committed many offenses, but in spite of them he managed to become viceroy of Mexico and to continue his dishonest acts by engaging in smuggling with Jamaica.[18] Five men who won the royal approval because of their experience in Chile were viceroys of Peru, and Juan Pimienta, governor of Cartagena, became the chief executive of Nueva Granada, though death claimed him in four days.[19]

Promotion from one viceroyalty to another was frequent, and to be invited to go to Peru was the greatest honor of all. This custom began with the great Mendoza, whose administration in New Spain had been so successful that the king decided to send him to the more turbulent region of Peru. Nine viceroys of New

[16] Rivera Cambas, I, 284, 326; Bancroft, *History of Mexico*, III, 349-350, f. 355.

[17] Priestley, *The Mexican Nation*, 185; Bancroft, *History of Mexico*, III, 360, 371; *ibid.*, IV, 648; Moses, *Spain's Declining Power*, 275.

[18] Bancroft, *History of Mexico*, III, 385-386; Croix, Charles François, *Correspondance du Marquis de Croix, capitaine general des armées de S. M. C., viceroi du Mexique* (Nantes, 1891), 249; Cunningham, 143-144.

[19] *See* Appendix II.

Spain attained this high ambition, to serve in Peru, also Viceroy Guirior and Viceroy Gil of Nueva Granada and Avilés of Buenos Aires.[20] Not many South American viceroys were chosen for Mexico, the most notable case being Flórez who came from Nueva Granada.

No fixed term was decided upon for the early viceroys. Mendoza's term, practically speaking, was for life, since he died in office after being transferred to Peru, and the first Velasco governed fourteen years until his death. In some of the early instructions, it was stated that the viceroys enjoyed their positions during the pleasure of the king. Finally, it was thought best to limit the term, accordingly a cédula of March 10, 1555, referring to the appointment of the first Cañete to the viceroyalty of Peru, declared his term to be six years, beginning from the day that he arrived in Lima and took charge of the government. The same limit was implied in a decree of March 28, 1620, directed to Esquilache.[21] This rule was not strictly followed, as the king did not always send the viceroy's successor when the time had expired. Later the three-year period, which had been employed in Naples, Sardinia, and Sicily, was adopted, but the king extended the period whenever he saw fit, sometimes duplicating it in favor of those who were especially distinguished by their service.[22] For instance, the Count of Chinchón and Mancera of Peru held office for ten years under this rule. Others served for eight or nine years; Viceroy Cerda of Nueva Granada acted as colonial executive for twelve years. During the eighteenth century the term was made five years.[23] Few viceroys were appointed for a second term; either their years of service were extended or they were promoted to another viceroyalty. Of all the vice-

---

20 *See* Appendix II.

21 Solórzano, II, lib. 5, cap. 14, art. 24, p. 391.

22 Merriaman, Roger Bigelow, *The Rise of the Spanish Empire in the Old World and in the New* (New York, 1918), I, 506, 515; II, 310; *Recopilación* ley 71, tit. 3, lib. 3; ley 1, tit. 2, lib. 5.

23 Alamán, Lucas, *Historia de Méjico* . . . . (Mexico, 1849–52), I, 44.

roys, only the second Velasco, Mancera, and Montañez served two terms in one viceroyalty, and Mancera alone filled consecutive terms.

A number of viceroys died in office; therefore it became necessary to make some provision for governing in the interim until arrival of the succeeding viceroy.[24] In the sixteenth and early seventeenth centuries the audiencia usually served ad interim. It appointed one of its members president who virtually took the place of a viceroy.[25] The audiencia of Mexico ruled fourteen times during the colonial period, but that of Peru not so frequently, no doubt on account of remembrance of the early turbulent days in the southern viceroyalty. However, the audiencia usually governed in Peru for a longer period than in New Spain.[26]

Pliegos de mortaja, or letters sent by the king to designate who should fill the place of a deceased viceroy until his successor arrived, were finally adopted in order to prevent misunderstandings. The viceroy himself brought with him a sealed letter addressed to the audiencia, which could be opened only in case of his death.[27] In the latter part of the seventeenth century it became the custom to name the archbishop in the pliego de mortaja or providencia; but the ecclesiastics elevated to the high position of chief executive seemed no more successful than the average viceroy. A very few really great names like Moya de Contreras, the first inquisitor-general of Mexico, Palafox, Liñan of Peru, and Caballero y Góngora of Nueva Granada, were among them.[28]

As soon as it was reported that the viceroy had died, one of the government clerks hastened to the viceregal palace to confirm

---

24 Twelve viceroys of Mexico and nine of Peru died in office, but several others died before leaving the country. See González Obregón, Luis, *México viejo* . . . . (Paris, Mexico, 1900), 429–432; Appendix II.

25 Account concerning Cañete, *Documentos inéditos* . . . . *de Indias*, VIII, 390; Riva Palacio, II, 664.

26 For the dates refer to Orozco, Wistano Luis, *Legislación y jurisprudencia sobre terrenos baldíos* (Mexico, 1895), 169–180; Appendix II.

27 Pérez y López, Antonio Xavier, *Teatro de la legislación de España é Indias* . . . . (Madrid, 1791–98), XXVIII, 554–555.

28 For the other ecclesiastical viceroys *see* Appendices I, II, III.

the fact. The secretary of the viceroyalty then officially notified the audiencia, and immediately an extraordinary acuerdo of oidores was summoned to fill the vacancy. The pliego de mortaja was opened and read in the presence of the regent, the fiscals, and all the judges of the audiencia. If there was no pliego de mortaja, it was declared by auto that the audiencia should take charge of the government; the regent, or in case there was no regent, the senior oidor assumed the duties of viceroy. After all the judges had signed the pliego, it was submitted to the person named in it to perform the functions of administration.[29]

The salary of the viceroy was high enough to maintain the dignity of his office, but at first it was not regulated by rule. Mendoza received 6000 ducats to be paid from the day that he set sail from the port of San Lucar, and was granted an additional allowance of 2000 ducats for his bodyguard.[30] The first viceroy of Peru, Blasco Núñez Vela, received a salary of only 5000 ducats, but in a short time the amount was raised to 40,000, the sum which Francisco de Toledo and the second Marquis of Cañete received.[31] In 1614 a law of the Indies, confirmed by others in 1628, 1653, 1659, 1660, and 1663, fixed the emoluments of viceroys of Peru at 30,000 ducats and those of Mexican viceroys at 20,000, beginning from the day they took possession of their office and continuing until their successor began to serve. Fully six months were allowed for the voyage to Peru or New Spain and another six months for the return trip.[32] In the middle of the eighteenth century the salary of viceroys of Mexico was raised to 40,000 and even to 60,000 pesos.[33] The remuneration of the Marquis of Croix amounted to 70,000 pesos and that

---

[29] González Obregón, *México viejo*, 428–429.

[30] Puga, Vasco de, *Provisiones, cédulas, instrucciones de su Majestad, ordenanças de difuntos y audiencia* . . . . (Mexico (1563), 1878–79), I, foja 98, p. 353; *ibid.*, foja 99, p. 355.

[31] Account concerning Cañete, 1543, *Documentos inéditos* . . . . *de Indias*, VIII, 379, 390; Instruction of Toledo, *ibid.*, VIII, 220.

[32] *Recopilación*, ley 72, tit. 3, lib. 3.

[33] Alamán, *Historia de Méjico*, I, 44; Riva Palacio, II, 790; Rivera Cambas, I, 388; Zamacois, Niceto de, *Historia de Méjico* . . . . (Barcelona, Mexico, 1877–82), V, 579.

of Bucareli, who was one of the most popular viceroys of New Spain, was 80,000 pesos, which had a purchasing value in terms of today, of from 160,000 to 200,000 dollars.[34] Antonio de Caballos, the first viceroy of Rio de la Plata, received a salary of 40,000 pesos, and on the eve of independence the viceroys of Peru were granted 60,500 pesos.[35] A palace was also set aside for the use of the viceroys and the expense of its upkeep was defrayed from public funds.[36] Compared with the salaries of the highest colonial functionaries of other nations, the Spanish viceroys were well paid, and it has been seen how some of the more avaricious executives might increase their wealth.

Proper instructions for his successor were required of every viceroy before he departed from the country. They were provided by a written document recording the most notable events of the administration and the measures applied to them. The report included all departments of government, military, political, financial, and ecclesiastical. The instruction was left in a sealed package, with all the dispatches, letters, and cédulas sent by the king to the departing viceroy. It was intrusted to the care of a reliable person who gave it to the new viceroy as soon as he arrived, if the former viceroy did not do this himself.[37] The first Revillagigedo said that he sent to the king one copy of the instruction to his successor and kept another in the office of his secretary.[38] The penalty imposed upon an executive for the failure to submit to the new viceroy such an account was forfeiture of his last year's salary.[39]

---

[34] Alamán, *Historia de Méjico*, I, 44; Priestley, *The Mexican Nation*, 186; Zamacois, V, 619.

[35] Moses, *Spain's Declining Power*, 161; Avilés, Gabriel, *Memoria del virey del Peru* (Lima, 1901), Romero, Carlos, ed., Appendix IX; Moses, Bernard, *South America on the Eve of Emancipation* (New York, 1908), 8.

[36] *Recopilación*, ley 21, tit. 3, lib. 3; Croix, *Instrucción que . . . . dejó*, AGI, 88–5–13.

[37] *Recopilación*, leyes 23–24, tit. 3, lib. 3; Solórzano, II, lib. 5, cap. 14, art. 22, p. 390; *Memorias de los vireyes . . . .* I, Introduction, x–xiii.

[38] To Amarillas, 1755, *Instrucciones que los vireyes . . . .* art. 1, p. 5.

[39] *Recopilación*, ley 32, tit. 14, lib. 3; Polo, José Toribio, *Memorias de los vireyes del Peru* (Lima, 1896), Appendix VII.

The majority of the viceroys met their successors, either before leaving the capital or at some town on the way to the coast, where they held conferences with them, explaining the conditions of the country and making valuable recommendations as to policy. Cholula, that beautiful historic spot, was frequently the meeting place for the viceroys of Mexico. There Mendoza and Velasco first became acquainted, and for many days discussed matters relating to New Spain. Sometimes the former viceroy sent to his successor chocolate, wines, and whatever was needed for the journey to the capital.[40] At other times he arranged a splendid and costly reception, as Monterey did for Montesclaros.[41]

The reception of a viceroy was an important social event. The people eagerly waited for it, coming from far and near to attend the celebrations and pay their respect to the new executive. As the fleet approached Vera Cruz, one of the ships was sent ahead from Campeche to take the news of the viceroy's arrival and to bear letters for the authorities of Mexico. As soon as the viceroy landed, the ayuntamiento and governor met him at the wharf, and the ceremony of giving him the keys to the city was performed. After remaining in the port long enough to inspect the fortifications and to arrange for a conference with his predecessor, the viceroy began his journey to the capital. All along the way the governors, other officials, and the people made his trip a triumphant march, greeting him with chains of roses and the playing of trumpets. Great fiestas, lasting for several days, many bullfights, and sometimes banquets of twenty-four courses were held in his honor. There were masquerades by the gilds and cabildos, and dances by Indians in gala attire. The festivities culminated at Chapultepec. There sixteen days of entertainment and hospitality were provided for Escalona.

---

[40] Zamacois, V, 27; Rivera Cambas, I, 33, 57.

[41] Torquemada, Juan de, *Monarchia indiana* (Madrid, 1723), I, lib. 5, cap. 60, p. 727.

From Chapultepec the viceroy drove in a richly adorned carriage to the entrance of Mexico City, where the best horse in the whole district was sent to him and he was welcomed by various organizations. The gaily decorated streets and balconies were crowded with people who waved their greetings as he rode on his splendid horse through the city.[42] At the sanctuary of Guadalupe, a league from the city, the audiencia and the clergy sometimes met the viceroy and took part in the procession. They accompanied him into the city and near the church of Santa Domingo beneath a triumphal arch the ayuntamiento delivered to him the keys of the citadel. He was then conducted to the cathedral and after the Te Deum, he proceeded to the palace. Several days of celebration followed, the chief amusements being bullfights and allegorical plays.[43] Practically the same description may be given for the reception of viceroys of Peru.[44]

The viceroys were first received under the canopy, but this ceremony was discontinued for a time. As the colonial executives represented the king, it was thought that external observances, like making a public entrance into the city under the canopy, would impress the people with the proper respect due to such a high functionary; therefore a cédula of November 30, 1744, permitted the viceroys to renew this ceremony.[45]

---

[42] Rivera Cambas, I, 57–60; *Vireyes de Mexico, instrucciones, residencias* . . . . MS, serie 2, pp. 1–11; García Genaro, *Don Juan de Palafox* (Mexico, 1918), 66–78. In 1783 on account of the disputes occurring during the entry of Matías de Gálvez into Mexico City, the king ordered that the viceroy should no longer ride into the city on horseback, but should remain in the carriage (Alamán, Lucas, *Disertaciones sobre la historia de la república mejicana* . . . . (Mexico, 1844–49), III, Appendix 99).

[43] Croix, *Correspondance*, 200–201; Account concerning Cañete, *Documentos inéditos* . . . . *de Indias*, VIII, 311–327.

[44] For the best accounts *see* Juan, Jorge and Ulloa, Antonio de, *A Voyage to South America*, in Pinkerton, John, *A General Collection of the Best and Most Interesting Voyages* . . . . (London, 1808–14), XIV, 574–577; *Documentos inéditos* . . . . *de Indias*, VIII, 228–232; Fernández, Diego, *Historia del Peru* (Madrid, 1913–14), I, 53–54.

[45] Zamora y Coronado, José María, *Biblioteca de legislación ultramarina* . . . . (Madrid, 1844–49), VI, 217; Superunda to his successor, 1761, *Memorias de los vireyes* . . . . IV, 76–77; Lemos to Vallenari, 1796. *ibid.*, VI, 67.

The expenses of the reception grew so heavy that it became necessary to curtail them. As much as fourteen thousand pesos were expended on the reception of Matías de Gálvez; accordingly the second Revillagigedo advised his successor to reduce the amount. Several previous attempts had been made to decrease these charges; the government of Peru was limited to twelve thousand pesos and that of New Spain to eight thousand on the reception of the viceroy, but the rule was not well observed.[46] Viceroy Cerda of Nueva Granada tried to prevent the gilds of Santa Fé from contributing to his reception because he did not wish to be a burden to the people.[47] It is said that the ayuntamientos or municipal councils of Mexico City saved their money for the viceroy's arrival, and in order to meet the large expenditures held bullfights for about two weeks. Marquina refused to allow this sport, much to the disgust of the people, and paid six thousand pesos out of his own pocket toward his reception.[48]

An oath of office was required of every new viceroy. Shortly after he entered the capital, the viceroy went to the sala of the audiencia, where a clerk read his title, and in the presence of all the judges he

swore by God and the holy Mary to perform well and faithfully the duty of viceroy and president, attend to the service of his Majesty, obey the laws and ordinances of the kingdom, [to administer] justice to litigants and [keep] the secrecy of the audiencia.[49]

This was the substance of all the oaths, but occasionally the wording was slightly changed. Sometimes the religious element was emphasized more than in the oath quoted. Before the oath was taken, the royal seal was brought out of the chancillería with great pomp and returned afterwards with the same ceremony.

[46] Alamán, *Disertaciones* . . . . III, Appendix 99; *Recopilación*, ley 19, tit. 3, lib. 3.

[47] Groot, José Manuel, *Historia* . . . . *de Nueva Granada* (Bogotá, 1889–93), II, 74–75.

[48] Marquina to Iturrigaray, 1803, *Instrucciones que los vireyes* . . . . arts. 93–96, p. 175.

[49] Account concerning Cañete, *Documentos inéditos* . . . . *de Indias*, VIII, 381.

When the monarch died, it was not necessary to repeat this oath, but the viceroy and other functionaries went through the ceremony of swearing allegiance to the new king.[50] Many distinctions and privileges were granted to the viceroys from the time of their appointment until they returned to Spain. The Casa de Contratación, or Board of Trade, was to transport them and their families to America without charge, as it did also when they were transferred from one viceroyalty to another. They might take with them a certain number of arms and jewels, and import free of duty every year as much as eight thousand ducats' worth of articles for their household.[51] Of course they could ship other things at their own expense. Escalona spent six hundred ducats a day during his voyage and had on board two hundred fowls, twelve calves, two hundred sheep, many kegs of preserved fruit, rice, lentils, chestnuts, chick-peas, raisins, and wines. The king favored the Marquis of Croix by giving him twenty thousand pesos for his voyage, but the viceroy took with him articles worth much more.[52] During the early days, quite a large number of attendants accompanied the viceroys to America. The second Cañete was allowed one hundred attendants and ten or twelve slaves. When the people complained that the followers and servants desired the same privileges and immunities as the viceroys themselves, the king reduced their number somewhat, and prohibited them from intermeddling in matters of government.[53]

At first the title of Señoría was given to the viceroy, but soon the more distinguishing one of Clarísimo or Excelentísimo was permitted, and the troops honored him with the royal salute.[54]

---

[50] *Vireyes de Mexico* . . . . MS, serie 2, art. 4, pp. 12–13; Solórzano, II, lib. 5, cap. 14, arts. 15, 18, 23, pp. 289–290.

[51] *Recopilación*, leyes, 8–10, 14, tit. 3, lib. 3; Account concerning Cañete, *Documentos inéditos* . . . . *de Indias*, VIII, 391.

[52] García, *Don Juan de Palafox*, 60; Croix, *Correspondance*, 187, 189.

[53] *Documentos inéditos* . . . . *de Indias*, VIII, 391; Fuenclara, *Instrucción reservada* . . . . April 23, 1742, AGI, 90–2–17, arts. 10–11.

[54] *Recopilación*, ley 11, tit. 3, lib. 3; Rivera Cambas, I, 42; Solórzano, II, lib. 5, cap. 12, art. 17, p. 368; *Vireyes de Mexico* . . . . MS, serie 1, art. 9, p. 2.

A viceregal court was maintained in imitation of the court in Spain. There the wealthiest and most select persons of colonial society gathered, and the court naturally became the chief social center and displayed great pomp and magnificence. It fixed the styles and etiquette of polite society, and the people of high social standing eagerly awaited the coming of the new viceroy and his attendants to set the pace for them in these matters. The viceroy's guard of honor also lent dignity to his high position and gave a military aspect to the palace.[55]

Special favors were conferred upon certain viceroys who were highly esteemed by the king. For instance, Francisco de Toledo was authorized to give habits of the military orders to three of his attendants and appoint ten of his friends pikemen in his guard. The sovereign made him a steward in the royal household and gave orders for his salary to be paid from the time that he was appointed viceroy, while other men did not receive it until the date of their sailing. Montesclaros was allowed to keep control of the government in New Spain until the moment he sailed from Acapulco to Peru—a privilege not previously granted to any other viceroy. The king commanded that all the expenses of the residencia of the Marquis of Croix should be paid from the treasury of Mexico.[56] The viceroys had the right to receive some gifts from the people, but they were not to accept them on their journeys from one town to another. Viceroys like Iturrigaray made the most of the opportunity to enrich themselves. Others, as the Marquis of Croix, refused presents for themselves or their families. The annual parade of the royal standard on August 13 in memory of the conquest of Mexico City was a special time when gifts and sweetmeats were presented to the viceroys and their secretaries.[57] Other occasions for bestowing gifts upon the

---

[55] For a good description of the royal palace of Mexico in 1666 *see* González Obregón, *México viejo*, 312–321.

[56] Account concerning Toledo, *Documentos inéditos . . . . de Indias*, VIII, 219–220; Riva Palacio, II, 540; Croix, *Correspondance*, 230–231.

[57] *Recopilación*, ley 22, tit. 3, lib. 3; Villarroel, *Enfermedades políticas . . . .* MS, II, pt. III, pp. 58–60.

chief executive were his birthday, the king's birthday, at the birth of his children, and on almost any holiday.

The highest honors were paid to a viceroy who died in office. The funeral of the beloved first Velasco was a time of great splendor and pomp, as well as of mourning. All the civil and ecclesiastical organizations of the capital, the audiencia, the visitor, and the archbishop accompanied the remains to their resting place in the Dominican Convent. Four bishops were pall-bearers. The troops raised for the Philippines marched in the sad procession and were followed by the people of all classes who had come to mourn for their beloved viceroy.[58]

3. THE POWERS OF THE VICEROY

The powers of the early viceroys exceeded those of later ones, since the means of communication were slow, and they had to meet emergencies without waiting for decisions by the mother country. It often took several months before the king could be informed of a particular event and several more to receive an answer from him; therefore a wise executive took the proper measures in all practical issues, just as the sovereign would do if present. Even the later viceroys, until the eve of independence, acted upon their own responsibility in military and many other matters. Repression of revolts or plans of campaign against a foreign enemy had to be determined immediately by the viceroys. The king tried to plan everything in the New World, and legislated on almost every possible subject; but there were always many details relating to military and administrative matters which the innumerable royal instructions could not cover. When regular communication was established between Spain and the Americas and visitors-general were sent there, the viceroys became less independent and had to rely more upon instructions from the Council of the Indies.

---

[58] Torquemada, I, lib. 5, cap. 16, p. 627; Cavo, Andrés, *Los tres siglos de Méjico* . . . . (Jalapa, 1870), lib. 4, art. 22, p. 118.

The widest latitude was allowed in the time taken by the viceroys to obey instructions and royal cédulas. Frequently royal measures were delayed as long as a year. In 1604, when the royal decree came to Lima ordering that Indians should not be detained by force on the charcaras or large estates, the audiencia appealed to the viceroy and asked him to withhold the cédula, since it was the time for harvesting crops. The viceroy did not put the measure into effect and gave as his excuse to the king that he was hindered by the audiencia in obeying the decree.[59] The second Revillagigedo failed entirely to fulfil some of the royal orders within the five years of his administration, to the court's disgust. Yet this man was one of the most capable viceroys of New Spain.[60] The well-known and frequently used phrase "obedezco pero no cumplo" (I obey but do not execute) shows the attitude of the viceroys toward royal orders.[61]

The kings themselves permitted measures to be ignored by the viceroys which in their opinion seemed contrary to the public welfare. There was often doubt as to the interpretation of royal decrees. In such a case, Montesclaros said that when he received a decree which ordered something entirely different from what was in practice, he kept it back until further information was obtained. He advised his successor to compare the recent cédulas with those of former years, and if there was evidence that the new measures would soon be recalled, not to enforce them.[62] Viceroy Palata of Peru declared that, when a contradiction of decrees occurred, it was easier for an executive to do nothing under the pretext of reporting to the king; but in consulting the monarch sometimes a delay of two years resulted. He thought, however, that a viceroy would be blameworthy for causing such

---

[59] Velasco to Monterey, *Documentos inéditos* . . . . *de Indias*, IV, 422–423.

[60] Rivera Cambas, I, 487.

[61] Smith, Donald E., *The Viceroy of New Spain* (Berkeley, 1913), 130.

[62] Rivera Cambas, I, 123; Montesclaros to his successor, 1615, *Documentos inéditos* . . . . *de Indias*, VI, 207.

delay if he could otherwise remedy the situation.[63] The second
Revillagigedo received a royal order that was difficult to inter-
pret. It commanded the work of street-paving in Mexico City
to stop. The fiscal was of the opinion that the decree did not
apply to the streets already begun, but only to new ones, since
its application would make the chief thoroughfares impassable
and the nearest houses would be injured by the flowing of water.
While the king was being informed concerning the matter, the
viceroy caused the most urgent part of the work to be continued.[64]

Sometimes viceroys were empowered to modify royal orders.
In enforcing the rules of personal service for the Indians of Peru,
Viceroy Velasco was authorized to add to the cédulas or take
away what seemed best to him, if there was danger of causing
general discontent, but of course the king had to be advised concerning his action. The same viceroy modified a royal decree
commanding that manufactures should not be increased in Peru.
He realized the importance of the cloth industries and favored
them, informing the king that the people would be forced to go
about nude if the cloth mills were abolished.[65] Fuenclara was
permitted to take active measures of his own to check the delin-
quencies of judges, if conditions showed that the means already
advocated were not sufficient to stop abuses. He was also given
the same freedom to proceed against the contraband trade.[66]

There are some cases of the suspension of royal cédulas by the
viceroys. On November 16, 1676, Castellar of Peru was commanded to add at least one-half or more per cent to the two per
cent duty which the consulado collected from the avería for building ships of the armada. The viceroy thought this measure
impracticable and suspended it until a more favorable time, but

---

[63] Palata to Monclova, 1689, *Memorias de los vireyes* . . . . II, 40–41.

[64] Revillagigedo, conde de, *Instrucción reservada* . . . . (Mexico, 1831),
arts. 284–286.

[65] *Documentos inéditos* . . . . *de Indias*, VI, 120–121; Velasco to Monterey,
1604, *ibid.*, IV, 436–437.

[66] Fuenclara, *Instrucción reservada* . . . . April 23, 1742, AGI, 90–2–17,
arts. 6, 8.

notified the king of his action. Again, in 1788, Teodoro de Croix suspended a royal order of October 15, 1754, for the remeasurement of the land in the intendancies of Peru. Much injustice had been caused by the act, the public opposed it, and the rights of litigants were not considered; therefore the viceroy decided to take action against such an unpopular measure. The king was pleased and requested an investigation to be made concerning the harm which the Indians had suffered.[67]

The viceroys were always free to express their opinions to the king and recommend measures to him. Mendoza wrote to the sovereign saying that it seemed to him unwise to discontinue the aid given to the city of Los Angeles (Puebla) until it was able to support itself, but he added "what your Majesty orders concerning it will be done."[68] The viceroy's opinions were often sought by the king before he took action on certain matters. According to the wording of a special request to the viceroy of Peru, we read,

You will take very great care to know and advise what things it is fitting for us to order newly provided for the good of the country, and those which require prompt attention. Meanwhile, you may take the [proper] measures, advising us concerning what you have provided and about other [abuses] which it seems to you that we ought to order remedied.[69]

In 1599 Francisco de Toledo was asked to give his advice whether the salary of treasury officials ought to be increased, and in 1604 Montesclaros was required to express his ideas about whether it was best to impose a duty on exports from Acapulco for the Philippines.[70] Innumerable similar cases might be cited.

Sometimes the monarch heeded the advice of his chief representative in the colony; at other times it was simply pigeonholed.

[67] Castellar to Liñan, 1681, *Memorias de los vireyes* . . . . I, 170–171; Croix to Lemos, 1790, *ibid.*, V, 91–94.

[68] Letter of Mendoza to the emperor, Dec. 10, 1537, *Documentos inéditos* . . . . *de Indias*, II, 181.

[69] *Ibid.*, XXIII, 497.

[70] King to the viceroy and audiencia of Lima, *ibid.*, XIX, 95; Letter of Montesclaros, to the king, April 12, 1612, *ibid.*, VI, 304.

However, a wise king could not afford to treat slightingly the opinions of an experienced viceroy. When the consulado petitioned the irresponsible Philip III to stop all direct trade between Mexico and the Philippines, the advice of Montesclaros was taken and the commerce with those islands continued as usual. The viceroy shrewdly explained that the consulado would only be enriched by carrying merchandise to the Orient, and that France and Flanders would reap the benefits from the increased silk trade with Spain.[71]

Another power of the viceroy was his right to give instructions to governors and demand their obedience. About 1703, a case occurred wherein the viceroy of Mexico deposed Martín de Urzúa, governor of Yucatan, who was charged with the murder of an alcalde of Valladolid. Nevertheless, after going to Spain to plead his cause, Urzúa was pardoned and reinstated on June 6, 1706. The second Revillagigedo removed the governor of Texas from his office because he had killed within his own house five Lipan Indians who were friendly, and Manuel Muñoz was appointed to succeed him.[72] The chief executive had absolute power to suspend or remove any judges sent out on commission by the audiencia. In 1591 the king ordered the viceroy of Peru to remove all the judges repartidores of the Indians in the provinces of Quito and Charcas and cause the corregidor to oversee the repartimientos.[73] Also the viceroys frequently recommended to the king the removal of judges of the audiencia. For instance, in 1556 the first Cañete of Peru told the king to investigate the conduct of the oidores Savaría, Santillán, and Mercado, whom he thought unworthy to keep their positions.[74]

---

[71] Letter of Montesclaros to the king, April 12, 1612, *Documentos inéditos* .... *de Indias*, VI, 303–304.

[72] Ancona, Eligio, *Historia de Yucatan* .... (ed. 2, Barcelona, 1889), II, 316–323; Rivera Cambas, I, 479.

[73] Orozco, I, 126–129; King to García de Mendoza, 1591, *Documentos inéditos* .... *de Indias*, XIX, 67.

[74] Letter of Cañete to the emperor, May 25, 1556, *ibid.*, IV, 85–86.

Some of the early viceroys were permitted to legitimize children, even when the mothers were Indians, but in 1561 this power was revoked and given to the Council of the Indies.[75] The viceroy called the attention of the king to persons deserving to be rewarded for their services; however he usually performed the act of conferring the favor. The king often ordered his chief representative to attend to the needs of descendants of conquistadores, as he did in 1558 when the viceroy of Peru was commanded to confer upon Antonio Vaca de Castro, the son of the licenciado Vaca de Castro, a repartimiento of Indians yielding an income of sixteen thousand pesos a year.[76]

The viceroy's power of appointment depended entirely upon the will of the king. Some monarchs were more lenient with their favorite viceroys in respect to this matter than others. The officials of royal designation were the viceroys, governors, captains-general, oidores, regents, treasury officials, corregidores, and alcaldes mayores. All vacancies in these positions were to be reported to the king by the viceroy, who could mention the names of worthy persons to succeed in them.[77] Quite often the viceroys were granted the right to fill certain of these offices, especially those of the last two classes. The first Cañete, who had the authority to designate a number of officials in Peru, appointed the corregidor of Cuzco, to whom he intrusted the power to provide for the office of alguacil or bailiff. Later Viceroy Toledo appointed corregidores in Cuzco and Potosí.[78] In 1604 a law of the Indies permitted the viceroy of New Spain to choose the alcalde mayor of Acapulco, and in 1680 the viceroys of Mexico and Peru were empowered to continue the selection of corregidores and alcaldes mayores within their jurisdictions.[79]

---

[75] Letter of Montesclaros to the king, April 17, 1612, *Documentos inéditos . . . . de Indias*, VI, 284.

[76] Cédulas and provisiones for the viceroy of Peru, *ibid.*, XVIII, 484–486.

[77] *Recopilación*, ley 3, tit. 2, lib. 3.

[78] Letter of Cañete to the emperor, May 25, 1556, *Documentos inéditos . . . . de Indias*, IV, 92; *ibid.*, VIII, 289–290.

[79] *Recopilación*, ley 74, tit. 45, lib. 8; ley 70, tit. 2, lib. 3.

The viceroy could also confer some of his power upon the corregidores of the more distant towns of South America for confirming the elections of alcaldes ordinarios.[80]

Even governors were appointed by the viceroys, since this
saved a great deal of time and trouble for the far away king.
We hear of Mendoza appointing a governor of Pánuco to take
the place of Nuño de Guzmán, and making Coronado provisional
governor of Nueva Galicia.[81] The first Cañete chose his own son
governor of Chile, and when Gonzalo Mendoza, the governor of
La Plata died, although the colony had elected Vergara governor,
the marquis passed by his claims and nominated Ortíz de Zárate
in his stead.[82] In 1609, a law of the Indies reaffirmed the right
of the viceroy of New Spain to select the governors of New Mexico
and fix their salaries.[83] Mancera appointed a governor of Chile
and Buenos Aires. Liñan chose Castillo de Herrera, an oidor of
the audiencia of Lima, governor of Guancavelica, and the Marquis
of Croix appointed his nephew, Teodoro, governor of Acapulco.[84]
The viceroy of Mexico filled temporarily the post of governor of
the Philippines until 1664, when this right was revoked. However, it was restored again in 1670 and continued until about
1720.[85]

Minor appointments made by the viceroys were numerous.
but even these varied with the whims of the monarch. Sometimes the king designated the men who should serve and the vice-

---

[80] Cédulas and provisiones of the king 1589, *Documentos inéditos . . . .
de Indias*, XVIII, 204–207.

[81] Zamacois, IV, 613; Bancroft, *History of Mexico*, II, 465.

[82] Letter of Cañete to the emperor, Sept. 25, 1556, *Documentos inéditos
. . . . de Indias*, IV, 100; Moses, Bernard, *The Spanish Dependencies in
South America* (London, 1914), I, 198.

[83] *Documentos inéditos . . . . de Indias*, VIII, 290; *ibid.*, XV, 54–57;
Recopilación, ley 66, tit. 2, lib. 3.

[84] Mancera to his successor, *in* Polo, *Memorias de los vireyes . . . .* art.
134, p. 56; *ibid.*, art. 144, p. 62; Bancroft, *History of Mexico*, III, 160;
Liñan to Palata, 1681, *Memorias de los vireyes . . . .* I, 311; Croix,
Correspondance, 202.

[85] Orozco, I, 153; Mancera to Veraguas, 1673, *Instrucciones que los
vireyes . . . .* 266; Cunningham, 200.

roy merely performed the act of confirming the office.[86] Some viceroys chose treasury officials and officers for the mint, others selected ecclesiastical and secular visitors.[87] The laws of the Indies permitted the executive to appoint his own assessor, and as a mark of special favor the second Velasco was empowered to appoint a visitor of the audiencia of the Philippines.[88] A royal cédula of 1680 authorized the viceroys to fill twelve public offices with their friends and attendants, but during the term of the first Revillagigedo of Mexico this rule existed only on paper.[89] Viceroy Croix was allowed to appoint for two years six residents of Mexico City as honorary regidores to check the ayuntamiento or municipal council. Naturally the other councilmen resented this as an intrusion upon their rights; therefore a decree of 1794 granted the regidores themselves the privilege of selecting the honorary members.[90]

The viceroys appointed encomenderos and assigned the Indians to them. At first the encomiendas could be kept only for two generations, but this rule was not strictly enforced. Later, they were held by the same family for as long as four generations. Whenever they became vacant it was the duty of the viceroy to designate the successors and within five years his candidates had to be confirmed by the king or the encomiendas again became vacant. In 1542 the New Laws took away from the viceroy the power to appoint encomenderos when the encomienda became vacant by resignation. Such encomiendas were to revert to the crown, and also those made vacant by the death of the owners.[91]

---

[86] *Recopilación*, ley 67, tit. 2, lib. 3.

[87] Villagarcía to Superunda, 1745, *Memorias de los vireyes* . . . . III, 376; Mendoza to the king, 1537, *Documentos inéditos* . . . . *de Indias*, II, 191; *ibid.*, VIII, 259.

[88] *Recopilación*, ley 35, tit. 3, lib. 3; Riva Palacio, II, 451.

[89] Revillagigedo to Amarillas, 1754, *Instrucciones que los vireyes* . . . . art. 169, pp. 34–35.

[90] Croix, *Instrucción que* . . . . *dejó*, AGI, 88–5–13; Revillagigedo, *Instrucción reservada*, art. 158.

[91] Solórzano, I, lib. 3, cap. 1, arts. 37–38, p. 228; *ibid.*, cap. 7, art. 30, p. 263; *Recopilación*, leyes 1, 6, tit. 19, lib. 6.

Ad interim appointments, both civil and ecclesiastical, were numerous,[92] but even here the royal approval had to be obtained. The viceroy's appointees held their positions until the king either confirmed them or sent men from the mother country to fill the offices. Sometimes a number of years elapsed before the arrival of the persons designated by the sovereign; during this period the temporary officials appointed by the viceroy were to receive only half salary.[93]

The viceroys could declare persons of age so that they might be eligible to hold public offices. When this privilege seemed to be abused, a cédula of May 14, 1748, confirmed by another in 1749, prohibited the practice. The right was restored in 1752 because the king realized that the people had received benefit from it.[94]

Too much initiative on the part of the viceroys was always regarded by the king with suspicion, and frequently he refused to approve their acts. Viceroy Nieva of Peru gave the office of assayer of the mines of Potosí to one of his friends, at a salary of eight thousand pesos, without the king's permission. The office was bestowed upon a royal appointee and the viceroy's friend was disregarded.[95] The Marquis of Croix put into effect the ordinances passed by Visitor Gálvez concerning the gild of bakers and the king expressed surprise that he should have done this without first seeking his approval.[96] Later, when Bernardo de Gálvez on his own responsibility pardoned three criminals who were about to be executed, a great agitation arose in New Spain, which probably would have caused the viceroy's recall if it had not been for his sudden death. Although the crown confirmed

[92] *Recopilación*, leyes 47–50, tit. 2, lib. 3; *ibid.*, leyes 2–3, tit. 16, lib. 2.

[93] *Ibid.*, ley 51, tit. 2, lib. 3; *ibid.*, ley 13, tit. 19, lib. 1; Solórzano, II, lib. 5, cap. 13, art. 15, p. 378; Cédulas and provisiones of the king 1582, *Documentos inéditos* . . . . *de Indias*, XVIII, 150–151.

[94] Superunda to his successor, 1761, *Memorias de los vireyes* . . . . IV, 80.

[95] *Documentos inéditos* . . . . *de Indias*, XVIII, 20–21.

[96] Croix, *Instrucción que* . . . . *dejó*, AGI, 88–5–13.

the act of Gálvez, it added the reproof that the executive should not leave the palace while prisoners were being led to execution. This viceroy established close relations with the leading families of New Spain and courted popularity, thereby arousing suspicion that he intended to establish a throne for himself.[97] A safe rule laid down by an early viceroy was for the executive not to arrive at anything extraordinary when this was not needed.[98]

4. LIMITATION OF THE VICEROY'S AUTHORITY

The many limitations imposed upon the viceroy were intended to keep him absolutely under the royal control. Almost endless correspondence with the king was employed to attain this purpose. The viceroy had to inform the king concerning everything he did, no matter how trifling; the letters written to the monarch by a single executive extended into the thousands. Bucareli referred to letter number 4194, in which he recommended a miner to the king,[99] and other viceroys wrote hundreds or even thousands of letters.

The subject matter of these reports was so various that almost nothing escaped the eye of the king. There were accounts relating to religion, government, and finance; vacant ecclesiastical and secular positions and recommendations of deserving persons to fill them; the number of convents in each province and their rents; the audiencias, the administration of justice by the oidores, their qualifications and conduct; alcaldes mayores and other minor officials; those who sought favors and had received them; persons who lived scandalously and corrupted good customs; the treatment of Indians and salable offices; how the funds of the treasury could be increased; the salaries paid to all officials in the

---

[97] *Suplemento de Bustamante,* to Cavo, art. 72, pp. 357–358; Alamán, *Disertaciones . . . .* III, Appendix 75–76.

[98] Montesclaros to his successor, 1615, *Memorias de los vireyes . . . .* I, 3.

[99] *Suplemento de Bustamante,* to Cavo, art. 28, p. 322.

Indies and the rents from encomiendas; and whatever the viceroys thought necessary to be brought to the attention of the
monarch.[100] Special reports might be called for by the king at
any time, as in 1535, when Mendoza was ordered to send information relating to all the tributes paid in his viceroyalty. During
his administration in Peru, Velasco was requested to report on
manufactures, and Branciforte said that he advised the king every
month concerning his military measures for New Spain.[101] At the
end of their terms all viceroys were required to send a special
report of the condition in which they left the government.[102]

New and serious matters were always submitted to the sovereign.[103] Sometimes unimportant incidents, which would make
the present day administrator smile, were related to the king by
the viceroys. Mendoza wrote to the sovereign concerning the
marriages of the conquistadores and asked him to order the
people to cease using mules and neglecting horses, which were
more noble animals. Again, the viceroy had to ask permission to
erect a statue of Charles IV in Mexico City.[104]

The very paternalism of the home government served as a
hindrance to the initiative of the viceroy. Spain had a perfect
mania for regulation, best shown in the case of the Indians who
were treated as minors and put under the perpetual tutelage of
the whites. Acts signed by natives and contracts involving an
amount slightly above a peso were declared null, and all their
wants were carefully anticipated by the crown. This paternal
surveillance extended to all departments of government. The
most minute details were planned by legislation, as the laying

---

100 *Recopilación*, leyes 1–20, 32–33, tit. 14, lib. 3.

101 King to Mendoza, 1535, *Documentos inéditos . . . . de Indias*,
XXIII, 432; Velasco to Monterey, 1604, *ibid.*, IV, 436; Letter of Branciforte to Azanza, May 30, 1798, *Instrucciones que los vireyes . . . .* 149.

102 *Recopilación*, ley 27, tit. 6, lib. 2.

103 *Ibid.*, ley 51, tit. 3, lib. 3.

104 Letter of Mendoza to the emperor, Dec. 10, 1534, *Documentos
inéditos . . . . de Indias*, II, 211, 197–198; González Obregón, *México
viejo*, 564.

out of new towns and streets and the erecting of public buildings—details which today would be intrusted to a board of
works.[105] Regulations were made for the marriage of every
important public official, and even the dress worn by the members
of the audiencia was prescribed by the king.[106]

The audiencia was, perhaps, the principal limitation of the
power of the viceroy. It was the intention of the crown to establish such a system of checks and balances that one official or
institution would serve to control the other. Therefore, the
judges were permitted to correspond directly with the king, and
the viceroy could not interfere with this privilege.[107] At any
time the king might ask the audiencia for information, even
against the viceroy. This always had a restraining influence.
When a viceroy exceeded his power, the audiencia could warn
him, but without publicity and with due respect for his high
position. If the viceroy persisted in his actions, the judges might
report to the king.[108] No oidor alone could make public or secret
information against the viceroy without a special order from the
king, but in serious matters the majority of the judges had power
to receive secret information against the viceroy and give account
to the king.[109]

The real acuerdo or viceregal council likewise was a check
upon the authority of the executive, but not in the same degree
as the governor's council in the English colonies. During the
administration of the first Velasco in New Spain the judges of
the audiencia insisted that the viceroy should consult the acuerdo,

---

105 Humboldt, Alexander Von, *Political Essay on the Kingdom of New
Spain* (ed. 2, London, 1814), I, 188; Ordinances for new towns, 1563
Documentos inéditos . . . . de Indias, VIII, 523–524.

106 Cédulas and provisiones of the king, 1582, *ibid.*, XVIII, 148–149;
1581, *ibid.*, 142–143.

107 *Recopilación*, ley 40, tit. 15, lib. 2; Account for Juan de Obando of
the consejo, 1570, *Documentos inéditos . . . . de Indias*, XI, 59–61.

108 Cédulas and provisiones for the audiencia of Charcas, March 4,
1568, *ibid.*, XVIII, 118; King to the audiencia of Chile, 1590, *ibid.*, XXV,
542–543; *Recopilación*, ley 36, tit. 15, lib. 2.

109 *Ibid.*, leyes 39, 41, tit. 15, lib. 2.

alleging that Velasco's health would not permit him to attend to everything. As a result laws were passed which ordered the viceroy to confer with the acuerdo concerning all difficult matters.[110] A wise viceroy always submitted serious matters to the acuerdo and learned its opinions, but, after communicating with it, he might do as he thought best.[111] Esquilache declared that his consultations with the acuerdo were voluntary, but he considered them convenient since the audiencia would not oppose his measures if interested in them.[112]

The fiscal also acted as a restraint upon the viceroy, since he reported to the king everything relating to the treasury discussed or decided in the acuerdo.[113] Linares thought that the junta de guerra hindered his actions. He said that much time was lost and great confusion resulted because of the many votes in the junta. After three months of discussion, only two measures were passed, and one of them was opposed to a royal provision.[114]

In 1776 the establishment of the office of regent, a kind of chief justice, decreased the viceroy's power as president of the audiencia. This official relieved the president in the performance of his many duties, the viceroy merely retaining his nominal title. When serious matters were discussed the regent often notified the viceroy to attend the audiencia, and when oidores were to be reproved the viceroy had to confer with the regent concerning them. If the viceroy was absent from the capital, the regent dispatched all civil and political business for him, but not military matters.[115] The regent could attend any chamber he wished and serve as judge in both civil and criminal cases.

110 Zamacois, V, 45–46; *Recopilación*, ley 45, tit. 3, lib. 3.

111 King to Mendoza, 1535, *Documentos inéditos . . . . de Indias*, XXIII, 424; Palafox to his successor, 1642, *Documentos inéditos . . . . de Mexico*, VII, 32, 69–70; Liñan to Palata, 1681, *Memorias de los vireyes . . . .* I, 288.

112 Esquilache to Guadalcázar, 1621, *ibid.*, I, 99–100.

113 King to the fiscal of the audiencia of Lima, 1596, *Documentos inéditos . . . . de Indias*, XIX, 91–92.

114 Linares to Valero, 1716, *Instrucciones que los vireyes . . . .* 314.

115 Antequera, 494; Becker, Jerónimo, *La Política española en las Indias* (Madrid, 1920), 62–63.

Yet, when the viceroy was present, he was honored more than the regent and could still decide upon the formation of certain courts and assign special duties to the oidores.[116] In 1794 the second Revillagigedo declared that when the president was not a lawyer, his duties did not consist of much more than being present at public functions. Later Marquina stated that the chief obligation of the president consisted in sending the king every year a report of the services of the members of the audiencia and of the cases decided or still pending. Otherwise, the position of president was one of mere ceremonial preëminence.[117]

Even the people sometimes restrained the actions of the viceroy. There were always some influential persons in the viceroyalties who could easily gain the king's ear. When an individual wished to give account of something to the Council of the Indies, it was customary to do this through the viceroy, but if the information was against the executive himself, direct correspondence with the king was permitted.[118] Enríquez said that the people were always ready to judge the words and actions of a viceroy, and that they did not do this to praise, but to criticize him.[119] One case may be mentioned wherein the people asked for the recall of a viceroy of New Spain. They associated a period of public calamities, marked by the capture of a galleon by pirates, and by epidemics and earthquakes, with the administration of Villamanrique. Then too, the viceroy engaged in a dispute with the audiencia of Guadalajara because one of the oidores had married within his district without royal permission. The complaints had the desired effect and the king removed the viceroy.[120]

116 For a detailed account of the duties of the regents, *see* the royal instruction to the regents of the audiencias of the Indies, June 20, 1776, *in* Zamora y Coronado, *Biblioteca legislación ultamarina* . . . .V, 297–306.

117 Revillagigedo, *Instrucción reservada*, art. 21; Marquina to Iturrigaray, 1803, *Instrucciones que los vireyes* . . . . 223–224; *ibid.*, art. 16, p. 162.

118 Solórzano, I, lib. 2, cap. 14, art. 33, p. 126.

119 To Coruña, 1580, *Instrucciones que los vireyes* . . . . art. 1, p. 242.

120 Cavo, lib. 5, arts. 18–20, pp. 142–143; Riva Palacio, II, 429–440; Bancroft, *History of Mexico*, II, 754–755.

Peralta, the third viceroy of New Spain, was accused of aiding the encomenderos and Martín Cortés in their plans for a revolt, therefore the pesquisidores Muñoz and Carrillo were sent to Mexico to investigate the charges and Peralta was recalled.[121] Escalona was also relieved of office on suspicion that he was friendly with the Portuguese, because he quarreled with the archbishop visitor, Palafox, and was dishonest in accumulating wealth.[122] In 1716 Viceroy Ladrón de Guevara of Peru was deprived of office, accusations sufficient to arouse the king's suspicion having been made against him.[123]

The office of viceroy was temporarily suspended in Peru at the close of the administration of the Count of Nieva. For five years his successor, García de Castro, held only the titles of governor and captain-general. The title of viceroy was reëstablished in 1569 when Francisco de Toledo became administrator. In 1722 at the end of Villalonga's rule the viceregal office was suspended in Nueva Granada. As the viceroy of Peru was not able to exercise sufficient control over such a large territory, this viceroyalty was restored in 1740 under Sebastián de Eslava.[124]

Reprimands from the king usually restrained the actions of the chief executive and even favorite viceroys sometimes received them. In 1563 the viceroy of Peru was censured for having given Gerónimo de Silva an encomienda when he was rich and already had another. The king showed his displeasure to the Marquis of Gelves in 1623 because he had suspended an oidor of his audiencia and ordered him imprisoned.[125] Salvatierra was made to realize

---

[121] For the details concerning the deposition of Peralta *see* Cavo, lib. 4, arts. 27–29, pp. 120–124; Riva Palacio, II, 394–397; Zamacois, V, 122–124.

[122] Riva Palacio, II, 598–600; Bancroft, *History of Mexico*, III, 101–111.

[123] Moses, *The Spanish Dependencies* . . . . II, 273–274.

[124] Moses, Bernard, *The Establishment of Spanish Rule in America* (New York, London, 1898), 138–139; Moses, *Spain's Declining Power*, 50–55. The case of Torres de Rueda in New Spain is not a typical example of the suspension of the office of viceroy, since he was only an ad interim ruler and was given the title of governor. Cavo, lib. 7, p. 204.

[125] Solórzano, I, lib. 3, cap. 6, art. 58, p. 257; *ibid.*, II, lib. 5, cap. 4, art. 41, p. 292.

that he did not have power to appoint the general of the armada of the Windward Islands and was scolded because he prevented some bales of merchandise from being opened in Campeche, thereby spoiling the sale.[126] Mancera was reproved for a deficit of one hundred thousand pesos in the royal treasury and because of habitual tardiness at divine services. Likewise, the king severely chided Figueroa for saving a lap dog and none of his papers, at the time when he barely escaped being taken prisoner by the English during his voyage to New Spain.[127]

Some of the minor limitations imposed upon an executive must have been very annoying. Viceroys and their children were forbidden to marry within their jurisdictions during the time of their administration without a special license from the king.[128] The number of the viceroy's attendants was fixed by the crown, and they were not to include married sons and daughters or sons-in-law and daughters-in-law.[129] The viceroy did not have power to ennoble a town by giving it the title of a city, since this right was reserved exclusively for the king. He could not take part in new discoveries, or grant licenses for this without first consulting the king.[130] Viceroys could not give permission for people to come to the colonies, or return to Spain. A case has been found wherein the viceroy complained that he did not have sufficient authority to suppress the evils of a mining town without a special royal order prescribing the form of the measure to be taken.[131]

---

126 Rivera Cambas, I, 167–168. Escalona was reproved for making the same appointment. Riva Palacio, II, 598, 613.

127 Rivera Cambas, I, 171, 222; Riva Palacio, II, 788.

128 Solórzano, II lib. 5, cap. 9, arts. 5–6, pp. 330–331; Cédulas and provisiones of the king, 1575, *Documentos inéditos . . . . de Indias,* XVIII, 241. The punishment for violating this rule was loss of office.

129 *Recopilación,* ley 12, tit. 3, lib. 3; Account concerning Cañete, 1589, *Documentos inéditos . . . . de Indias,* VIII, 297.

130 Revillagigedo to the corregidor, Padilla, 1754, *Instrucciones que los vireyes . . . .* art. 28, p. 51; Becker, 318; Ordinances for new discoveries, 1563, *Documentos inéditos . . . . de Indias,* VIII, 486.

131 Court to Amarillas, 1755, *Instrucciones que los vireyes . . . .* arts. 16, 18, p. 65; Linares to Valero, 1716, *ibid.,* 312.

Custom also caused important limitations upon the power of the later viceroys. The early colonial executives had been granted the pardoning power, but custom forbade its use. Many viceroys were so accustomed to lax obedience that their orders were often worded so as to leave a loophole. The general tone at the capitals seemed to indicate that viceroys could enforce only those measures not in direct opposition to the wishes of local magistrates. Governors and other provincial officials were apt to take their own time in carrying out the viceroy's commands. Matters were frequently disposed of according to the recommendation of the fiscal. A common form of decree was "Como pide el Señor fiscal," "Let it be as the fiscal requests," indicating that the professional advice of the state's attorney was accepted[132]

The almost endless delay in putting viceregal measures into effect detracted greatly from the executive's power. An interesting example occurred in the relief of the San Sabá mission in Texas. The mission and the presidio of Las Amarillas were established in 1757, but the Indians were unwilling to remain in the mission. Therefore Colonel Parrilla proposed to the viceroy that both the mission and the presidio should be placed nearer San Antonio. In the meanwhile, the Indians attacked the mission and burned it. It was more than a month and a half before the report of Parrilla on the disaster reached the capital. Then the documents were submitted to the fiscal, and after three weeks he made his decision, which agreed with the advice of the colonel, that the mission should not be reëstablished in the same location.[133] The viceroy next sent the papers to the auditor de guerra and on June 12 this official made his recommendations. He also favored the abandonment of the San Sabá site and advised that a general junta be called. On the 27th the junta was sum-

---

132 Montesclaros to his successor, 1615, *Memorias de los vireyes* . . . . I, 3; Priestley, H. I., *José de Gálvez* (Berkeley, 1916), 59.

133 Dunn, Wm. E., ''The Apache Mission,'' in *The Southwestern Historical Quarterly*, XVII, 389–390; *Testimo. de los autos sobre el asalto y attaque* . . . . *en el presidio de San Luis de las Amarillas* . . . . AGI, 92–6–22, pp. 126–127, 141–183.

moned by the viceroy and, in opposition to the opinions of Parrilla, the fiscal and the auditor de guerra decided that it would be dishonorable to relinquish the post, and that the northern tribes should be punished. The viceroy accepted this report and on July 5 send instructions to the frontier, but it was another month before they reached their destination.[134]

5. THE VISITOR AND THE VICEROY

The visitor-general, that direct representative of the king whose authority was restricted only by his special instructions, was another effective check upon the power of the viceroys. He was to report to the monarch every abuse which could be found, the conduct of no official from the highest to the lowest escaping his attention. The office of visitor had proved to be a valuable asset in Spain, but was not so successful in the New World because the visitor generally did not have experience in colonial affairs, and aroused the hostility of the officials on account of the secret information which he collected respecting them.

The power of visitation was occasionally granted to the viceroys themselves, especially in the early days. The king ordered Mendoza to visit Mexico City and all the other towns of the province, so that he might know their condition and provide what was fitting for them. Sometimes a newly appointed viceroy was commanded to make a visitation of the acts of his predecessor, as Nieva did in the case of the first Marquis of Cañete.[135] Francisco de Toledo, perhaps, spent more of his time in making visitations than any other viceroy, since for five years he traveled nearly five thousand miles throughout Peru, when travel was almost impossible.[136] In 1570 Viceroy Enríquez of New Spain

---

[134] *Testimo. de los autos sobre el asalto y attaque* . . . . *en el presidio de San Luis de las Amarillas* . . . . AGI, 92–6–22, 198–221.

[135] King to Mendoza, 1535, *Documentos inéditos* . . . . *de Indias,* XXIII, 427; Instruction of Nieva, 1559, *ibid.,* XXV, 55.

[136] Memorial of Toledo, 1596, *ibid.,* VI, 530–531.

was ordered to visit personally his principal towns and see that the local officials performed their duties faithfully. He considered it a very necessary means of good government for the viceroy to witness with his own eyes conditions as they really were.[137] By a decree of May 12, 1651, it was commanded that the viceroy should visit the military orders every five years.[138] There were two instances in Mexico wherein the executive possessed the concurrent powers of archbishop, viceroy, and visitor. The archbishop, Moya y Contreras, received his appointment as viceroy while he was performing the tasks of visitor, and the same thing happened, in 1642, to Palafox. As late as the latter part of the eighteenth century, the second Revillagigedo devoted his idle moments to visiting the various tribunals and the treasury.[139]

The coming of a visitor was always dreaded by a viceroy and the audiencia, and as a result relations with him were usually strained. Montesclaros expressed the sentiment of most of the viceroys when he said that the visitations were

comparable to the whirlwinds often seen in the public squares and streets, which serve no purpose save to stir up dust, straw, and other trash, and scatter them about the heads of the people.[140]

He added that

the injuries which are pretended to be remedied . . . . have scarcely ever been removed. . . . Only caution and secrecy in committing them are improved.[141]

Viceroys were ordered to aid the visitors and give them the information for which they asked, but this was hard to do when they knew that their own conduct might also be the subject of investigation.[142] Visitors might enter the audiencia at any time

---

[137] Memorials and papers of Diego de Robles, *ibid.*, XI 5; *Instrucciones que los vireyes* . . . . art. 17, p. 249.

[138] Solórzano, II, lib. 5, cap. 10, art. 17, p. 346.

[139] Rivera Cambas, I, 478.

[140] Solórzano, II, lib. 5, cap. 10, art. 19, p. 346.

[141] Montesclaros to the king, 1607, *Instrucciones que los vireyes* . . . . 252.

[142] *Recopilación*, leyes 10, 13, tit. 34, lib. 2; Solórzano, II, lib. 5, cap. 10, art. 15, p. 345.

and hear what was being discussed, but they did not have a vote in business pertaining to the court. They could inspect its books and suspend disobedient judges from office.[143] The king expected that the best of relations should be maintained between the viceroy and visitor, since they were both his representatives and sought the same end—the performing of the royal service.[144]

The arrival in New Spain of the first visitor, Tello de Sandoval, was the occasion of much excitement, since he came to enforce the New Laws. The encomenderos decided to dress in mourning and go out to meet him, but the good sense of Mendoza would not permit this, as it woud only irritate Sandoval and offend the king. In spite of all that Mendoza could do, there was some friction with Sandoval, who tried to show his superior authority. When asked, ''What about the viceroy?'' he answered, ''Ship him to Spain when it seems best to me.'' The visitor also published Mendoza's residencia twice, as if he were the lowest official in the viceroyalty.[145] In self defense the viceroy was forced to ally himself with the clergy against the visitor, who did not succeed in putting the New Laws into effect.

The next visitor to come to New Spain was Valderrama, who soon became a favorite of the Cortés faction. He criticized the administration of the first Velasco so severely that the viceroy became very much displeased at his assumption of power. Velasco was even declared to be inefficient and his term of office was considered too long. The ayuntamiento planned to have Valderrama appointed governor and Martín Cortés made captain-general, but the king was horrified at this wild scheme and the visitor was recalled to Spain.[146]

The pesquisidores, Muñoz and Carrillo, invested with the powers of visitors, were sent to Mexico during Peralta's adminis-

[143] *Recopilación*, leyes 12, 16, 26, 31, tit. 34, lib. 2.

[144] Palafox to his successor, 1642, *Documentos inéditos . . . . de Mexico*, VII, 32.

[145] Riva Palacio, II, 338–339; Fernández, *Historia del Peru*, I, 27–32; *Documentos inéditos . . . . de Indias*, III, 509.

[146] *Ibid.*, IV, 357–359, 364.

tration. They bore a letter ordering the viceroy to appear at
court and give account of his conduct in relation to the conspiracy
of Cortés. The judges assumed complete control of the government and acted in a very arbitrary and cruel manner. When
reports of their conduct reached the king, Villanueva and Vasco
de Puga were sent to New Spain to investigate matters, and
the terrible Muñoz was recalled. In 1650 Pedro de Gálvez
came to Mexico to complete the unfinished visitation of Palafox.
He was to take the residencia of the viceroy, of his servants, and
of the alcaldes mayores whom he appointed. One part of his
instruction provided that the viceroy and the audiencia were
not to take cognizance of cases tried by the visitor.[147]

A peculiar incident occurred in 1683 after the capture of
Vera Cruz by the pirates. It was thought that the king appointed
Antonio Benavides visitor, but when he reached Puebla he was
arrested and taken to the capital, where he was imprisoned for
a year and on July 10, 1684, executed in the principal plaza.
There were many murmurs against the viceroy and the audiencia
for daring to impose such a penalty upon a representative of the
king. The truth about Benavides has always remained a mystery.
Some people thought that he was an agent of the pirates, and
others that he was merely an imposter.[148]

In 1715 the inquisitor, Francisco Garzarón, was commissioned
to visit the audiencia and other courts of New Spain, but at first
he had to consult with Viceroy Valero concerning certain matters. He therefore represented to the Council of the Indies
that the visitation would be useless if he did not have complete independence of the viceroy. When the request was
granted Garzarón began the visitation in earnest. The next
visitor-general of New Spain, Francisco de Pagave, was ordered
in 1770 to appeal to the viceroy and the audiencia for temporary
decision in all doubtful litigation, until the will of the Council of

---

[147] Zamacois, V, 123–133; Priestley, *José de Gálvez*, 113.
[148] Riva Palacio, II, 640–641.

the Indies might be known. Neither could the viceroy and audiencia listen to appeals from the visitor's decision, except in cases wherein he sought their advice.[149]

José de Gálvez, the great visitor, came to Mexico in 1765. He had been charged with regulating the public treasury, establishing the tobacco monopoly, introducing customs reforms, and examining the conduct of civil employees. He had secret instructions from Arriaga, the minister of the Indies, to investigate certain accusations of embezzlement against Viceroy Cruíllas. In a short time the viceroy and the visitor quarreled, since Gálvez refused to show Cruíllas the copies of his instructions from the Council of the Indies, which he ought to have done as soon as he arrived. Then the question of the division of their powers occupied their attention. The viceroy insistently refused to give up any of the prerogatives of his office, and Gálvez was equally determined that his authority should not be decreased.[150] The visitor's instructions specifically ordered him to consult the viceroy in regard to custom-house reforms. In spite of àll the objections of Gálvez, the rule which provided this remained unchanged. It said:

It is understood, however, that if any measure be deemed necessary which changes the practice established by earlier orders, you shall not take such measure yourself, but refer it to the viceroy, to whom you shall make manifest the reasons which justify it.

Again the instruction adds:

It will be very desirable for you, during such time as you may reside in Mexico, to confer with the viceroy in a junta which you should hold every week concerning the best method of securing the proposed ends and the measures which may be thought conducive to them. . . .[151]

---

[149] Solórzano, II, lib. 5, cap. 10, art. 60, p. 353; Priestley, *José de Gálvez*, 114–115.

[150] Rivera Cambas, I, 400; Riva Palacio, II, 822; Priestley, *José de Gálvez*, 128–138.

[151] Gálvez, *Instrucción reservada*, March 14, 1765, AGI, 136–5–3, arts. 2, 32.

Cruíllas continued to hinder the work of the visitor in every way possible, even countermanding the orders of Gálvez to the governor of Vera Cruz concerning the sale of smuggled goods. Finally, the visitor obtained the removal of Cruíllas, and the king appointed the Marquis of Croix to replace him.[152] Croix proved to be subservient to the visitor, but it was for this purpose that he had been chosen. He was given very specific orders to aid Gálvez in the affairs with which he was intrusted, and to maintain harmonious relations with him.[153]

The case of Antonio de Areche must be mentioned as an example of a visitor who lacked knowledge in colonial matters. Areche arrived in Lima in 1777 and immediately made plans to increase the royal revenue. His proposal to raise the alcabala, or tax on sales, from four to six per cent, caused much dissatisfaction. The protests grew louder when the visitor interfered with other existing taxes and imposed new ones. A struggle arose between Areche and Viceroy Guirior concerning the founding of the college of lawyers and appointments to its staff. The viceroy won in the contest, for a cédula of June 1, 1785, approved all that he had asked and ordered him to establish the college. The visitor, however, made so many charges against Guirior that the king finally recalled him and appointed a new viceroy.[154]

6. THE INTENDANCIES

The system of intendancies as a limitation upon the power of the viceroy must now be discussed. The primary purposes of this system were to relieve the viceroy of many duties and to provide for a more efficient financial administration. Then too. the shortness of the term of the later viceroys prevented them from being familiar with all the conditions of their viceroyalties,

---

[152] Priestley, *José de Gálvez*, 157 *et seq.*
[153] Croix, *Instrucción que* . . . . *dejó*, AGI, 88–5–13.
[154] Croix to Lemos, 1790, *Memorias de los vireyes* . . . . V, 143–144; Moses, *Spain's Declining Power*, 177–178.

while the intendants could be better informed and were able to specialize in their line of work.[155] Viceroy Croix, in 1768, submitted the plan for the intendancies of New Spain to Charles III, who approved it; but the measure was not put into effect in Mexico until 1786. The institution of the intendancies, borrowed from France, had proved successful in Spain, therefore the king decided to introduce it into America. The experiment was first tried in Cuba in 1768. It was then extended to the viceroyalty of Río de la Plata in 1782 and to the other governments by 1786.[156]

Twelve intendancies and three provinces were created in New Spain.[157] The viceroy was to continue to exercise all his powers according to his instructions and the laws of the Indies, except those relating to the superintendency of the treasury. These latter were to be intrusted to the intendente-general, who was to reside in the capital in order to preside over the junta superior de hacienda, or board of finance.[158] Municipal juntas with delegated powers were established in the capitals of the provinces. The viceroy could attend the junta superior, which was composed of the regent of the audiencia, the fiscal, the senior judge of the tribunal of accounts, and the senior contador, or the treasurer-general of the army and treasury.[159]

The intendants took full charge of finances and were directly responsible to the intendente-general, who in turn was directly

---

[155] Revillagigedo to Floridablanca, Oct. 30, 1790, AGI, leg 1, num. 55; Villarroel, *Enfermedades políticas* . . . . MS, I, pt. II, p. 16; Lemos to Vallenari, 1796, *Memorias de los vireyes* . . . . VI, 202.

[156] Croix, *Instrucción que* . . . . *dejó*, AGI, 88–5–13; Navarro y Lamarca, Carlos, *Compendio de la historia general de America* (Buenos Aires, 1913), II, 412.

[157] For the names of the intendancies see the *Real ordenanza para el establecimiento é instrucción de intendentes de exército y provincia en el reino de la Nueva España* (Madrid, 1786), art. 1, pp. 2–3; Rivera, *Principios criticos* . . . . I, 72.

[158] *Ordenanza* . . . . *de Intendentes* . . . . art. 2, pp. 4–5.

[159] The local juntas were composed of the alcalde ordinario or the senior member who presided, two regidores, the procurador general (attorney-general), or the síndico (defender) without a vote. Becker, 64; *Ordenanza* . . . . *de intendentes* . . . . art. 4, p. 7.

subject to the Council of the Indies. They were appointed by
the king and performed the duties of the former governors in
civil administration and cases of justice, but the viceroy gave
them instructions. The intendants were obliged to inform the
viceroy concerning all the appointments which they made.[160]
They were subordinate to him in affairs relating to policia or
general administration, worship, public instruction, and the
judiciary; however they were the direct agents of the general
intendant in matters of revenue and all fiscal control. In matters
of war they were subordinate to the general of the army and
had to respect all the rights that belonged to the viceroy and
the commandant-general of the frontier. An assessor deputy
chosen by the king, who served as a judge in civil and criminal
cases, aided the intendant. Appeals from his decision went to
the audiencia, and in the absence of the intendant the assessor
performed all the duties of that official except those of the vice-
patronage.[161]

A complete change also took place in the local government.
It had been discovered that corregidores and alcaldes mayores
caused disorder, and that a considerable amount of money was
lost to the treasury every year on account of their dishonesty.
The salaries of those functionaries had been low, and they did
not hesitate to appropriate funds from their districts to make
up for this and for the expenses involved in purchase of their
positions. The ordinances of intendants abolished these old
offices and created sub-delegates, who were put in charge of the
partidos or divisions of each intendancy. They were directly
subordinate to the intendant of the province, who at first
appointed them, but later in 1787 the viceroy was granted this
power.[162]

[160] *Ordenanza . . . . de intendentes . . . .* art 7, p. 11; Rivera Cambas,
I, 469.

[161] Moses, *Spain's Declining Power*, 244; *Ordenanza . . . . de intendentes
. . . .* arts. 299–302, pp. 398–402; Pinkerton, *Modern Geography*, III, 541.

[162] Revillagigedo, *Dictamen . . . . sobre la ordenanza de yntendentes
. . . .* May 5, 1791, MS, num. 402, arts. 131–132; Revillagigedo, *Instrucción reservada*, arts. 859–861.

There were eight intendancies in the viceroyalty of Rio de la Plata and later another was added which included the Patagonian coast and the Falkland Islands.[163] The salary of the governor-intendants in this viceroyalty was six thousand pesos and an additional six hundred for secretarial expenses and visitations. In the case of Potosí the intendant received ten thousand pesos, since he was also the director of the mint. The intendant-general who presided over the tribunal of accounts and audited all the accounts of the viceroyalty was paid ten thousand pesos.[164] In 1784 eight intendancies were established in Peru, and two years later the intendancies of Santiago and Conceptión were created in Chile. There was also one intendancy in Cuba, one in Charcas, and one in Guatemala.[165]

The question whether the intendant system was successful in the New World was much debated. The interference with the viceroy's powers was one of its objectionable points. Viceroy Flórez of Mexico said that his term was too short for him to know all the results of the new ordinances and that he had proceeded cautiously, not daring to enact a great number of measures or give decisive advice. He thought that there was room for improvement in many of the articles of the ordinance, for, judging from the laments of the people, the kingdom and the treasury were about to be ruined.[166] Among the intendants and their sub-delegates there were few outstanding figures. They seemed to be men of limited capabilities and were not much of an improvement over the former officials, while under the old system there had been a number of renowned governors, some of whom became viceroys.

---

[163] For the names of these intendancies consult Moses, *Spain's Declining Power*, 243; Pinkerton, *Modern Geography*, III, 541–542.

[164] *Ibid.*, III, 541, 539.

[165] The names of the Peruvian intendancies are found in Moses, *Spain's Declining Power*, 246; Croix to Lemos, 1790, *Memorias de los vireyes* . . . . V, 70–72; Navarro y Lamarca, II, 412; Altamira y Crevea, Rafael, *Historia de España y de la civilización española* (ed. 3, Barcelona, 1913–14), IV, 195.

[166] Flores to Revillagigedo, 1789, *Instrucciones que los vireyes* . . . . arts. 46–50, pp. 123–124.

Revillagigedo was more frank than his predecessor in expressing his opinion. He believed that the twelve intendants ought
to be directly subordinate to the viceroy in everything. They
should privately take cognizance of the sales, regulations, and
repartimientos of unoccupied lands, but recognize the viceroy's
power to approve and confirm titles. In spite of the defects of
the new system, this viceroy thought that it ought not to be
abandoned, because of the difficulty in reëstablishing the old
order. He also considered the number of intendancies small for
such a vast territory. In order to settle disputed matters Revillagigedo advocated the forming of a special council to be presided
over by the viceroy, and consist of the regent, the senior oidor,
two other judges appointed annually by the viceroy, and the
fiscal. Also it was deemed necessary that the vice-patronage
reside only in the viceroy.[167]

The superintendency-general of the treasury was restored to
the viceroy in 1788; at the same time the management of municipal finances (propios y arbitrios), cognizance of the income
from land tax (censos), and management of the proceeds from
Indian communities were again conferred upon him.[168] Experience proved that ''A viceroy of the treasury and a viceroy
of the political government were incompatible;'' therefore the
intendente-general was made subject to the viceroy. By a
cédula of December 2, 1794, it was declared that the supervision
of all public works, like roads and bridges, pertained to the
viceroy, just as before the intendancies were established.[169]

A case has been found wherein Viceroy Teodoro de Croix
removed an intendant from office. It shows that, although some
of the viceroy's powers had been decreased by the establishment
of the intendant system, he still was able to exercise a great deal
of authority. Francisco Hurtado engaged in commerce with the

---

[167] Revillagigedo, Sept. 1, 1791, MS, num. 128, AGI, 24; Revillagigedo,
Dictamen . . . . sobre la ordenanza de intendentes . . . . MS, num. 402,
arts. 280, 298, 22, 32, 112, 125.

[168] *Ibid.*, arts. 230–231.   [169] Coroleu, III, 52; Becker, 65.

island of Chiloé, and in spite of the viceroy's warnings, persisted in continuing his misdeeds. He became angered and denounced both the viceroy and his assessor. Croix then gave an account of his conduct to the king, but this had no effect upon the intendant, who insulted the viceroy and even went so far as to say that the island of Chiloé was not subject to the jurisdiction of Chile or Peru. The viceroy finally had him removed, brought to Lima, and from there sent to Spain.[170]

7. THE RESIDENCIA

The residencia was the principal means employed by the king to keep viceroys and other functionaries under control. At the expiration of their term of service, all officials from the highest to the lowest had to undergo this official investigation of their conduct during incumbency. The residencia, like all other Spanish colonial institutions, was transported from Spain, and, no doubt, the very fear of it was often an incentive to efficient service. The viceroys were held responsible for taking the residencias of governors, and a law of the Indies ordered that they should dispatch a commission for this purpose every five years, but the real acuerdo had to be consulted concerning this matter. Also, the viceroy was to provide for the residencias of corregidores, alcaldes mayores, and treasury officials. At the beginning of every year, it was his duty to appoint a judge of the audiencia to take the residencia of regidores, and of the fieles ejecutores, who were the judges of a special court which had charge of the supply of foodstuffs and the adjustment of prices.[171] A book containing all the decisions made by the judges of residencia was ordered kept in the archive of the audiencia, and at the end of each year it had to be submitted to the viceroy for examination.[172]

---

[170] Croix to Lemos, 1790, *Memorias de los vireyes* . . . . V, 125–129.

[171] *Recopilación,* leyes 4–7, 21, 14, 11, tit. 15, lib. 5.

[172] Cédulas and provisiones for the audiencia of Charcas, 1591, *Documentos inéditos* . . . . *de Indias,* XVIII, 200. The practice of taking the residencia of minor officials was abandoned in 1799. Cunningham, 129.

The residencia of a viceroy was an important event which was widely published so that accusations might be received from any part of the viceroyalty. Six months was the time set for this investigation and the examination of witnesses, but sometimes many years elapsed before it was finished. It took Palafox two years to complete the residencias of viceroys Cerralvo and Cadereyta.[173] As a general rule, the viceroy had to submit to the residencia before leaving his post. Occasionally it was completed in Spain when the viceroy was a man of good character. As a mark of special favor the king might dispense with it entirely. In New Spain Bucareli was the first viceroy to receive this great honor.[174] Matías de Gálvez also was relieved of the residencia. Flórez was not only free from the expenses of a residencia but had six months' salary placed at his disposal for the return voyage to Spain.[175]

Some of the visitors were authorized to take the residencia of the executive, as in the case of Mendoza of New Spain. Sandoval tried to convict him of certain charges made by Cortés, who declared that the viceroy had committed many misdeeds, like carrying on illicit commerce, misappropriating funds, engaging in expeditions of discovery, allowing his attendants to be corrupt, and committing acts of cruelty during the Mixtón War, but he was not found guilty.[176]

The most incriminating charges were frequently made against the viceroys in their residencias. For instance, the Marquis of Cerralvo was accused of appropriating for his own use four thousand pesos, of denying the jurisdiction of the Council of the Indies, on account of his using four thousand pesos for a chapel without consulting that body, and of making false accusation against Francisco de la Torre, his enemy.[177] The second Albur-

173 *Recopilación*, ley 1, tit. 15, lib. 5; García, *Don Juan de Palafox*, 115.
174 Gómez, Diario, *Documentos para la historia de Mexico* (Mexico, 1853–57), serie 2, pt. VII, pp. 85–86.
175 *Ordenes de la corona*, MS, III, pp. 56, 82.
176 Priestley, *The Mexican Nation*, 66–67.
177 *Vireyes de Mexico* . . . . MS, serie 1, arts. 16–17.

querque was said to have permitted more than seventy foreign ships loaded with merchandise to enter Vera Cruz within four years, so that he might gain profit for himself. It was also stated that the viceroy received fees from alcaldes mayores by forcing them to pay for their offices the amount which they cost in Spain, that he received twelve to twenty per cent from all warrants on the treasury, that he kept half of the money assigned to the Indian parishes and for the armada of the Windward Islands, and a portion of all the rents in the kingdom. Likewise, the viceroy was thought to have levied one hundred thousand pesos on each ship coming from China, and to have formed a monopoly of maize.[178] Vizarrón was accused of violating the rules of the visitation, appointing men of his own choice and disregarding the judges of the audiencia, to whom those duties belonged. It was charged that he would not permit cases in first instance to go to the audiencia; that he denied the passing of autos appealed from the superior government to the audiencia, and that he allowed persons to be appointed to office whose residencia had not been taken.[179]

Viceroys were seldom punished severely, in spite of such accusations. Occasionally slight fines were imposed upon them. Monterey was said to have spent 200,000 pesos uselessly on the Indian reductions, or settlements in towns, and was ordered to restore the amount to the treasury, but after his appeal to the king the sentence was revoked. A small fine of 1000 ducats was paid to the treasury of New Spain by Salvatierra before he began his service in Peru.[180] Vizarrón was not declared guilty and it was stated that all the qualities of a perfect viceroy were found in him. Even Cruíllas, against whom numerous charges were made by Visitor Gálvez, was found blameless in all matters concerning the treasury and justice, and no proof could be

---

178 *Consulta en vista del papel que hace acusación contra Alburquerque*, June 2, 1711, AGI, 60–5–2.

179 *Vireyes de Mexico* . . . . MS, serie 1, art. 18, pp. 1–7.

180 Zamacois, V, 251; Rivera Cambas, I, 80, 165, 169.

obtained of his having given positions for compensation. The king also complimented him on the good results of his residencia.[181] The penalty of the residencia fell heavily upon one viceroy at least. The Council of the Indies ordered Iturrigaray to pay the huge sum of 400,000 pesos for his interests in the mining tribunal of Mexico, also 119,000 pesos for merchandise illegally introduced into New Spain at his arrival in 1803, and twice the amount of 9684 ounces of gold, and 4000 pesos which he and his wife had received as favors in the distribution of quicksilver and in contracts for paper for the manufacture of cigarettes. Execution of this sentence was deferred because of the declaration of Mexican independence in 1821. Meanwhile, Iturrigaray had died, and in 1824 the Mexican Congress stopped the proceedings and restored the 400,000 pesos to his family.[182]

The length of the residencia and its expenses were hardships for the viceroy. For instance Villamanrique, who was charged with wasting public funds, lost nearly all his possessions in his residencia, which lasted for six years. Finally, the Council of the Indies excused the marquis from the accusations, but he died before everything was settled.[183] Perhaps the second Revillagigedo, one of the best viceroys of Mexico, suffered the most inconvenience from his long residencia. He was permitted to sail for Spain and the investigation of his deeds was conducted during his absence, but the last days of the ex-viceroy were embittered by the unjust arraignments of his enemies, and his death occurred before the residencia was decided. The inestimable worth of Revillagigedo was discovered at last and the vascillating Charles IV ordered the regidores of Mexico City to pay the costs of his residencia.[184]

---

181 *Vireyes de México* . . . . MS, serie 1, art. 18, pp. 166–173, 182. For the charges against Cruíllas *see* Priestley, *José de Gálvez*, 166–168.

182 Alamán, *Historia de Méjico*, I, 264–266.

183 Rivera Cambas, I, 64; Riva Palacio, II, 441.

184 Alamán, *Disertaciones* . . . . III, Appendix, pp. 81–82.

The process seems to have lost much of its effect during the latter days of Spanish rule in America. The second Revillagigedo certainly had no use for it, when he said,

The residencias have been considered as a means of avoiding disorders in the administration of justice; but experience clearly proves how little progress is made by this means, [which] as a rule is the more burdensome to the good servants of the king, whom it obliges to go to an expense which they cannot afford. . . .[185]

There was always the possibility that a viceroy who was rich and powerful would bribe the judges to decide the residencia in his favor or overlook his worst misdeeds. Juan and Ulloa describe how this could be done in Peru. As soon as the judge arrived in Lima, the persons whose residencias were to be taken set their friends to win his support so that he would absolve the officials of all charges. In other words the residencia of every corregidor and public functionary could be made to turn out well for a price.[186]

The establishment of the four viceroyalties of New Spain, Peru, Nueva Granada, and Rio de la Plata required a powerful personage, the direct representative of the sovereign, to rule over each. Several grandees from Spain, some ecclesiastics, many military leaders, and four American-born men were considered worthy to hold this high honor, and for the most part, with of course some exceptions, they proved faithful to their duties. Exceptionally successful governors or captains-general in America might hope to be summoned to fill the high office of viceroy; likewise the chief executive himself always looked forward to being promoted to some other viceroyalty. At first his term was practically for life, but later it was fixed at three years, then gradually extended to five years.

When a viceroy died in office the pliego de mortaja designated the person who should rule in the interim, the archbishop, as a

---

[185] Revillagigedo, *Instrucción reservada*, art. 140.

[186] Juan, Jorge, and Ulloa, Antonio de, *Noticias secretas de America* (Londres, 1826), pt. II, pp. 255 *et seq.*

rule, being preferred. The executive's salary was always high enough to correspond to the dignity of his important position. Upon the arrival of a new viceroy, if possible a conference was arranged with his predecessor; but in any event, a written instruction to his successor, describing the condition in which he left the kingdom, was always required of the retiring executive and was usually forthcoming. The reception of a recently appointed viceroy was one of the chief social events in the colony. An oath of office which was necessary for every new viceroy was taken in the presence of the audiencia.

The early viceroys exercised more powers than later ones, since they had to meet many emergencies arising in a country newly settled and because of the great distance from Spain. The greatest freedom was permitted in the time taken by colonial executives to put into effect their instructions and the royal decrees. The monarch himself allowed his orders to be modified, and even suspended. The viceroy issued instructions to governors and others officials, recommended their removal from office, and called the attention of the monarch to their excellent service. The power of appointment depended entirely upon the will of the king, and as a result some viceroys exercised this right more frequently than others. Too much initiative on the part of a viceroy was regarded by the crown with suspicion.

The limitations imposed upon viceroys, especially later ones, were many. Colonial executives were commanded to report to the king with the greatest detail on all matters, so that nothing might escape his eye. The very paternalism of the home government often proved to be a hindrance to viceroys in America. The audiencia, which communicated directly with the sovereign, was one of the principal checks upon the viceroy's authority, and the viceregal council also had a slight restraining influence upon him. The office of regent of the audiencia, created to relieve the president of that body of some of his many duties, at the same time, naturally decreased his powers somewhat, making him more of an honorary presiding officer. The people whom he governed served to cause a viceroy to act with caution, for some of them had influence at the royal court. There was danger of the king deposing the viceroy if he was not careful of his conduct, and reprimands were received frequently.

The visitor was another effective check upon the power of the executive; his coming was dreaded and strained relations often resulted between the two officials because of the overlapping of their powers. Likewise, the intendant system limited the authority of the later viceroys, since the intendant-governors assumed many viceroyal duties, especially in financial matters. The residencia was the principal means adopted by the king to keep the viceroys faithful in the performance of their duties. Yet, during the latter days of Spanish rule in America, even this check lost some of its terror and effectiveness, for there was the possibility of a rich and powerful executive bribing the judge who had come to try him.

CHAPTER II

CIVIL ADMINISTRATION

The viceroy's duties pertaining to civil administration were just as essential, although perhaps not so conspicuous, as his military and other functions. The real problem was the development of the colonies in order to make them profitable for the mother country. The civil administration was continuously busy with the distribution and colonizing of lands, public works, and questions of municipal government. It must be realized that many of the civil functions of the viceroy were so closely united with those of other departments of government that it is difficult to separate them; accordingly it becomes necessary to treat some of them under justice, the royal patronage, and the duties of captain-general.

One of the important titles of the viceroy was that of governor. Montesclaros thought that it gave him the most preëminence and authority in gubernatorial affairs,[1] and it was under this title, as well as that of viceroy, that the executive supervised all the matters of civil administration in the whole viceroyalty.[2] There was always much to be done in the populous cities of Mexico, Lima, and later Santa Fé de Bogotá and Buenos Aires; hence the relation of the viceroy-governor with the provinces wherein these capitals were located, was more intimate than with the other parts of the viceroyalties, where many of the matters of civil administration were intrusted to the governors in the name of the chief executive.

---

[1] To his successor, 1615, *Documentos inéditos* . . . . *de Indias,* VI, 192.

[2] Donald E. Smith in his work entitled *The Viceroy of New Spain* emphasizes the fact that the viceroy was the governor of the province of Mexico and that he exercised in this central district only the duties of any one of the many other ordinary governors. As it will be seen in this study, the view is taken that, under the title of governor, the viceroy performed the tasks of civil administration for the whole viceroyalty. The documentary evidence supports this view.

1. THE SECRETARIAT

A secretariat, usually controlled by two chief secretaries, assisted the viceroy in his administrative duties. These offices were bought at high prices and were much desired. The business of the government was divided between them; that is, all civil matters, since cases relating to justice were not received in the secretary's office. It was there that many details of administration were worked out and the numerous dispatches of the viceroy formed. The secretaries were bound by an oath to observe secrecy.[3] The two chief secretaries might have assistants, and it was the duty of the viceroy to see that these were capable men.[4] The great cumbersomeness of Spanish administration, involving masses of papers, reports and opinions concerning the most minute details, made the viceroy dependent to a high degree upon his secretaries. Villarroel declared that the most burdensome duty of a viceroy was to spend from four to six hours daily in the dispatch of contentious expedientes which the two secretaries of the government showed him for proper reference. Thus much valuable time was lost which might have been spent on more important matters.[5]

We do not hear of any very famous secretaries, and, no doubt, they were men of average abilities. Before the administration of Fuenclara in New Spain, it seems that the secretaries had belonged to the viceroy's attendants or family, but at this time the king decided to appoint them. He designated Fernández Molinillo, who had served Casafuerte well and was experienced in matters of government, and Fuenclara was requested to confer with him concerning gubernatorial matters. The viceroy was to sign with his own name all the official letters which he asked the secretary to write. Certain rooms were set aside for the

---

³ Croix, *Instrucción que* . . . . *dejó*, AGI, 88–5–13; Palafox to his successor, 1642, *Documentos inéditos* . . . . *de Mexico*, VII, 68.

⁴ Liñan to Palata, 1681, *Memorias de los vireyes* . . . . I, 287.

⁵ Villarroel, *Enfermedades políticas* . . . . MS, I, pt. II, pp. 2–3.

secretariat. One room was assigned to the archives and another contained the desks of the secretaries and their assistants.[6]

The first reorganization of the secretariat was made by Amarillas in 1756, when three salaried positions were established. This arrangement did not long remain satisfactory. Croix added two more officials, but even these were not sufficient and Bucareli was forced to make another change. The staff then consisted of six officials who received regular pay and six others who served without. In 1778 Bucareli appointed two more undersecretaries, two copyists and a porter, making a force of seventeen subordinates subject to a chief secretary.[7] During the administration of Flórez the secretariat was divided into departments in which the work was more equally distributed.[8] In 1790 Revillagigedo had five departments comprising a staff of thirty. He separated the materials in the achive into two divisions named corriente and antiguos. In the former he put all papers pertaining to his administration and those of his predecessor, and in the latter all old documents. Thus the papers most frequently consulted were made easily accessible.[9]

In the dispatch of administrative matters the viceroy was aided by an assessor. The early laws of the Indies permitted this to be done by means of the clerks of the cámara or by the viceroy's deputy, but only in cases of secrecy could the president employ his secretaries for such a purpose. A law of 1618, confirmed by others during the next three years, granted the viceroy the right of appointing an assessor without salary for all matters relating to government. He was not to take cognizance of contentious jurisdiction or cases of justice, which belonged to the prerogative of the audiencia. The assessor gave advice

---

[6] Fuenclara, *Instrucción reservada* . . . . April 23, 1742, AGI, 90–2–17, arts. 15, 12–13; Croix, *Instrucción que* . . . . *dejó,* AGI, 88–5–13.

[7] Revillagigedo to Valdes, Jan. 11, 1790, translated by Smith, 189–190. Unfortunately this letter has been mislaid and was not accessible to the present writer in the original.

[8] *Suplemento de Bustamante,* to Cavo, art. 86, p. 369.

[9] Revillagigedo to Valdes, March 27, 1790, AGI, num. 388 (28).

to his chief in all other questions of law. ''As counselor to the president, this official bore the same relation to the executive as the fiscal did to the audiencia.''[10]

2. DISTRIBUTION OF THE LANDS AND COLONIZATION

Titles to lands were granted as remuneration for the services of the conquerors, but the king also permitted his friends, who either went to the colonies or remained at court, to receive them. Lands were given by the viceroys in the king's name to discoverers, the descendants of conquistadores, and colonists, who were not to sell them to the church or monasteries.[11] Several laws of the Indies ordered the viceroy to consult with the cabildos of the cities and towns before distributing lands. Wistano Orozco in his study of the legislation concerning uncultivated lands in Mexico, states that from the earliest date these laws were not enforced and that titles were habitually bestowed by the viceroy without consulting the cabildos.[12] In the conferring of lands upon Spaniards, the Indians were not to be injured. If harm resulted to them, the titles of the estates were to be declared null by the viceroy. The executive was to see that all lands for raising cattle were located far enough from Indian towns that their crops would not be destroyed, and he could use his own judgment in deciding which regions were best adapted to irrigation. He was to have all cattle removed from such lands in order that wheat might be cultivated.[13] He had authority to inspect land titles, the laws of the Indies commanding him to protect the rights of persons having legitimate titles, but to restore all other lands to the crown. He was to take away part of the estates from people having a legal title, but who had

---

10 *Recopilación*, leyes 4–5, tit. 16, lib. 2; leyes 46–47, 35, tit. 3, lib. 3; Cunningham, 208.

11 Riva Palacio, II, 670; *Recopilación*, leyes 4, 10, tit. 12, lib. 4.

12 *Ibid.*, ley 5; Orozco, I, 32.

13 *Recopilación*, leyes 9, 12–13, tit. 12, lib. 4.

usurped more than their share of uncultivated territories, and grant them new titles.[14]

The viceroys were authorized to sell public lands and see that within reasonable time the royal confirmation for holding them was obtained. Grants made by the cabildos could be revoked if they were not confirmed by the king.[15] Because of the great expenses for the defense of Christianity against the heretics and for the armada to protect the colonies, the sovereign commanded the second Cañete to sell estates at just prices to those who wished to buy them in the city of La Plata, the towns of Cochabamba, Tarija, Tomina, and neighboring places. During the administration of Mancera in Peru, the money which entered the treasury from the sale of lands amounted to two million pesos.[16] A royal decree of August 27, 1747, directed to the first Revillagigedo, permitted appeal to the Council of the Indies concerning the sale and distribution of land, but only with the viceroy's approval. Another order of October 15, 1754, to the same viceroy, empowered him to appoint judges of commission to take charge of the sale and distribution of unoccupied royal lands.[17]

The viceroy confiscated estates and personal property whenever the king ordered him to do so. During the administration of Vizarrón a cédula came from the king authorizing him to confiscate all the property which the Duke of Monteleone, the marquis of the valley of Oaxaca, had in Mexico, because he sympathized with the Germans in the kingdom of Naples. The viceroy took necessary measures to confiscate all the goods and papers of the duke, but a special agent came from Spain to dispose of them.[18]

---

[14] King to viceroy of Peru, 1540, *Documentos inéditos . . . . de Indias*, XXIII, 492; Cédulas and provisiones for García Hurtado Mendoza, 1591, *ibid.*, XVIII, 235–236; *Recopilación*, leyes 14–15, tit. 12, lib. 4.

[15] *Ibid.*, leyes 16, 20; Orozco, I, 118.

[16] Cédulas and provisiones for Cañete, *Documentos inéditos . . . . de Indias*, XVIII, 547–548; Polo, *Memorias de los vireyes . . . .* art. 71, p. 25.

[17] Orozco, I, 128–130, 60.   [18] Riva Palacio, II, 781.

The encouragement of colonization was another duty of the viceroy under his title of governor. Mendoza gave impetus to the establishment of new settlements in Mexico by granting men who married Spanish girls the position of corregidor in the towns to be erected.[19] In 1591, after some uprisings of the Chichimec Indians, a treaty made with the natives stipulated that the second Velasco might send Christianized native families to assist them in forming settlements. Accordingly four hundred families of Tlaxcaltecs were settled among the Chichimecs. Under the direction of the Franciscans the four colonies of San Luis Potosí, San Miguel Mesquitic, San Andrés, and Sudueste were founded, thereby uniting the fierce Chichimecs to the crown and guaranteeing permanent peace with them.[20] Monterey permitted Diego de Montemayor to settle the province of Nuevo León in 1596, and sent to New Mexico Juan de Oñate, who took with him families for colonization.[21] Almost a century later Laguna sent three hundred families to establish the colony of Santa Fé. The second Alburquerque also dispatched some families of Tlaxcaltecs to inhabit the post of Santa María de Galve in Florida, and Azanza founded a new colony in Nuevo León, giving it the name of Candelaría de Azanza.[22]

The viceroy supervised in a general way the building of all new towns and cities. He informed himself concerning the best and most healthful sites on which to locate towns. Not only were the sites to be good, but the viceroy had to consider also the fertility of the surrounding country, the water supply, whether there were building materials for the houses, and Indians to instruct in the Gospel, whether there was an outlet to the sea and the possibility of making good roads, whether the

---

[19] Priestley, *The Mexican Nation*, 68.

[20] Cavo, lib. 5, arts. 23–24, p. 146; Zamacois, V, 202.

[21] Bancroft, *History of Mexico*, III, 779–780; *Documentos inéditos . . . . de Indias*, XVI, 97, 193.

[22] Rivera Cambas, I, 253, 303; Bancroft, *History of Mexico*, III, 497.

region could be easily defended, and whether the natives would suffer injury from proximity to the Spanish settlements.[23]

The first Cañete of Peru caused the five towns of Tomebamba, Cuenca, Cañete, Truxillo, and Santa to be founded during his administration. He aided them by the remission of the tributes and by providing funds for roads, bridges, and public buildings. Shortly after his reception in Lima, Viceroy Toledo gave orders for the town of Santiago del Cercado to be built. This example may be mentioned as typical in the planning of all Spanish towns. A prominent place was chosen for the hospital and the parochial church. Another section was assigned to the Indian houses, which were not to be crowded. The remainder of the town was laid out in squares. Walls surrounded it and the gates were to be closed at night so that the inhabitants might be safe.[24] Sometimes the king gave substantial assistance for the erection of new towns, as he did when Superunda was governing Peru. At this time the energetic Charles III placed twenty thousand pesos for public works at the disposal of all the towns established in Chile. The elder Velasco caused the towns of San Felipe and San Miguel to be erected to guard the roads leading from the rich mines of Zacatecas against Indian attacks. Córdoba was also established to defend the road to Vera Cruz from Negro uprisings.[25]

Taking the census was another task of the viceroy. During the sixteenth century several attempts of this kind were made in Mexico, but the results were far from accurate. In the seventeenth century, however, the census was taken seven times in New Spain, and on several occasions in the following century. In 1790 the second Revillagigedo learned from his census report,

---

[23] King to the viceroy of Mexico, April 6, 1550, *Documentos inéditos . . . . de Indias*, XXIII, 534–535; Ordinances for new towns, 1563, *ibid.*, VIII, arts. 34–41, pp. 498–500; Ordinance of 1573, *ibid.*, XVI, 154–157.

[24] Letter of Cañete to the emperor, May 25, 1556, *ibid.*, IV, 97–98; Account concerning Toledo, 1569, *ibid.*, VIII, 233–234.

[25] Superunda to his successor, 1761, *Memorias de los vireyes . . . .* IV, 209–210; Riva Palacio, II, 364; González Obregón, *México viejo*, 325.

which was more accurate than previous ones, that the population of his viceroyalty was three and a half millions.[26] Palata undertook an enumeration of the population of Peru. He intrusted the counting of the people of their districts to the corregidores, who were assisted by a clerk and the alguacil, and ordered the priests to show baptismal and burial records and assist the corregidores as much as possible.[27]

3. PUBLIC WORKS AND IMPROVEMENTS

The viceroy's duties as superintendent of public works occupied much time. The construction of aqueducts for the cities and towns was one of his chief cares. Viceroy Toledo made many wise provisions for the water supply of Lima. No person might close, repair, or open a new ditch without the consent of the cabildo or the superintendent of waterworks, and everybody was to keep the ditches on his own property clean. All running water which crossed a street was to be covered with flat stones, and carts were not permitted to enter the city, since they polluted the water. Waste of irrigating water was also prohibited.[28]

The bringing of water from Chapultepec to Mexico City was undertaken by Montesclaros in 1604, but the aqueduct could not be finished until 1620, during the administration of Guadalcázar. This structure consisted of nine hundred arches, some of which still stand, and cost one hundred and fifty thousand pesos. Later Croix caused the part of the aqueduct which brought the water to the front of the palace to be constructed with lead pipes so that it would be more durable. At his arrival in the capital, the second Revillagigedo found that the water supply had been

---

[26] King to Mendoza, April 17, 1535, *Documentos inéditos . . . . de Indias*, XXIII, 425. For the other dates when the census was taken *see* Riva Palacio, II, f. 682; Robertson, Wm., *The History of America* (ed. 1, London, 1777), Appendix, pp. 494–495; Revillagigedo, *Instrucción reservada*, art. 143.

[27] Palata to Monclova, 1689, *Memorias de los vireyes . . . .* II, 237–250; Solórzano, I, lib. 2, cap. 18, art. 66, p. 151.

[28] Moses, *The Spanish Dependencies . . . .* I, 167.

badly neglected. He took measures to make the necessary repairs and appointed two guards to report concerning any leaks and prevent people from using more than their share of water. New lead pipes were laid along the sides of the streets, instead of in the center of them, since passing carriages had caused much damage. The viceroy also provided for the improvement of the ten public fountains in order to economize the water and keep it more sanitary.[29]

Road-building was another problem of the viceroy-governor. The king desired the colonial executives to open highways in convenient places so that all parts of the viceroyalty might be accessible. Then too, road construction was a humanitarian measure. Since pre-conquest days the Indians had been the burden bearers, but the Spanish monarch considered this work inhumane, and therefore commanded his viceroys to make roads in order that beasts of burden could be used, thereby relieving the native carriers. Mendoza gave orders for roads leading from the mines to be opened, because it was there that the Indians suffered most from carrying heavy metals.[30] This was to be done, however, with the least possible expense to the treasury, and the persons who received benefit from those works were expected to help pay the cost.[31]

One of the greatest enterprises of this kind was the highroad from Mexico City to Toluca. Since the valley of Toluca was the principal source of the grain supply in New Spain, there was need of better facilities to transport wheat and maize. An engineer by the name of Ricardo Ailmert made a survey for the road in 1768, and a judge of the audiencia, Domingo Trespalacios,

29 Riva Palacio, II, 540, 562; González Obregón, *México viejo*, 62; Croix, *Instrucción que . . . . dejó*, AGI, 88–5–13; Revillagigedo, *Instrucción reservada*, arts, 304–308.

30 Solórzano, I, lib. 2, cap. 13, arts. 23, 25–26, p. 119; King to the viceroy of Mexico, April 16, 1550, *Documentos inéditos . . . . de Indias*, XXIII, 526; Mendoza to Velasco, *Instrucciones que los vireyes . . . .* 230, 237.

31 *Recopilación*, ley 53, tit. 3, lib. 3; ley 1, tit. 16, lib. 4; Court to Amarillas, 1755, *Instrucciones que los vireyes . . . .* art. 37, pp. 71–72.

drew up a plan, but the matter was suspended until the administration of Croix, who again ordered Ailmert to consider the
matter. Because of other pressing business, Croix was forced
to drop the project; however he emphasized to his successor the
need of the highway. Finally 'the work was begun in 1793 under
the second Revillagigedo, but it was not finished until the time
of Branciforte.[32]

The Vera Cruz highway was of even greater importance than
that of Toluca, since over it would be brought all the merchandise
from Europe. When he traveled from Vera Cruz to the capital,
Croix noticed how badly the roads were neglected, and ordered
that new thoroughfares from the port should be constructed.
The great Revillagigedo was also interested in this public work;
therefore he permitted two plans to be made. When the papers
were submitted to the consulado, that organization found many
objections to details, and the viceroy was not able to realize the
undertaking. It was not until 1803 that the much desired highroad from Vera Cruz was begun in earnest.[33]

Another dream of Revillagigedo was the construction of a
road leading northward to Tampico, but this was never completed in his day. It is interesting to note that this liberal viceroy did not favor building a road through Texas and Louisiana
to encourage trade between Texas and New Orleans, because of
his suspicion of foreigners.[34] In South America one of the
greatest problems was the opening of roads to Chile. This was
the province most exposed to foreign aggressions and most
ravaged by hostile Indians; accordingly it was necessary to be
able to send there troops and supplies as quickly as possible.
Several viceroys of Peru were interested in the project of road-

---

[32] Revillagigedo, *Instrucción reservada,* arts. 173, 185; Croix, *Instrucción
que . . . . dejó,* AGI, 88–5–13; Marquina to Iturrigaray, 1803, *Instrucciones que los vireyes . . . .* art. 131, p. 180.

[33] Croix, *Instrucción que . . . . dejó* AGI, 88–5–13; Revillagigedo,
Instrucción reservada, arts. 187–188, 192–193, 195; Marquina to Iturrigaray,
1803, *Instrucciones que los vireyes . . . .* art. 130, p. 180.

[34] *Instrucción reservada,* arts. 196, 198, 448.

building,[35] but at the threshold of the nineteenth century O'Higgins found the thoroughfares of Chile in lamentable condition. This energetic viceroy had the very necessary highway from Lima to Callao constructed.

A stage line was established in Mexico in 1791, the coaches running regularly from the capital to Puebla and from there to San Andrés, a distance of sixty-nine leagues. Eight coaches transported the people from one part of the capital to another in 1793. On days of fiesta and bullfights this number was increased to accommodate the people.[36] Viceroys were ordered to see that inns were established for travelers and that just prices were charged for the conveniences given. They were to supervise in a general way the good administration of all public houses. In the latter part of the eighteenth century Villarroel complained about the inconvenience for travelers in the town of Antigua, where the only lodgings were made of cane or reeds. In these everyone from viceroys and archbishops to the most miserable native had to spend the night, and it did not occur to any one to improve conditions.[37]

Canals did not play a very important part in transportation during the viceroyal days. Mendoza gave orders that a river coming from the lake of Citaltepeque and another arising in the town of Teutiguaca should be extended into a canal so that lime, stone, and grain might be brought into the city by it. This canal proved very serviceable, and the viceroy requested his successor to keep it in repair. Revillagigedo was an advocate of canal construction. In 1794 he said: "Much more advantageous than roads would be the construction of canals, or rendering navigable certain rivers, which could be done at slight cost." He therefore commanded the director of engineers, Miguel del

---

[35] Croix to Lemos, 1790, *Memorias de los vireyes* . . . . V, 161–165; Lemos to Vallenari, *ibid.*, VI, 163–169.

[36] Gacetas de Mexico, 1790–1791, IV, 347; *ibid.*, 1792–1793, V, 419–423.

[37] *Recopilación*, ley 1, tit. 17, lib. 4; Villarroel, *Enfermedades políticas* . . . . MS, III, pt. IV, p. 116.

Corral, to form plans for an internal system of canals to be tributary to the port of Vera Cruz; this was done and on March 24, 1790, the plans were submitted to the king for his approval. Because of the cost and more urgent matters, nothing was done to put these projects into effect.[38]

Bridges were needed, especially for crossing the dangerous rivers in South America. Many passengers and Indians had drowned in the Barranca and Apurimá rivers, which traversed the highroad between Santa Cruz and Cuzco. Velasco saw that durable wooden bridges were built across these rivers. A bridge was required to cross the river of Mara, fourteen leagues from Lima. There much loss of baggage and many accidents had occurred every year; therefore Mancera ordered Captain Benito Pérez to construct a bridge in that place. Later, during the administration of Teodoro de Croix, was built the bridge of Jequetepeque on the highway carrying the traffic from Lima and adjacent towns. The priest Contreras, to promote the public welfare, undertook to get a bridge erected over the river of Santa. Viceroy Lemos was pleased that an ecclesiastic should be interested in such a work, so he took the matter up with his council and the junta de hacienda, and it was decided to put the plan into effect.[39]

The wharves at Vera Cruz and Callao, and later those at San Blas were objects of the viceroy-governor's care. After the transfer of Vera Cruz to its present site in 1591, much merchandise was lost in unloading cargoes in the narrow channel between San Juan de Ulúa and the mainland; therefore the second Velasco decided to provide a wharf on the coast. The work had not been completed by 1595 when the viceroy's term ended, because some vessels bringing lumber for the structure

[38] Mendoza to Valero, *Instrucciones que los vireyes* . . . . 231; Revillagigedo, *Instrucción reservada,* arts. 199–200, 201, 205.

[39] Velasco to Monterey, 1604, *Documentos inéditos* . . . . *de Indias,* IV, 429; Mancera to his successor, 1648, *in* Polo, *Memorias de los vireyes* . . . . art. 52, p. 17; Croix to Lemos, 1790, *Memorias de los vireyes* . . . . V, 137; Lemos to Vallenari, 1796, *ibid.,* VI, 193–197.

had met with accidents. Velasco urged his successor to finish the wharf. Viceroy Croix caused a dry dock to be established at San Blas to aid the explorations in California.[40] Castel-Fuerte and Superunda both had a wharf built at Callao, but it was not large enough for the increasing commerce. Viceroy Guirior made great preparations to construct a new wharf; as little was accomplished, Teodoro de Croix decided to continue the work with the aid of the consulado.[41]

The powder factories of Mexico City, Lima, and Cuzco were considered very important, since it was from these centers that supplies of powder were sent to the frontier. The people of Mexico City never felt at ease because the powder magazine was situated only half a league from the city. Therefore, Mancera had the establishment removed to a greater distance and caused the explosive to be stored in several depositories so that if one blew up, the city would not be endangered.[42] Teodoro de Croix also had the powder magazine of Cuzco located a league from the city on account of the danger from fires. Viceroy Amat permitted the powder factory of Lima to be constructed against the wall of the city. Because of the possibility of an explosion, Viceroy Guirior gave orders that a place should be found some distance from the capital, but at that time the king did not favor building a new and costly magazine. In 1782 the royal approval was obtained for placing the establishment between Pando and Marango. Then it was decided that two factories were needed and nothing was done. On January 31, 1792, the old powder magazine blew up, and this incident hastened the erection of the new plant during the administration of Lemos.[43]

---

[40] *Los advertimientos que el virey Don Luis Velasco dejó al conde de Monterey,* 1595, AGI, 58–3–13, cap. 17; Cagigal to Cruillas, 1760, *Instrucciones que los vireyes* . . . . 117–118; Croix, *Instrucción que* . . . . *dejó,* AGI, 88–5–13.

[41] Croix to Lemos, 1790, *Memorias de los vireyes* . . . . V, 151–160.

[42] Mancera to Veraguas, 1673, *Instrucciones que los vireyes* . . . . 265–266.

[43] Croix to Lemos, 1790, *Memorias de los vireyes* . . . . V, 177–192; Lemos to Vallenari, 1796, *ibid.,* VI, 89.

Mendoza took measures to provide for the preservation of forests. Early colonizers have always caused much damage to virgin forests, and the settlers of New Spain were no exception to the rule. Therefore, the first viceroy realized that if they continued to do this, the supply of timber would fail. He urged his successor to keep his ordinances for the preservation of the forests, modifying them only when the timber lands had been sufficiently increased.[44]

The drainage of the valley of Mexico was, perhaps, one of the greatest public works ever undertaken in Spanish America. Even under the Aztec rule floods had occurred in this valley, being caused during the rainy season by the excess waters of Lake Cristóbal overflowing into that of Tézcuco. The Aztecs tried to keep the waters of this lake away from their capital by means of dikes, which were cut during the conquest. The first inundation under viceregal administration was in 1553, when for three or four days canoes had to be used in the streets of the city. The first Velasco did all that he could to check the course of the waters, and worked like a day laborer, with spade in hand, on the canals and dikes which the Spaniards had neglected to repair after the conquest. The critical situation was finally relieved by changing the bed of a small river.[45]

Elaborate plans were drawn up in 1604 for a drainage canal to cost four hundred and sixty-eight thousand pesos, but it was decided to repair the dikes and clean the canals already in existence. The viceroy, Montesclaros, gave orders for a dike to be built in Mexicaltzingo to check the waters of Lake Chalco. This work freed the capital from floods, but the rich country on the other side of the embankment suffered more. In 1607, after the next flood, the drainage of the valley was begun in earnest by Enrico Martín, a Portuguese engineer. The project accepted

---

[44] Mendoza to Velasco, *Instrucciones que los vireyes* . . . . art. 10, p. 228.

[45] Torquemada, I, lib. 5, cap. 14, pp. 618–619; Cavo, lib. 4, art. 12, pp. 109–110.

by the second Velasco was practically the same as the one suggested in 1580 by Obregón y Archiniega, whereby the waters of
the plateau lakes were carried through the Tula and Pánuco
rivers to the Gulf of Mexico. On May 9, 1609, the viceroy,
oidores, ayuntamiento, and many members of the clergy went out
to the work to witness the flowing of the waters of the lakes
Zumpango and Citlaltepetl by way of the Nochistonga Canal to
the valley of Tula. This work soon proved disappointing, since
the conduit was too small and the sediment clogged it. Martín
was criticized severely for the inefficiency of the drainage and
in 1616 he tried to repair it, but only with additional expense
to the treasury.[46]

Again in 1627 the waters broke the dike of Cuautitlán,
inundated the city, and remained until 1631. Viceroy Cerralvo
hesitated to take immediate action without the royal approval.
In 1637 the torrents swept away part of the work constructed
by Martín, hence it was decided to make an open cut now called
the cut of Nochistongo or the Huehuetoca Canal. Many Indian
laborers lost their lives on this work and by the year 1700 the
enormous sum of 4,229,582 pesos had been spent on it. During
the administration of Croix the project of widening the river bed
was begun in order to prevent the stream from being closed by
débris. The drainage was continued by Branciforte and later
viceroys, but the Huehuetoca Canal was not finished until the
administration of President Díaz.[47]

---

[46] Riva Palacio, II, 538–540, 542–545, 562; Cavo, lib. 6, art. 9, pp.
163–164.

[47] Riva Palacio, II, 585–586, 590, 665. A good description of the cut
of Nochistongo, also of the measures taken after the different floods is
given by Mancera in *Instrucciones que los vireyes* . . . . 261–265; Branciforte to Azanza, *ibid.*, art. 90, p. 141; Croix, *Instrucción que* . . . . *dejó*,
AGI, 88–5–13.

4. THE RELATION OF THE VICEROY TO THE CAPITAL

The first relation of the viceroy-governor toward his capital was the protection of the inhabitants. This was not always an easy task, for according to Villarroel

Each subject lived as he chose, without order or system, causing commotion in the street day and night, and disturbing the rest of the people, while the lower classes gained control with no one to check their daring, restrain their excesses, or punish their insolence.

He went on to say that misery and grandeur held equal sway and that Mexico City was a haven for vagrants and a resort for rogues. In order to rid the city of criminals the viceroy usually used great vigilance in causing patrols to be made, even calling out the troops if necessary.[48]

The cabildo or town council was elected originally by the citizens, and the viceroy might not hinder their actions in any way. This was the only trace of self-government in the Spanish-American colonies, but even this privilege was limited when the cabildo tended to become a closed corporation, membership in which was purchased or inherited. Finally the cabildo became entirely self-perpetuating and the election a mere farce. The viceroy himself was president of the cabildo of Lima, and he often indicated verbally the persons who seemed suitable to him to serve as alcaldes ordinarios.[49] Ordinarily there were six regidores or councilmen and two alcaldes ordinarios or justices elected by the regidores, but in the larger cities the number might be increased. In the latter part of the eighteenth century the cabildos of Lima and Mexico consisted of sixteen members each. The towns were permitted to dispatch agents to represent their interests before the Council of the Indies, but the viceroys

---

[48] *Enfermedades políticas* . . . . MS, II, pt. III, pp. 5–6; Castel-Fuerte to Villagarcía, 1736, *Memorias de los vireyes* . . . . III, 276.

[49] *Recopilación*, ley 7, tit. 9, lib. 4; Moses, *The Spanish Dependencies* . . . . II, 371; Revillagigedo to Amarillas, 1754, *Instrucciones que los vireyes* . . . . art. 88, p. 22.

were not to allow them to send attorneys. The residents of
Lima, in a cédula of November 19, 1769, obtained the privilege
of electing the alcaldes of the wards (de barrio), whose duty
consisted of attending to the lighting and cleaning of streets
and fountains and general police matters.[50]

The functions of the cabildo comprised local legislation, provision for sanitation, regulation of prices and supplies, suppression of monopolies, prevention of graft, repair of aqueducts
and causeways, and the cleaning and paving of streets. The first
Revillagigedo divided Mexico City into four wards and placed
a regidor over each in order to keep it clean and to make improvements. He thought, however, that the regidores became very
careless in the performance of their duties unless the viceroy
watched them continually.[51] In order to obtain greater efficiency
in their management, the viceroys found it necessary to absorb
many of the powers of the cabildo.

The viceroy had to see that the regidores were the right kind
of persons to hold public positions. Linares said that the executive got the blame for everything which went wrong; therefore it
was necessary that the councilmen should be men whom the
people respected. Before the administration of Croix regular
salaries were not paid, but the regidores were merely allowed
their expenses in the commissions of which they had charge.
Among the regulations which Visitor Gálvez made, was a provision that they were to receive fixed salaries. Sometimes
rivalries between the cabildo and the audiencia were very embarrassing to the viceroy, since both organizations claimed that the
election of alcaldes ordinarios belonged to their jurisdiction.
Marquina was disturbed by a disagreement between these bodies,
the cabildo objecting to the judge conservador of the audiencia

---

[50] Lemos to Vallenari, 1796, *Memorias de los vireyes* . . . . VI, 83;
Croix, *Instrucción que . . . . dejó*, AGI, 88–5–13; *Recopilación*, leyes 4–5,
tit. 11, lib. 4; Avilés to Abascal, 1806, *Memoria del virey del Peru*, 32–33.

[51] Villarroel, *Enfermedades políticas* . . . . MS, II, pt. III, pp. 14–15;
Revillagigedo to Amarillas, 1754, *Instrucciones que los vireyes* . . . . arts.
82, 87, pp. 21–22.

and to the general assessor of the administration. The difficulty was finally settled by the viceroy who suggested the forming of an impartial council to discuss the matter.[52]

The two alcaldes elected annually by the cabildo took cognizance in first instance of judicial matters in the city and for five leagues around it. Several laws of the Indies authorized them to take the place of the governor, when he died without leaving a deputy, until the viceroy could provide for the vacancy. Viceroy Linares himself performed the duties of the corregidor in Mexico City and he considered that the office would be a good one for the executive to fill permanently, since it gave him much authority. After 1786, the intendant who resided in the capital took the place of the corregidor, but in 1803 we find Marquina entreating the king to reëstablish the old office. However, the monarch did not seem to heed the viceroy's request.[53]

The viceroy had power to declare town elections void in cases of corruption, as did Toledo in ʿCuzco. When the executive visited this city, he found that only two regidores had voted for alcaldes, therefore he ordered a new election. When it was held only four persons appeared, and the viceroy then called out the soldiers to compel the councilmen to vote properly. In 1758 the residents of the same city had a dispute with the corregidor over the election of alcaldes. Following the example of his predecessors, Viceroy Superunda suspended the cabildo's power of election for that year, and himself chose the alcaldes. Because of special entreaties by the people other alcaldes were elected by the cabildo, but the viceroy fined the corregidor and ordered the councilmen to give place to his appointees. In order to prevent disorders in Lima, Viceroy Palata caused the cabildo

---

[52] Linares to Valero, 1716, *Instrucciones que los vireyes* . . . . 305, 310; Croix, *Instrucción que* . . . . *dejó*, AGI, 88–5–13; Marquina to Iturrigaray, 1803, *Instrucciones que los vireyes* . . . . arts. 73–76, p. 171.

[53] *Recopilación*, ley 3, tit. 8, lib. 4; ley 12, tit. 3, lib. 5; Croix, *Instrucción que* . . . . *dejó*, AGI, 88–5–13; Linares to Valero, 1716, *Instrucciones que los vireyes* . . . . 305; Marquina to Iturrigaray, 1803, *ibid.*, art. 72, p. 171.

to confer with him concerning the candidates two or three days before the election.[54]

To provide a sufficient food supply in a country where famine prevailed was an important duty of the viceroy. The very first viceroy of New Spain was confronted by this problem; accordingly he ordered the corregidores of the neighboring towns to bring wheat and maize to the public plaza of the capital where it was sold to persons who needed it. There was also a scarcity of fodder for cattle, so Mendoza caused a part of the marshy land surrounding the lake to be planted with grass. The plan was so successful that in a short time more land was prepared for this purpose.[55]

Provisions were not only needed in the capital to relieve the misery of the people, but the position of the viceroy himself was not secure without them. Palafox tells us that the lack of food caused the people to be thrown into confusion and to act rashly. Linares said that ''The enemy to be feared most was hunger and shortage of food.'' Villarroel adds:

. . . . For this reason [Linares] was vigilant in seeing that there was an abundance of comestibles, in order that he might feel secure from popular insurrection. . . . Only when there is dire need and things have become irremediable do [the viceroys] begin to worry, call meetings, pass hasty resolutions and [make] inadequate decisions for remedying matters. Everywhere the clamor of the people is for bread and meat. If these are lacking because of poor management on the part of those who govern, they cannot be sure of living long in peace, for the populace is an untamed beast that is easily aroused.[56]

This fear was not a mere false alarm on the part of the viceroys, since a number of food riots actually occurred. The most notable one was in 1692, at which time a mob surrounded the public granary of Mexico City and started fires. Viceroy Galve fled

---

[54] Account concerning Toledo, *Documentos inéditos . . . . de Indias,* VIII, 257–258; Superunda to his successor, 1761, *Memorias de los vireyes . . . .* IV, 316–317; Palata to Monclova, 1689, *ibid.,* II, 68.

[55] Mendoza to Velasco, *Instrucciones que los vireyes . . . .* 237, 231.

[56] Palafox to his successor, 1642, *Documentos inéditos . . . . de Mexico,* VII, 29; Villarroel, *Enfermedades políticas . . . .* MS, II, pt. III, pp. 75–76.

to the convent of San Francisco for safety while the palace was besieged and burned. The viceroy thought that the use of the intoxicant, pulque, was one of the causes for those disturbances; therefore he prohibited its consumption.[57]

The first public granary was established in Mexico during the administration of Enríquez, in order that there might be plenty of grain for years of scarcity. Two regidores were appointed to sell the wheat, flour, barley, and other grains stored in it. No one might buy or sell these articles outside of the granary, nor might bakers purchase a larger quantity of wheat or flour than was needed for two days.[58]

The meat supply had to be safeguarded by the viceroy, just as that of grain. The meat ordinarily came from a distance, since the cattle lands were farther from the large cities than the grain fields; therefore the monopoly of furnishing the capital and other populous cities with meat was granted to persons who were willing to pay the highest price for this privilege. The contracts were sold at auction, but had to be confirmed by the government. When there was a lack of meat in the capital the funds from the granary might be applied for purchasing cattle to be slaughtered.[59]

Prevention of food profiteering, when rich and influential persons were engaged in it, was a real problem for the viceroy to solve. A well-known case of this kind occurred in Mexico under Gelves. Some wealthy individuals who were friends of the oidores, and especially Pérez de Várez, the alcalde mayor of Metepec, tried to form a monopoly of maize; accordingly the viceroy ordered the regidores to deposit the maize in the public granary and fixed the price at twenty reales a fanega. Várez was arrested for tampering with the food supply, but he claimed

---

[57] Cavo, lib. 9, arts. 19–20, p. 235; Riva Palacio, II, 652–654; Rivera Cambas, I, 274–276; Zamacois, V, 458–465.

[58] Enríquez to Coruña, 1580, *Instrucciones que los vireyes* . . . . art. 12, p. 247; Riva Palacio, II, 517; *Recopilación*, leyes 4, 7, tit. 14, lib. 4.

[59] Revillagigedo, *Instrucción reservada*, arts. 325–326; Revillagigedo to Amarillas, 1754, *Instrucciones que los vireyes* . . . . art. 83, p. 21.

sanctuary at the convent of Santa Domingo, thereby causing complications wherein Archbishop Serna was involved. The viceroy was finally excommunicated and recalled to Spain. In 1659 the first Alburquerque suspended García Tello de Sandoval, the corregidor of Mexico City, from office for six months, deposed his deputy permanently, and imprisoned the alguacil and four regidores for trying to decrease the weight of loaves of bread under pretense that there was a scarcity of wheat. The viceroy visited the flour mills in person to find out how much grain was on hand and appointed a new corregidor.[60]

Viceroys frequently took a hand at the regulation of prices. Viceroy Casafuerte fixed the price of meats according to the quality of the cattle and the place from which they came. The crop of 1769 was scant, and the farmers concealed some of the grain so as to raise its price. Viceroy Croix set the price at fourteen pesos a carga on produce of the first grade and thirteen pesos for that of the second. He also sent councilmen to the places where the grain had been stored in order that they might bring it to the mills in the suburbs of Mexico City. In a short time the normal value of ten pesos a carga was attained.[61] During the Napoleonic wars the rates of wheat rose considerably. Marquina then sent letters to the prelates and cabildos of the neighboring towns asking them to coöperate with the collectors of the tithes in sending grain to the public depositories. He also ordered the intendants to give a report of the harvests, and commissioned the judge of the criminal chamber, Joaquín de Mosquera, to investigate the scarcity of wheat.[62]

The supervision of street cleaning and paving was an additional task of the viceroy. In those days of medieval sanitation property owners were very careless about throwing garbage and refuse into the streets. Viceroy Croix tried to solve this problem

---

[60] Rivera Cambas, I, 114; Zamacois, V, 380.

[61] Rivera Cambas, I, 329; Croix, *Instrucción que . . . . dejó*, AGI, 88–5–13.

[62] *Suplemento de Bustamante*, to Cavo, art. 63, pp. 353–354; Marquina to Iturrigaray, 1803, *Instrucciones que los vireyes . . . .* art. 82, p. 172.

and to reduce the annual expense of twelve or fourteen thousand pesos for street sweeping by assigning one hundred and sixty convicts to the work.[63]

This same viceroy tried to beautify the capital by paving the chief thoroughfares, after having the stepping stones, so dangerous to the passage of carriages, removed. The streets of San Francisco were paved and repaired at the expense of the property owners. When the cost was high, these individuals objected and made it difficult for the city councilmen to collect the money; therefore Croix advanced a project to be discussed in the municipal council, whereby other funds were to be appropriated for this work. The second Revillagigedo realized the difficulty of trying to collect taxes from carriage drivers and house owners every time the streets were to be paved or repaired, so he decided to impose a regular tax of one-half real for each square rod of abutting property.[64]

Street lighting did not occur until the latter part of the eighteenth century, but as early as the administration of Montesclaros crude attempts were made to have lights placed after dark in the principal public buildings of Mexico City. In 1763 Viceroy Cruíllas ordered all the residents of the city to keep a light on one of the balconies of their houses from dusk until ten o'clock in order to prevent crimes from being committed under cover of darkness. The penalty for neglect was a fine of two or three pesos and six days' imprisonment. The inhabitants of the streets of Juan Manuel and San Agustín had, since 1780, performed this duty of illumination so successfully and without any cost to the treasury that Matías de Gálvez ordered the other citizens to do the same, but his death prevented the measure from being put into effect. Finally, in 1790, Revillagigedo had the lighting of the streets paid for by imposing a tax of three reales on each carga of flour brought into the city. In Buenos Aires,

---

[63] Villarroel, *Enfermedades políticas* . . . . MS, II, pt. III, pp. 100–102; Croix, *Instrucción que* . . . . *dejó*, AGI, 88–5–13.

[64] *Ibid.*, AGI, 88–5–13. This tax amounted to 44,060 pesos annually. Revillagigedo, *Instrucción reservada*, arts, 276–277.

Viceroy Vertíz imposed a tax of two reales on each house door opening on the street, to pay for municipal lighting.[65] Viceroy Amat caused all the houses of Lima to be numbered and the names of each street to be indicated on the corner.[66] The creation and improvement of public parks was another duty of the viceroy. It was the second Velasco who caused the Alameda to be established for the purpose of beautifying the city of Mexico and for the recreation of its residents. Later Viceroy Croix enlarged this park, inclosing it by a palisade around which were placed benches. A grove of trees surrounded the palisade and in the center were five fountains. The proceeds from a bull-fight were used to meet the expenses of these improvements. The fines imposed by justices of the cities and by judges of the audiencia for minor offenses were sometimes used on public works of this kind.[67]

When cities were damaged by earthquake, the viceroys usually came immediately to the rescue. After the earthquake of June 17, 1678, in Lima, Viceroy Castellar commanded the maestro de obras or superintendent of public works to repair all the damaged buildings, including the viceregal palace, other public edifices, churches, convents, and the houses of the people. Lima was pratcically rebuilt by order of the viceroy after an earthquake ten years later. The day following the earthquake of October 28, 1746, in the same capital, Superunda rode among the ruins to see how the city might be aided. An earthquake caused much destruction in Mexico City in 1711, and Viceroy Linares at once took charge of the repairs and of assisting the poor to rebuild their homes.[68]

[65] Rivera Cambas, I, 86; González Obregón, *México viejo*, 507–508; Riva Palacio, II, 876; Revillagigedo, *Instrucción reservada*, arts. 292–296; Moses, *Spain's Declining Power*, 250.

[66] Coroleu, II, 139.

[67] Rivera Cambas, I, 69; Croix, *Instrucción que . . . . dejó*, AGI, 88–5–13; Cédulas and provisiones for the treasury officials of Charcas, 1589, *Documentos inéditos . . . . de Indias*, XVIII, 427.

[68] Castellar to Liñan, 1681, *Memorias de los vireyes . . . .* I, 192–194; Palata to Monclova, 1689, *ibid.*, II, 119–120; Superunda to his successor, 1761, *ibid.*, IV, 110–113; Zamacois, V, 525.

Protection against fire was another matter to occupy the attention of the viceroy.   It seems that in Lima fireworks used in fiestas had caused conflagrations; therefore Teodoro de Croix, following the example of Amat, prohibited the manufacture of all fireworks except those needed to show respect to members of the royal family who had died.   In Mexico City fire pumps were established in 1790 to protect the custom-house, the tobacco factory, the mint, and other important buildings.   At this time Revillagigedo caused a list of rules to be drawn up concerning fighting fires and protection of property.   Marquina decided that a special judge was needed a try cases growing out of fires.   He made arrangements for the viceroy's guard to be sent immediately to burning buildings and as soon as the fire bell rang a company of infantry and a division of dragoons were to assemble in front of the viceregal palace in order to protect it.   A subaltern and twenty men, also a company of dragoons were to keep order and prevent looting in the burning districts.[69]

The viceroys had to see that public offices were sold to efficient persons.   It was considered perfectly proper to sell offices, and this was one of the means taken to replenish the treasury.   Offices for sale were of great variety, ranging from those of public clerks, notaries, town councilmen, fieles ejecutores, receivers of the fines of the cámara, attorneys, alguaciles, alfereces reales or standard-bearers, treasurers and other officers of the mint, letter carriers, brokers, to tax collectors.   These positions were sold only for short periods or for life, not becoming hereditary as in Spain.   In order to prevent frauds in the sale of offices, the viceroy had to be informed concerning just prices to be charged for them.[70]   In 1591 the king ordered the viceroy of Peru to sell all vacant offices in the cities and towns, to increase the number of salable offices, to sell for life as many as he deemed profitable,

---

[69] Croix to Lemos, 1790, *Memorias de los vireyes* . . . . V, 146–151; Revillagigedo, *Instrucción reservada,* arts. 298–299; Marquina to Iturrigaray, 1803, *Instrucciones que los vireyes* . . . . art. 87, pp. 173–174.

[70] Solórzano, II, lib. 6, cap. 13, arts. 7, 9, p. 484; *ibid.,* arts. 18–19, p. 488; *ibid.,* art. 38, p. 491.

and to send a report concerning the proceeds to the Council of the Indies. The practice of selling offices was one of the reasons for the creation of a number of useless positions. Velasco said that the king commanded him to establish in Lima another office of clerk so that it might be sold, although one was sufficient for the business of the government. Montesclaros advised the king to suppress the position of contador de resultas or accountant of results, since he thought that there were enough officials without him.[71]

Confirmation had to be obtained from the Council of the Indies for all salable and renunciable offices. A royal order of May 31, 1597, required all persons who had purchased offices to show their certificates of confirmation or give up their positions.[72] Resignations from office were not permitted without the king's consent. Those of naval officials had to be made in the presence of the governor or justice of the port at which their vessel landed.[73] The viceroys were to see that a third of the income from renounced offices was given to the treasury, and that the position was sold again to the best advantage of the treasury. According to a decree of July 8, 1598, the king did not favor more than one resignation, for if this occurred more frequently, it might be injurious to the good government of the colonies.[74]

Over all public ceremonial functions held in the capital, the viceroy was expected to preside. The parade of the royal banner in Mexico City on August 13 in memory of the conquest was one of these occasions. A great celebration took place when the royal seal arrived in Lima in 1544. The viceroy, Blasco

[71] Cédulas and provisiones for García Hurtado de Mendoza, 1591, *Documentos inéditos . . . . de Indias*, XVIII, 217–219; Velasco to Monterey, 1604, *ibid.*, IV, 416; Montesclaros to the king, Jan. 15, 1604, AGI, 58–3–15.

[72] *Recopilación*, leyes 1, 3, tit. 22, lib. 8; Cédulas and provisiones for García Hurtado de Mendoza, *Documentos inéditos . . . . de Indias*, XVIII, 454.

[73] Cédulas and provisiones for the audiencia of Charcas, 1585, *ibid.*, XVIII, 162; *Recopilación*, leyes 4–5, tit. 21, lib. 8.

[74] Cédulas and provisiones for Martín Enríquez, 1591, *Documentos inéditos . . . . de Indias*, XVIII, 214–216; Royal cédula of Feb. 10, 1601, *ibid.*, XIX, 130–131; *ibid.*, XVIII, 283–284.

Núñez Vela, and many of the people of the city went out on horseback to receive it. When they came to the place where the seal was, the viceroy gave orders for the case to be opened by the clerks of the audiencia, and a round silver seal stamped with the royal arms was drawn out and shown to the people, who made obeisance to it. It was then conveyed with much pomp into the city. At the entrance of the capital the cabildo met the procession, the regidores placed a canopy of crimson satin over the seal, and it was carried to the viceregal dwelling. At the foot of the stairs the viceroy and the oidores took the case off the gaily caparisoned horse and intrusted it to the alcaldes, who bore it to the executive's apartment.[75]

When an oath of allegiance was made to a new king, the viceroy was the center of attraction. The first Cañete, the audiencia, the functionaries of Lima, and the people, all in gala attire, assembled in the public plaza to swear allegiance to Philip II. The imperial arms and those of the city were displayed amidst the music of trumpets. The viceroy, mounted on a white horse, handed to Pedro de Avendaño, the clerk of the audiencia, a letter from Charles V which he read word for word. He then read another letter from Philip II and when he had finished the viceroy grasped the royal banner in his right hand and in a loud voice said, "Castile! Castile! Peru! Peru! for the king Don Philip our Lord." Then all the officials repeated the same words and all the people in the plaza shouted, "Long live the king! Long live the king!" The viceroy and the archbishop scattered throughout the plaza silver reales, stamped with the image of Philip and Queen Mary. A procession was made through the city to the largest church where the mass of Santiago, the patron saint of Spain, was said. After the benediction, the crowd accompanied the viceroy to his home.[76]

---

[75] The ceremony of bringing out the royal seal was discontinued Jan. 7, 1812. González Obregón, *México viejo*, 54–56; Account concerning Cañete, *Documentos inéditos* . . . . *de Indias*, VIII, 383–385.

[76] Account concerning Cañete, *ibid.*, IV, 395–401.

The viceroy also took charge of the ceremonies performed in honor of a deceased monarch. He sent instructions to all towns of the viceroyalty telling their officials how to conduct the ceremonies. The people were required to dress in mourning, but sometimes an exception was made to this rule in the case of the Indians and the poor. In order to prevent the exactions of merchants, Viceroy Moctezuma fixed the price of black materials at twenty reales a yard and fined those who sold it for a larger amount.[77] The death of King Charles II was solemnly proclaimed in the viceregal palace of Mexico, and the bells of the cathedral tolled three hundred times. Similar announcements were made in the palace of the archbishop, of the Inquisition and in the cabildo. Several days later Viceroy Moctezuma received visits of condolence from the different functionaries and from the people. Almost a week later the obsequies were celebrated by the tolling of the vespers for the dead and a Latin oration in eulogy of the deceased king. Next day at sunrise the service for the dead was attended by the viceroy and other officials; a funeral sermon ended the ceremonies.[78]

Supervision of public health was another viceroyal duty. Epidemics were common in the viceroyalties because of the physical uncleanness of the people and of bad climatic conditions in some sections. Smallpox, introduced into Mexico during the Narváez expedition, caused the destruction of many Aztecs. A pernicious disease called matlazáhuatl, which attacked the natives but not the whites, appeared in the time of Mendoza. Many thousands of Indians died from these diseases through lack of quarantine and proper treatment.[79] The plague of 1545 carried off whole towns and the fields were without cultivators. Mendoza

---

77 Rivera Cambas, I, 387; Cavo, lib. 10, art. 1, p. 245.

78 Cavo, lib. 10, arts. 2–3, pp. 246–247.

79 Humboldt, I, 117; Priestley, *The Mexican Nation*, 64. No doubt the disease matlazáhuatl was a form of influenza. The native methods of treating diseases were bleeding and the roots of the country for fevers, and plunging into cold water and sweats for smallpox. García Icazbalceta, Joaquín, *Nueva colección de documentos para la historia de México* (Mexico, 1886–92), III, 56–57, 64–65.

did all that he could to relieve the distress by assigning buildings to the care of the sick, ordering the governors of the provinces to render the necessary aid, and by giving large sums of money. When the terrible matlazáhuatl broke out again in 1576 and lasted for five years, Viceroy Enríquez and the archbishop were tireless in providing temporary hospitals, medicines, food and clothing.[80]

In 1736 another scourage attacked the natives and Viceroy Vizarrón established eight provincial hospitals and five drug stores where the poor might obtain free medicine. He also paid four doctors to visit the sufferers and a commission was sent from house to house to distribute food. The image of Guadalupe was brought out into the street as a means of relieving the plague. During the epidemic of smallpox in 1779, Viceroy Mayorga arranged that one hundred more beds should be established by the ayuntamiento in the hospital of San Juan de Dios, and permitted the archbishop to found another hospital of four hundred beds in the ex-Jesuit college of San Andrés. The order by the second Revillagigedo in 1792 to kill all dogs in the capital may have been a measure to prevent disease or simply to get rid of a public nuisance.[81]

The lack of cemeteries outside of the cities was considered one of the chief causes for disease, therefore the second Revillagigedo turned his attention to this matter. A graveyard was finished at Puebla in 1790, and the viceroy wrote to the cabildo of Vera Cruz concerning a similar work, but these wise measures were interrupted two years later when a royal cédula permitted ecclesiastics to continue to be buried in the churches and convents of Vera Cruz. Viceroy Croix of Peru assigned four places for cemeteries outside of Lima, but the scarcity of funds prevented

---

[80] Zamacois, IV, 711–712; Cavo, lib. 5, arts. 6–7, pp. 134–135.

[81] Rivera Cambas, I, 345–346, 441; Cavo, lib. 2, art. 6, p. 273. After the plague of 1736, the dead in the capital and its suburbs were estimated at 40,500 and in the whole country at 192,000. Gómez, Diario, *Documentos para la historia de Mexico*, serie 2, pt. VII, p. 381.

the work from being realized. A cédula of July 30, 1803, ordered Viceroy Avilés to put the measure into effect. He also could not do this because of the shortness of his term.[82] Some attempts were made to prevent the spread of epidemics. Revillagigedo saw that the rules suggested by the protomedicato, or board of physicians, in regard to burning the clothing and beds of persons who had contagious diseases, were carried out in Mexico City, and he ordered the intendants to do it in their provinces. Avilés quarantined a boat named the *Prince of Asturias* when it arrived at Callao because three persons had died on board from what seemed to be a plague. Likewise, he commanded that boats trading from one port to another should be inspected for diseases.[83]

The security and prompt delivery of the mails had to be guaranteed by the viceroy. The laws of the Indies were very strict concerning the matter of tampering with the mails. No one was to open letters sent to the viceroys, governors, or individuals, under the penalty of loss of office, banishment, lashes, or service in the galleys. Viceroys had a perfect right to investigate crimes relating to the opening of the mails and severely punish the guilty. The king was informed that sometimes letters and packages of dispatches coming from Peru were opened and detained, and that secrets of the government were learned and communicated to other persons. Therefore he ordered the second Cañete to publish orders in all the towns of his viceroyalty that no one, either ecclesiastic or secular, should dare to open letters or hinder any one in sending them.[84]

The viceroys were to see that the Indian chasquis or mail carriers were well paid. Mancera took measures to stop the sufferings and grievances of the Indian letter carriers in Peru,

---

[82] Revillagigedo, *Instrucción reservada*, arts. 208–213, 222–224; Avilés to Abascal, 1806, *Memoria del virey del Peru*, 34–35.

[83] Revillagigedo, *Instrucción reservada*, arts. 230, 234–236; Avilés to Abascal, 1806, *Memoria del virey del Peru*, 35–36.

[84] *Recopilación*, leyes 6–8, tit. 16, lib. 3; Cédulas and provisiones for Cañete, 1592, *Documentos inéditos . . . . de Indias*, XVIII, 262–263.

and as a result, much time was saved, it being possible for a letter to come from La Plata and Potosí to Lima in twenty-four or twenty-six days. A letter could be sent from Cuzco and the answer be obtained within the same month. In 1659 the first Alburquerque gave orders for small dispatch boats or avisos to be sent to Spain with the mail from Mexico every four months. Finally, on account of mismanagement, in 1765 the crown took charge of the mail service and many advantages were obtained from the change.[85]

Many minor administrative matters needed the attention of the viceroys. The wine shops, peanut shops, and retail grocery stores frequently became places of vice and laziness where the poor and especially working men pawned even their clothing and tools. When these people no longer had articles of their own to pawn, they committed robberies of homes and churches. The tribunal of the fiel ejecutoría passed an ordinance which commanded that nobody should receive any jewel in pawn, when it could not be proved that it belonged to the person pledging it. This measure was not sufficient to destroy the evil; therefore Viceroy Croix ordered all the shopkeepers and wine merchants of Mexico City to show the articles which they had received. A surprisingly large number of personal effects were found and among them eight hundred forbidden weapons. The viceroy fixed by decree a period of time in which the owners might redeem their former possessions.[86]

The viceroy also had to oversee the collection of laws, statistics, and geological specimens. It was the first Velasco who gathered together the royal cédulas, letters, provisions, ordinances, instructions, and other dispatches for the monumental work of the *Recopilación de leyes de los reynos de Indias.* The

---

[85] *Recopilación,* ley 21, tit. 16, lib. 3; Mancera to his successor, 1648, *in* Polo, *Memorias de los vireyes* . . . . arts. 63–64, pp. 21–22; Bancroft, *History of Mexico,* III, 639–640.

[86] Croix, *Instrucción que* . . . . *dejó,* AGI, 88–5–13; Villarroel, *Enfermedades políticas* . . . . MS, III, pt. IV, pp. 127–128.

viceroy likewise caused all the ordinances necessary for the government of the towns to be collected for publication.[87] Viceroy
Solís of Nueva Granada undertook to assemble all the statistics
of that viceroyalty in order to form a department of statistics.
Marquina received two royal orders to gather the various natural
specimens, metals, and precious stones in Mexico and send them
to Spain.[88]

5. THE RELATION OF THE VICEROY TO CIVIL OFFICIALS

The relation of the viceroy to civil officials must now be considered. The governor and adelantado were the highest officials
next to the viceroy. The title of adelantado was given only to
a discoverer or pacifier of a new region not previously included
under the jurisdiction of the viceroy or of an audiencia. This
functionary performed all the duties of a governor and had both
civil and criminal jurisdiction in the district over which he ruled,
hearing all the appeals from subordinate judges, which did not
go to the Council of the Indies. If the new discovery included
land belonging to the regions governed by the viceroy or audiencia, however, appeals could be made to them. The adelantado
was immediately subject to the Council of the Indies, and the
viceroy or the audiencia was not to intermeddle in his province.[89]
The well-known quarrel between Viceroy Monterey and Juan de
Oñate, the adelantado of New Mexico, was due to the lack of
clarity in the wording of the ordinances concerning new discoveries, dated July 13, 1573, which gave rise to different inter-
pretations as to whether the newly discovered provinces were
within the jurisdiction of the viceroy and the audiencia, or

---

[87] Antequera, 480–481; King to the viceroy of Peru, *Documentos
inéditos . . . . de Indias*, XXIII, 496–497.

[88] Coroleu, I, 336; Marquina to Iturrigaray, 1803, *Instrucciones que los
vireyes . . . .* art. 144, p. 182.

[89] Ordinances for new discoveries, 1563, *Documentos inéditos . . . . de
Indias*, VIII, arts. 87, 69, pp. 513, 508; *Recopilación*, leyes 14, 25, 15, tit.
3, lib. 4.

whether Oñate was immediately responsible to the Council of the Indies. The viceroy tried to compel Oñate to allow appeals to the audiencia and treated him like an ordinary governor, much to the digust of the adelantado.[90] Governors were subordinate to viceroys, even when appointed by the king. In the more distant provinces, however, they exercised almost independent authority in purely local affairs. All important matters of administration, like the founding of new colonies, presidios or missions, and questions of defense or military campaigns were submitted directly to the viceroy. In 1602 the king ordered Pedro de Acuña, governor of the Philippines, to consult with the viceroy of New Spain whenever it was necessary to do so. When the governor of Santa Cruz de la Sierra received the royal order to retain for defense of the kingdom half the income from the encomiendas during a period of four years, he immediately wrote to the viceroy of Peru explaining to him the poverty of his district, and Palata sent word for him not to carry out the king's decree.[91] Governors were to give account to the viceroy of any new discoveries made within their provinces. When Joseph de Escandón undertook the pacification of the province of Nuevo Santander at his own expense and was appointed governor of that region, he corresponded regularly with the first Revillagigedo and related everything to him, including the resources of the country, its industry and commerce. He also consulted with the viceroy concerning the founding of new towns and missions.[92]

Governors had to have the permission of the viceroy in order to confirm the election of alcaldes ordinarios in the towns under their control, and they might not absent themselves from the principal town of the province without his consent.[93]   When

---

[90] *Documentos inéditos . . . . de Indias*, XVI, 165, 513, 42–43.
[91] Cunningham, 20; Palata to Monclova, 1689, *Memorias de los vireyes* . . . . II, 416.
[92] *Recopilación* ley 3, tit. 1, lib. 5; ley 1, tit. 3, lib. 5; Revillagigedo to Amarillas, 1755, *Instrucciones que los vireyes* . . . . 36–37.
[93] *Recopilación*, ley 10, tit. 3, lib. 5; leyes 10, 34–35, tit. 2, lib. 5. Governors usually served for three years.

governors were not lawyers, the viceroy was to see that their deputies had legal training and were properly examined. The viceroy was to prohibit governors or their deputies from engaging in trade, since the laws of the Indies forbade it.[94] This was difficult to do, however, as many of the governors, especially those of the frontier provinces, were military men, and the task of fighting Indians would not have been very attractive without the possibility of trading with the soldiers. For instance, Governor Martos i Nararrete became wealthy from the profits made on the goods which he sold to his men at Los Adaes and his trade with the French and the Indians.[95]

Occasionally governors refused to obey the viceroy, as in the case of the governor of Nueva Vizcaya during the administration of Guadalcázar. This viceroy wrote to the king saying that he could not intervene in putting down an Indian rebellion in the province mentioned because the governor would not obey him. A royal cédula was soon forthcoming on June 18, 1624, which ordered the governor to be submissive to the viceroy. Viceroy Croix had received bad reports concerning Joseph Escandón, who was governing the province of Nuevo Santander; accordingly he summoned the council of war and finance to decide what should be done. Palacios and Llamas were sent to visit the region, and were empowered to investigate the conduct of Escandón and regulate the troops.[96]

The corregidores caused the viceroys much trouble because of their engaging in trade, oppressing the Indians, and getting into disputes with the ecclesiastics. Complaints came from Peru that they appropriated the best pieces of land for themselves, took away water rights from the Indians, and practically enslaved the poor by making them work their estates. Villarroel

---

[94] *Ibid.*, leyes 37, 39, 47, tit. 2, lib. 5.

[95] Bolton, H. E., *Texas in the Middle Eighteenth Century* (Berkeley, 1915), 9.

[96] *Recopilación*, ley 20, tit. 15, lib. 5; Rivera Cambas, I, 106; Croix, *Instrucción que . . . . dejó*, AGI. 88–5–13.

declared that the corregidores in New Spain did not report the true state of affairs in their towns to the viceroy on account of wishing to make a good impression upon him and to win his favor by rendering him idolatrous attentions. An uprising in the province of Andahuaylas against the corregidor obliged Viceroy Castel-Fuerte of Peru to intervene.[97] Many similar cases of the downtrodden people dealing roughly with overbearing corregidores might be mentioned. As early as the administration of the first viceroy of New Spain, the king was advised by the executive himself that the office of corregidor ought to be abolished and be replaced by that of alcalde mayor. Corregidores were usually appointed for three years, but sometimes the king indicated in their titles that they might serve for five years. When the viceroy did not appoint the corregidor, he submitted the names of three persons to the king, who chose one of them for the position. The names were to be sent to Spain one year and a half before the retiring official's term expired.[98]

The duties of a corregidor were multitudinous, especially if he happened to reside in a mining town. All public buildings, roads, and other municipal works were intrusted to his care. He had to provide for the food supply, just as the viceroy did in the capital, and carry out viceregal and royal measures, after he published them in his district. The punishment of criminals was not an easy task for him, since deserters from ships, vagabonds and criminals—all the offscourings of civilization—rushed to the mining regions. The corregidor examined the many legal proceedings which were pending before the ordinary justices, and saw that criminal and civil cases were dispatched as briefly as possible, but he permitted appeal to the audiencia. In order to

[97] *Memorias de los vireyes* . . . . III, 365; Friar Xuarez de Escobar to the king, *Documentos inéditos* . . . . *de Indias,* XI, 197; Letter of Alonso Messia to Velasco, *ibid.,* VI, 130; Villarroel, *Enfermedades políticas* . . . . MS, I, pt. II, pp. 99–100; Castel-Fuerte to Villagarcía, 1736, *Memorias de los vireyes* . . . . III, 78.

[98] Letter of Mendoza to the emperor, Dec. 10, 1537, *Documentos inéditos* . . . . *de Indias,* II, 183–184; Cédulas and provisiones for the conde de Villar, 1584, *ibid.,* XVIII, 177; *Recopilación,* ley 10, tit. 2, lib. 5.

prevent robberies and disorders he tried to make the inhabitants engage in honest occupations. He could appoint persons to take charge of public works, remove them from office if need be, and demand contributions from the taverns and pulque shops to meet the expenses of these projects. He regulated weights, measures, and prices in order to prevent profiteering, and might summon the most influential residents and miners of the town to discuss the best means for increasing the taxes or to decide upon other public necessities. Ecclesiastics conferred with the corregidor about the building of churches or convents, and all prisons were under his supervision, the baliffs being appointed by him. The corregidor was to maintain friendly relations with other officials and with any military companies that might be stationed at a neighboring presidio on the frontier; provide for the good treatment of the natives; aid tax collectors; give account to the viceroy concerning the maladministration of treasury officials, and at the same time suggest to him means whereby treasury funds might be increased. In other words, he was to consult the viceroy about all important measures. He was to keep a book in which all the fines imposed by the justices were recorded. The failure to do this was one of the charges brought against Joan de Ávila, corregidor of the city of La Plata, in his residencia.[99] With the permission of the viceroy the corregidor might confirm the election of the alcaldes ordinarios of his district, and in Peru he had charge of the mitas, it being his duty to see that the miners did not oppress their Indian laborers.[100]

Alcaldes mayores governed the smaller divisions of each province called alcaldías. About two hundred of these officials served in New Spain. They were generally poor, since their salaries were not paid, and as a result they were forced to trade

---

[99] Instruction of Revillagigedo to the corregidor, Padilla, 1754, *Instrucciones que los vireyes* . . . . 48–53; Cédulas and provisiones for the audiencia of Charcas, 1596, *Documentos inéditos* . . . . *de Indias*, XVIII, 273–274.

[100] Cédulas and provisiones of the king, 1589, *ibid.*, XVIII, 203–204; Velasco to Monterey, 1604, *ibid.*, IV, 411–429.

or to tyrannize over the natives. Speaking of the trade of these officials, Palafox declared that the Indians had to handle merchandise, work day and night, sometimes without pay, and buy what they did not need. Ferdinand VI permitted alcaldes mayores to engage in a somewhat restricted form of trade, but the viceroy had to be informed whether they were keeping within the legitimate bounds of this regulation.[101] Frequently alcaldes were lax in the performance of their duties and made the sentences of criminals lighter for a consideration. The priests sometimes took the part of the natives in their lawsuits against the alcaldes mayores, only making matters worse. A case has been found wherein the king took the part of an alcalde against the viceroy. The alcalde mayor of Puebla came to the capital using four mules to draw his carriage. Viceroy Fuenclara tried to stop this ostentation because he himself was only permitted to have six mules. This insignificant ceremonial matter finally was reported to the king, who decided in favor of the alcalde.[102] The tasks of alcaldes mayores were of a judicial and civil nature, similar to the duties already described for the corregidores. At first under Cortés they were intrusted merely with judicial matters, but they soon came to exercise civil functions also.

6. OPPOSITION TO VICEREGAL ADMINISTRATION

There are some notable cases of opposition to viceregal administration. Relations between Cortés and Mendoza were strained from the beginning because their powers seemed to overlap. The organization of the viceroyalty interfered with the conquistador's powers as captain-general, and his large estate in the valley of Oaxaca, containing twenty-three thousand Indian vassals, was

---

101 Priestley, *José de Gálvez,* 49; Palafox to his successor, 1642, *Documentos inéditos* . . . . *de Mexico,* VII, 71–72; Revillagigedo to Amarillas, 1754, *Instrucciones que los vireyes* . . . . arts. 36–39, p. 12.

102 Linares to Valero, 1716, *ibid.,* 304; Villarroel, *Enfermedades políticas* . . . . MS, I, pt. II, p. 27 *et seq.;* Rivera Cambas, I, 363.

a hindrance to centralized government.   Then too, Mendoza asked permission from the king to engage in discoveries—a right which, hitherto, had belonged to Cortés, and quite naturally the viceroy's request caused friction.   The rupture came when Cortés decided to go to conquer the cities of Cíbola, and the viceroy forbade him to do so.   Cortés disobeyed and prepared an expedition which was put under the command of Ulloa.   Later Mendoza seized some of the ships of the marquis and imprisoned the crew which was about to undertake another voyage of discovery.[103]

The most serious case of opposition to viceregal administration was that of Blasco Núñez Vela, the first viceroy of Peru. From the moment he landed in Panamá, Vela began to put into effect with great rigor the New Laws.   All along the way to Lima he adhered to the letter of the new regulations, declaring the natives to be free and refusing to permit them even to carry his baggage or that of any of his attendants.   His tactlessness and arrogance filled the people with consternation, as it was announced everywhere that he would put the New Laws into effect without delay.   At first the people of Lima decided not to receive Vela, but they finally gave him the accustomed reception.   The captain-general, Vaca de Castro, and the encomenderos were hostile to the new executive, and all kinds of wild rumors spread abroad concerning the viceroy's desire to kill the oidores and Captain Martín de Robles.   At last, Gonzalo Pizarro took up arms against Vela, and a veritable civil war occurred wherein Peru was divided into two factions, one supporting the viceroy and the other the conquistador.   After some indecisive skirmishes between the two forces, Vela was killed in the battle of Anaquito, January 19, 1546.[104]

---

[103] Letter of Mendoza to the emperor, Dec. 10, 1537, *Documentos inéditos . . . . de Indias*, II, 211; Cavo, lib. 3, arts. 20–22, pp. 88–89.

[104] Fernández, *Historia del Peru*, I, 50 *et seq;* Herrera, Antonio, *Historia general de los hechos de los Castellanos en las islas y tierra firme del mar oceano* (Madrid, 1601–15), IV, decada 7, lib. 7, pp. 187 *et seq.; ibid.*, decada 8, lib. 1, pp. 1 *et seq.; Documentos inéditos . . . . de Indias*, XLII, 305–326; Robertson, II, 235.

The humanitarian measures of the first Velasco for the protection of the Indians caused antagonism to him on the part of the encomenderos and Martín Cortés. The marquis tried to hold the first place in New Spain by means of his wealth, and his great arrogance angered the viceroy. When Cortés had a silver seal made for himself almost as large as the one used by the king, Velasco informed the monarch about the matter, and the use of the seal was prohibited. The feud became so bitter that Cortés refused to be present at the reception of Visitor Valderrama, but hastened out of the city to meet him before the the viceroy had a chance to do so. Velasco was irritated still more when the visitor became a friend of Cortés and frequented social affairs at his home. After the death of the viceroy, conditions grew worse during the interregnum of the audiencia. Cortés was accused of wishing to become a monarch, and some of his friends were convicted of treason, the Áviles brothers being executed.[105]

There was some opposition even to Montesclaros, who was considered a good viceroy of New Spain. When he was on his way to Acapulco in order to set sail for Peru, he received a letter from forty influential gentlemen of the capital, denouncing him to the audiencia because he had not appointed them to the offices to which they had a right as descendants of conquistadores. The audiencia permitted them to have recourse to the king, much to the annoyance of the ex-viceroy, who believed that he had governed honorably. The attempts to assassinate the first Alburquerque and Viceroy Valero were not due as much to hostility as to the rash acts of madmen.[106]

The uprising in Paraguay under Antequera in 1721 has been thought by some persons to have been an attempt to establish a free state, but it seems to have been more like a case of pure disobedience on the part of a usurping governor. The inhabit-

---

[105] Cavo, lib. 4, art. 18, pp. 114–115; Riva Palacio, II, 372–387; Zamacois, V, 53–56, 71–119.

[106] Riva Palacio, II, 540; *Vireyes de Mexico* . . . . MS, serie 1, art. 24, pp. 1–3; Zamacois, V, 542–543.

ants of Asunción sent complaints to the audiencia of La Plata concerning the supposed dishonesty of their governor, Diego de los Reyes. The oidor Antequera was sent to investigate matters; and he himself took charge of the government, imprisoning the governor. Los Reyes appealed to the viceroy of Peru, who ordered him to be restored to office. Antequera refused to do this, although the viceroy repeated his command three times and demanded that the oidor cease governing. Meanwhile, Los Reyes escaped from prison, raised a force, and began to wage war upon the audiencia and Antequera. The viceroy dispatched troops to put down the civil strife, but at first they were defeated. In the struggle Los Reyes and his family were put to death by Antequera, many lives were lost and much property was destroyed. A reign of terror lasted until 1724. The new viceroy, Castel-Fuerte, took a strong hand in the matter and sent Bruno de Zabala, governor of Buenos Aires, with a sufficient number of men to conquer Antequera, who was soon brought to trial as he deserved [107]

The first Revillagigedo accused the president of Guatemala of assuming an independent attitude toward the viceregal administration. This president was the only official in the whole viceroyalty who had found reasons to suspend a measure for the secularization of parishes, although the preliminary steps had been taken by his predecessor. He gave account of his action to the king, but without having written a word to the viceroy.[108]

A notable case of insubordination was the insurrection of the comuneros in Nueva Granada. The people of this viceroyalty were groaning already under a heavy burden of taxes, tithes, and monopolies, when the visitor, Gutiérrez de Piñeres, was sent to increase them, and to regulate the alcabala and dues for the armada. The ruthless manner in which those imposts were col-

---

[107] Superunda to his successor, 1761, *Memorias de los vireyes* . . . . IV, 207; Castel-Fuerte to Villagarcía, 1736, *ibid.*, III, 294–321.

[108] Letter of Revillagigedo to Amarillas, 1754, *Instrucciones que los vireyes* . . . . 43.

lected led to a revolt, the purpose of which was to redress all wrongs, not to attain independence. The uprising was quelled in 1782, after the viceroy of Peru came to the assistance of the executive of Nueva Granada.[109]

Popular discontent in Chile found expression in the movement for independence led by certain intellectuals like Antonio Rojas, José Orejuela, and Francisco de Borja Araos. The king was informed that an independent republic similar to the one formed by the revolted English colonies, was to be established. The viceroy of Peru apprehended the conspirators and in 1784 sent them to Spain, thereby causing the plot to collapse. It was in 1790 that Miranda entreated Great Britain to aid the Spanish-American colonies in winning their freedom, but not until 1806 did his small expedition leave the United States for Venezuela [110]

The machete conspiracy of 1799, which might have produced a dangerous revolution in Mexico, was detected during the administration of Azanza. The instigator of the plot was Pedro Portílla, collector of the duties of the capital, and his associates were drawn from the lower classes whose only weapons were the broad short swords called machetes, from which the rebellion took its name. Prisoners were to be freed, the property of the wealthy confiscated, and a new government was to be established by the people, who were to decide whether it ought to be like that of the United States. A cousin of Portílla revealed the plans to the viceroy, who immediately summoned the audiencia to decide upon the necessary measures. Without disturbance the thirteen chief conspirators were surprised at their rendezvous, arrested, and tried. From this time until the outbreak of the struggle for independence in both Mexico and South America the germs of rebellion were strengthened by the growing hatred of the American-born Spaniards for the peninsulars.[111]

---

[109] Groot, II, 188 *et seq.;* Moses, *Spain's Declining Power,* 205–225.

[110] *Ibid.,* 233–240, 324–331.

[111] Riva Palacio, II, 888; Alamán, *Historia de Méjico,* I, 132–134; *Suplemento de Bustamante,* to Cavo, art. 195, p. 649.

The people of Mexico seemed to oppose the coming of Marquina, since little was known about him and they thought that he was only a tool of the minister Godoy. Bad reports concerning him came from the Philippines where he had been governor; therefore the residents of the colony were not very enthusiastic about having him for their executive. The audiencia even hesitated to accept his papers, believing they were not authentic. During Marquina's administration a conspiracy to reëstablish the Aztec empire was discovered among the natives of Nueva Galicia. The leader of the movement was an Indian by the name of Mariano, who was supposed to have been abetted by Count Miravalles of Mexico City because of his having large estates in the vicinity of Tepic, the home of the chief conspirators. The plot was revealed to the viceroy, but the evidence was not sufficient to convict any of the participants.[112] In 1805 the president of the audienca of Cuzco informed the viceroy that oidor Berriozábal was planning an insurrection among the inhabitants and officials of the city. There again the plot did not prove dangerous, since the leaders were arrested and executed by order of the viceroy.[113]

In the sketch which has been presented it is seen that, under his title of governor, the viceroy performed all the duties of civil administration for the whole viceroyalty. He was assisted by a secretariat which worked out all the cumbersome details involved in civil government. The viceroy was empowered to distribute lands to discoverers, their descendants, and other worthy persons, and guarantee them proper titles. He took charge of the sale of public lands and saw that the purchasers received the royal confirmation for their property. The promotion of colonization was another very important duty of the viceroy-governor, since by this means only could he hope to hold the more distant parts of the discoveries against foreign aggressions. The founding of

---

112 *Ibid.*, arts. 206–208, p. 657; Rivera Cambas, I, 508.
113 Avilés to Abascal, 1806, *Memoria del virey del Peru*, 45–49.

new towns and cities and the taking of the census were always objects of interest and care for the executive.

Some executives spent much of their time as superintendent of public works. There was always need of aqueducts, roads, bridges, and wharves; for protection of powder factories, and preservation of forests. The drainage of the valley of Mexico was a titanic project which required the careful attention of many viceroys.

In the capital the executive had to keep order, protect the town councils in their elections, and settle any rivalries that might arise between those organizations. In order to preserve peace and to maintain his own security it was necessary for the viceroy to keep continually on hand a sufficient supply of food; for those purposes public granaries were built. Profiteering had to be checked and prices regulated for the good of the community; the cities had to be beautified by street cleaning, paving, and lighting; damages caused to public buildings by earthquakes had to be repaired; precautions had to be taken against fires, and public parks laid out for the recreation and welfare of the people. The viceroy saw that public offices were sold to efficient persons; he presided over all public functions occurring in the capital; he passed measures relating to the department of public health, and he tried to insure the protection and prompt delivery of the mails.

The relations of the chief executive with other officials were to be as harmonious as possible. Discoverers who had been granted the title of adelantado were not to be interfered with in the districts over which they ruled. Governors were subordinate to the viceroys, whom they had to consult before adopting any important measures. Whenever complaints arose against them, the viceroy could send trustworthy persons to investigate their conduct. Corregidores and alcaldes mayores caused the viceroy a great deal of trouble because of their engaging in trade, oppressing the Indians, and getting into quarrels with ecclesiastics.

There were some notable cases of opposition to viceregal administration. Cortés became the enemy of Mendoza on account of the viceroy's seeming to usurp the conquistador's powers of captain-general and his rights to make new discoveries. A civil war was waged in Peru against the arbitrary Blasco Núñez Vela, who was finally killed by the forces of Gonzalo Pizarro. The humanitarian measures of the first Velasco for the protection of the Indians caused the encomenderos and Martín Cortés to be hostile to him. There was some opposition to Montesclaros, and the people of Mexico hesitated to receive Marquina as their viceroy. The civil strife in Paraguay grew out of the disobedience of Governor Antequera. The conspiracy of the comuneros in Nueva Granada, the movement of certain intellectuals in Chile, and the machete rebellion in Mexico were forerunners of the struggle for Spanish-American independence.

CHAPTER III

THE SUPERINTENDENT OF THE TREASURY, AND PROMOTER OF INDUSTRY AND COMMERCE

As superintendent of the treasury the viceroy exercised supervision over the whole financial system of the viceroyalty. His duties relating to this department of government were very important, since he had to oversee the collection of sums of money so enormous that they dazzled the imagination of Europeans. If the viceroy could increase the funds of the treasury he was considered a successful administrator and was sure of royal approval; therefore most viceroys gave matters of public finance their greatest attention. The promotion of industry and commerce was another task of the executive, for by this means, even under the restrictive mercantile theory, it was hoped that the treasury might receive benefit.

1. THE VICEROY AND THE TREASURY

The administration of the treasury was intrusted to the special care of the viceroy, who acted as its superintendent until the era of Spanish-American independence, except during the first two years of the intendancies, from 1786 to 1788. Although the title of superintendent was not conferred upon the viceroy until the middle of the eighteenth century, he had performed all the duties of such an office from the earliest days of the viceroyalties. Much of his time had to be spent in studying the condition of the treasury in order to administer it well. At a moment's notice he had to be able to know the exact funds in the treasury by consulting the reports kept in the secretariat.[1]

---

[1] In 1741 the title of superintendent was conferred upon the first Revillagigedo of Mexico. Priestley, *José de Gálvez*, 58; Palata to Monclova, 1689, *Memorias de los vireyes* .... II, 133.

Economizing for the treasury was considered one of the most essential virtues of administration. The feeble-minded Charles II gave special thanks to Viceroy Rivera of Mexico for reducing the expenses of his secretariat.[2] The monarchs were always greatly pleased to hear that expenses had been reduced, since this meant that larger sums could be sent to Spain. The viceroys were empowered to apply the means which seemed best to them for the collections of moneys owed to the treasury. Fuenclara was commanded to see that the fiscal and the treasury officials honestly collected the large amounts of tribute money. Some negligence occurred in the collection of accounts in New Spain during the rule of the elder Revillagigedo; therefore the king informed the new viceroy Amarillas that he, as well as the treasury officials and the tribunal of accounts, would be held responsible for them.[3]

Under ordinary conditions warrants on the treasury were not valid without an order from the king, and treasury officials who paid them without this provision, even if they were the viceroy's drafts, were in danger of being deprived of their positions. In this matter the treasury officials and the tribunal of accounts acted as a check upon the power of the viceroy. If the executive insisted on drawing money in violation of these rules, the treasury officials could report to the Council of the Indies concerning his conduct.[4] In cases of emergency, however, as a protective measure when there was not time to consult the king, the viceroy might authorize extraordinary expenditures after consulting the acuerdo. A royal decree of July 30, 1588, permitted the viceroy of Peru to do this if he merely communicated with the audiencia and the treasury officials. The same right had been granted to Viceroy Mendoza of Mexico, but when the treasury officials complained that this caused inconveniences, a cédula of December 29,

---

[2] Revillagigedo to Amarillas, 1754, *Instrucciones que los vireyes* . . . . art. 120, p. 26; Cagigal to Cruíllas, 1760, *ibid.*, 112; Rivera Cambas, I, 246.

[3] *Recopilación*, ley 14, tit. 8, lib. 8; Court to Amarillas, 1755, *Instruc ciones que los vireyes* . . . . 81, 75; Fuenclara, *Instrucción reservada*, April 23, 1742, AGI, 90–2–17, art. 5.

[4] *Recopilación*, leyes 1–6, tit. 28, lib. 8.

1593, required that the draft be ordered in a general acuerdo. In 1627 the viceroys were empowered to expend funds in emergencies without consulting the acuerdo.[5] After the title of superintendent was conferred upon the viceroy, money could be drawn from the treasury at his order, and a royal decree of April 14, 1789, provided that expenditures for exploration could be made by him without obtaining the consent of the junta real de hacienda.[6]

The viceroys issued orders to the subtreasuries (cajas reales) in all the larger cities. The principal treasury was always in the capital and the executive might command that the money from the smaller treasuries be sent there. The treasury of Vera Cruz was almost as important as that in Mexico City, since the wealth to be transported to Spain went there from many of the other subtreasuries.[7] Whenever irregularities occurred in the divisions of the treasury, it was the duty of the viceroy to send visitors to investigate their condition. It has been mentioned that one of the chief duties of the visitor-general appointed by the king was to examine the treasury and the state of finances in the viceroyalty.[8]

The viceroy had to protect the gold and silver coming from the mines, and certain dues were imposed to meet the expenses of this obligation. In Peru, Viceroy Toledo had the treasury officials

---

[5] *Recopilación*, ley 57, tit. 3, lib. 3; Solórzano, II, lib. 6, cap. 15, arts. 6–7, p. 504.

[6] Priestley, *José de Gálvez*, 77; Flores to Revillagigedo, 1789, *Instrucciones que los vireyes* . . . . art. 65, p. 126.

[7] Palafox to his successor, 1642, *Documentos inéditos* . . . . *de Mexico*, VII, 83. For the names of the subtreasuries of Mexico and Peru consult Croix, *Instrucción que* . . . . *dejó*, AGI, 88–5–13; Revillagigedo to Amarillas, 1754, *Instrucciones que los vireyes* . . . . art. 101, p. 24; Priestley, *José de Gálvez*, 81; Salvatierra to Aliste, 1651, *in* Polo, *Memorias de los vireyes* . . . . art. 47, p. 47. For a good account of the subtreasury of Vera Cruz *see* Fonseca, Fabian, and Carlos Urrutia, *Historia general de real hacienda* (Mexico, 1845–53), IV, pp. 536 *et seq*. This is a very valuable work which was compiled by order of the second Revillagigedo in 1791–1792. It contains many copies of royal cédulas relative to every branch of revenue, and traces the origin of each division of finance.

[8] Court to Amarillas, 1755, *Instrucciones que los vireyes* . . . . 76–77; Croix, *Instrucción que* . . . . *dejó*, AGI 88–5–13.

send the precious metals to Lima every six months. During the administration of Viceroy Croix of Mexico the task of conveying the precious metals to Vera Cruz for transportation was granted to Pedro Vertíz, a wealthy and trustworthy man. He collected all the gold and silver for one hundred leagues around the capital and took it safely to the coast for twelve pesos on each six thousand.[9]

The dispatch of the treasure to Spain was an important event. The date for the departure of the fleet having been determined, the viceroy began to take measures for the collection of the moneys, notifying the treasury officials, the tribunal of accounts, the cruzada, the tribunal of quicksilver, and all other tribunals which had royal funds under their control, to take prompt action in transporting their wealth to the coast. The viceroy had to send special word to the more distant provinces like Yucatan and Guatemala, so that they might deliver their precious metals to the port a little before the sailing of the fleet.[10]

Serious financial problems were always submitted to the junta superior de real hacienda, which was established in Peru in 1548–1549 and in New Spain in 1554.[11] In 1626 this junta was composed of the viceroy, the senior judge of the audiencia, the fiscal, the contador of accounts where there was a tribunal of accounts, and the senior treasury official. Under the intendancies the membership of this body in Mexico City comprised the regent, the fiscal—with a vote in all matters in which he was not an advocate—the senior judge of the tribunal of accounts, and the senior contador of the treasury   In 1796 the junta at Lima was composed of the same officers, except that an oidor of the audiencia was added. At this time the viceroy still served as presi-

---

[9] Marfil to Cagigal, 1760, *Instrucciones que los vireyes* . . . . 107; Ordinances of Toledo for the treasury officials of Guamanga and Guancavelica, *Documentos inéditos* . . . . *de Indias*, VIII, art. 28, p. 477; Croix, *Instrucción que* . . . . *dejó*, AGI, 88–5–13.

[10] Mancera to Veraguas, 1673, *Instrucciones que los vireyes* . . . . 297–298.

[11] Palafox to his successor, 1642, *Documentos inéditos* . . . . *de Mexico*, VII, 85; Revillagigedo, *Instrucción reservada*, art. 816.

dent of the council of finance.[12]   At first the viceroys summoned
meetings of the junta every Thursday afternoon, but increase
of financial business made it necessary to hold these meetings
every Tuesday, Wednesday, and Thursday afternoon. Money
was drawn from the treasury by vote, the viceroy casting the
decisive vote if need be, and all the members signed the warrant,
even those of opposing opinion. Montesclaros said that the chief
service of the junta was to decide points of law which the viceroy
could not understand unless he were a lawyer.[13]

Cognizance of judicial cases of the treasury belonged to the
viceroy as superintendent, not to the audiencia. Appeals went
to this body, however, and it was the special duty of the fiscal to
attend to all financial matters referred to it.[14]   The treasury
officials and the accountants (contadores) of the tribunal of
accounts exercised the power of hearing fiscal cases in first
instance. The contadores might not be absent from these sessions
without the consent of the viceroy, and the porter (portero) kept
him informed of all their absences.[15]

The viceroy had to be on the alert for means whereby the
revenues might be increased to the highest amount possible, so
that larger sums of money could be sent to Spain.[16]   Many executives tried financial reforms in order to attain this end. When
Castellar came to Peru in 1672, he found that a number of
persons were indebted to the treasury and that there was an

---

[12] *Recopilación*, ley 8, tit. 3, lib. 8; Revillagigedo, *Instrucción reservada*,
art. 817; Lemos to Vallenari, 1796, *Memorias de los vireyes* . . . . VI, 82;
Marquina to Iturrigaray, 1803, *Instrucciones que los vireyes* . . . . art. 303,
p. 203.

[13] *Recopilación*, ley 56, tit. 3, lib. 3; ley 8, tit. 3, lib. 8; ley 12, tit. 28,
lib. 8; Montesclaros to his successor, 1615, *Documentos inéditos* . . . . *de
Indias*, VI, 256–257.

[14] Superunda to his successor, 1761, *Memorias de los vireyes* . . . . IV,
83–84; Croix, *Instrucción que* . . . . *dejó*, AGI, 88–5–13; Cédulas and provisiones for the fiscal of the audiencia of Charcas, 1580, *Documentos inéditos*
. . . . *de Indias*, XVIII, 465.

[15] Ordinances of Toledo for the treasury officials of Guamanga and
Guancavelica, *ibid.*, VIII, art. 33, p. 479; Court to Amarillas, 1755,
Instrucciones que los vireyes . . . . 77–78.

[16] *Recopilación*, ley 17, tit. 14, lib. 3.

annual deficit of two hundred thousand pesos. He therefore ordered the officials to inform him daily of the receipts of the treasury and to make no payment without his approval. As the result of his strict regulations, the critical condition was improved; but he made many enemies by his reforms, and they made accusations against him which led to his recall. In Mexico during the administration of Croix the resources of the treasury were increased through the reforms of the visitor, Gálvez. The chief financial reform of the second Revillagigedo was the systematization of the expenditures and receipts of the treasury. He arranged that on Monday, Wednesday, Friday, and Saturday mornings warrants for salaries, pensions, annuities, and for similar things might be paid; in the afternoons the royal fifths (quintos), and tithes (diezmos) were to be received from the treasuries outside of the capital. In spite of the opposition of the tribunal of accounts, the king approved this reform on May 1, 1792. When Branciforte came to New Spain in 1794, he said that the treasury was empty and had to depend on loans, but in a short time it began to be filled and large remittances were sent to Spain. The means employed may have been questionable, since Branciforte had a peculiar power to collect funds and at the same time to increase his own wealth.[17]

The treasury officials, or oficiales reales, were the most important functionaries in the viceroyalties after the viceroys and judges of the audiencia. They were national rather than local officials. In each town there were three treasury officials, the factor, the accountant, and the treasurer, and they lived in a special public building called the casa real. In the provinces they were directly subordinate to the governor, but in the capitals to the viceroy. They had to give bonds for their positions, and could not absent themselves from the town wherein they served

---

[17] Moses, *The Spanish Dependencies* . . . . II, 183–185; Croix, *Instrucción que* . . . . *dejó*, AGI, 88–5–13; Revillagigedo, *Instrucción reservada*, arts. 886–888; Branciforte to Azanza, 1797, *Instrucciones que los vireyes* . . . . art. 21 *et seq.*, pp. 131–133.

without the permission of the viceroy. They had to take an oath to keep secret all matters concerning the treasury.[18]

The powers and duties of treasury officials during the first century after the conquest were very extensive. In the next century the tribunal of accounts and the audiencia took charge of some of their functions. Their authority had been so great that they could easily perform the tasks of the alcaldes mayores or alcaldes ordinarios when those officials were absent or in case of their sudden decease, but a royal order of February 6, 1584, and another of May 1, 1588, declared that henceforth they were not to serve in those positions. They collected the taxes and customs within their jurisdiction; they were empowered to pursue and arrest debtors of the treasury without calling upon the justices; they paid salaries and pensions from the funds under their control, and sent the money collected to the treasury in the capital.[19] In their home there was a strong box called the caja real into which they put the taxes. Each official had a key to a separate lock thereon, and it could not be opened except in the presence of the three men. According to the ordinances made by Viceroy Toledo of Peru, the cajas were to be opened twice a week, on Tuesday to make payments and on Saturday to deposit funds.[20]

Account had to be rendered by the treasury officials to the viceroy whenever he desired. The first Revillagigedo said that he received a weekly report concerning all that entered the treasury. Shortly before the arrival of Visitor Gálvez in Mexico, a monthly balance sheet signed by all the officials of the treasury

---

[18] *Recopilación*, leyes 1, 5, 18, tit. 4, lib. 8; Ordinances of Toledo for the treasury officials of Guamanga and Guancavelica, *Documentos inéditos* . . . . *de Indias*, VIII, art. 32, p. 478.

[19] Cédulas and provisiones for viceroys and presidents of audiencias, *ibid.*, XVIII, 166–168; Montesclaros to his successor, 1615, *ibid.*, VI, 246; Superunda to his successor, 1761, *Memorias de los vireyes* . . . . IV, 236–237.

[20] Instruction to the treasury officials of Guamanga, 1582, *Documentos inéditos* . . . . *de Indias*, VIII, 467; Ordinances of Toledo for the treasury officials of Guamanga and Guancavelica, *ibid.*, VIII, art. 10, p. 471.

was required by the viceroy, so that he might know the exact amount of the funds. At least every year treasury officials had to submit to the viceroy a sworn report. This statement was to show how much money was due the treasury, who its debtors were, and what action had been taken against them, as well as the deposits actually on hand. If this obligation was not fulfilled by the treasury officials, the viceroy could prevent them from receiving the last third of their annual salary.[21]

The financial report for the year was finally sent to the king by the viceroy or the audiencia in January or February, just two months after it was begun.[22] Each official was required to keep a book wherein was set down the amount entering and going out of the subtreasury. A common or daybook was to be locked securely in the strong box and at the end of the year all the books were to be compared so that a correct general report might be made. The intention was that one record should serve as a check on another, but it did not prove so in actual practice, since the officials were careless in making entries. Visitor Gálvez learned how they copied one account from the other, and made up the daybook at the end of the year from their own books.[23]

The viceroy continually watched over the treasury officials in order that they might perform their duties faithfully. It was also his duty to promote harmony among the employees of the treasury and settle their differences with the greatest impartiality.[24]

---

[21] *Recopilación*, ley 22, tit. 3, lib. 8; ley 15, tit. 4, lib. 8; Revillagigedo to Amarillas, 1754, *Instrucciones que los vireyes* . . . . arts. 108, 110, p. 25; Court to Amarillas, 1755, *ibid.*, art. 44, p. 74; Priestley, *José de Gálvez*, 194.

[22] Ordinance of 1554, *Documentos inéditos* . . . . *de Indias*, XII, 143–144; Cédulas and provisions for the audiencia of Charcas, 1564, *ibid.*, XVIII, 331–332; Memorial for Juan Obando of the consejo, 1570, *ibid.*, XI, 60; Court to Amarillas, 1755, *Instrucciones que los vireyes* . . . . 77.

[23] Court to Amarillas, 1755, *ibid.*, art. 43, p. 73; Instruction to the treasury officials of Guamanga, 1582, *Documentos inéditos* . . . . *de Indias*, VIII, 468–469; Priestley, *José de Galvez*, 195.

[24] Court to Amarillas, 1755, *Instrucciones que los vireyes* . . . . art. 42, p. 72; Marquina to Iturrigaray, 1803, *ibid.*, art. 395, p. 217; Villagarcía to Superunda, 1745, *Memorias de los vireyes* . . . . III, 575; Palafox to his successor, 1642, *Documentos inéditos* . . . . *de Mexico*, VII, 84–85.

In 1535 mints were established at Mexico City, Santa Fé in Nuova Granada, and Potosí. Later in 1683 a mint was erected at Lima.[25] The viceroys had to oversee the building of mints, and they exercised the same vigilance over the principal officials of the mint as they did over the treasury officials. Like other public positions, mint offices became salable, but the viceroy continued to appoint judges to take the residencia of their holders every two years.[26] Civil suits relating to the mint were tried in first instance by the tribunal of the mint. Matters relating to the king's fifth (quinto) could be handled by the ordinary justices, however, and the audiencia took cognizance of cases of forgery. It was not until 1733, when the mint of Mexico was reorganized, that it was incorporated with the treasury and the superintendent made directly subordinate to the viceroy.[27]

The superintendent had to give account of everything to the viceroy. When vacancies occurred, the superintendent submitted three names to the viceroy who chose one for the office. The position of inspector of the mint was greatly desired, and much overbidding took place for the purchase of it; but the superintendent and the viceroy always had to consider the character of the claimant, since the office was a very responsible one. The visitation of the mint was another duty of the viceroy, and the superintendent could not interfere with it in any way.[28] With the aid of the latter the viceroy was to prevent any dishonesty in the mint. Annually the superintendent had to report to the viceroy concerning the metal on hand and any other matters worthy of attention. The superintendent had jurisdiction in first instance over all the employees, allowing appeal to the

---

[25] *Recopilación*, ley 1, tit. 23, lib. 4; Fonseca and Urrutia, I, 110; Palata to Monclova, 1689, *Memorias de los vireyes* . . . . II, 148, 226.

[26] King to Mendoza, 1535, *Documentos inéditos* . . . . *de Indias*, XXIII, 432; *Recopilación*, leyes 13–14, tit. 23, lib. 4.

[27] *Ibid.*, ley 18; Fonseco and Urrutia I, 113–114, 225–226.

[28] *Ibid.*, I, 247; Revillagigedo to Amarillas, 1754, *Instrucciones que los vireyes* . . . . arts. 47–51, pp. 14–15; Gómez, Diario, *Documentos para la historia de Mexico*, serie 2, VII, 216.

superior government only when the first hearing had been decided, but the viceroy was empowered to settle differences between the officials of the mint over salaries and other matters. Bentura Santelices, superintendent of the mint at Potosí, doubted the authority of the viceroy over such cases; therefore he acted as a private judge with no superior. After consulting the real acuerdo, the viceroy ordered him to obey and informed him that he was merely a subordinate of the executive.[29]

The viceroy had also to oversee the coining of money and to decide upon the quantity needed for public use. Coinage began in 1536 under the first viceroy of Mexico. The coins were irregular polygons of copper. The Indians showed a repugnance toward this money and refused to accept it. When silver currency was made, the viceroy experienced even more difficulty, since the Indians could not realize its value and were frequently cheated.[30] The largest sum of money coined in New Spain at one time during the sixteenth and seventeenth centuries was thirty-eight million pesos of silver which the Marquis of Cerralvo ordered made. The viceroy was likewise to see that coins contained full value according to the weight determined by royal order.[31]

Few banks existed in the viceroyalties during the colonial period. In 1716 Linares said that there were only two in Mexico; one was under the control of the family of Tagles and the other under Isidro Rodríguez. It was in the time of Matías de Gálvez that the famous bank of San Carlos was founded in Mexico City. Whenever excessive interest was charged for the loan of money

---

[29] Fonseca and Urrutia, I, 155, 146, 226; Revillagigedo to Amarillas, 1754, *Instrucciones que los vireyes* . . . . art. 117, p. 26; Croix, *Instrucción que* . . . . *dejó* AGI, 88–5–13; Superunda to his successor, 1761, *Memorias de los vireyes* . . . . IV, 256–258.

[30] *Recopilación*, ley 5, tit. 23, lib. 4; Rivera Cambas, I, 30; Zamacois, IV, 599.

[31] For the amounts of money coined in Mexico by other viceroys of these centuries *see*, Riva Palacio, II, 686; Cédulas and provisiones for treasury officials, 1578, *Documentos inéditos* . . . . *de Indias*, XVIII, 409–411, 420.

the viceroy was expected to make the proper regulations. Azanza was forced to intervene in a case of this kind occuring at San Blas.[32]

Over the different monopolies the viceroy exercised a general supervision. The principal monopoly was that of tobacco, which was established in Peru in 1752, although the royal approval had been obtained for the project as early as 1746. The Count of Superunda, then viceroy, was given full power to appoint the manager, to assist in forming the monopoly, and to draw up instructions for the officials. The manager was permitted to choose his own subordinate officials. The results were so satisfactory that in 1753, the viceroy decided to extend the monopoly to Chile. He chose the three chief officials as he had done in Peru and provided a junta to settle disputes and judicial affairs relating to the monopoly, but appeals were to be sent to Lima. Later Superunda established the tobacco monopoly in the bishoprics of Trujillo, Guamanga, Cuzco, Arequipa, La Paz, Santa Cruz de la Sierra, and in the archbishhopric of La Palata, appointing in each district a chief official with the title of contador.[33]

In New Spain Cruíllas took the first step to create this monopoly in 1764, but the real task of founding it was left to the visitor, Gálvez. Viceroy Croix said that the revenue from the monopoly reached one million two hundred thousand pesos in 1770, and that the cultivation of tobacco ought to be one of the chief cares of an executive. In 1803 the rents from this division of finance continued to be the richest in the kingdom, and for this reason the monopoly was intrusted to the care of the viceroy. The settling of disputes between the director and the employees of the monopoly was one of his many duties.[34]

---

[32] Linares to Valero, 1716, *Instrucciones que los vireyes* . . . . 312; Marquina to Iturrigaray, 1803, *ibid.*, arts. 347–348, p. 210; *Suplemento de Bustamante,* to Cavo, art. 58, p. 345.

[33] Superunda to his successor, 1761, *Memorias de los vireyes* . . . . IV, 238–246.

[34] Priestley, *José de Gálvez,* 142 *et seq;* Croix, *Instrucción que* . . . . *dejó,* AGI, 88–5–13; Marquina to Iturrigaray, 1803, *Instrucciones que los vireyes* . . . . arts. 333–334, p. 208. The tobacco monopoly was established in Nueva Granada by Viceroy Cerda (1761–73). Groot, II, 135.

Salt was also monopolized by the government, since large quantities of it were needed in mining, especially for the extraction of quicksilver. The salt monopoly was established in New Spain in 1580, but it never flourished until the time of the Gálvez visitation.[35] Stamped paper bearing the royal coat of arms was required for written documents of all kinds, and on December 28, 1638, it was made a monopoly. The revenue from playing cards was also leased and administered exclusively for the king. The other monopolies were gunpowder, snow brought from the mountains, leather, cockfighting, alum, copper, lead, tin, and alcohol.[36]

The divisions of finance controlled by the viceroy were almost too numerous to mention. The great bulk of the royal revenue came from the fifth on all precious metals and stones. Viceroys were enjoined again and again to see that the king was not defrauded in this right, and the extravagant Philip III gave special thanks to Viceroy Montesclaros of Peru for having remedied abuses relating to the quintos. Other dues on metals came from the assaying of gold and silver (derecho de ensaye), the manufacture of jewelry (bajilla), coinage, and from the baser metals of alum, copper, lead, and tin.[37]

The tribute brought much money into the royal treasury. The viceroy had the tribute lists examined frequently so that nobody might escape the tax, and he was to see that it was collected on time. It was the duty of the collector (contador) of tributes to inform the viceroy about everything relating to this division of finance. Viceroy Cagigal of Mexico arranged for a council to

---

[35] Croix, *Instrucción que* .... *dejó*, AGI, 88–5–13; Revillagigedo, *Instrucción reservada*, arts. 1001–1003; Revillagigedo, *Doctamen* .... *sobre* .... *la ordenanza de intendentes* .... May 5, 1791, MS, num. 402, art. 479.

[36] Riva Palacio, II, 699, 701; Montesclaros to his successor, 1615, *Documentos inéditos* .... *de Indias*, VI, 254; Castel-Fuerte to Villagarcía, 1736, *Memorias de los vireyes* .... III, 275; Moses, *Spain's Declining Power*, 99; Priestley, *José de Gálvez*, 153, f. 314, p. 321, 346.

[37] Cédulas and provisiones by the king, 1563, *Documentos inéditos* .... *de Indias*, XVIII, 358–360; Ordinances of Toledo for the treasury officials of Guamanga and Guancavelica, *ibid.*, VIII, art. 30, p. 478; Croix, *Instrucción que* .... *dejó*, AGI, 88–5–13; Solórzano, II, lib. 5, cap. 1, arts. 27–28, p. 429; *ibid.*, lib. 6, cap. 1, art. 24, p. 428; Priestley, *José de Gálvez*, 314–322.

be held every week for the purpose of discussing means to improve the collection of tributes.[38]

The alcabala or sales tax, the most hated form of revenue, was established in Mexico in 1575 and in Peru in 1591. The second Cañete of Peru began its collection as a 2 per cent ad valorem duty. Riots broke out in Quito against it, but the viceroy soon quelled them. In the eighteenth century the duty became as high as 14 per cent. It was levied on all salable articles except a few that were taxed in other ways, and included both the first and second sales.[39] When Mancera came to Mexico in 1665 he found that the collectors of the alcabala had been negligent, and he put this branch of finance under the charge of the consulado. In the time of the first Revillagigedo the alcabala was placed again under the government by a royal order. The visitor Gálvez found that the collection of the alcabala had been leased to towns and districts (villas y partidos), but he soon made plans to put it under the administration, and Viceroy Bucareli carried out the measure.[40] The viceroy exercised vigilance over many minor divisions of revenue. Most of which were in reality trust funds for various public beneficences, in addition to caring for the important revenues of the colony.[41]

The organization of the treasury could not be called successful, for a number of viceroys found it empty and had to employ loans and gifts to replenish the funds. When Philip II announced his marriage to Queen Mary of England, he asked

[38] In Fonseca and Urrutia, I, 411 *et seq.*, there is a very comprehensive account of this branch of revenue. Revillagigedo to Amarillas, 1754, *Instrucciones que los vireyes* . . . . arts. 79, p. 20; Cagigal to Cruíllas, 1760, *ibid.*, 113.

[39] Solórzano, II, lib. 6, cap. 8, arts. 17–19, p. 465; Priestley, *The Mexican Nation*, 132; Esquilache to Guadalcázar, 1621, *Memorias de los vireyes* . . . . I, 128.

[40] Mancera to Veraguas, 1673, *Instrucciones que los vireyes* . . . . 295–296; Croix, *Instrucción que* . . . . *dejó*, AGI, 88–5–13; Priestley, *José de Gálvez*, 355. For a detailed treatment of the division of alcabalas *refer to* Fonseca and Urrutia, II, 1 *et seq.*

[41] Priestley, *José de Gálvez*, 312–383, gives the most available account in English.

Velasco of New Spain to send him financial aid for his wars
and the spread of the faith. In Peru the second Cañete collected
1,426,680 ducats to be used against the rebellious provinces of
Flanders and other enemies, and on September 25, 1591, the
bellicose Philip thanked him for this generous donation. In
1624 Cerralvo of Mexico sent to the king a gift of 432,343 pesos,
and five years later he dispatched another 1,100,000 pesos
because the monarch begged him for a fund to replace in part
losses due to the sinking of his ships with 16,000,000 pesos on
board. Again in 1634, when the palace at Madrid burned, the
king asked for 2,000,000 pesos from New Spain.[42]

When the monarch sent a request to Cadereyta for a voluntary loan, the marquis informed him that this was a bad way to
raise money, but his letter was not well received. As the king
kept repeating his entreaties, the viceroy sold some Negroes at
San Juan de Ulúa and sent the proceeds of 42,030 pesos on the
fleet. A contribution of 350,000 pesos was collected by the viceroy of Peru when there was danger from the Portuguese because
of the uprising of the Duke of Braganza. Another order came
to Mexico in 1665 for a donation on account of the death of the
king and Mancera raised 115,144 pesos, giving 6000 from his
own purse.[43] Viceroy Castellar of Peru was in need of money
for defensive purposes, therefore he resorted to asking the people
for a gift, and he obtained in this way 87,793 pesos. In 1706
Viceroy Alburquerque sent to the king one million pesos and
another million two years later, both of which sums were 'voluntary' donations from the inhabitants of Mexico. The tribunal
of mining of New Spain in 1782 gave a loan of 1,000,000 pesos at
5 per cent interest, and in a few years made a similar loan besides
gifts amounting to 550,000 pesos. In 1791 the king wished to

42 King to Velasco, 1556, *Documentos inéditos . . . . de Indias,* IV, 403;
Account concerning Cañete, *ibid.,* VIII, 341, 361–363; Riva Palacio, II,
703–704; Priestley, *José de Gálvez,* 370–371.

43 Riva Palacio, II, 592–593; Mancera to his successor, 1648, *in* Polo,
Memorias de los vireyes . . . . art. 72, p. 27; Mancera to Veraguas, 1673,
Instrucciones que los vireyes . . . . 295.

publish a list of American plants, but not at the expense of the treasury; accordingly four years later the viceroyalty of Peru contributed 17,966 pesos for the work.[44]

2. INDUSTRY

The viceroy was expected to be the promoter of all unprohibited industries in the colonies. Agriculture soon occupied the attention of the conquerors and the early viceroys. The Spaniards introduced into the Indies some of the most useful plants, like the orange, lemon, olive, the vine, sugar cane, coffee and rice. At the same time they brought domestic animals and took over the cultivation of a number of American plants—maize, cacao, and cotton—which became valuable commercial products. Viceroy Mendoza of New Spain was ordered to provide for planting wheat and other crops, and assist the natives in their agriculture. He was also to take measures to prevent the cattle of neighboring ranches from destroying the crops of the Indians.[45]

Although Mexican wheat did not yield as many bushels to the acre as in Europe, Humboldt says that it was of the very best quality. Near Puebla white wheat remarkable for its abundant yield was raised, but in 1677 its use was declared by the protomedicato to be injurious to health, and it was therefore prohibited. However, when, in 1692, a famine threatened Mexico, Viceroy Galve permitted its cultivation again. Chile became the great source of the wheat supply for South America and after 1687 this grain began to be exported. In spite of the fear that the competition of Chilean wheat would be injurious to Peruvian production, wheat-raising in the southern province was not checked.[46] Other European cereals were not extensively

---

[44] Castellar to Liñan, 1681, *Memorias de los vireyes* . . . . I, 243; Lemos to Vallenari, 1796, *ibid.*, VI, 286–287; Riva Palacio, II, 758; Revillagigedo, *Instrucción reservada*, art. 473.

[45] King to Mendoza, Aug. 23, 1538, *Documentos inéditos . . . . de Mexico*, XV, 63; King to the viceroy of Mexico, April 16, 1550, *Documentos inéditos . . . . de Indias*, XXIII, 533.

[46] Humboldt, III, 2; *ibid.*, II, 434; Cavo, lib. 8, art. 8, p. 219; Bancroft, *History of Mexico*, III, 612; Moses, *Spain's Declining Power*, 42–43.

cultivated, since greater profits could be obtained from the "colonial products," cochineal, indigo, vanilla, and cacao. In 1545 a law of the Indies commanded viceroys to cause flax and hemp to be raised. The king repeated the order for New Spain in 1777, because not much progress had been made in the industry. Viceroy Bucareli was told to promote the cultivation with energy. The second Revillagigedo received similar decrees, but he thought it was useless to hope for success, since the natives were not familiar with flax, and there was too much foreign competition.[47]

The native product, cacao, brought large returns and was much sought for in Europe because the beverage chocolate was made from it. At first this plant was regarded by the Spaniards with much suspicion, since they thought that it caused the death of many Indians. Francisco de Toledo ordered that the planting of cacao in Peru should cease, but it was found that cultivation of this product could not be stopped, for many Spaniards and Indians were engaged in it. When the value of the product was realized the king took measures to protect it. Mancera found it necessary to regulate the price of cacao for New Spain, and Marquina tried to encourage its cultivation by offering rewards.[48]

In New Spain cochineal, chiefly from Oaxaca and Yucatan, was one of the principal exports. The Indians were especially adapted to the work of raising the little spider or cochineal insect which grew on the cactus, and to extracting the scarlet dye product from it, since the process was slow and it gave them plenty of leisure during certain seasons of the year. It therefore came to be the chief occupation of the natives in many parts of New Spain and Nueva Granada. The growing of tobacco to supply the needs of the famous monopoly was another profitable occupa-

[47] *Recopilación*, ley 20, tit. 18, lib. 4; Revillagigedo, *Instrucción reservada*, arts. 390–394.

[48] Memorial of Diego de Robles, 1570, *Documentos inéditos . . . . de Indias*, XI, 40; Account concerning Toledo, *ibid.*, VIII, 260–262; Mancera to Veraguas, 1673, *Instrucciones que los vireyes . . . .* 267; Marquina to Iturrigaray, 1803, *ibid.*, art. 387, p. 216.

tion in both Mexico and South America. On April 16, 1550, a royal order to the viceroy of Mexico asked him to favor the sugar-growers by giving them lands.[49]

Hernán Cortés introduced the cultivation of mulberry trees and silkworms into New Spain. The marquis pledged himself to plant in the provinces of Guajocingo, Cholula, and Tlascala one hundred thousand mulberry trees. He asked Viceroy Mendoza to furnish him the workmen needed, and promised to give the king half of the income. It is said that some of the ecclesiastics objected to silk-raising and manufacture because it kept the laborers from attending church during Lent.[50]

On April 16, 1550, the king ordered the viceroy to see that the Indians cared for the forty thousand mulberry trees which had been neglected in the province of Guajocingo, to make special effort to inform the king concerning lands that were adapted to silk-raising, and to interest the Indians in the industry. The Andalusian silk-growers became alarmed at the rapid spread of the occupation in the New World, and in 1679 it was abolished by royal order. It fell to the lot of Viceroy Rivera to publish throughout New Spain the decree to uproot all the mulberry trees and to destroy the silkworms. The second Revillagigedo tried to revive interest in this industry, but was not successful.[51]

Many restrictions were imposed upon colonial agriculture, but fortunately they never were strictly enforced. The Spanish court always viewed with suspicion American cultivation of the olive, the vine, the mulberry tree, hemp, and flax. Royal orders came repeatedly after 1595 asking the viceroys to prohibit the planting of vineyards. As late as the beginning of the nineteenth century the viceroy of New Spain was commanded to destroy the vines in the northern part of the country, where the wine industry flourished, because the merchants of Cádiz complained that

---

[49] *Documentos inéditos . . . . de Indias,* XXIII, 532.

[50] *Ibid.,* XII, 563–567; Mendoza to Velasco, *Instrucciones que los vireyes . . . .* art. 19, p. 230.

[51] *Documentos inéditos . . . . de Indias,* XXIII, 531; Riva Palacio, II, 675.

their commerce in wines had decreased; happily this decree like many former ones was never put into effect. The prohibitive measures also applied to olive-growing and Humboldt stated that few of those trees existed in Mexico by the nineteenth century.[52] Cattle-raising likewise became important in the New World. Viceroy Mendoza established the mesta or grazers' court in New Spain in order to promote this industry. Although domestic animals multiplied very rapidly, it was necessary for the viceroys to pass measures to protect them, since the people often killed them for their hides and left the meat to spoil. As a result licenses for slaughtering cattle had to be obtained from the viceroys, and sometimes government commissioners were sent to inspect the ranches.[53] Viceroy Enríquez hoped that the wool industry would become profitable in New Spain; therefore he appointed a judge to go to the places where the sheep were raised to encourage the Indians in increasing wool production. The means employed in wool-growing were very crude, and Villarroel said that much of the fleece was wasted because proper methods and tools were not known.[54] The wool industry flourished on the mission lands and in the distant provinces, as for instance, in California and in some parts of South America.

Manufacture was even more limited than agriculture. Only such textiles and articles which could not compete with the production of the mother country were permitted to be made. In spite of the illiberal regulations colonial manufacture made some progress. Mendoza established a few textile industries in New Spain, and the king ordered him to instruct the natives in the handicrafts, but it was the second Velasco who was the great promoter of manufacture. He explained to the king that when the fleet failed to arrive the prosperity of the colony decreased;

---

[52] *Recopilación*, ley 18, tit. 17, lib. 4; Humboldt, II, 469.

[53] King to the viceroy of Peru, 1540, *Documentos inéditos* . . . . *de Indias*, XXIII, 499–500; Mancera to Veraguas, 1673, *Instrucciones que los vireyes* . . . . 267; Revillagigedo to Amarillas, 1754, *ibid.*, arts. 98–99, pp. 23–24.

[54] Enríquez to Coruña, 1580, *ibid.*, arts. 6–7, p. 246; *Enfermedades políticas* . . . . MS, III, pt. IV, pp. 22–23.

accordingly he succeeded in obtaining the royal permission to reopen the factories for weaving and spinning founded by the first viceroy. The results were good, the price of cloth soon fell, and the inhabitants were greatly benefitted.[55] The second Revillagigedo was a great advocate of manufacturies for New Spain. He thought that new branches of commerce might be created by the export of raw materials and the handiwork of the natives. He also advised that the Indians should be taught spinning. O'Higgins, who ruled in Peru during the last years of the eighteenth century, likewise gave his support to mills for spinning cloth, flax, and hemp.[56]

The manufacture of linen was considered a safe occupation for the colonies because not much of this fabric was made in Spain but had to be imported. It was believed that since the Indians could make blankets and had done some cotton-weaving in pre-conquest days, they would be able to make linen cloth. Canvas and ropes were needed for ships; therefore Palafox was ordered to encourage the manufacture of hemp and flax at Atlixco for these purposes.[57]

The city of Puebla was famous for its cloth factories, of which there were forty-three in 1794. The industries of this city included the making of earthenware, blankets, some weaving of cotton and silk besides the woolen cloth, which was the principal output. In the intendancy of Oaxaca there were two factories of indigo and five hundred looms for rebosos of cotton and seven for silk. In Valladolid thirty-four establishments existed for making coarse woolen materials, light weight cloth, and blankets. Many looms for weaving were found in the intendancy of Guana-

---

[55] King to Mendoza, Aug. 23, 1538, *Documentos inéditos . . . . de Mexico,* XV, 63; Velasco to the king, Feb. 25, 1593, AGI, 58–3–11, cap. 1; Riva Palacio, II, 448.

[56] Revillagigedo, *Instrucción reservada,* arts. 374–377; Moses, *Spain's Declining Power,* 393.

[57] King to the viceroy of Mexico, 1550, *Documentos inéditos . . . . de Indias,* XXIII, 532; Palafox to his successor, 1642, *Documentos inéditos . . . . de Mexico,* VII, 49.

juato, and cotton and leather goods were cheaper in the colonies than in Spain. There were two hundred and fifteen looms and fifteen hundred workmen at Querétaro. In 1802 the intendancy of Guadalajara alone supplied cotton and woolen cloth to the value of 1,601,200 piastres, tanned hides amounting to 418,900 piastres, and soap worth 268,400 piastres. There were more than twelve hundred weavers of cotton in Puebla at this time, and over five thousand persons were employed in the cigar factories of Mexico City.[58]

In Peru the chief manufactures of the eighteenth century were blankets, cotton cloth, leather goods of all kinds made in Cuzco, glass in the town of Ica, stamped and gilded leather and canopies for beds produced at Huamanga, and crude fabrics of cotton, wool, and linen. Arequipa was celebrated for the casting of bells and at Guayaquil there was a good shipyard. The first cloth factory of South America was established by Inés Muñoz in 1545, and the last one founded under Spanish rule was in 1824. During this period the looms in Peruvian territory alone increased to four thousand.[59] Spanish disapproval of manufacture was intermittent. On November 4, 1711, Viceroy Ladrón de Guevara of Peru received a royal order for the destruction of all textile factories, and as late as the beginning of the nineteenth century similar decrees were still being sent to Mexico.[60] Because of such disregard of their interests, it is not surprising that the people of the Spanish-American colonies were eager to cast off the yoke of the mother country when the proper moment arrived.

Early viceroys granted licenses for founding cloth mills and factories, but in 1680, 1684, and 1690, the king prohibited their

---

[58] Revillagigedo, *Instrucción reservada*, arts. 367, 370, 373; Humboldt, III, 461–463; Pinkerton, *Modern Geography*, III, 201. *Piastre* is the French word for *peso*.

[59] Becker, 122; Navarro y Lamarca, II, 392–393.

[60] Moses, *Spanish America on the Eve of Emancipation*, 313–314; Marquina to Iturrigaray, 1803, *Instrucciones que los vireyes* .... art. 285, p. 216.

establishment without consent of the Council of the Indies. Conditions in the manufactories were very bad. Little attention was paid to sanitation. Free men, Indians, Negroes, and criminals, assigned to these establishments by the justices to serve their terms, all worked together, usually in the same room. Many of the employees were covered with rags, deformed, and ill. Only on Sundays were they permitted to see their families, and they were cruelly punished for their mistakes.[61]

Mining was by far the most essential industry, and all viceroys were expected to encourage it as much as possible, since it was the principal source of revenue. The first rush to the mining regions always brought many undesirable persons; therefore one of the great problems of the viceroy was to prevent frauds and disorders of all kinds. The first viceroy of Mexico found it necessary to make ordinances for the mines, as this was before the *Recopilación de leyes* . . . . *de las Indias* was written. Much of the silver from Potosí had fallen into the hands of foreigners; accordingly Viceroy Mancera of Peru made strict regulations for registering it at Callao and appointed special guards to prevent the evil. When Viceroy Croix came to New Spain, he too learned that precious metals were being exported to foreign countries, so he also drew up an ordinance prescribing how gold and silver should be conveyed from the mines in such way that none might go astray. In 1767 the viceroy had these rules published in the capital, the large towns, and mining districts.[62]

The discovery of rich bonanzas usually caused many lawsuits between powerful persons in which the viceroy was obliged to intervene. Amarillas dispatched the oidor Calvo to the mine of Iguana for this purpose. At the mine of Real del Monte, near Pachuca, there was prolonged litigation between the families of

[61] Solórzano, I, lib. 2, cap. 12, art. 37, p. 114; Humboldt, III, 463–464; Croix, *Instrucción que* . . . . *dejó,* AGI, 88–5–13.

[62] Mendoza to Velasco, *Instrucciones que los vireyes* . . . . art. 9, p. 228; Mancera to his successor, 1648, *in* Polo, *Memorias de los vireyes* . . . . 36; Croix, *Instrucción que* . . . . *dejó,* AGI, 88–5–13.

the deceased Marquis of Valleameno and Romero de Terreros over property rights. The viceroy did not succeed in stopping this lawsuit, as a result of which both families were ruined.[63]

The aiding of miners was a special duty of the viceroy, for when the mines were prosperous he could hope to meet his financial obligations to the king more easily. In order to attain this end, Viceroy Toledo of Peru appointed a veedor, Pedro los Rios. His chief duties consisted of attending to financial matters in the mines, reporting every four months to the viceroy concerning conditions, and distributing quicksilver. The miners of Peru being too poor to pay for the quicksilver used in the extraction of silver, Palata annually set aside a sum of 125,000 pesos to help them. The king sent German experts to Mexico and Peru to increase the output of the mines and instruct the miners in the latest methods. The first Revillagigedo of New Spain decided to encourage mining by measures for working abandoned veins of metal, and the results of his efforts were very successful.[64]

The problem of providing enough quicksilver for the process of amalgamation, which was discovered by Bartolomé de Medina of Pachuca in 1557, was one of the chief cares of the viceroy.[65] The supply for Mexico came on the fleets from Almadén in Spain. There was plenty of this mineral at Guancavelica in Peru, but it was rarely sent to New Spain. The rich deposits in Nueva Galicia were not worked. At first quicksilver was sold to the miners by the treasury officials. It was soon learned, however, that they favored their wealthy friends, and that small mine owners could not obtain the quantity of this metal which they needed, so the viceroys had to intervene.

[63] Riva Palacio, II, 810; Marfil to Cagigal, 1760, *Instrucciones que los vireyes* . . . . 108–109.

[64] Ordinances of Toledo for the treasury officials of Guamanga and Guancavelica, *Documentos inéditos* . . . . *de Indias*, VIII, art. 35, pp. 480–483; Superunda to his successor, 1761, *Memorias de los vireyes* . . . . IV, 159; Lemos to Vallenari, 1796, *ibid.*, VI, 156–157; Revillagigedo, *Instrucción reservada*, art. 481 *et seq.*; Avilés to Abáscal, 1806, *Memoria del virey del Peru*, 73; Revillagigedo to Amarillas, 1754, *Instrucciones que los vireyes* . . . . art. 115, p. 26.

[65] Rivera Cambas, I, 35; Fonseca and Urrutia, I, 298.

The Count of Coruña arranged that the amalgamating material should be distributed to the miners under the nature of a deposit and not as a sale, hoping that greater profit would thus be obtained for the treasury from the increased output of the mines. Later Villamanrique gave orders for the metal to be sold by the alcaldes mayores for cash, but much corruption resulted from this and the miners suffered many hardships. The second Velasco requested the king to send to Mexico as much quicksilver as possible and reduce its price. When the king lowered the price to one hundred pesos de minas per quintal, the viceroy expressed his grateful appreciation, and gave the miners a year's time within which to pay. Even so the miners did not meet their obligations and deficits resulted for the treasury.[66]

Whenever there was a scarcity of mercury in New Spain mining decreased. Likewise, when the price of quicksilver was raised the miners could not pay expenses. In 1767 Croix succeeded in getting the king to decrease the price by a fourth part and it was found that within the next three years over ten million more pesos entered the mint of Mexico City than in the three previous years. Matías de Gálvez even tried to procure mercury from China, but the project was a failure.[67]

In Peru the question of distributing quicksilver was not quite as acute as in New Spain, since the supply did not have to come on the fleets. In 1590 the second Cañete caused the mines of Guancavelica to be worked, but the king retained the ownership of them and the quicksilver was extracted under a lease. In Potosí a storehouse for mercury was constructed, and from there it was distributed to the miners.[68] In 1645 when a

---

[66] Riva Palacio, II, 683–684; Velasco to Philip II, Dec. 22, 1590, AGI, 58–3–11; Velasco to the consejo, AGI, 58–3–11; Velasco to the king, Oct. 30, 1591, AGI, 58–3–11.

[67] Cagigal to Cruíllas, 1760, *Instrucciones que los vireyes* . . . . 114; Croix, *Instrucción que* . . . . *dejó*, AGI, 88–5–13; Humboldt, III, 286.

[68] Account concerning Cañete, *Documentos inéditos* . . . . *de Indias*, VIII, 365–366; Velasco to Monterey, 1604, *ibid.*, IV, 409–410, 412; Montesclaros to his successor, 1615, *ibid.*, VI, 243–245. After two centuries the quicksilver mines of Guancavelica were known to have yielded metal to the value of 67,000,000 pesos. Pinkerton, *Modern Geography*, III, 611.

scarcity of quicksilver was reported, Mancera decided to go in person to investigate the condition of the mines of Guancavelica; the king required viceroys to send special accounts on all the fleets concerning the mercury provided for each mine and the silver extracted by means of it.[69]

The labor problem in the mines also occupied the attention of the viceroys. As the protectors of the Indians, it was they who tried to enforce in the mines the royal measures to better their condition. Only the viceroy had power to distribute the natives among the various mines under the repartimiento and mita systems.[70] When thousands of Indian laborers perished in the mines, the early viceroys began to entreat the king to send Negro slaves to perform the arduous tasks of mining. Mendoza was ordered to consult the judges of the audiencia, the chief public officials, and other influential persons in Mexico as to whether it was best to use Negro slaves. Enríquez of New Spain recommended to the king that Negro slaves should be distributed among all the mines. In 1593 the second Velasco told the sovereign that if Negroes were not sent to New Spain the mines would have to close. He said that the only way to remedy the labor situation without Negro slaves would be to have the Indians brought to the mines from a distance of fifty miles, making them serve for a month at a time, but this could not be done because of the objections raised by ecclesiastics.[71]

Industry, particularly in the cities, was performed under the medieval gild system. There was a judge of the gilds who saw that all the ordinances, which the viceroy confirmed, were

---

[69] Mancera to his successor, 1648, *in* Polo, *Memorias de los vireyes* . . . . art. 93, p. 37; *Recopilación*, ley 12, tit. 23, lib. 8.

[70] Solórzano, I, lib. 2, cap. 15, arts. 38–40, 42, pp. 130–131; *ibid.*, cap. 18, art. 8, p. 147.

[71] King to Mendoza, April 25, 1535, *Documentos inéditos* . . . . *de Indias*, XXIII, 436; Enríquez to Coruña, 1580. *Instrucciones que los vireyes* . . . . art. 5, p. 245; Velasco to the king, Feb. 25, 1593, AGI, 58–8–11, cap. 2; *Los advertimientos que el virey D. Luis Velasco dejó al conde de Monterey*, 1595, 58–3–13, cap. 13.

observed.[72] Outside of these organizations, a man might not engage in the occupation of his choice except as an apprentice of some master. The apprentice had to produce a masterpiece and undergo an examination before he could open a shop of his own. He was examined by a council of the gild or by masters specially appointed for the purpose. Indians and Negroes were debarred from the gilds. Most of the associations of laborers were found in the capitals of the viceroyalties. There were no less than one hundred in Mexico City during the seventeenth century, but they also existed in all the larger towns and were under municipal control. The gilds became subject to the authority of the church through their cofradías or brotherhoods. Some of the best known gilds were those of the bakers, barbers, silk-growers, manufacturers, saddle-makers, weavers, hatters, pottery-makers, butchers, candle-makers, confectioners, tailors, silversmiths, carpenters, shoemakers, tanners, blacksmiths, and basket-makers. In Peru there had even been a miners' gild, but it was abolished in 1779 by the visitor Areche.[73]

The bakers' gild of Mexico City was first established by Visitor Gálvez who, with the approval of Viceroy Croix, made regulations for it. The number of bakeries was reduced from thirty-eight to thirty and they were placed at uniform intervals throughout the city for the convenience of the public. A granary used as a depository for supplies was built at the expense of the gild, and the tribunal of the fiel ejecutoría fixed the price of bread and guaranteed its purity. By 1803 the organization of bakers became a real monopoly and Marquina said that it had been discussed whether it would not be better to discontinue the

---

[72] For the different ordinances of the gilds in Mexico *see* Barrio Lorentzot, Francisco de, *Ordenanzas de gremios de la Nueva España* (Mexico, 1920), Genaro Estrada ed.; Revillagigedo, *Instrucción reservada*, art. 345.

[73] Barrio Lorentzot, Introduction I–II, and for the minor gilds *see* Index, pp. 289 *et seq.;* Riva Palacio, II, 680; Zamacois, IV, 629–630; Avilés to Abascal, 1806, *Memoria del virey del Peru*, 75.

gild, but no other means had been found to supply the people with bread.[74]

The gild of silversmiths was also quite strong in the capital of Mexico. The first Velasco prohibited the other towns from having this organization and as a result the society in Mexico City became very important. In 1580 Viceroy Enríquez ordered the silversmiths to have their shops only in San Francisco Street so that he might be able to exercise greater vigilance over them. Monterey also adopted this arrangement, but he gave the gild more freedom in renting the houses that it wished. Until 1799 women had been excluded from the gilds of New Spain; however at this time Viceroy Azanza ordered a proclamation to be published permitting them to be employed in any occupation that was suitable for them.[75]

3. COMMERCE

Under Spain's restrictive commercial policy before the late Bourbon days, all supplies for the colonies were brought on fleets sailing from the port of Seville where they had been collected by the Casa de Contratación. Later Cádiz obtained control of the American commerce and held it until the reglamento of free trade in 1778 when the ancient monopoly was destroyed. It did not take certain commercial houses of Seville, Mexico City, and Lima, which were under the protection of the consulado, long to exercise their authority over the limited trading system, but companies did not play as great a part in the Spanish as in the Dutch, English, and French colonies. Perhaps the most noted Spanish company was that of Guipúzcoa organized in 1728 to take charge of the trade of Caracas because the efforts of the government to

---

[74] Croix, *Instrucción que . . . . dejó*, AGI, 88–5–13; *Correspondance*, 263; Marquina to Iturrigaray, 1803, *Instrucciones que los vireyes . . . .* art. 80, p. 172.

[75] Riva Palacio, II, 688; Revillagigedo, *Instrucción reservada*, art. 346; Azanza, *Instrucción . . . . á su sucesor . . . .* April 29, 1800, MS, num. 17, pp. 58–59.

prevent smuggling had failed, and to develop the resources of Venezuela. Six years later the company of Galicia was permitted to send annually two registered ships to Campeche, and, if there was any merchandise left, to sell it at Vera Cruz. Still other companies, like that of Honduras for trading with Central America, that of Havana, of Barcelona, Cumaná, Margarita, Escaray, Burgos, the Philippines, and two organizations for the transportation of Negro slaves to America, were formed, but none of them ever proved very successful.[76]

The annual arrival of the fleet was a great event in the Spanish colonies. It touched first at Cartagena, then at Porto Bello, and later went on its way to Vera Cruz. Large fairs were held at these towns which before the coming of the armada were almost deserted villages. When it was almost time for the fleet to appear, throngs of merchants, hucksters, gamblers, and even thieves hastened to the port. Colonial products were collected from far and near to be exchanged for European merchandise, and everything was seething with activity. The towns were so crowded that dwellings rented for enormous prices, and many people lost their lives because of the unhealthful climate. The size of the flotas varied according to the state of American trade and the security of the seas. In 1550 there were eleven or twelve trading vessels convoyed by an armada of eight, and the fleet of 1552, consisted of forty ships, twenty-four for Tierra Firme and sixteen for New Spain. Toward the close of the sixteenth century the number of vessels varied from thirty to ninety. In the next century this number decreased somewhat, since the ships were larger and trade had not grown.[77]

When the Manila galleon came from the Philippines with its rich cargoes from China and the Orient, a similar fair took place

[76] Haring, C. H., *Trade and Navigation between Spain and the Indies in the Time of the Hapsburgs* (Cambridge, London, 1918), 138; Bourne, Edward Gaylord, *Spain in America* (New York, cop. 1904), 295–296; Altamira, IV, 297.

[77] Robertson, II, 402–403; Haring, *Trade and Navigation* . . . . 211–212. For a description of ships and navigators *see* pp. 258 *et seq.*

at Acapulco. The fair of January, 1697, was especially lively
because a Peruvian vessel landed at the port, having on board two
million pesos with which to buy Chinese merchandise. In 1720
the first fair occurred at Jalapa, but it was only through the
influence of Viceroy Casafuerte that it was continued. A fair of
a local nature grew out of the religious pilgrimages, beginning
in 1633, to San Juan de Lagos in the same viceroyalty.[78] The
viceroy supervised these fairs and saw that everything was
conducted in the proper manner.

An import and export duty, the almojarifazgo, was required
on all merchandise. The usual rates were two and a half per cent
on goods going out of the country and five per cent on imports.
The viceroy was to see that these duties were collected. As soon
as the fleet arrived, the treasury officials had to make an evaluation of all the merchandise, one of them always being present
while the vessel was being unloaded. A law of 1593 provided
that when the treasury officials sent the evaluation to the viceroy,
he was to summon a council of finance to decide what import
duty ought to be collected. The decision was sent to the port to
be enforced by the treasury officials, who also served as customs
officials.[79] The fact was that the almojarifazgo varied under
different administrations. In 1566 the rate was raised to fifteen
per cent, of which five per cent was paid as export duty at Seville
and ten per cent upon American entry. Goods passing from one
colonial port to another paid from two and one-half to five per
cent duty.[80]

The consulado or organization of merchants was the principal
means whereby commerce was carried on. In 1592 Philip II gave
his consent for the founding of consulados in Mexico City and

---

[78] Cavo, lib. 9, art. 27, p. 240; Rivera Cambas, I, 324, 327, 333; Casafuerte, Summary of events in the kingdom, April 16, 1733, AGI, 61–2–14.
The Jalapa fair was held until 1777. Bancroft, *History of Mexico*, III, 640.

[79] Solórzano, II, lib. 6, cap. 9, art. 8, p. 468; King to the viceroy and
audiencia of Lima, 1595, *Documentos inéditos . . . . de Indias*, XIX, 81;
Order of the king to Velasco, 1600, *ibid.*, XIX, 112; Cédulas and provisiones
for the audiencia of Charcas, 1554, *ibid.*, XVIII, 337–339; *Recopilación*,
ley 16, tit. 16, lib. 8; Fonseca and Urrutia, V, 6–59.

[80] Priestley, *José de Gálvez*, 361.

Lima in imitation of those at Seville and Burgos. Other consulados were created at Santiago de Guatemala in 1793, at Buenos
Aires in 1794, and in Chile under the governorship of Ambrosio
O'Higgins (1788–1796).[81] The consulado of Lima was called the
"university of charity" and that of Mexico "university of
merchants." The chief officials were one prior, two consuls, and
six deputies for Lima and five for Mexico. There were lesser
functionaries like the assessors, the attorney, the solicitor, the
treasurer, the alguacil, the portero, and the receptor.[82] The prior
and two consuls constituted a judicial tribunal which took
cognizance of all cases relating to commerce, but on the whole
the consulado was somewhat similar to a modern chamber of
commerce.

The consulado undertook the financing of many public works,
since it had large sums of money at its disposal. It rented the
collection of the alcabalas, erected public buildings, like custom-
houses and hospitals, opened roads, constructed bridges and
wharves, and in Mexico it gave funds for the great drainage
canal of Huehuetoca. It also aided hospitals, charitable institutions, the religious communities, widows, and the poor.[83] The
consulado of Buenos Aires drew up plans for the building of the
port, erected lighthouses, deepened harbors, constructed highways, and introduced new machinery into the viceroyalty.[84]

Its diputados or agents attended to commercial interests in
the smaller cities which did not have a consulado. Viceroy
Villagarcía succeeded in obtaining the royal consent for placing
deputies in Potosí and Chile so that judicial cases concerning
trade would be removed from the jurisdiction of the ordinary

---

[81] *Recopilación*, ley 1, tit. 46, lib. 8; Rivera Cambas, I, 53; Solórzano,
II, lib. 6, tit. 14, art. 24, pp. 499–500; Becker, 93; Navarro y Lamarca,
II, 312.

[82] *Recopilación*, leyes 2–3, 15, 21–24, tit. 46, lib. 8.

[83] Alamán, *Historia de Méjico*, I, 59–60; Palafox to his successor, 1642,
Documentos inéditos . . . . de Mexico, VII, 89; Revillagigedo to Amarillas,
1754, *Instrucciones que los vireyes . . . .* art. 94, p. 22; Chapman, Charles E.,
The Spanish Consulados of the Eighteenth Century (M. A. Thesis, Berkeley,
1909), 67–73.

[84] Altamira, IV, 295–296.

justices. The merchants were empowered to elect one of their own number deputy; appeals from his decisions in judicial suits went to the consulado of Lima. In 1752 the governor of Buenos Aires asked the viceroy for a judge of merchants for that city, and the Count of Superunda, who was the executive of Peru at that time, permitted two agents to be appointed.[85]

After 1785 the accounts of the consulado of Lima were submitted to the viceregal government for inspection, instead of being sent directly to the Council of the Indies as had been done before this date. Since the contador and treasurer were often the same person, Teodoro de Croix thought that there ought to be a careful audit by the tribunal of accounts before sending the reports to Spain.[86] There were two classes of merchants in the consulado, the Montañeses and the Biscayans, and everybody was grouped under these no matter what was their nationality. Annually the prior and the two consuls were elected alternately from among the two divisions. Great controversies sometimes arose in the elections, causing the viceroy to intervene.[87] This was true especially in Lima because of the peculiar method of election employed there. The university of merchants first selected thirty of their own number, and this group in turn chose fifteen persons who elected the prior and consuls. Nevertheless, according to Viceroy Linares of Mexico, the disputes always ended well if the viceroy showed kindness to the merchants.[88] Contentions between the consulado and other tribunals the viceroy also decided, declaring whether the matter belonged to the consulado or ought to be submitted to another court.[89]

[85] Haring, *Trade and Navigation* . . . . f. 45; Superunda to his successor, 1761, *Memorias de los vireyes* . . . . IV, 129–130.

[86] Croix to Lemos, 1790, *ibid.*, V, 333–337.

[87] Fuenclara, *Instrucción reservada*, 1742, AGI, 90–2–17, art. 18; Croix, *Instrucción que* . . . . *dejó*, AGI, 88–5–13; Revillagigedo to Amarillas, 1754, *Instrucciones que los vireyes* . . . . art. 91, p. 22.

[88] Croix to Lemos, 1790, *Memorias de los vireyes* . . . . V, 340–341; Linares to Valero, 1716, *Instrucciones que los vireyes* . . . . 310.

[89] Revillagigedo to Amarillas, 1754, *ibid.*, art. 92, p. 22; Croix, *Instrucción que* . . . . *dejó*, AGI, 88–5–13; Superunda to his successor, 1761, *Memorias de los vireyes* . . . . IV, 129.

Quarrels took place in Buenos Aires over the choosing of deputies during the administration of Superunda, and the right of election had to be suspended. In 1787 Teodoro de Croix intervened in an election in Lima by summoning the merchants to meet in his office in order to discuss the matter, and it was settled peacefully. Again the tribunal of the consulado imprisoned a lieutenant in the public prison of Lima for a debt of twenty-five pesos. On the way to prison the chief sergeant ordered him to be taken to the barracks of his battalion for custody, but the consulado paid no attention to the command and the lieutenant was conducted to the public jail. The matter was appealed to Viceroy Croix, who gave the tribunal a slight reproof, saying that it had a perfect right to arrest soldiers, but that it ought to respect military orders.[90]

Complaints made against the consulado by some of the later viceroys of Mexico indicate that the institution was getting beyond control. In 1716 Viceroy Linares referred to many annoying irregularities in the conduct of the members of the consulado. He implied that its agents sometimes tried to undermine the influence of the viceroy at court. They obtained monopolies of certain kinds of merchandise, hid their goods, or went into bankruptcy, and injured the common people by raising prices. Marquina objected to the independence of the regiment of commerce under the consulado, and to the confused condition of its finances. This regiment had refused to be reviewed by the commander of the brigade.[91]

Supervision of the Philippine trade was an important duty of the viceroy of New Spain. He was to see that no commerce was carried on between any other part of the Indies and those islands. Usually in the early autumn or by the first of the year ships laden with 250,000 pesos' worth of merchandise set sail

---

90 Superunda to his successor, 1761, *Memorias de los vireyes* . . . . IV, 308; Croix to Lemos, 1790, *ibid.*, V, 342, 87–88.

91 Linares to Valero, 1716, *Instrucciones que los vireyes* . . . . 310–311; Marquina to Iturrigaray, 1803, *ibid.*, arts. 245–250, pp. 195–196.

from the port of Acapulco by order of the viceroy, and returned
in the spring with a cargo often valued as high as 2,000,000
pesos, although the amount fixed by the laws was to be only
500,000 pesos.[92] The viceroy gave the necessary orders to the
crews of outgoing vessels. He granted licenses for people to go
to the Philippines, and regulated the rates of transportation of
freight and passengers. About fifteen days before the arrival
of the returning galleon, the viceroy appointed a contador of
the tribunal of accounts, a treasury official of Acapulco, and a
member of the consulado, to evaluate its cargo. If these three
men did not agree, the executive selected a new committee for
this purpose, but if they in turn disagreed he himself could make
the evaluation.[93] The rich merchandise from the Orient was
eagerly awaited every year by the people of New Spain, who considered themselves favored to be granted the privilege of this
trade. The first Revillagigedo said that Peru was clamoring
continually for the Philippine commerce, which had been forbidden to that viceroyalty.[94]

Coastwise trade between the ports of the different viceroyalties, and even between those of the same viceroyalty, was
prohibited under Spain's restrictive commercial policy. In 1595
the viceroy of Peru was empowered to give permission for two
ships to trade annually with Mexico, but because of violations
of this privilege, in 1596 it was taken away. In spite of this
regulation, however, Montesclaros complained that in 1612 four
or five Peruvian vessels had arrived at Acapulco under various
pretexts.[95] Viceroys and other colonial officials often paid no

---

[92] *Recopilación*, leyes 1, 5–6, tit. 45, lib. 8; Enríquez to Philip II, Dec. 13,
1577, AGI, 58-3-96; Revillagigedo to Amarillas, 1754, *Instrucciones que los
vireyes . . . .* art. 58, p. 17; Pinkerton, *Modern Geography*, III, 229.

[93] *Recopilación*, leyes 25, 29, 59, 62, tit. 45, lib. 8.

[94] King to Velasco, 1600, *Documentos inéditos . . . . de Indias*, XIX, 124;
Solórzano, II, lib. 6, cap. 10, art. 24, p. 474; Revillagigedo to Amarillas, 1754,
Instrucciones que los vireyes . . . . art. 59, p. 17. For further details con-
cerning the Philippine trade *consult* Fonseca and Urrutia, IV, 451 *et seq.*,
and Schurz, Wm. L., *A Study in the Beginnings of Trans-Pacific Trade*
(Thesis for Master of Letters, Berkeley, 1912), chap. 3, pp. 109 *et seq.*

[95] Riva Palacio, II, 512; *Recopilación*, ley 72, tit. 45, lib. 8; Montesclaros
to the king, 1612, *Documentos inéditos . . . . de Indias*, VI, 343.

attention to the coastwise ships coming to Mexico, for it was not until the administration of Viceroy Croix in Mexico that the harbors of Campeche, Yucatan, and the Windward Islands were opened to the entrance of European merchandise coming from Vera Cruz. The first Revillagigedo, who had most liberal views concerning commerce, suggested the advisability of reopening the trade with Peru as a means of increasing revenue and promoting the general welfare, but it was not until 1774 that Viceroy Bucareli of New Spain received a royal cédula permitting his viceroyalty to trade with Peru, Nueva Granada, and Guatemala.[96]

The commercial dependence of Buenos Aires upon Peru was a real hardship. This port was not open to European trade because the region did not produce precious metals, and it was feared that the gold and silver of Peru would be sent out of the country by way of it, or the merchandise entering there might be cheaper and interfere with the fair of Porto Bello. As a result of this illiberal policy, European merchandise was sent to the isthmus, then transmitted to Peru, and carried over the mountains by mules to Buenos Aires, increasing the price of the goods outrageously.[97] Finally the reglamento of free trade in 1778 relieved the situation in Buenos Aires and other similar places, and their commercial prosperity was soon increased.

Smuggling was the means employed to satisfy the needs of the colonies as a result of Spain's narrow commercial policy. The principal strongholds of illicit trading were the Dutch and English West Indies, the Louisiana frontier, Panamá, and the Brazilian borders. The asiento with England in 1713 only increased for the viceroys the problem of dealing with contraband traffic. In spite of their efforts to stop this evil, thousands of pesos were lost to the treasury annually. During the administration of Croix in Mexico the treasury was defrauded of about one million pesos by smuggling, and including the other vice-

---

[96] Priestley, *José de Gálvez,* 202; Revillagigedo to Amarillas, 1754, *Instrucciones que los vireyes* . . . . art. 119, p. 26; Rivera Cambas, I, 432.

[97] Haring, *Trade and Navigation* . . . . 142.

royalties the amount rose to twelve million pesos annually.[98] It was impossible for an executive to wipe out even for one year illicit trading in his viceroyalty because the people were only too eager to obtain merchandise from traders who sold it at lower prices than did Spanish merchants. For instance, Philip Reste, an Englishman, resided for three years in Lima where he defrauded the king by engaging in forbidden commerce and seems to have been protected by the residents.

In New Spain Viceroy Aliste found it necessary to place guards along the rivers crossing the roads leading from Tlaxcala and Guatemala to Vera Cruz in order to prevent contraband silver being sent to the fleets. Although the officials of Vera Cruz were expected to be especially vigilant in detecting smuggling, it was quite common in that region and profits from it enormous. In 1803 Marquina said that he believed there was direct correspondence carried on between the Spaniards of Mexico and the English in Jamaica.[99] From Acapulco to Guatemala on the western coast of Mexico the viceroys had power to take cognizance of all confiscations of vessels coming from Peru, but before the time of Croix some of the viceroys of New Spain had secretely encouraged this trade and won much wealth for themselves thereby. Then too, the galleons from Manila brought large quantities of contraband goods; accordingly Viceroy Croix appointed his nephew, Teodoro, commissioner to check the irregularities at Acapulco. The younger Croix boarded the galleon when it arrived and had all the smuggled merchandise confiscated. The king was well pleased with the energetic measures taken by Croix against illicit commerce, especially when the confiscations brought into the treasury 1,800,000 crowns.[100]

---

[98] Priestley, *José de Gálvez*, 198; Cédulas and provisiones for the audiencia of Lima, 1583, *Documentos inéditos . . . . de Indias*, XVIII, 158.

[99] Rivera Cambas, I, 180; Marquina to Iturrigaray, *Instrucciones que los vireyes . . . .* art. 314, 316, 318, pp. 205–206.

[100] Revillagigedo to Amarillas, 1754, *ibid.*, art. 60, p. 17; Croix, *Correspondance*, 202, 205–206, 209.

Many captains of vessels found pretexts to land on the western coast of Mexico or South America, saying that they had been driven there by storms. Sometimes only a few hours were sufficient for unloading and taking on board large cargoes of contraband. In 1799 a notable case of this kind occurred. A frigate named *Nuestra Señora del Pilar* was sent to take aid to the Manila galleon, but it returned before the galleon, the crew declaring that it was obliged to do so because of a tempest. After the vessel landed at San Blas, over 200,000 pesos' worth of its smuggled goods were sold.[101]

In South America illicit trading was even greater than in Mexico, even ecclesiastics obtaining their share of the spoils. Bales of contraband goods were often hidden in the convents and on the charcaras or large estates to escape the vigilance of the customs guards. If the offenders were caught and a trial resulted, they were absolved from their crime or punished lightly, since the justices sympathized with them. Friar Francisco de Vitoria, bishop of Tucumán, seems to have been the first person to send a cargo of goods to his Brazilian neighbors. The results were so favorable that a second expedition was sent out in 1587, but it was captured by the English corsair, Thomas Cavendish, on his way to the Pacific. In 1602 Bishop Loyola of Buenos Aires succeeded in getting the ban against the commerce of his town with Brazil raised for six years, because he explained to the easily persuaded Philip III the poverty of the people and their needs.[102] No matter what measures the viceroy might take against smuggling in Rio de la Plata, at any time a bark was able to cross the river to the Portuguese town of Sacramento and bring back the articles desired. Much Portuguese cloth entered Buenos Aires and found its way back to Potosí. Foreign whalers fre-

---

[101] Humboldt, III, 91–92; Marquina to Iturrigaray, 1803, *Instrucciones que los vireyes* . . . . arts. 349–350, p. 210.

[102] Montesclaros to the king, 1612, *Documentos inéditos* . . . . *de Indias*, VI, 341–344; Cédulas and provisiones of the king, 1602, *ibid.*, XVIII, 323–326; Velasco to Monterey, 1604, *ibid.*, IV, 427–428; Haring, *Trade and Navigation* . . . . 140–141.

quently landed along the western coast of South America to obtain water and supplies, and at the same time unload cargoes of merchandise.[103] Again and again the viceroys of Peru gave orders for such goods to be confiscated, but the officials were on the side of the people and seldom put these commands into effect.

As superintendent of the treasury the viceroy had to oversee all the financial matters in his viceroyalty, and his consuming ambition was to increase the revenue of the treasury to the highest amount possible. Although warrants on the treasury were not valid without an order from the king, in cases of emergency the viceroys were authorized to make extraordinary expenditures after consulting their council. The viceroy issued orders for the subtreasuries, protected precious metals coming from the mines to the local depositories, and dispatched the treasure to Spain; but all serious financial problems had to be submitted to the junta superior de real hacienda. The promotion of harmony among treasury officials was another duty of the viceroy, and he had to see that they faithfully performed their tasks. The superintendent of the mint was also subordinate to the viceroy, who determined the amount of money to be coined and caused it to be put into circulation. The executive exercised control over the different monopolies and over the many divisions of finance. When the treasury became empty or the king was in need of funds for some special purpose, he resorted to forced loans and gifts from the people.

The viceroy was the promoter of all the industries which were not prohibited in the New World. He encouraged agriculture, cattle-raising, and the few manufactures which the colonies were permitted to have. All the viceroys considered mining the most important industry, since it was the principal source of revenue for the treasury. They settled serious disputes among the miners and aided them as much as possible. The viceroy also provided

---

[103] Superunda to his successor, 1761, *Memorias de los vireyes* . . . . IV 179–180; Castel-Fuerte to Villagarcía, 1736, *ibid.*, III, 250–257.

laborers for the mines under the repartimiento and mita systems. In the cities industry of all kinds was performed by means of the medieval gild organization and the viceroy had to see that the members observed the ordinances of their particular gild.

The viceroy was expected to enforce in America the regulations of Spain's restrictive commercial policy, see that everything went smoothly at the great fairs which were held annually when the fleet arrived, and settle all disputes in the consulado. The Philippine trade was under the special care of the viceroy of New Spain, who was to prevent any other colony from trading with the Orient. The viceroy had to be informed whether the people of one port under his jurisdiction traded with those of another, or with some other viceroyalty. He tried to punish individuals who persisted in the coastwise trade which the laws of the Indies forbade. Smuggling was one of the greatest annoyances of the viceroys. Although many executives tried to stop the evil, it grew worse when popular opinion began to favor it secretly, and many thousands, even millions of pesos were lost annually to the royal treasury.

CHAPTER IV

THE VICEROY AND THE AUDIENCIA

As president of the audiencia, the viceroy had charge of the enforcement of the laws, and it was in this capacity that he had opportunity to become intimately acquainted with the legal needs of the viceroyalty. He possessed exclusive authority over all cases in which the Indians were involved, since he was the chief of the juzgado de Indios or Indian Court. Under his title of captain-general he was the supreme military judge in the viceroyalty. If he was not a lawyer, the president of the audiencia could not vote in judicial matters, but he had the final word in purely administrative affairs, and decided whether disputed cases should be classified as strictly civil or judicial. It was here that the viceroy exercised a strong hand. The right of deciding whether a contention was of judicial or gubernatorial character, and of settling rivalries among the courts themselves made the viceroy the principal judicial arbiter in the colony.

1. LEGISLATION

Legislation in its modern aspect did not exist at all in the viceroyalties. The laws were made by the Council of the Indies and sent to America to be enforced by the viceroy and the audiencias. Under the Bourbon centralizing policy, however, the king assumed all legislative functions and sent out his orders through his ministers only, or ''por la vía reservada.'' These commands came to the chief executive as cédulas or decrees and royal orders.[1] By 1797 one hundred and fifty-six massive volumes

---

[1] Danvila y Collado, Manuel, *Significación que tuvieron en el gobierno de América la Casa de la Contratación* . . . . (Madrid, 1892), 36; Scelle, *La traite négrière aux Indes de Castille* (Paris, 1906), I, 18–22. Cédulas were laws passed by the Council of the Indies and signed by the counsellors, while ordenes were measures communicated by the king to the Council of the Indies to be put into effect. Alamán, *Historia de Méjico*, I, f. 36.

of royal cédulas and ordenes had been collected in New Spain alone. In cases of doubt the viceroys were expected to consult this collection, and obey the laws directed to their predecessors.[2] When a decree contrary to what had been ordered in the past came, the viceroy was to consider it in the light of experience. If it was evident that it could not be put into practice and would soon be revoked, he could, after consulting with trustworthy persons, delay the execution of the measure until further action in Spain. Montesclaros did this with respect to a cédula which he had received in Peru, and similar instances were frequent.[3]

Bandos or proclamations and ordenanzas or measures were passed by the viceroys, and autos or court decisions by the audiencias. This was the nearest approach to lawmaking in Spanish America. Proclamations issued by the viceroys were to be obeyed without any appeal; but all bandos, ordenanzas and autos were sent to the Council of the Indies for approval.[4] In Peru the ordenanzas of Francisco de Toledo were observed for many years. Viceroy Liñan suspended one of Castellar's measures concerning the tribunal of the cruzada. The latter viceroy had arranged that no one might enjoy the privileges of the cruzada, except in matters relating to the bulls. The tribunal explained the inconveniences that had resulted from this; therefore Liñan issued a bando on January 29, 1680, ordering the setting aside of his predecessor's action.[5]

Mendoza made ordenanzas concerning the sale of Negroes, retailers of wheat, wood and stone, trade and labor gilds, amusements, barter, granting credit to children who were under parental authority, the loading and unloading of ships, and the defense of San Juan de Ulúa. Likewise, the viceroy's proclamations included the protection of Indians, cultivation of the soil,

---

2 Branciforte to Azanza, *Instrucciones que los vireyes . . . .* art. 10, p. 130; *Recopilación*, ley 13, tit. 1, lib. 2.

3 To Esquilache, 1615, *Memorias de los vireyes . . . .* I, 17–18.

4 *Recopilación*, leyes 33–34, tit. 1, lib. 2.

5 Montesclaros to Esquilache, 1615, *Memorias de los vireyes . . . .* I, 17; Liñan to Palata, 1681, *ibid.*, I, 269.

education, and the mines. The viceroy of Peru issued a bando separating the province of Tucumán from Chile, and the king approved it in 1563. In the same viceroyalty Salvatierra gave orders forbidding Negroes and mulattoes to carry arms. Croix announced the expulsion of the Jesuits from New Spain, and Matías de Gálvez published the peace made by Spain and England in the same way, but the last two were measures enforcing orders from Spain, and not original with the viceroy.[6]

2. POWERS AND DUTIES OF THE AUDIENCIA

The audiencias in the New World had more powers than those in Spain. In the mother country they were composed of officials who were learned in the law and represented the king in the administration of justice, but in America they exercised political functions as well. In the absence of the viceroy they also controlled military matters. The audiencia had the privilege of corresponding directly with the king and was under no compulsion to show its letters to the viceroy.[7] It was the highest judicial authority in the colonies, there being no appeal from it, except in serious criminal matters and in civil suits involving large sums. Such appeals went to the Council of the Indies.[8]

In case of the death or absence of the viceroy the audiencia's powers were increased. The first law of the Indies permitting the audiencia to take charge of the government when the viceroy of Peru died, was in 1550. This law was repeated in 1586 and 1606, and in 1600 a similar measure was passed for Mexico. The senior oidor served as president and performed all the duties of

---

[6] Mendoza to Velasco, *Instrucciones que los vireyes* . . . . 231; Palafox to his successor, 1642, *Documentos inéditos* . . . . *de Mexico*, VII, 69; Moses, *The Spanish Dependencies* . . . . II, 29; Salvatierra to Aliste, 1651, *in* Polo, *Memorias de los vireyes* . . . . art. 46, p. 47; Riva Palacio, II, 841, 859.

[7] Montesclaros to his successor, 1615, *Documentos inéditos* . . . . *de Indias*, VI, 266; Account for Juan de Obando of the consejo 1570, *ibid.*, XI, 59; *Recopilación*, ley 40, tit. 15, lib. 2.

[8] Moses, *The Spanish Dependencies* . . . . I, 265; *Recopilación*, ley 1, tit. 13, lib. 5.

an executive. He could even act as captain-general until a successor was appointed or the viceroy had recovered from his infirmity. This meant that the subordinate audiencias also had to obey him.[9]

Thirteen audiencias had been established in the colonies by 1661.[10] The number of members varied according to the importance or location of the audiencia. The largest audiencias were Lima and Mexico. When founded, they consisted of eight oidores or judges, four alcaldes del crimen (criminal judges), two fiscales, an alguacil mayor or court bailiff, and many minor officials.[11] Later this number was increased to take care of the growing business. In 1689 Viceroy Palata spoke of ten oidores, four alcaldes del crimen, and two fiscales in the audiencia of Lima, but it seems that the former number was found again in 1761, 1796, and 1807. In the latter part of the eighteenth and early nineteenth century there were ten oidores, five alcaldes de corte, and two fiscales in the audiencia of Mexico. The smaller audiencias had four or five oidores and a fiscal.[12]

The audiencias subordinate to the viceroy of Mexico were in Guatemala and Guadalajara. In matters of justice they were permitted to control their own administration, but in affairs of finance and war they were subject to the superintendent-general

---

[9] *Recopilación,* leyes 46–48, tit. 15, lib. 2; leyes 57, 16, tit. 16, lib. 2.

[10] They were as follows: 1526 Santo Domingo, 1527 Mexico, 1535 Panamá, 1542 Lima, 1543 Guatemala, 1548 Guadalajara, 1549 Nueva Granada, 1559 La Plata or Charcas, 1563 Quito, 1583 Manila, 1609 Santiago de Chile, 1661 Buenos Aires. *Recopilación,* leyes 2–14, tit. 15, lib. 2; Antequera, 477. According to the New Laws of 1542 and 1543, the audiencia of Panamá was abolished and that of Los Confines founded in place of it. The audiencia of Panamá was reëstablished at the close of the sixteenth century, the exact date not being known, and Los Confines disappeared. Bancroft, H. H., *History of Central America* (San Francisco, 1882–87), II, 241, 464.

[11] *Recopilación,* leyes 3, 5, tit. 15, lib. 2. The lesser functionaries of the audiencia of Mexico numbered over eighty and two hundred attorneys practiced before it. Priestley, *José de Gálvez,* 61.

[12] Palata to Monclova, 1689, *Memorias de los vireyes . . . .* II, 65; Superunda to his successor, 1761, *ibid.,* IV, 106; Lemos to Vallenari, 1796, *ibid.,* VI, 82; Pinkerton, *Modern Geography,* III, 587; Revillagigedo, *Instrucción reservada,* art. 66; Alamán, *Historia de Méjico,* I, 49.

of the treasury and to the captain-general of the viceroyalty.[13] The same conditions prevailed in the audiencias of Panamá, Chile, Quito, and Los Charcas, which were dependent upon the viceroy of Peru. Viceroy Esquilache believed in allowing these audiencias to do as much as possible, since in this way measures could be put into effect more quickly. It was the duty of the subordinate audiencias to keep the viceroy informed of all matters within their district and obey his commands concerning military and political affairs. According to a specific law,

The president and judges of the royal audiencia of Guadalajara, in New Galicia, shall obey the viceroy in everything, and hold with him the good relation which is befitting one who represents the king.[14]

The chief power of the audiencia was its right to decide all judicial matters, both civil and criminal. However, cases in first instance were to be handled by the proper authorities without the interference of the oidores. Two alcaldes ordinarios who took cognizance of lawsuits in first instance, were chosen by the cabildos every year for the larger towns and cities.[15] The viceroy had certain duties to perform with respect to these judges of first instance. He was to see that no treasury officials or debtors to the treasury were chosen alcaldes ordinarios. Moreover, he was not to permit them to be reëlected until two years had passed and their residencia had been taken. Viceroys or those to whom they delegated the power could confirm the election of alcaldes ordinarios, and had authority to settle all disputes connected with it.[16] In 1761 the king disapproved of an appeal concerning

---

[13] Revillagigedo to Amarillas, 1754, *Instrucciones que los vireyes* . . . . art. 3, p. 6; Croix, *Instrucción que* . . . . *dejó*, AGI, 88–5–13.

[14] Esquilache to Guadalcázar, 1621, *Memorias de los vireyes* . . . . I, 103; Palata to Monclóva, 1689, *ibid.*, II, 94; *Recopilación*, leyes 49–50, 52, tit. 15, lib. 2.

[15] *Ibid.*, leyes 66–67, 70, tit. 15, lib. 2; *ibid.*, ley 1, tit. 3, lib. 5. By the latter part of the eighteenth century twenty-eight cities and towns of New Spain had these officials who were chosen by free elections ordered by the viceroys. Revillagigedo, *Instrucción reservada*, art. 80; Antequera, 486.

[16] *Recopilación*, leyes 6–7, 9–10, tit. 3, lib. 5; Esquilache to Guadalcázar, 1621, *Memorias de los vireyes* . . . . I, 103; Mancera to his successor, 1648, *in* Polo, *Memorias de los vireyes* . . . . art. 50, p. 16.

the election of the alcalde, Gerónimo Herrera, and refused its admission by the audiencia of Chile, since the viceroy had the right to dispose of such matters.[17] Linares said that he always courted the alcaldes for his own convenience, because they supported and blindly obeyed him and were interested in his honor.[18]

Other officials who attended to cases in first instance were governors, corregidores, alcaldes mayores, and later the intendants and their sub-delegates, also alcaldes de barrio or judges of wards in the cities. However, they were not to interfere in cases the cognizance of which belong to the alcaldes ordinarios.[19] The viceroy had first instance in Indian and military cases and in all matters that pertained to administration. The elder Revillagigedo was willing that the ordinary justices should take cognizance of as many lawsuits as possible, and thereby relieve the government. He thought that the viceroy ought only to admit cases belonging to his privilege and submit all others to their respective justices.[20] First cognizance was granted to ecclesiastical courts in certain matters relating to religion, to the consulado in disputes between merchants, to the protomedicato in lawsuits among men of the medical profession, to the rector of the university in dissensions among students, to the tribunal of accounts in financial affairs, to the tribunal of the mesta in disagreements among cattle-raisers, to the tribunal of mining in cases belonging to miners, to the tribunal of the mint in incidents affecting coining of money, to the tribunal of prohibited drinks in matters concerning intoxicants, and to the superintendent of the custom-house in regard to duties on exports and imports. The audiencia was not intended to be a court of first instance. The alcaldes del crimen took cognizance of criminal cases in the

---

[17] Avilés to Abascal, 1806, *Memoria del virey del Peru*, 25–26.

[18] Linares to Valero, 1716, *Instrucciones que los vireyes* . . . . 307–308.

[19] Revillagigedo, *Instrucción reservada*, arts. 78–79; *Recopilación*, ley 14, tit. 2, lib. 5.

[20] Letter of Mendoza to the emperor, Dec. 10, 1537, *Documentos inéditos* . . . . *de Indias*, II, 185; Revillagigedo to Amarillas, 1754, *Instrucciones que los vireyes* . . . . art. 27, pp. 10–11.

city wherein the audiencia resided and for five leagues around it. In the smaller audiencias where there were no criminal judges the oidores had this power.[21] A certain order of precedence was observed in the decision of cases by the audiencia. Lawsuits concerning the treasury came first. Other cases followed according to the date when they were submitted, but those relating to the poor were to be preferred.[22] Indian lawsuits were not to be delayed, and matters of slight importance could be decided by decrees of the viceroy.[23]

The audiencia was primarily a court of appeals. Alcaldes ordinarios could appeal their cases to the alcaldes mayores and from them to the corregidores and governors or directly to the audiencia. There was recourse to the audiencia from the various tribunals, from the governors, alcaldes mayores, and other justices.[24] After the intendancies were established, each intendant had a deputy who was a lawyer, duly examined and approved by the audiencia. All persons who felt aggrieved in the partidos or districts could go directly to the intendant, who took cognizance of their cases by means of his deputy. Appeals from the deputies went to the audiencia.[25] In 1545 the sentence of civil cases had to exceed six thousand maravedís in order to be admitted on appeal by the audiencia. Some later laws of 1563 and 1596 stated that the amount was to be one thousand pesos.[26] Whenever individuals felt dissatisfied with the decisions of the viceroys in administrative matters, they might have recourse to the audiencia, and executives could not prevent these appeals. When the litigant took his suit to the audiencia from the viceroy's decision, it was the custom of that body to send a memorial to

---

[21] *Recopilación*, leyes 89, 111, tit. 15, lib. 2.

[22] Montesclaros to his successor, 1615, *Documentos inéditos* . . . . *de Indias*, VI, 266; *Recopilación*, leyes 76, 82, tit. 15, lib. 2.

[23] *Ibid.*, leyes 75, 83, 85, tit. 15, lib. 2.

[24] *Ibid.*, leyes 12–13, tit. 12, lib. 5; ley 68, tit. 15, lib. 2.

[25] *Ordenanza* . . . . *de intendentes*, art. 15, pp. 23–24; *ibid.*, art. 121, p. 143; *ibid.*, art. 19, p. 28.

[26] *Recopilación*, ley 29, tit. 12, lib. 5; ley 42, tit. 16, lib. 2.

the viceroy telling him that the case had been appealed. Military matters in which the viceroy was the supreme judge were never appealed to the audiencia, but only to the junta de guerra of the Council of the Indies.[27] Sometimes people brought their cases directly to the viceroy. He gave these matters a preliminary hearing, and, if they were not serious, referred them to the courts of first instance.[28] Under certain conditions second appeals were permitted to go to the Council of the Indies, but the value of the lawsuits had to be at least six thousand pesos before they could be taken to the Council. In order to prevent recourse in trifling matters, a fine of one thousand ducats was to be imposed upon persons who dispatched cases to Spain which had no right to a second appeal. Lawsuits appealed from governors and ordinary justices were understood to have no second recourse. In appeals to the Council of the Indies the proceedings had to be entirely finished and the sentence decided before the case could be taken to Spain.[29]

The audiencia was directly responsible to the Council of the Indies for all its actions and decisions. At the end of each year it was to send to that body special reports concerning its work, but when it was governing during an interregnum reports were required every month. If the oidores were agreed that money ought to be expended on some public work, they did not have power to draw the amount from the treasury, but had to present their cause to the Council of the Indies, and in case the project was approved by it, an order authorizing the expenditure would

---

[27] *Recopilación*, leyes 35, 43, tit. 15, lib. 2; Court to Amarillas, 1755, *Instrucciones que los vireyes* . . . . art. 35, p. 70; Azanza, *Instrucción sobre las provincias de la Nueva España* . . . . April 29, 1800, MS, num. 17, p. 18; Solórzano, II, lib. 5, cap. 13, art. 41, p. 383. The junta de guerra was a special committee of the Council of the Indies composed of four councilors and four members from the council of war. Its duty was to attend to military and naval affairs concerning the defense of the colonies. The president, the conde de Medellin to the king. AGI, 141–5–8.

[28] Croix, *Instrucción que* . . . . *dejó*, AGI, 88–5–13; *Correspondance*, 263.

[29] *Recopilación*, leyes 1, 6, 8, tit. 13, lib. 5; ley 4, tit. 10, lib. 5; King to the audiencia of Lima, 1596, *Documentos inéditos* . . . . *de Indias*, XIX, 85–86.

be sent back.[30] Every year the fiscal drew up for this body a
statement of the action taken in the general acuerdos, in which
the viceroy and oidores were present, relating to matters of the
treasury and its lawsuits, and the Council had to be notified
annually concerning all fines collected by the audiencia.[31] On
all occasions accounts respecting visitations of the country were
to be sent to the Council by the fleets. Again when an oidor
finished his term of service another report was required of him.[32]
Viceroys and audiencias were to submit to the Council all cases
cerning the legitimization of children, and it also took cognizance of all the residencias of governors, corregidores, alcaldes
mayores or other justices.[33] It was utterly impossible for anything very important to escape the attention of the Council of
the Indies, since the accounts demanded by it were so detailed
and covered such a variety of subjects.

When judges of the audiencia decided cases sentences were
passed by a majority vote. When there was a tie the fiscal might
be called upon to give his opinion. If the oidores still disagreed,
one, two, or three lawyers might be appointed to make the proper
decision. All the judges had to sign the sentences.[34] The president also attached his signature to them, except in criminal cases.
He could refuse to sign the measures of the audiencia, but if they
were agreed to by a majority of the oidores, they passed without
his sanction.[35] The votes of the judges were recorded in books
kept for the purpose, and the president swore that he would not
reveal the records to anyone without the king's permission.[36]

[30] *Recopilación*, leyes 21, 59, 132, tit. 15, lib. 2.
[31] *Ibid.*, leyes 20–21, tit. 18, lib. 2; ley 1, tit. 25, lib. 2.
[32] King to the audiencia of Lima, 1595, *Documentos inéditos . . . . de
Indias*, XIX, 81; *Recopilación*, ley 26, tit. 31, lib. 2; ley 40, tit. 32, lib. 2.
[33] *Ibid.*, leyes 120, 69, tit. 15, lib. 2; Montesclaros to the king, April 17,
1612, *Documentos inéditos . . . . de Indias*, VI, 284.
[34] *Recopilación*, leyes 97, 106–107, tit. 15, lib. 2; Cédulas and provisiones
for the audiencia of Charcas, 1565, *Documentos inéditos . . . . de Indias*,
XVIII, 58–59.
[35] Rivera Cambas, I, 29; Court to Amarillas, 1755, *Instrucciones que los
vireyes . . . .* art. 28, p. 68; *Recopilación*, ley 29, tit. 17, lib. 2; leyes 32, 115,
tit. 15, lib. 2.
[36] *Ibid.*, leyes 156–157, tit. 15, lib. 2.

The visitation of the provinces, sometimes of a judicial, but more often of an administrative nature, was another important duty of the audiencia. Every three years an oidor was to make a tour of inspection throughout the entire district of the audiencia. If the viceroy saw fit, however visitations might be made more frequently. In 1588 the king gave orders that the province of Tucumán should be visited every year.[37] The visiting oidor was to inform himself concerning the economic conditions of the people, and of the churches and monasteries, whether the Indians still made idolatrous sacrifices, whether those in the mines were instructed in religion, whether the natives were enslaved, and as to the conduct of the corregidores and other public officials. He was to find out whether the tributes were just and see that caciques did not make the Indians pay more than was necessary. The mines also were to be inspected in order to insure better treatment of the natives. The visiting judge was to learn for the viceroy whether justices engaged in trade in contravention of the laws, or took possession of the wealth of persons who died intestate, and how encomenderos treated the Indians on their estates.[38]

The senior oidor began the work of visitation and the viceroy-president appointed the others by turns, assigning to them the places where they were to begin. The visiting oidor also acted as a circuit judge and was to prevent cases which ought not to be appealed from going to the audiencia, thereby burdening that court with unnecessary responsibilities. He was to receive two hundred thousand maravedís a year, besides his regular salary, during the time that he was occupied in the tour of inspection, and under no condition was he to take any bribes from the Indians in the provinces.[39]

<hr/>

[37] Cédulas and provisiones for the audiencia of Charcas, 1588, *Documentos inéditos . . . . de Indias*, XVIII, 192–193.

[38] *Recopilación*, ley 1, tit. 31, lib. 2; Queen to Mendoza, 1536, *Documentos inéditos . . . . de Indias*, XXIII, 464; King to the viceroy of *Mexico*, 1550, *ibid.*, 526–530; Memorial of Diego de Robles, 1570, *ibid.*, XI, 5–17.

[39] *Recopilación*, leyes 2–3, 20, 29, tit. 31, lib. 2; Cédulas and provisiones for the audiencia of Charcas, 1570, *Documentos inéditos . . . . de Indias*, XVIII, 516–517, 92–93.

The visitation of treasury officials was also intrusted to judges of the audiencia. Montesclaros said that members of the audiencia of Mexico were subject to corruption when visiting treasury officials; but they were no worse than the visitors from Spain who entered into the investigation like blind persons. He therefore advised that this task be given to the viceroy.[40] For six months continuously the oidores, in turn, were to attend the public auctions of the treasury. The president empowered a judge to inspect the registers of public clerks in all Spanish cities, and in Lima an oidor examined the armadas which returned each year to the port of Callao. Another served as a commissioner of mesadas, medias anatas, and stamped paper;[41] one took cognizance of appeals from the consulado relating to merchants, and another scrutinized cloth from China and contraband merchandise. Jails were frequently inspected by oidores, but, as Villarroel states, no doubt this was done in a perfunctory manner without interest or knowledge concerning the cases of the criminals.[42]

Certain restrictions were imposed upon visiting oidores so that their impartiality would not be impaired. They were not permitted to take their immediate family, relatives, or servants with them. Only one clerk and a sheriff (alguacil) could accompany each judge.[43] The king was informed that in the viceroyalty of Peru corregidores came out to receive visiting oidores and went to great expense to show them hospitality; therefore in 1596 it was ordered that they should not receive such entertainment under the penalty of one thousand ducats fine.[44]

---

[40] *Recopilación*, ley 22, tit. 31, lib. 2; Montesclaros to the king, 1607, *Instrucciones que los vireyes* . . . . 253.

[41] *Recopilación*, ley 34, tit. 16, lib. 2; ley 29, tit. 31, lib. 2; Solórzano, II, lib. 5, cap. 2, arts. 51–52, p. 279.

[42] *Recopilación*, ley 37, tit. 46, lib. 9; ley 76, tit. 45, lib. 9; ley 38, tit. 16, lib. 2; Villarroel, *Enfermedades políticas* . . . . MS, I, pt. II, p. 81.

[43] Provisiones reales, 1518, *Documentos inéditos* . . . . *de Indias*, XIX, 33–34; *Recopilación*, ley 90, tit. 16, lib. 2; leyes 30, 32, tit. 31, lib. 2.

[44] Cédulas and provisiones for the audiencia of Charcas, *Documentos inéditos* . . . . *de Indias*, XVIII, 264–265.

Pesquisidores or judges of commission could be sent out by the audiencia and the viceroy to investigate special crimes or violations of laws. For example, if governors, alcaldes mayores, and other justices failed to fulfil the instructions which the audiencia gave them, such persons might be dispatched, at the expense of the guilty, to inquire into their conduct. The viceroy as president of the audiencia appointed these judges with the consent of his council or the sala del crimen, and decided upon the length of the term of their commission.[45] It seems that the viceroys of Peru did not always consult with the audiencia in this matter, hence a special cédula of June 19, 1620, prohibited them from dispatching pesquisidores without the advice of the acuerdo. The king was informed that judges on commission with high salaries were sent to the provinces of Tucumán and Rio de la Plata, which in 1598 were poor. As complaints came from those regions concerning the burdens which the judges caused, the sovereign ordered that they should not be dispatched there for civil suits and not often in criminal cases, and then only at moderate salaries.[46]

Courtesy due to their rank was to be shown to the members of the audiencia. The people were to address them by the title of "Vuestra Merced" and when absent they were to speak of them as "Señores." Upon going to the viceregal palace for official business, the viceroy was to give them seats and not keep them waiting long. Viceroys were to correspond with the audiencia by letters written in the proper style and not make their wishes known by direct commands. They were to see that its rights of preëminence were kept at all times.[47] On important religious

---

[45] *Recopilación*, leyes 117, 176, tit. 15, lib. 2; leyes 1–2, 11, tit. 1, lib. 7; Montesclaros to his successor, 1615, *Documentos inéditos . . . . de Indias*, VI, 266.

[46] Esquilache to Guadalcázar, 1621, *Memorias de los vireyes . . . .* I, 101–102; King to the audiencia of La Plata, 1598, *Documentos inéditos . . . . de Indias*, XIX, 93–94.

[47] Palafox to his successor, 1642, *Documentos inéditos . . . . de Mexico*, VII, 76; *Recopilación*, leyes, 57–59, 63, tit. 15, lib. 3.

holidays, like Easter, Corpus Christi, the Ascensión, and the Avocation, the oidores and other members of the audiencia were to accompany the viceroy to mass, but on other occasions only the senior oidor went with him. When the senior oidor became president of the audiencia at the viceroy's death, he received the honors accorded to the executive, but a cédula of September 11, 1610, sent to Lima, stated that he was not to have the seat of honor in the audiencia or the ceremonies performed for the president, in case of the mere absence of the viceroy.[48]

During the sessions of the audiencia matters of ceremony and style were determined by the president according to the rules of the chancillerías of Valladolid and Granada. Palafox thought that the viceroy ought not to undervalue small matters like ceremony, but should carefully regulate them. On the other hand, the oidores were to honor the viceroy at all times as the king's representative by taking off their caps and capes whenever they saw him.[49] On the occasions when the viceroy came to the audiencia in state, much attention was paid to ceremony.

A deputation of judges attended him from his palace to the hall; on his arrival at the door, the porter called aloud, 'the president!' whereupon all the attorneys, advocates, and others met him and conducted him to his chair; the judges continued standing until he was seated and nodded permission for them to resume their seats.

At the end of the session all the members of the audiencia "accompanied him to the door of his apartment in the palace, the regent walking on his left, and the other members preceding him two and two.'"[50]

In New Spain a question arose concerning the viceroy's guard not paying due respect to the audiencia when that body

---

48 *Ibid.*, ley 6, tit. 3, lib. 3; leyes 51, 77, tit. 15, lib. 3; Solórzano, II, lib. 5, cap. 3, art. 46, p. 278.

49 Montesclaros to his successor, 1615, *Documentos inéditos . . . . de Indias*, VI, 265; Palafox to his successor, 1642, *Documentos inéditos . . . . de Mexico*, VII, 29–30; Palata to Monclova, 1689, *Memorias de los vireyes* . . . . II, 74.

50 Stevenson, W. B., *Twenty Years' Residence in South America* (London, 1825), I, 174–175.

went out of the palace or entered it. Viceroy Cruíllas said that it was the subinspector-general, Villalba, who had given orders for those honors to be discontinued by the palace guard. A royal decree of August 3, 1765, commanded that they be resumed, but the matter was not satisfactorily settled until 1792. At this time it was decided that the guard of the palace should raise their arms and beat the drums as soon as they saw the first judges entering or coming out of the palace to attend public functions when the viceroy was not present, and those honors were still being observed in 1803.[51]

3. RESTRICTIONS UPON THE AUDIENCIA

Many restrictions were imposed upon the audiencia by the laws of the Indies so that it might not become too powerful. Oidores were not to take part in discoveries or in mining. They might not have more than four slaves, and their wives were not to intervene in any matters. Neither they nor their children were allowed to receive gifts or loans of money, marry within the district of the audiencia, become sponsors at marriages or baptisms, attend betrothals and burials, or frequent the homes of litigants.[52] In 1570 Diego Robles reported that the first thing which oidores did was to allow their children to marry the richest persons in the country, thereby making impossible impartial decisions against the wealthy. Hence the need for a marriage law of the nature mentioned was imperative. Oidores might not be absent from their jurisdiction or return to Spain without a license from the king, nor could they hold more than one office.[53] Lawsuits relating to their interests were not to be brought to the

[51] Revillagigedo, *Instrucción reservada*, arts. 524, 526–527; Revillagigedo to Porlier, Jan. 10, 1790, AGI, 89–6–13; Marquina to Iturrigaray, 1803, *Instrucciones que los vireyes* . . . . art. 294, p. 201.

[52] *Recopilación*, leyes 60, 65, 67, 69, 82, tit. 16, lib. 2; Court to Amarillas, 1754, *Instrucciones que los vireyes* . . . . art. 32, p. 69.

[53] Memorial of Diego Robles, 1570, *Documentos inéditos* . . . . *de Indias*, XI, 41; *Recopilación*, leyes 88, 96, tit. 16, lib. 2.

audiencia in first instance, but had to be submitted to the ordinary justices of the cities and towns where they resided. The audiencia was not to take cognizance of criminal cases of viceroys or presidents. Members were not to engage in any profitable occupations, like cattle-raising, agriculture, commerce, or pearl fishing, but this law was hard to enforce and was frequently violated.[54] If an oidor had decided a case and it was appealed to the whole audiencia, he might not be present or vote at the final decision; he was not permitted to attend the lawsuits of his relatives and retainers. No judge was to make public any secret information against the president without a special order from the king, and in the absence of the presiding officer, no matter the cognizance of which belonged strictly to his jurisdiction could be introduced into the audiencia. The audiencia as a body was also enjoined to keep all matters secret.[55] The viceroy had to see that all these prohibitive laws were obeyed.

Information might be taken by the viceroy against the oidores and sent to the king at any time. However the executive did not have power to expel a guilty judge from the viceroyalty. If any misdemeanor was discovered, the viceroy could summon the guilty oidor and reprove him secretly. When the misdeed was of a serious nature or if the judge did not heed warning, information was to be sent to the king.[56] The monarch desired the viceroy to give his opinion as to how to deal with the situation and state all the details concerning the nature of the crime, but

---

[54] *Ibid.*, leyes 42, 45, 54–55, 59; Cédulas and provisiones for the audiencia of New Spain, 1549, *Documentos inéditos . . . . de Indias*, XVIII, 37, *et seq.*; King to the viceroy of Mexico, 1550, *ibid.*, XXIII, 540–541.

[55] *Recopilación*, leyes 25, 31, 39, 45, 65, tit. 15, lib. 2.

[56] *Ibid.*, ley 39; ley 38, tit. 3, lib. 3; Queen to Mendoza, 1536, *Documentos inéditos . . . . de Indias*, XXIII, 465; Croix, *Instrucción que . . . . dejó*, AGI, 88–5–13; Arriaga to Amarillas, 1755, *Instrucciones que . . . . los vireyes . . . .* art. 1, p. 94. A law of the Indies in 1620 provided that the oidor should be censured in the secrecy of the acuerdo when only the oidores were present. In cases which were not serious it was done in the presence of the senior oidor, but in actual practice this measure was not carried out literally. *Recopilación*, ley 51, tit. 16, lib. 2.

according to Palafox, the executive could not sentence or condemn the judge even in a serious offense.[57] The powers of the viceroy were sufficient to suspend an oidor and give account of the action to the king, if by chance his conduct was of such a nature that it might cause serious public scandal. Palafox suspended three oidores because of their irregularities. During the administration of Castellar in Peru, some of the judges of the probate court committed abuses; the defensor was temporarily deprived of his office, and the clerk was subjected to a fine and to perpetual loss of his position. Viceroys also recommended to the king the retirement of members of the audiencia, as the second Revillagigedo did in the case of the oidor Modesto de Salcedo who was old, feeble, and unable to attend properly to his duties.[58]

It was the duty of the president to keep check on the attendance of members of the audiencia. Oidores had to be present in court at least three hours in the morning, the penalty for absence being the deduction of half the day's salary.[59] The first Revillagigedo spoke of reprimanding judges for being tardy, but sometimes it required a great deal of tact on the part of the viceroy to correct oidores without stirring up open hostility. Viceroy Croix of Mexico seems to have been adept in administering reproofs without causing offenses.[60]

---

[57] Fuenclara, *Instrucción reservada*, April 23, 1742, AGI, 90–2–17, art. 6; Palafox to his successor, 1642, *Documentos inéditos . . . . de Mexico*, VII, 78.

[58] Croix, *Instrucción que . . . . dejó*, AGI 88–5–13; *Recopilación*, ley 44, tit. 16, lib. 2; Rivera Cambas, I, 144; Castellar to Liñan, 1681, *Memorias de los vireyes . . . .* I, 181; Revillagigedo to Porlier, April 30, 1790, AGI, 89–6–13.

[59] *Recopilación*, ley 21, tit. 15, lib. 2; Court to Amarillas, 1755, *Instrucciones que los vireyes . . . .* art. 29, p. 68; Superunda to his successor, 1761, *Memorias de los vireyes . . . .* IV, 77.

[60] Revillagigedo to Amarillas, 1754, *Instrucciones que los vireyes . . . .* art. 68, p. 18; Croix, *Correspondance*, 248.

4. THE PRESIDENT AND HIS DUTIES

Mendoza became president of the audiencia on the same day that he was appointed viceroy, thereby representing the king as the fountain of justice, as well as in his absolute gubernatorial capacity. Although it was not until 1614 that the viceroy was formally declared by law to hold the office of president of the audiencia, the custom was thoroughly established before this date.[61] The president was seldom a lawyer; therefore his activities in the audiencia were directive rather than judicial. He did not have a vote in matters of justice.[62] The same prohibition applied to appeals which were pending before the audiencia, nor was the viceroy allowed to be present when lawsuits which had been appealed from his sentence were being voted upon.[63]

The promotion of harmony and a friendly spirit in the audiencia was one of the arduous tasks of the president. He was expected to abstain from acts which would create hostility among the members. A cédula of September 17, 1616, ordered viceroys not to call oidores to their palace at inconvenient hours unless the seriousness of the matter to be considered demanded this.[64] Judges were always to obey their president, and heed his summons to come to his home or to attend juntas. They were to fulfil all his measures concerning war, administration, and finances, and keep all his orders relating to the royal patronage of the church.[65] Even when viceroys exceeded their authority,

---

[61] Rivera Cambas, I, 29; Riva Palacio, II, 229; *Recopilación,* ley 4, tit. 3, lib. 3.

[62] King to Mendoza, 1535, *Documentos inéditos . . . . de Indias,* XXIII, 423; Account concerning Cañete, 1543, *ibid.,* VIII, 379; Court to Amarillas, 1755, *Instrucciones que los vireyes . . . .* art. 28, p. 68; Marquina to Iturrigarary, 1803, *ibid.,* art. 16, pp. 161–162.

[63] *Recopilación,* ley 36, tit. 3, lib. 3; leyes 44, 24, tit. 15, lib. 2.

[64] Mendoza to Velasco, *Instrucciones que los vireyes . . . .* art. 1, p. 227; Palafox to his successor, 1642, *Documentos inéditos . . . . de Mexico,* VII, 76; *Recopilación,* ley 9, tit. 16, lib. 2; Solórzano, II, lib. 5, cap. 13, art. 38, p. 383.

[65] *Recopilación,* ley 12, tit. 16, lib. 2; leyes 50–51, tit. 15, lib. 2.

they were to be respected by the oidores as the king's highest representative, and judges were never to interfere with matters belonging strictly to them.[66] The viceroy could ask information of the audiencia whenever he desired it. Usually this was done when the audiencia met as an acuerdo or council of state on certain appointed days. Ordinarily the viceroy presided at the acuerdos, but in case of other pressing business he might be excused. [7] In New Spain acuerdos seem to have been held shortly after the audiencia was established and before there was a viceroy. One of these meetings occurred as early as September 25, 1529, since it was customary for all dispatches from the king to be opened in the presence of the whole audiencia, and not by the president alone.[68] Some viceroys found that the opinions of the oidores were well worth considering. The second Cañete gave orders for a general acuerdo to be held in the audiencia of Lima to determine the best way to put royal measures into effect, and Salvatierra of Peru stated that he always availed himself of the opinions of the judges in grave matters of administration. In the middle of the eighteenth century Viceroy Castel-Fuerte of the same viceroyalty said that most of his time was occupied with his frequent attendance at the acuerdos where various matters were debated. Viceroy Cagigal declared that the oidores of Mexico always gave him wise advice, and Branciforte implied the same thing. In 1808 Iturrigaray met with the acuerdo to decide upon the action that ought to be taken in Mexico because of the relinquishment of the throne by the royal family.[69]

---

[66] King to the audiencia of Chile, 1590, *Documentos inéditos* . . . . *de Indias*, XXV, 542–543; *Recopilación*, ley 34, tit. 3, lib. 3.

[67] Cédulas and provisiones for the audiencia of Charcas, 1591, *Documentos inéditos* . . . . *de Indias*, XVIII, 211–212, 222; *Recopilación*, leyes 49, 21, 26, 23, tit. 15, lib. 2; Croix, *Instrucción que* . . . . *dejó*, AGI, 88–5–13.

[68] Accusation of the marqués del Valle against the licenciados Matienzo and Delgadillo, *Documentos inéditos* . . . . *de Indias*, XXIX, 319; *Recopilación*, ley 28, tit. 15, lib. 2.

[69] Account concerning Cañete, 1590, *Documentos inéditos* . . . . *de Indias*, VIII, 344–345; Salvatierra to Aliste, 1651, *in* Polo, *Memorias de los vireyes*

The attendance of the president on Saturdays at all residencias was required.   On other occasions litigants asked him to be present during the process of their lawsuits, since they thought that their cases would thus be judged with more fairness.[70] When visiting the subject audiencias of Panamá, La Plata, or Quito, the viceroy of Peru might enter the acuerdos with the president and occupy the most eminent place.[71]

The duties of the viceroy as president were numerous.   If the boundary of an audiencia needed to be changed, the king intrusted the work to him.   When new oidores entered into their office the president received their oath.   In 1544 after the first viceroy of Peru, Blasco Núñez Vela, took his oath of office, the oidores put their hand upon the cross held by the viceroy and swore in the name of God, the holy Mary and four of the apostles to perform faithfully their tasks, fulfil the laws and ordinances of the king, and to keep the secrecy of the audiencia.[72]

The viceroy was to be solicitous for the welfare of the judges and see that they received justice   A law of the Indies of 1550 confirmed by others in 1552 and 1605 authorized the president and the alcaldes ordinarios to take cognizance of criminal cases of oidores.   Viceroy Castel-Fuerte, with the advice of the acuerdo, ordered the oidor, Sebastián Bonde Leos, who was imprisoned by the president of the audiencia of Panamá, to be released and treated with the respect due to a person of his rank.   Later when news came that the judge had died in prison, the viceroy and the acuerdo immediately took measures to punish the president and

. . . . art. 39, p. 40; Castel-Fuerte to Villagarcía, 1736, *Memorias de los vireyes* . . . . III, 266; Cagigal to Cruíllas, 1760, *Instrucciones que los vireyes* . . . . 113; Branciforte to Azanza, 1797, *ibid.*, art. 96, p. 142; Riva Palacio, III, 39.

[70] Palafox to his successor, 1642, *Documentos inéditos* . . . . *de Mexico*, VII, 74, 76.

[71] *Ibid.*, VII, 78; *Recopilación*, leyes 19–20, 36, tit. 17, lib. 2; ley 29, tit. 3, lib. 3.

[72] Cédulas and provisiones of the king, 1563, *Documentos inéditos* . . . . *de Indias*, XVIII, 28–29; *ibid.*, VIII, 380–381; Account concerning Toledo, 1569, *ibid.*, VIII, 232.

gave account of their action to the king.[73] The viceroy had to
inform himself concerning the salaries of all judges and officials
of the audiencia and send an annual statement to the king. Also
he was to report all vacancies in that body. On such an occasion
he could recommend an increase of their salary, as the second
Velasco did in New Spain. Later Viceroy Croix did the same
thing. Since the cost of living had gone up considerably, the
marquis explained to the king that the four thousand pesos which
the oidores received were not sufficient for them.[74]

The president had to settle disputes among the judges and
the different tribunals according to certain laws of the Indies
that gave him the authority to determine to which tribunal the
cognizance of doubtful cases belonged, but he could not do this
when it was a contest over the jurisdiction of the executive and
the audiencia wherein he presided, for only the Council of the
Indies could decide such a matter. If the cases were declared to
be civil, the oidores dealt with them, and if criminal, the alcaldes
del crimen tried them. When there were differences between the
audiencia and the consulado, the viceroy or senior oidor decided
them. The same rule applied when conflicts occurred with the
alcaldes ordinarios.[75] In fact the viceroy had power to pass
judgment upon all rivalries between the audiencia and the government. Nevertheless Palafox thought that when serious consequences were foreseen from the viceroy's decision, it was better
to suspend the matter and give account to the king. Liñan wisely
adjusted one of those contentions over a lawsuit between the
oidores and the judges of the criminal chamber.[76]

The viceroy maintained correspondence with the audiencias
of his viceroyalty outside the capital. Liñan said that he wrote

[73] *Recopilación*, ley 43, tit. 16, lib. 2; Castel-Fuerte to Villagarcía, 1736,
Memorias de los vireyes . . . . III, 268–269.

[74] *Recopilación*, ley 168, tit. 15, lib. 2; Velasco to Philip II, Dec. 22,
1590, AGI, 58–3–11; Croix, *Instrucción que* . . . . *dejó*, AGI, 88–5–13.

[75] *Recopilación*, leyes 2–5, tit. 9, lib. 5.

[76] Palafox to his successor, 1642, *Documentos inéditos* . . . . *de Mexico*,
VII, 31; Liñan to Palata, 1681, *Memorias de los vireyes* . . . . I, 289–290.

to the four audiencias of Charcas, Quito, Chile, and Panamá during his administration, and the viceroys of Mexico did the same thing with the audiencias of Guatemala and Guadalajara. Likewise the viceroy could issue orders for the good government of the cities and towns within his jurisdiction, and the oidores were not to hinder the cabildos from obeying.[77] The viceroy-president had to prevent delays in judicial proceedings so that the rich would not trample upon the poor by causing them needless expense. Perhaps the best examples of this kind were Mendoza, the two Velascos, and Palafox, who took measures to prevent lawsuits from being prolonged indefinitely.[78]

As previously mentioned, one of the greatest powers of the viceroy as president was his right to decide what affairs belonged strictly to civil administration and what matters might be considered within the province of the audiencia.[79] He might request the audiencia to abstain from taking cognizance of certain cases, when they were declared to pertain entirely to the government. Frequently points of administration were so closely united with matters of justice that it was not easy to separate the two kinds of jurisdiction. As a result disputes arose between the chief executive and the audiencia. Revillagigedo proposed a remedy to Branciforte, which he thought would preserve at the same time the decorum of the viceroy and the authority of the judge; that is, "to have the decision appealed from the viceroy heard before himself with two or three of the judges associated with him." By this arrangement he believed that no one would be embarrassed and the power of the viceroy would not be diminished.[80] Closely allied with the right to determine guber-

---

[77] Liñan to Palata, 1681, *Memorias de los vireyes* . . . . I, 289; *Recopilación*, ley 10, tit. 16, lib. 2.

[78] Court to Amarillas, 1755, *Instrucciones que los vireyes* . . . . art. 28, p. 68; García, *Don Juan de Palafox*, 117.

[79] *Recopilación*, ley 38, tit. 15, lib. 2; Montesclaros to his successor, 1615, *Documentos inéditos* . . . . *de Indias*, VI, 264; Court to Amarillas, 1755, *Instrucciones que los vireyes* . . . . art. 33, pp. 69–70.

[80] *Recopilación*, ley 42, tit. 15, lib. 2; Revillagigedo, *Instrucción reservada*, arts. 84, 90–91.

natorial matters, was the important prerogative, already discussed, of deciding disputes between the judges themselves or with other tribunals, after they had been heard by the civil fiscal.[81] Viceroys sometimes intruded into judicial affairs in their capacity of passing judgment upon what pertained to administration. Perhaps it was because of the great distance from the seat of control that they ventured to assume this power. The audiencias were powerless to do anything in these instances.

They may advise, they may remonstrate; but in the event of a direct collision between their opinion and the will of the viceroy, what he determines must be brought into execution, and nothing remains for them, but to lay the matter before the king and the Council of the Indies,

says William Robertson.[82]

Let us see what one of the viceroys had to say about the judicial powers of the executive. Montesclaros thoroughly believed that the viceroy had authority in matters of justice. He based his view upon many royal cédulas, especially the one which treated of the titles of the viceroys. When speaking of the audiencia the king said

. . . . You shall understand and are able to know in the future my will concerning the method and form which must be taken in the dispatch and carrying out of the business, and these [matters] which belong only to the viceroy to provide, and those which are under our care and pertain to the administration of justice, in which I have ordered and commanded these viceroys that you allow them to do it freely without being interfered with.

Montesclaros again quotes the king,

. . . . In order to do and administer justice alike to all our subjects and vassals, and therefore in all other matters and business of any kind and condition which may exist and arise, the viceroy [shall do] what appears and seems best.

---

[81] Revillagigedo, *Instrucción reservada*, art. 93; Montesclaros to his successor, 1615, *Documentos inéditos . . . . de Indias*, VI, 263; Azanza, *Instrucción sobre las provincias de la Nueva España . . . .* April 29, 1800, MS, num. 17, pp. 9–11.

[82] *History of America*, II, pt. VIII, p. 357.

Montesclaros also claimed that the viceroy had jurisdiction even in criminal cases. In another cédula the monarch said he had learned that persons committed serious crimes and escaped punishment by wandering throughout the provinces and cities of the kingdom. He then addressed the viceroy in the following words:

.... You shall inform yourself and know very particularly what crimes have been committed in these provinces, for which the guilty have not been punished nor has any action been taken against them. After summoning and hearing the litigants affected, you shall provide officially for justice to be administered with brevity in both civil and criminal cases .... against any of my governors, justices and treasury officials .... as against any person of whatever estate, rank or preëminence he may be; for this I give you sufficient and complete power.

Other letters and decrees granted the viceroy power to inform himself concerning the administration of justice in the audiencia. For example, one stated that he should have

.... special care to understand with all punctuality and truth how justice is administered and executed in all the audiencias of this district, and by all my governors and corregidores. . . .

Montesclaros declared that there was no recourse from the decisions of the viceroy, since appeal ordinarily went from an inferior to his superior and the viceroy had no peer in the colony.[83] Thus it may be realized that there was much room for variously interpreting the laws of the Indies.

Supervision of patrolling the capital at night was another duty of the president. Since the streets were not lighted after dark until the latter part of the eighteenth century, it was necessary to adopt some effective measure to prevent night crimes. Mexico City was divided into wards, over each of which the viceroy appointed a judge of the audiencia. Within his ward the oidor was to see that all disorders and robberies were prevented.[84] The palace guard was sometimes called out to assist in the patrol-

---

[83] Montesclaros to his successor, 1615, *Documentos inéditos . . . . de Indias*, VI, 258–261.

[84] Marfil to Cagigal, 1760, *Instrucciones que los vireyes . . . .* 109–110; Castel-Fuerte to Villagarcía, 1736, *Memorias de los vireyes . . . .* III, 266.

ling of the wards. The same method of keeping order was employed in Lima. Viceroy Liñan commanded that the city should be patrolled by a company of infantry from early evening until ten o'clock and by a squadron of cavalry from twelve o'clock until dawn. Later Teodoro de Croix found it necessary to commission Juan Lostaunu, the captain of the infantry, to patrol the capital, its suburbs and the surrounding country, in order to capture not only malefactors but also runaway slaves who sought refuge in the city and in the neighboring mountains. In 1805 night watchmen were established in Lima at the expense of the residents, and arrangements were made for lighting the wards.[85]

The president had to keep certain records, which might be consulted when necessary. One book included all the repartimientos of Indians, and another the fines imposed by the audiencia.[86] Viceroys were ordered to take special care to execute, in all their districts, the wills of persons who died in the Indies without heirs. Whenever it was necessary for the judge of the probate court to send out collectors against remiss and negligent persons, the president fixed their salaries. Likewise, he had power to admit or reject information brought before the audiencia. He did not allow everybody to give evidence, but only such persons as could be relied upon for truthfulness.[87]

The viceroy determined the days for sessions of the audiencia, designated the judges for special cases, and had authority to remove them if they ought not be permitted to vote on the matter in question. Croix said that when an occasion of withdrawing a judge arose, it would be convenient to do it with dissimulation by giving him some charge or by assigning him to another chamber.[88]

---

[85] Liñan to Palata, 1681, *Memorias de los vireyes* . . . . I, 290; Croix to Lemos, 1790, *ibid.*, V, 145; Avilés to Abascal, 1806, *Memoria del virey del Peru*, 33–34.

[86] *Recopilación*, ley 62, tit. 3, lib. 3; ley 163, tit. 15, lib. 2.

[87] *Ibid.*, leyes 58, 11, tit. 32, lib. 2; ley 8, tit. 33, lib. 2.

[88] Croix, *Instrucción que* . . . . *dejó*, AGI, 88–5–13; *Correspondance*, 265; Palafox to his successor, 1642, *Documentos inéditos* . . . . *de Mexico*, VII, 77.

The president divided the audiencia into salas and selected the judges who served in them.[89] At first there were two chambers in the audiencias of Lima and Mexico, one for civil and the other for criminal cases. Later, when the business of the courts increased, three salas were formed, two for deciding civil suits, and one for criminal matters. This arrangement lasted until the eve of independence.[90] The principal difference between the chambers of the audiencias in the two capitals was that in Lima the president appointed the judges at the beginning of each year, while in Mexico City the distribution of the salas was made daily. Viceroy Palata first introduced this custom into the former audiencia, and his measure was approved by a royal cédula in 1687. In Peru the union of the salas was prohibited in 1765, but a royal order of July 3, 1801, declared that when serious or important business occurred they might be combined by order of the viceroy, who should inform the regent.[91]

The judges of the criminal chamber in Lima were at first called alcaldes de corte. The king esteemed them next to the viceroy, since they were men of good judgment, who punished criminals and pacified the country just as if it were a village in Spain. Unfortunately this good reputation did not always last. Viceroy Linares of Mexico complained that the alcaldes came to the sala late in the morning and left early, intrusting many matters entirely to their subordinates. They also had disputes with the civil oidores, which the viceroy settled with difficulty.[92]

[89] *Recopilación,* leyes 61–62, tit. 15, lib. 2; Palata to Monclova, 1689, *Memorias de los vireyes* . . . . II, 100; Solórzano, II, lib. 5, cap. 3, art. 63, p. 281.

[90] *Ibid.,* art. 64, p. 281; Account concerning Cañete, 1590, *Documentos inéditos* . . . . *de Indias,* VIII, 387–388; Rivera Cambas, I, 349; Revillagigedo, *Instrucción reservada,* art. 66; Alamán, *Historia de Méjico,* I, 49; Lemos to Vallenari, 1796, *Memorias de los vireyes* . . . . VI, 82; Pinkerton, *Modern Geography,* III, 587.

[91] Azanza, *Instrucción sobre las provincias de la Nueva España* . . . . April 29, 1800, MS, núm. 17, pp. 10, 20–21; Avilés to Abascal, 1806, *Memoria del virey del Peru,* 24.

[92] *Documentos inéditos* . . . . *de Indias,* V, 486–487; Linares to Valero, 1716, *Instrucciones que los vireyes* . . . . 303.

The alcaldes del crimen tried all criminal cases that came before the audiencia, and there was no appeal from their decision except to the Council of the Indies. A law of the Indies in 1571, reiterated by others in 1574 and 1598, permitted two alcaldes to determine cases during the absence of the other members of the sala, except when the death penalty or mutilation was to be inflicted, when all the judges had to be present. In 1802 delays occurred when one of the members of this sala was absent; therefore the next year the king authorized an oidor from the civil chamber to be present if a death sentence, or one of whipping, or of banishment to the presidios for ten years had to be decided.[93] The criminal judges did not need to attend the ordinary acuerdos of the president and civil judges unless some serious business was to be discussed.[94] An order from the viceroy was necessary for alcaldes of Lima to sentence prisoners to the galleys. When the civil chamber was so rushed with work that it was not able to dispatch all its cases, the viceroy could send some of them to the criminal sala. In 1802, Viceroy Avilés said that in a few months fifty civil cases were handled by the sala del crimen in Lima.[95] Criminal judges could not arrest the corregidor of Mexico City without first consulting the viceroy. Their greatest privilege was the right to correspond directly with the king.[96]

The punishment of crime was one of the special functions of the viceroy. He was also held responsible for those committed during the rule of his predecessor. In spite of all the measures applied by the colonial executives, vice had not decreased very much in New Spain up to the latter part of the eighteenth century. Porlier, the secretary of the second Revillagigedo,

---

[93] *Recopilación*, leyes 3, 7, tit. 17, lib. 2; Avilés to Abascal, 1806, *Memoria del virey del Peru*, 25.

[94] *Recopilación*, ley, 20, tit. 17, lib. 2.

[95] *Ibid.*, leyes 24, 26; Avilés to Abascal, 1806, *Memoria del virey del Peru*, 25.

[96] *Recopilación*, leyes 31, 35, tit. 17, lib. 2.

records many notable crimes. Not even the clergy escaped, some of them being treacherously murdered in their convents.[97] Perhaps the laxness or corruption of the criminal chamber was one of the causes for this. Linares made numerous objections to the court. Rich criminals laughed at the idea of meeting with their deserts, but the poor were sometimes treated with the greatest severity. The judges took bribes, and a portion of the profits from brigandage was used to obtain immunity for robbers. Villarroel complained of the endless red tape involved in lawsuits.[98]

There were several well-known occasions on which certain viceroys made special efforts to bring the guilty to just punishment. Shortly before the arrival of the second viceroy of Mexico, a man, accompanied by a woman from Seville, landed at Vera Cruz and announced that he was the licenciado Vena, come as visitador from Spain. When Mendoza asked to see his papers, he said that Velasco would bring them. This aroused suspicion, and Mendoza was able to expose ·and punish this impostor, who was sentenced to four hundred lashes and to serve in the galleys for ten years. This was the last act of Mendoza in New Spain and it won much applause from the people.[99]

During the administration of Castellar the treasury officials of Peru committed some thefts, and the viceroy gave the corregidor, Luis Henríquez, a secret commission to investigate them. The treasury had been robbed of four hundred thousand pesos; accordingly two of the officials were hung, the contador was deprived permanently of his position, and the other officers banished. The king approved of the viceroy's action and asked him to thank the corregidor.[100]

---

[97] *Ibid.*, leyes 25–26, tit. 3, lib. 3; *Suplemento de Bustamante*, to Cavo, arts. 128–133, p. 385.

[98] Linares to Valero, 1716, *Instrucciones que los vireyes* . . . . 303–304; Villarroel, *Enfermedades politicas* . . . . MS, I, pt. II, p. 78.

[99] Cavo, lib. 4, art. 8, pp. 105–106; Zamacois, V, 24–27; Rivera Cambas, I, 33.

[100] Castellar to Liñan, 1681, *Memorias de los vireyes* . . . . I, 175–176.

In the same viceroyalty a case similar to Vena's was dealt with by Teodoro de Croix. Manuel Antonio Figueroa, a native of Galicia, came to Peru and assumed many high sounding titles, like Cardinal Patriarch of the Indies and Governor of the Council of Castile. In 1785 Croix ordered the auditor de guerra to seize the man and examine his papers, which were found to be forged, so Figueroa was sentenced to ten years in the presidio of Africa.[101]

A terrible crime was committed in Mexico City nine days after the arrival of the second Revillagigedo. Joaquín Dongo, a rich man, was murdered in his home and all his wealth taken. His servants shared his fate. The viceroy immediately gave orders to the tribunal of La Acordada, to the criminal chamber of the audiencia, and to the alcaldes in the wards of the city, that the criminals should be apprehended. In fifteen days the proceedings were over and the guilty executed; the residents of the capital were greatly astonished by the prompt action.[102]

Another celebrated case which the viceroy was called upon to look into was that of Toribio del Mazo, lieutenant of a battalion in Yucatan, who was suspected of killing the intendant of Mérida, Lucas de Gálvez. Since Mazo was the nephew of the bishop of that diocese, the clergy defended him. When it was realized that a just decision could not be reached in Yucatan, a royal decree of August 20, 1795, ordered Branciforte to remove the case to Mexico. At this time the sala del crimen was overburdened with cases; therefore the next year the viceroy obtained royal permission to appoint an extraordinary junta of judges to try Mazo. Branciforte selected the junta and submitted all the papers to it, but his successor, Azanza, advised the Council of the Indies to suppress this junta and restore the case to the criminal chamber, which was done by a cédula of October 10, 1798. The Mazo case was finally decided during the administra-

101 Croix to Lemos, 1790, *Memorias de los vireyes* . . . . V, 111–122.
102 Riva Palacio, II, 877–879.

tion of Marquina, more than ten years after the crime was committed, the accused being declared innocent.[103] The usual punishment for smaller crimes was to dispatch the guilty to the presidios of the frontiers or to the Philippines. Palafox favored the plan of sending vagabonds who came from Spain without licenses to those dependencies, because they were liable to become robbers and highwaymen, and thereby disturb the peace. What they might do in the Philippine Islands was a matter of indifference. Amarillas was commanded to cause mulattoes, Negroes, and vagabonds of the castes to work on the roads to expiate their crimes, and so save money for the treasury. They were also to serve in bakeries and workshops, where they could be useful while being chastised.[104] The criminal chamber of the audiencia assigned minor culprits to the cloth mills, bakeries, and butcher shops, selling them for a period of eight or ten years at prices of one hundred and eighty pesos down to fifty.

. . . . A leader was appointed over a gang of these criminals, which was called the collera. He led them through the cities and towns of the kingdom where the workshops were situated, forcing their owners to buy them and collecting a certain amount if any owner on account of not wishing to take such offenders, refused to receive them.

Since great abuses were committed and many persons were opposed to this institution, Viceroy Croix ordered the criminals to be sent to penitentiaries and public works as in Spain. The death penalty could not be inflicted by order of the viceroy without concurrence of the audiencia and the acuerdo.[105]

---

103 Branciforte to Azanza, 1798, *Instrucciones que los vireyes* . . . . 151–154; Marquina to Iturrigaray, 1803; *ibid.*, arts. 27–32, pp. 163–164; Azanza, *Instrucción sobre las provincias de la Nueva España*, April 29, 1800, MS, núm. 17, pp. 78–80.

104 Palafox to his successor, 1642, *Documentos inéditos* . . . . *de Mexico*, VII, 78; Revillagigedo, *Instrucción reservada*, arts. 134–135; Marquina to Iturrigaray, 1803, *Instrucciones que los vireyes* . . . . art. 262, p. 197; Court to Amarillas, 1755, *ibid.*, 85.

105 Croix, *Instrucción que* . . . . *dejó*, AGI, 88–5–13; *Recopilación*, ley 16, tit. 8, lib. 7.

The pardoning power was granted to the early viceroys. The wording of a law of the Indies in 1614 said,

> .... We grant the power to the viceroys of Peru and New Spain to pardon any crimes and excesses committed in the provinces of their government, which we according to the rights and powers of these kingdoms are able to pardon.[106]

Custom prescribed, however, that this law should not be carried out literally. Only in rare cases of rebellion and wars could the chief executive safely use the pardoning power. The risk was too great for many viceroys to try it, as in the cases of Peralta and Bernardo de Gálvez. As president of the audiencia the viceroy could excuse the fines of the oidores for being absent or tardy, and for minor offenses.[107]

The viceroy also supervised prisons by means of the oidores whom he designated for this purpose, but they were always to consult him in serious matters. Every Saturday the executive sent judges to inspect the Indian jails of Mexico City, and occasionally he himself went to visit prisons, as Branciforte did on March 18, 1796.[108] Poor prisoners were maintained at the expense of religious brotherhoods which controlled certain pious funds, and the king requested viceroys to aid those societies by paying the salaries of their chaplains.[109] Viceroy Croix caused some important changes to be made in the court prison of Mexico City. He found that there was only one room for both men and women; therefore he had the prison enlarged so that a room for women, an infirmary, and a chapel might be provided.[110]

The hearing of petitions and complaints was another duty that occupied much of the viceroy-president's time. Mendoza

---

[106] *Recopilación*, ley 27, tit. 3, lib. 3.

[107] Solórzano, II, lib. 5, cap. 13, art. 35, p. 382; Instruction of Nieva, 1559, *Documentos inéditos* .... *de Indias*, XXV, 52; King to the audiencia of Peru, 1593, *ibid.*, XIX, 77–78; *Recopilación*, ley 170, tit. 15, lib. 2.

[108] *Ibid.*, leyes 7, 12, tit. 6, lib. 7; Gómez, Diario, *Documentos para la historia de México*, serie 2, pt. VII, p. 448.

[109] Revillagigedo, *Instrucción reservada*, art. 131; King to the viceroy of Peru, 1595, *Documentos inéditos* .... *de Indias*, XIX, 79.

[110] Croix, *Instrucción que* .... *dejó*, AGI, 88–5–13.

said that he always listened patiently to the entreaties of the Indians who came before him, although he knew they were lying. Juan and Ulloa said that the viceroy of Peru daily gave public audience to all kinds of people and for this purpose three spacious rooms were set aside. In the first, which was decorated with the portraits of all the viceroys, the executive received the Indians and other castes. In the second he listened to Spaniards and in the third, adorned with the pictures of the reigning king and queen placed under a canopy of rich silk, he received ladies who wished to speak to him in private and without being known.[111] Viceroy Branciforte of Mexico received everybody without distinction of persons. The viceroys arranged for these conferences whenever it was most convenient. Marquina fixed them for four o'clock on four afternoons a week.[112] Some of the matters presented at these confidential meetings related to civil affairs; therefore they were submitted to the secretariat. Others, of a judicial nature, had to be referred to the viceroy's assessor. Another troublesome task which tried the patience of an executive was the answering of letters of complaint. Palata said that the viceroy himself had to attend to the opening of these letters, since in Peru persons of integrity could not be found to do it.[113]

The taking of the residencias of all officials who served in the Philippines was an additional task of the viceroy of New Spain when on August 9, 1589, the audiencia of Manila was abolished. Villamanrique sent the licenciado Herver del Coral to Manila for this purpose. He arrived in the islands in 1590 accompanied by the new governor, Gómez Dasmariñas.[114]

During a session the audiencia of Mexico was a scene of great activity. Outside in the corridors of the palace were large num-

<hr />

111 Mendoza to Velasco, *Instrucciones que los vireyes* . . . . art. 15, p. 299; ''A Voyage to South America,'' *in* Pinkerton, *Voyages and Travels*, XIV, 572.

112 Zamacois, V, 693; Marquina to Iturrigaray, 1803, *Instrucciones que los vireyes* . . . . art. 409, p. 220.

113 Palata to Monclova, 1689, *Memorias de los vireyes* . . . . II, 58–59.

114 Cunningham, 71.

bers of litigants, business agents, and attorneys. Some walked hurriedly, others slowly, some shouted in their disputes and others were silent. In the patio there was a stairway leading to the sala of the audiencia. It was necessary to uncover the head and enter the room with respect, speaking in a low voice. The chamber was large, well adorned, and awe-inspiring. In a prominent place Viceroy Velasco was seated surrounded by four oidores. Only the ministro semanero or inspector of dispatches was speaking. The other judges seldom addressed the president, except in serious matters or when an explanation was asked. The viceroy was seated on a large velvet-cushioned chair, and below him were ranged the fiscal, the alguacil mayor, the attorney of the poor, the protector of the Indians, and the other lawyers who had lawsuits. A wooden partition at the back of the room segregated the common people, who did not have seats.[115]

Next to the president, the fiscal was perhaps the most important official of the audiencia. There were two fiscales in the larger audiencias, one for civil and another for criminal matters. The fiscal attended the acuerdos and extraordinary juntas, since many matters pertaining to the treasury were discussed in them, and he sent to the Council of the Indies reports of the actions relating to the treasury taken in these general acuerdos.[116] He had to attend cases of administration of which the viceroy or president had cognizance and see that no injury resulted to the treasury. The fiscales defended all lawsuits affecting the treasury and were present at all such cases which came to the audiencia by appeal. They had to witness the auction of treasury positions, and know whether the men who bought them received the royal confirmation. They were to expedite the residencias of treasury officials and dispatch all fiscal cases promptly.[117]

[115] Gonzáles Obregón, *México viejo*, 72–73.

[116] *Recopilación*, leyes 1, 5, 20, tit. 18, lib. 2; Cédulas and provisiones for the audiencia of Charcas, 1564, *Documentos inéditos . . . . de Indias*, XVIII, 47.

[117] *Recopilación*, ley 26, tit. 15, lib. 2; leyes 10, 12–13, 15–17, 26–27, 40, tit. 18, lib. 2.

5. JUDICIAL POWERS OF THE VICEROY

A real judicial power was exercised by the viceroy in his cognizance of Indian cases in first instance. On Monday and Thursday morning of each week the interpreter of the audiencia brought Indians having petitions before Mendoza. He heard them and decided all minor cases as quickly as possible, referring matters of no great importance to the alcaldes mayores and other local justices so that the natives need not leave their homes, Cases which demanded more attention were handed over to one of the oidores.[118] The first Velasco personally heard Indian matters on Mondays and Wednesdays in the morning and on Friday afternoons. All business was dispatched without delay or expense to the natives. The audiencia could help decide whether it was necessary to send judges against corregidores and alcaldes mayores who vexed the Indians, but the viceroy appointed them.[119]

The multitudinous Indian lawsuits which began shortly after the conquest were always a source of annoyance to the viceroy. By this method the natives hoped to win back the lands of which they had been unjustly despoiled. As a result a veritable social warfare was created. In their ignorance, the Indians permitted the mestizos and crafty Spanish settlers to induce them to keep up litigation about their lands. Sometimes by a corrupt alliance with officials those instigators of legal proceedings were able to secure for themselves a part of the court fines and expenses that the natives were forced to pay. In order to remedy the situation many laws of the Indies commanded that mestizos and Spaniards should not be permitted to live in Indian towns.[120]

---

[118] *Ibid.*, ley 30, tit. 17, lib. 2; ley 65, tit. 3, lib. 3; ley 13, tit. 10, lib. 5; Mendoza to Velasco, *Instrucciones que los vireyes* . . . . art. 15, p. 229.

[119] Velasco to Philip II, June 2, 1592, AGI, 58-3-11; Solórzano, II, lib. 5, cap. 13, art. 23, p. 379.

[120] *Recopilación*, leyes 21–22, 24, tit. 3, lib. 6; Enríquez to Coruña, 1580, *Instrucciones que los vireyes* . . . . art. 3, p. 244; Montesclaros to his successor, 1615, *Documentos inéditos* . . . . *de Indias*, VI, 224–225.

Conscientious viceroys always tried to protect the natives in their legal proceedings. The first Velasco provided that no civil suit in which an Indian was a litigant should be prolonged, and that all cases involving a sum greater than ten pesos were to be brought before him. Viceroy Toledo of Peru tried to shorten and even abolish, if possible, Indian lawsuits. He appointed the fiscal and a learned judge of the audiencia as their defenders.[121] Viceroys were ordered to appoint protectors of the natives who were Christians and persons of ability. They were to have easy access to the executive, to whom they had to give account of the condition of the Indians, and the viceroy then sent those reports to the Council of the Indies.[122]

The second Velasco was known to be a friend of the Indians. He obtained permission to reëstablish the practice introduced by his father concerning lawsuits of the natives. A royal decree of April 9, 1591, fixed the salaries of all officials who took charge of Indian matters, thereby abolishing all legal fees imposed upon the natives. The expenses of their suits were to be defrayed by the assessment of a half real upon each Indian paying tribute. Velasco permitted the Indians to bring their cases before him every day and held conferences with legal advisers concerning their lawsuits.[123]

Also the viceroy as the supreme military commander-in-chief took cognizance in first and second instance of all civil and criminal cases concerning persons who enjoyed the military privileges. The audienca and other justices might not take cognizance of the civil or criminal suits of any soldier until he

---

[121] Torquemada, I, 670; Instructions for defensores of the Indians, 1574, *Documentos inéditos . . . . de Indias*, XXI, 287–291.

[122] Solórzano, I, lib. 2, cap. 29, arts. 47–48, p. 212; *Recopilación*, leyes 1, 5, 10, 12, tit. 6, lib. 6. In Lima, in 1621, there was a protector-general, two lawyers (abogados), and two solicitors (procuradores) for Indian cases. Esquilache to Guadalcázar, 1621, *Memorias de los vireyes* . . . . I, 93.

[123] Velasco to the king, Oct. 8, 1590, AGI, 58–3–11, cap. 1; Vetancurt, Agustín de, *Teatro mexicano* (Mexico, 1870–71), II, 312; Rivera Cambas, I, 68; Velasco to the king, June 2, 1592, AGI, 58–3–11.

left the army.[124] If further recourse was necessary than to the viceroy himself, who with the advice of a fiscal sat as a court of appeal in final judgment of military trials, it went directly to the junta de guerra of the Council of the Indies.[125] In matters of military justice in first instance the viceroy was relieved by the captains of the army, the castellán of a fortress, the maestre de campo, admirals of the navy, and the judges of military tribunals.[126] Generals of the armadas were not permitted to take charge of lawsuits of soldiers in the ports, nor could a captain in the army have anything to do with marine cases.[127]

For the decision of military cases the viceroy appointed an oidor of the audiencia with the title of auditor de guerra to serve as an assessor, but he was free to reject the opinions of this assistant. Viceroy Croix of Mexico seldom sent the auditor de guerra a case, since he depended upon his own assessor whom he brought with him from Spain.[128] At any time when it seemed best to him the viceroy might summon other lawyers to help him determine cases.[129]

Teodoro de Croix has described the working of a military trial in Lima. The crime instanced was committed in 1781, in the town of Belille of the province of Chumbibilca when various companies were assembled to check the raids of the rebellious

[124] Montesclaros to his successor, 1615, *Documentos inéditos* . . . . *de Indias,* VI, 268; Revillagigedo to Amarillas, 1754, *Instrucciones que los vireyes* . . . . art. 123, p. 27; Croix, *Instrucción que* . . . . *dejó,* AGI, 88–5–13; *Recopilación,* leyes 1–2, tit. 11, lib. 3.

[125] Solórzano, II, lib. 5, cap. 13, art. 41, p. 383; Revillagigedo to Amarillas, 1754, *Instrucciones que los vireyes* . . . . art. 124, p. 27; Court to Amarillas, 1755, *ibid.,* art. 40, p. 72.

[126] *Recopilación,* leyes 6–7, 9, tit. 11, lib. 3; ley 15, tit. 10, lib. 5; ley 77, tit. 15, lib. 9; Lerdo de Tejada, Miguel, *Apuntes históricos de la héroica ciudad de Vera Cruz* . . . . (Mexico, 1850–51), pt. v, p. 391.

[127] *Recopilación,* ley 60, tit. 15, lib. 9.

[128] Montesclaros to his successor, 1615, *Documentos inéditos* . . . . *de Indias,* VI, 368; Revillagigedo to Amarillas, 1754, *Instrucciones que los vireyes* . . . . art. 124, p. 27; Croix, *Instrucción que* . . . . *dejó,* AGI, 88–5–13.

[129] Revillagigedo to Amarillas, *Instrucciones que los vireyes* . . . . art, 124, p. 27; Court to Amarillas, 1755, *ibid.,* art. 40, p. 72.

Indians stirred up by the patriot, Cacique Condorcanqui, better known as Tupac Amarú. A certain captain, Lasco de la Vega, had imprisoned a sergeant of his company by order of the commander. The officer's father forcibly removed him from prison. Then the comandante, Pedro Nieto, and all his forces hastened to the scene of disturbance, but the soldiers were ordered to withdraw except Captain Vega. They did not obey, and the captain himself rashly gave an order to fire, snatching a gun from a soldier of his company. Vega was taken to Lima to be tried by the council of war. The viceroy appointed Joaquín de Yubillaga, fiscal, to help try the case. This fiscal decided that the death penalty ought to be given, but the oidores who were called upon for assistance disagreed with him. They alleged that, since Vega was not a regular captain, but had only assumed the title in order to raise troops, he should not come under the regular military ordinances. The sentence imposed was banishment for ten years to the presidio of Juan Fernández, and it was not to be ended without an order from the viceroy. Croix signed the sentence with the other judges and a royal decree of August 21, 1786, commanded it to be put into effect.[130]

6. QUARRELS BETWEEN THE VICEROY AND THE AUDIENCIA

Many quarrels occurred between the viceroy and the audiencia. The sad fate of Blasco Núñez Vela has already been related. The audiencia of Mexico opposed the policy of the elder Velasco limiting the jurisdictional powers of encomenderos and causing them to pay taxes for the use of the Indians, and because he did not consult the audiencia as frequently as its members desired. Some of the most influential residents and ecclesiastics of the capital, however, upheld the viceroy by declaring that he always consulted the audiencia in important matters.[131]

---

[130] Croix to Lemos, 1790, *Memorias de los vireyes* . . . . V, 206–209.

There was another dissension between Peralta and the audiencia of Mexico. When they could not convince this viceroy that the country was threatened by the conspiracy of Martín Cortés, the oidores began to undermine his influence at the royal court. The viceroy refused to grant their demand for the sequestration of the estates of the Marqués del Valle, and modified the death sentence of Luis Cortés to banishment to North Africa for ten years. Hence the audiencia accused Peralta of neglect of his duties and of favoring the plot of Cortés. It intercepted the viceroy's report to the king and finally was the cause of his deposition.[132]

The most notable instance of a quarrel between the viceroy and a subordinate audiencia was that of Villamanrique and the audiencia of Guadalajara. A law of the Indies of 1575, reaffirmed by another in 1619, forbade oidores or their children to marry within the districts under their jurisdiction.[133] One of the oidores married a daughter of Juan de Lomas, a rich inhabitant of Guadalajara. Viceroy Villamanrique heard of it and tried to deprive the judge of his office, ordering that his salary should not be paid. The audiencia denied that the executive had power to do this. Villamanrique decided to compel the haughty court to obey him at any cost and sent fifty soldiers to reduce it to submission. Only through the intervention of the bishop and the clergy was armed resistance avoided. This incident caused the viceroy the loss of his office, since the suspicious Philip II thought that the country was on the verge of a civil war. There were also some differences between the viceroy of New Spain and the audiencia of Manila over matters of a commercial nature. The chief bone of contention concerned the jurisdiction of the galleons which sailed between Manila and Acapulco.[134]

---

[131] Cavo, lib. 4, arts. 18–19, pp. 114–115; *Cartas de Indias* (Madrid, 1877), 121–122.

[132] Cavo, lib. 4, art. 28, p. 123; Zamacois, V, 117–122.

[133] Riva Palacio, II, 614; *Recopilación*, ley 82, tit. 16, lib. 2.

[134] Cavó, lib. 5, art. 19, p. 145; Riva Palacio, II, 439–440; Villamanrique to Philip II, Jan. 17, 1589, AGI, 58-3-11; Cunningham, 67–68.

Likewise, the Marquis of Gelves had trouble with certain oidores who had been accustomed to act with a great deal of freedom during the administration of the preceding viceroy. The senior oidor, Pedro Gaviria refused to play the subordinate after his taste of power. Gelves appointed him assessor, but he was in the habit of giving commands without consulting the viceroy. Finally the patience of the marquis became exhausted and he ordered Gaviria to be confined to his house.[135]

The viceroy of Peru had difficulties with the audiencia of Panamá over appointments. The audiencia refused to accept the official selected as governor by Viceroy Chinchón; therefore in 1639 he gave account of its disobedience to the king. Again in 1641, with the advice of his acuerdo, Mancera appointed Fernando Agüero to govern the province. The audiencia opposed him also, saying that the right of appointment belonged to it. The Council of the Indies was notified and a royal cédula was dispatched on May 10, 1643, ordering that the same method of filling vacancies should be observed in Panamá as was used in Chile. Three persons were to be appointed and should succeed according to their rank, in case the first one who became governor died. The audiencia still refused to obey, thereby causing a new decree to be sent to it on May 4, 1645. At the end of Mancera's rule in 1648 the judges had not been brought into subjection, and the arduous task was passed on to his successor.[136] The insubordination of the audiencia of La Plata to the will of the viceroy of Peru, in supporting José de Antequera, the rival claimant to the governorship of that province, has already been noticed in another connection.[137]

The audiencia of Mexico would not receive Viceroy Figueroa, since he had lost his papers during his escape from an English

[135] Bancroft, *History of Mexico*, III, 40–41.
[136] Mancera to his successor, 1648, *in* Polo, *Memorias de los vireyes* . . . . arts. 58–62, pp. 20–21.
[137] Castel-Fuerte to Villagarcía, 1736, *Memorias de los vireyes* . . . . III, 249–321.

warship on the way to Vera Cruz. The archbishop, Vizarrón, had to show the oidores the dispatches sent to him concerning Figueroa's appointment before they would permit him to take charge of the government. The first Revillagigedo found the oidores agreeable enough as private individuals, but when they convened in audiencia they always conspired to diminish the powers of the viceroy and extend their own Marquina thought that disagreement between the viceroy and the audiencia prejudiced the public against him. Therefore he yielded in minor matters to the audiencia in order to prevent scandalous misunderstandings.[138]

7. ECCLESIASTICAL AND PRIVATE JURISDICTION

The viceroy was not to interfere with the ecclesiastical courts, and the audiencias were ordered to uphold the ecclesiastical judges and not intermeddle in their affairs. If a town was put under an interdict, however the audiencia could proceed according to its right and the laws of Castile. Lawsuits relating to the military orders of Santiago, Calatrava, and Alcántara came under the jurisdiction of the audiencia, and cases against Indians were not to be encouraged in ecclesiastical courts. Nor might the president and audiencia take cognizance of matters belonging to the tribunal of the Inquisition. Appeal from it lay only before that of the Inquisition in Spain.[139]

When matters of the church were brought before the audiencia it merely decided whether the ecclesiastical judges had power to try them. Ecclesiastical cases might be appealed to the audiencia. Sometimes they were sent back to the bishops and their judges, who returned to the audiencia the papers concerning the proceedings after the cases had been tried a second

138 Riva Palacio, II, 787–788; Revillagigedo to Amarillas, 1754, *Instrucciones que los vireyes* . . . . art. 63, p. 18; Marquina to Iturrigaray, 1803, *ibid.*, art. 48, p. 166.

139 *Leyes de Indias*, MS, ley 71, tit. 2; *Recopilación*, leyes 150, 148, 96, 138, 153, tit. 15, lib. 2; ley 4, tit. 19, lib. 1.

time.[140]   Certain kinds of appeals were not to be admitted in the audiencia. The audiencia was not to condemn archbishops, bishops, or ecclesiastical judges under their jurisdiction to pecuniary fines to be collected from the rents of the church. In case of unusual disobedience, after a fourth letter had been sent to the prelate and if he refused to heed it, then a measure for seizing the temporalities might be passed as an example for others.[141]

In each bishopric there was a church court, where essentially the same form of procedure prevailed as in the secular tribunals. Civil cases which arose between priests, or when laymen brought action against them, were tried in these courts. According to Escriche the archbishops and bishops exercised jurisdiction in first instance in the dioceses through their provisores or vicarios, who corresponded to ordinary secular justices. The metropolitan handled cases of second instance in appeals from the suffragans and the papal delegate took cognizance of third instances. The cases that came before ecclesiastical courts concerned benefices, patronage, tithes, marriage, legitimation, funerals, and donations. There were some cases like polygamy which belonged to the fuero mixto. Under this privilege they could be tried either by an ecclesiastical or lay judge.[142]

The viceroy had a right to decide questions concerning competency of jurisdiction between the church and civil courts, just as he did those among the various civil tribunals.[143]   A notable case of this kind occurred in the town of Chancay in the viceroyalty of Peru. Javier de Vargas, a priest, exceeded his powers by making himself judge of cases pertaining to the civil authorities and by controlling the public prison of that town in order to

[140] *Recopilación*, leyes 135–136, 142, tit. 15, lib. 2.

[141] *Ibid.*, ley 143, tit. 15, lib. 2.

[142] Esriche, Joaquín, *Diccionario razonado de legislación y jurisprudencia* (ed. 3, Madrid, 1847–51), II, 453; *ibid.*, I, 832–833.

[143] Palafox to his successor, 1642, *Documentos inéditos . . . . de Mexico*, VII, 86; Mancera to Veraguas, 1673, *Instrucciones que los vireyes . . . .* 270–271; Croix, *Instrucción que . . . . dejó*, AGI, 88–5–13; Revillagigedo, *Instrucción reservada*, art. 97.

put his debtors in it. When the deputy of the corregidor took possession of the keys, Vargas shamefully denounced him on the street. Finally, Viceroy Superunda was ordered by the king to take action against the ecclesiastic and not permit any priest to arrest people for not paying obventions.[144]

Most of the differences with ecclesiastical judges arose over questions of immunity. The right of sanctuary had been permitted since the church was first established. By a bull of Clement XIV it was limited to a few churches, the number depending upon the population of the community, crimes of heinous character being excluded. The government and civil courts bent their energies upon abolishing the rights of immunity, since many persons abused them. Sanctuary did not extend to soldiers and sailors who came to the Indies and had remained without license. They could be taken from the sacred places by the civil authorities and handed over to their commanders.[145]

While serving in Peru, Mancera said that the public demanded the punishment of criminals and delinquents according to the royal jurisdiction; but ecclesiastics persisted in their right and the audiencia did the same with respect to theirs, thereby causing restlessness and disturbances among the people. In 1646 the viceroy was annoyed considerably by a contest over immunity which lasted for three days, although the ordinary justices, the sala del crimen and the acuerdo had decided that the matter did not belong to ecclesiastical judges.[146]

Another case of immunity occurred in Peru during the administration of Viceroy Castellar. Juan de Villegas, a treasury official, committed the crime of forging the viceroy's rubric. He was condemned to the galleys, but escaped and hid in certain chapels. The civil authorities demanded that he be surrendered, and this time it was done without resistance. Villegas was then

---

[144] *Memorias de los vireyes* . . . . III, 22–25.

[145] Escriche, I, 353; *Recopilación*, ley 3, tit. 5, lib. 1.

[146] Mancera to his successor, 1648, *in* Polo, *Memorias de los vireyes* . . . . art. 5, pp. 2–3.

hung by order of the criminal judges and the king thanked the viceroy in a cédula of May 14, 1676. In Mexico City a religious was imprisoned with the approval of the audiencia, but the archbishop claimed the right of immunity and excommunicated one of the secretaries of that body for intervening in the matter. Viceroy Cruíllas came to the rescue of the official and had the sentence removed by the prelate.[147]

Viceroy Amat also decided a dispute over local immunity in Lima. The question arose whether ecclesiastical or civil judges had the right to send criminals to the presidios. The viceroy decided the matter in favor of the civil authorities and the religious yielded without any trouble. A royal cédula of April 5, 1764, commanded that the royal judges were to take cognizance of all grave crimes and even remove offenders from the churches.[148]

Private jurisdiction over his estates was granted to Hernando Cortés shortly after the conquest. He exercised this power through alcaldes mayores or corregidores of his own appointment for the towns in his possessions. These alcaldes took cognizance of all cases in first instance, and appeals in second instance went to the private judge of state, who was an oidor, and finally to the audiencia. The heirs of the Marqués del Valle still possessed this privilege at the end of the eighteenth century. The estate of the valley of Oaxaca had its judge conservator, but he was removed by royal order. In 1770, however, the marquis obtained the right to reappoint this official. At about the same time a controversy arose concerning whether the cognizance of Indian cases on the estate of the Marqués del Valle belonged to the jurisdiction of the conservator or to the juzgado de Indios. The matter was still pending when the administration of Croix came to an end, and the retiring viceroy told Bucareli that it

---

[147] Castellar to Liñan, 1681, *Memorias de los vireyes* . . . . I, 171–172; Rivera Cambas, I, 395.

[148] Amat to his successor, 1773, *Memorias de los vireyes* . . . . IV, 344; Lemos to Vallenari, 1796, *ibid.*, VI, 51–52.

would be best to have the question settled by a consultative vote of the acuerdo.   The second Revillagigedo advised that other favors be given to the descendants of Cortés in exchange for their judicial privileges.[149]

8. JUDICIAL TRIBUNALS

A court for Indian cases, known as the juzgado de Indios, was established after the audiencia became occupied with more important business.   The lawsuits were conducted by officials called protectors of the Indians, but the viceroy was the chief of this tribunal and took cognizance of all cases in first instance through an assessor, who signed all measures and referred them to the viceroy for his signature.   In actual practice he made all the decisions, and submitted them to the viceroy for his approval. The salaries of protectors were paid from a tax of half a real added to the tribute.[150]

Another famous tribunal was that of La Acordada which was an outgrowth of the Santa Hermandad, an organization established in New Spain under the elder Velasco in 1552, for the apprehension and summary punishment of bandits.   La Acordada was created in 1710 by royal decree, Miguel Velásquez being its first judge.   The special duty of this court was to guard the roads.   A cédula of November 26, 1747, likewise added to it the task of regulating prohibited drinks.   The tribunal employed nearly two thousand five hundred men and had jurisdiction over practically the whole viceroyalty.   It scoured the country for brigands and after a hurried trial the culprit would soon be hanging from the nearest tree.   A cédula of December 21, 1765, ordered that the judge and two assessors should hear the defender

---

149 Revillagigedo, *Instrucción reservada*, arts. 107, 120; Croix, *Instrucción que* . . . . *dejó*, AGI, 88–5–13.

150 *Ibid.*, AGI, 88–5–13; Azanza, *Instrucción sobre las provincias de la Nueva España* . . . . April 29, 1800, MS, num. 17, pp. 11–13; Marquina to Iturrigaray, 1803, *Instrucciones que los vireyes* . . . . art. 51, p. 167; Court to Amarillas, 1755, *ibid.*, art. 10, pp. 62–63.

appointed for the criminals and they all were to sign the sentences, there being no appeal from their decision.[151]

This tribunal was subject to the viceroy, but he merely advised with it concerning decisions, in order that he might confirm or amend them. When there were complaints or appeals he also heard these, and if controversies occurred with the ordinary justices or other tribunals, the viceroy decided them. Marfil thought that the viceroy ought always to support La Acordada, since it was the principal means of preserving peace in the viceroyalty and of checking malefactors. Villarroel also believed that the court should be upheld in its daily disputes with the other magistrates, who were jealous of its prerogatives.[152] Under the second Revillagigedo all the sentences had to be submitted for his approval. He might even revoke those of capital punishment, imposing lighter penalties with the advice of a junta. The result was that cases in the criminal chamber of the audiencia increased, although in the preceding ten years La Acordada had dispatched four times as many lawsuits as the criminal sala.[153]

Azanza had some difficulty with the judge of La Acordada, who claimed that he could try cases with only one assessor present, but the viceroy compelled him to comply with the royal cédula. The junta, consisting of the judge and two assessors, could not handle the number of cases awaiting it rapidly enough; therefore Azanza decided to add two more counsellors.[154] At the beginning of the nineteenth century La Acordada lost most of its terror for culprits. In 1803 Marquina said that it was very necessary for the viceroy to be watchful lest cases be postponed by the

---

[151] González Obregón, *México viejo*, 455; Revillagigedo, *Instrucción reservada*, arts. 108; Alamán, *Historia de Méjico*, I, 55; Priestley, *The Mexican Nation*, 183.

[152] Croix, *Instrucción que* . . . . *dejó*, AGI, 88–5–13; Marfil to Cagigal, 1760, *Instrucciones que los vireyes* . . . . 110; Villarroel, *Enfermedades políticas* . . . . MS, I, pt. II, p. 105.

[153] Revillagigedo, *Instrucción reservada*, arts. 109–110.

[154] Azanza, *Instrucción sobre las provincias de la Nueva España* . . . . April 29, 1800, MS, num. 17, pp. 30–31, 20–30.

tribunal and criminals remain long in prison, an unheard of situation in the early history of the court.[155]

In Lima the tribunal of policía created in 1786 was a kind of substitute for the celebrated La Acordada of New Spain. The viceroy was superintendent of this court, the expenses of which were met by a tax of one real on each fanega of wheat brought from Chile. In 1806 its officers consisted of a deputy, two subalterns, four inferior judges, a maestro de obras, and one actuario or clerk.[156]

Perhaps the tribunal of accounts was the most important special court, as it exercised administrative and judicial functions in connection with the royal treasury. The tribunal of Mexico, founded in 1605, took cognizance of all cases in first instance concerning the treasury, first appeal lying before three oidores selected by the viceroy. At first the court was composed of six officials, but as its business increased more were added.[157] The viceroy, an oidor and a contador decided disputes of jurisdiction between the audiencia and this tribunal.[158] The viceroy was its president and could attend meetings in order to advise what seemed best. He could not provide any measure for the tribunal, however, without first consulting the contadores. He used his influence to help collect the debts of the treasury, and had power to make *ad interim* appointments. Croix was permitted to appoint the five accountants of the province (ordenadores de provincia), also the two bookkeepers of the tribunal in Mexico City.[159] Villarroel spoke of this court as the "third chamber of the audiencia."

155 González Obregón, *México viejo*, 457; Marquina to Iturrigaray, 1803, *Instrucciones que los vireyes* . . . . art. 56, p. 168. La Acordada was abolished in 1812.

156 Lemos to Vallenari, 1796, *Memorias de los vireyes* . . . . VI, 83; Avilés to Abascal, 1806, *Memoria del virey del Peru*, 29.

157 *Recopilación*, ley 36, tit. 1, lib. 8. *See* Priestley, *José de Gálvez*, 68, for these later officials.

158 *Recopilación*, ley 78, tit. 15, lib. 2; leyes 3, 42, tit. 1, lib. 8.

159 Marquina to Iturrigaray, 1803, *Instrucciones que los vireyes* . . . . art. 305, p. 203; *Recopilación*, leyes 44, 91, 76, tit. 1, lib. 8; ley 5, tit. 2, lib. 8; Croix, *Instrucción que* . . . . *dejó*, AGI, 88–5–13.

Lima likewise had a tribunal of accounts. It was founded in 1607 and exercised jurisdiction from Panamá to Quito and to the borders of Brazil. The viceroy was also president of this tribunal. Viceroy Esquilache said that he consulted the tribunal in serious financial matters, and every three years he appointed one of the contadores to audit the accounts of the treasury of Potosí. The third tribunal of accounts was in the city of Santa Fé in Nueva Granada.[160]

There was a tribunal of treasury officials in Mexico before the establishment of the tribunal of accounts. It held weekly sessions in the presence of the audiencia, and was composed of five members: a factor, an auditor, a treasurer, a contador of tributes, and one for alcabalas. It seems that this court still existed in the time of Croix and was composed of three treasury officials, the senior member serving as accountant, the second as secretary, and the third as treasurer. The three members appointed their own subordinates and the viceroy confirmed them.[161]

There were also tribunals of the consulado in Mexico and South America which took cognizance of lawsuits concerning merchants. The prior and two consuls who constituted the court were judges in first instance, and appeals went to an oidor of the audiencia if the sum involved exceeded one thousand pesos.[162] When differences arose between this tribunal and the other magistrates over matters of jurisdiction, the viceroy determined them with the assistance of the fiscal and his assessor. There was no further appeal.[163] The judges of the tribunal might appoint one or more persons from the organization of commerce or some

---

160 Lemos to Vallenari, 1796, *Memorias de los vireyes* . . . . VI, 297–298; Esquilache to Guadalcázar, 1621, *ibid.*, I, 144–145; *Recopilación*, ley 2, tit. 11, lib. 2.

161 Villa-Señor y Sánchez, *Teatro Americano* . . . . (Mexico, 1746–48), I, 39; Croix, *Instrucción que* . . . . *dejó*, AGI, 88–5–13.

162 *Recopilación*, leyes 28, 37, tit. 46, lib. 8. The second Revillagigedo spoke of two other accompanying judges who assisted this oidor. *Instrucción reservada*, art. 111.

163 Lerdo de Tejada, pt. v, pp. 328–329; *Recopilación*, leyes 39–40, tit. 46, lib. 8; Croix, *Instrucción que* . . . . *dejó*, AGI, 88–5–13.

lawyer to relieve them when they were rushed with business. They had an asssesor who went to the audiencia whenever it summoned him and gave his opinion orally or by writing. The lawsuits were decided secretly, and the prior and consuls were respected as judges of the king.[164]

The tribunal of the mesta or grazers' court, dating from the rule of Mendoza, took cognizance in first instance of cases relating to cattle-raisers. Its alcaldes were elected annually by the cabildo of the city. All persons who owned three hundred head of cattle might become members of the organization, and two meetings were held every year. The council of the mesta could make ordinances for the association, but they had to be approved by the viceroy before being put into effect.[165]

There was a probate court (de bienes de difuntos) which attended to matters concerning estates of deceased persons. The judges of the audiencia, appointed by the viceroy every two years, took turns in administering it.[166] The viceroy was ordered to protect the jurisdiction of this court and not permit cases belonging to it to be admitted into any other tribunal. If the judge exceeded his rights he was to be removed by the viceroy. The judge of the probate court kept account of all funds paid out of its treasury and sent a report to the audiencia every year concerning the amount due from the estates. Individuals inheriting the property of deceased persons had to appear personally before the court to prove their claims. When no heirs could be found, the proceeds with all papers were sent to the Casa de Contratación of Seville.[167]

A tribunal of mining similar to that of the consulado was founded in New Spain in 1777. It was composed of deputies from the different mining districts, who took cognizance of cases in

---

[164] *Recopilación*, leyes 41, 47–48, tit. 46, lib. 8.

[165] Rivera Cambas, I, 31; *Recopilación*, leyes 2, 6, 3, 7, tit. 5, lib. 5.

[166] Croix, *Instrucción que* . . . . *dejó*, AGI, 88–5–13; *Documentos inéditos . . . . de Indias*, XIX, 83; Court to Amarillas, 1755, *Instrucciones que los vireyes* . . . . art. 31, p. 69; *Recopilación*, ley 1, tit. 32, lib. 2.

[167] *Ibid.*, leyes 3, 5, 10, 20, 34, 38, 45, 48, tit. 32, lib. 2.

first instance according to the mining ordinances. In second instance the cases were decided by the intendant of the province assisted by two miners. In case of disputed authority the viceroy decided the matter as he did concerning the other tribunals. A college of mining was formed in connection with the tribunal, but the greatest contribution was the celebrated ordenanzas de minería of 1779, which became the first complete code of colonial mining laws.[168] A tribunal of mining similar to that of Mexico was established in Peru in 1786. Later it also had its bank and college of metallurgy.[169]

There were a great many minor tribunals. Among them may be classed the protomedicato, which had jurisdiction of all cases concerning the medical profession. Appeals from its decision went to the government.[170] There was a tribunal of tributes controlled by a general accountant appointed by the king. The viceroy made ad interim appointments and confirmed the subordinate officials chosen by the manager. By a cédula of January 26, 1731, the king ordered the viceroy to establish a junta or tribunal of the mint for the suppression of counterfeiting. The members of this court were to be thoroughly instructed in the methods of coining money, of the silversmiths, and workers in gold.[171]

A tribunal of quicksilver was created in Mexico by Viceroy Guadalcázar. At first it had judges appointed by the king, but later the viceroy chose them.[172] There was a tribunal of alcabalas in Mexico City, the officials of which were appointed by the vice-

---

168 Lerdo de Tejada, pt. v, p. 390; Cavo, art. 28, p. 321; Revillagigedo, *Instrucción reservada*, arts. 112–113, 479; Alamán, *Historia de Méjico*, I, 60–63. The tribunal consisted of an administrator-general who acted as president, a director-general, and two or three general deputies elected by the miners. Ordinance 7.

169 Croix to Lemos, 1790, *Memorias de los vireyes* . . . . V, 362–365. This tribunal was composed of a judge of appeals, an administrator, a director, a secretary and a bureau of accounts.

170 Revillagigedo, *Instrucción reservada*, art. 114; Villa-Señor, 1, 57–58.

171 Croix, *Instrucción que* . . . . *dejó*, AGI, 88–5–13; Fonseca and Urrutia, I, 131–132.

172 Revillagigedo to Amarillas, 1754, *Instrucciones que los vireyes* . . . . art. 96, p. 23; Rivera Cambas, I, 104.

roy, who gave account of his action to the king.[173]   A tribunal of
medias anatas and lanzas was formed in Lima, appeals only
being permitted to the Council of the Indies.   A cédula of
April 27, 1747, however, annulled this provision.   There was a
similar tribunal in Mexico.   In the port of Vera Cruz there was
a tribunal of registers (matricula) which had separate jurisdiction with respect to matters of marine.   It was presided over by
the governor of the fortress.[174]

Another tribunal took cognizance of all cases arising from the
sale of prohibited drinks.   During the administration of Azanza,
this court was united with La Acordada.[175]   Mexico City had a
tribunal, called the fiel ejecutoría, composed of three judges who
were the corregidor and two councilmen elected in turn.   Its
duties were to provide for the food supply and regulate prices,
especially the price of bread.   It also determined the weight of
each loaf and informed itself every four months concerning the
value of wheat in order to fix the rates justly.[176]

Other tribunals in New Spain mentioned by the first Revillagigedo were those of stamped paper, lands and waters, and the
tribunal of the estate of the valley.   In all of these courts, except
the latter, cases arose of which the viceroy took cognizance,
because the matters in question were so closely connected with
the treasury.   When the judges of the tribunal of the estate of the
valley passed the death sentence, there might be appeal to the
viceroy, and if some irreparable injury to the vassals was feared
he could see that justice was secured.[177]

---

[173] The officials of this court were: a superintendent, one general accountant, a minor accountant, a treasurer, two inspectors, two chief clerks with
other inferior clerks, an alcalde, a doorkeeper, a chief sentry, a deputy of
the night patrols and a guard of entrance and posts. *Croix, Instrucción que
. . . . dejó*, AGI, 88–5–13.

[174] Superunda to his successor, 1761, *Memorias de los vireyes . . . .* IV,
81; Revillagigedo to Amarillas, 1754, *Instrucciones que los vireyes . . . .*
art. 96, p. 23; Lerdo de Tejada, pt. v, p. 391; Revillagigedo, *Instrucción
reservada*, art. 116.

[175] Azanza, *Instrucción sobre las provincias de la Nueva España . . . .*
April 29, 1800, MS, num. 17, p. 32.

[176] Croix, *Instrucción que . . . . dejó*, AGI, 88–5–13.

[177] Revillagigedo to Amarillas, 1754, *Instrucciones que los vireyes . . . .*
art. 96, p. 23; Letter to Amarillas, 1755, *ibid.*, 40.

The viceroy as president of the audiencia was not a mere presiding officer. Although legislation in its modern aspect did not exist in the viceroyalties, the executive enforced all the laws passed by the Council of the Indies for the colonies, his own proclamations and ordinances, and the decisions of the audiencia. The powers of the audiencias in the dependencies were greater than those exercised by these courts in Spain, and in case of the death or absence of the viceroy they were increased much more, for the audiencia often governed during an interregnum. The chief task of the audiencia was to decide all judicial matters, but cognizance in first instance was left to the ordinary courts, since the audiencia was primarily a court of appeals. However, sometimes the people brought their cases directly to the viceroy as the highest authority in the country. The visitation of the provinces, which was more of an administrative function, was one of the principal duties of the audiencia.

The viceroy served as a check upon the audiencia by seeing that all the laws of the Indies which restrained its authority were observed. He might send information to the king at any time concerning the conduct of the judges and advise their recall. In serious cases he even had power to suspend an oidor from office. As president the viceroy represented the king as the fountain of justice. One of his difficult tasks was the promotion of harmony among the judges. The president was to attend all residencias so that he might know whether the officials had performed their duties faithfully. He provided for the changing of boundaries of an audiencia; he saw that the judges were treated well and received justice; he maintained correspondence with the other audiencias of the viceroyalty; and he tried to prevent delays in judicial proceedings. One of his greatest powers was the right to decide what affairs belonged strictly to civil administration and what matters might be considered within the province of the audiencia. It was in this capacity that the viceroys now and then intruded into judicial proceedings. Numerous other duties belonged to the viceroy as president, such as determining days for sessions, designating judges for special cases, dividing the audiencia into salas, seeing that crimes were punished justly, hearing complaints, overseeing prisons, and, when the audiencia of Manila was abolished in 1589, taking the residencias of all officials who served in the Philippines.

Real judicial power was exercised by the viceroy in his cognizance of Indian and military cases in first and second instances. He was assisted in these matters by his assessor, who always had legal training, and by the auditor de guerra. A number of violent conflicts occurred between viceroys and audiencias, most of them concerning their respective powers. The viceroy decided questions of competency of jurisdiction between ecclesiastical and civil tribunals, and exercised general supervision over all the courts.

CHAPTER V

THE VICE-PATRON: RELIGIOUS ORGANIZATIONS

The patronato real or royal patronage was an important department of viceregal administration which became the chief agency for the propagation of the faith and the dissemination of civilization in the New World. The vice-patron had manifold duties arising from his relations with the ecclesiastical organizations, namely, the secular clergy, the various religious orders, the church councils, the Inquisition, and the tribunal of the cruzada. The vice-patron's control over education, hospitals, and institutions of charity made this phase of the viceroy's administration widely influential. In cases of friction between church and state he was the representative of the interests of the latter.

The patronato real implied the power of planting, protecting and promoting the Catholic faith and the conversion of the Indians in newly discovered lands by endowing churches and missions. No individual or organization might use this right, except the person who exercised it in the name of the monarch.[1]

1. ORIGIN OF THE ECCLESIASTICAL PATRONAGE

The ecclesiastical patronage in the kingdom of Granada and in the Indies was granted as a special favor to the Catholic Kings because of their service in the wars against the Moslem infidels. The second of the three bulls of Pope Alexander VI concerning America, dated May 4, 1493, conferred upon Ferdinand and Isabella all the islands already known in the Indies and those that should be discovered in the future. The privileges of the patronage were increased on November 16, 1501, when the same pope conferred upon the Spanish sovereigns the use of the tithes in

---

[1] Revillagigedo to Amarillas, 1754, *Instrucciones que los vireyes* . . . . art. 143, p. 30; *Recopilación*, ley 1, tit. 6, lib. 1.

order to protect the faith and to convert the Indians, the king assuming the obligation of making gifts to the churches which were to be built and of sustaining the clergy. The right of appointment in the church of Granada and the Indies was given to the Spanish monarchs, July 28, 1508, by Pope Julian II and this power was reaffirmed by a bull of Clement VII on September 9, 1534, and by Benedict XIV, January 11, 1753.[2]

The authority possessed by the kings of Spain over the church in America was more extensive than that of any other nation and was jealously guarded; the right of patronage being considered the most resplendent jewel in the royal crown.[3] Many royal cédulas show the zeal of the king to protect this right. In 1574 it was ordered that any ecclesiastic who tried to reduce or modify the patronage should be punished severely and cast out of the Indies.[4]

It soon became difficult for the king to perform all the duties pertaining to the patronage, especially in the making of appointments, as he did shortly after the conquest, because of the great distance between Spain and her colonies. Therefore a cédula of 1574, intrusted this power to the viceroy or president of the audiencia.[5] When presidents of audiencias were permitted to exercise these privileges, however, it was always understood that they were subordinate to the viceroy. After the intendancies were established, the intendants were granted a few of the rights of patronage so that the viceroy might be relieved somewhat of these duties in the provinces.[6]

---

[2] Ribadeneyra, Antonio Joachin, *Manual compendio de el regio patronato-indiano* (Madrid, 1755), 387, 106, 325, 405; Becker, 67.

[3] Mancera to Veraguas, 1673, *Instrucciones que los vireyes* . . . . 285; Croix, *Instrucción que* . . . . *dejó*, AGI, 88–5–13; Palata to Monclova, 1689, *Memorias de los vireyes* . . . . II, 4; Solórzano, II, lib. 4, cap. 2, art. 20, p. 11.

[4] Montesclaros to his successor, 1615, *Documentos inéditos* . . . . *de Indias*, VI, 200; *Memorias de los vireyes* . . . . I, 12; Solórzano, II, lib. 4, cap. 2, art. 21, p. 11.

[5] Amat to his successor, 1733, *Memorias de los vireyes* . . . . IV, 358; Solórzano, II, lib. 4, cap. 3, art. 19, p. 16; *Recopilación*, ley 47, tit. 6, lib. 1.

[6] Superunda to his successor, 1761, *Memorias de los vireyes* . . . . IV, 25–26; *Ordenanza* . . . . *de intendentes*, art. 8, pp. 12–13.

The viceroys always considered the prestige of the vice-patron very important. Marquina declared that the authority of the viceroy was made evident by his functions as vice-patron, which caused him to be distinguished even by the ecclesiastics, who were always objects of veneration among the populace. The ceremonies whereby he was honored gave him a certain dignity of his own, which surpassed that of the highest functionary.[7]

2. AIDING THE CLERGY

Aiding the clergy and promoting their friendship were the first and very necessary duties of the vice-patron. Therefore he had to conduct himself with great circumspection toward ecclesiastics in order to avoid causing offense. The preservation of the rights of prelates, their dignity and jurisdiction was recommended by numerous royal decrees. Palafox advised his successor to answer with kindness all letters or messages showing respect to the viceroy sent to him on church holidays or at any other time. It was not thought best to permit an inferior to do this, since misunderstanding might arise. Even when the viceroy had some complaint to make against the clergy, he was expected to do it in reasonable and discreet words.[8]

It was also the duty of the executive to help prelates in their efforts to reform inferiors and to encourage those who were distinguished in virtue and learning. When commissioner-generals came to the kingdom for the purpose of correcting abuses among the clergy, the viceroy was to give them the necessary information concerning the condition of the religious. On January 25, 1600, Viceroy Velasco of Peru was ordered by the excessively devout Philip III to give assistance to the commissioner of the cruzada in matters pertaining to the good administration of the

---

[7] Marquina to Iturrigaray, 1803, *Instrucciones que los vireyes* . . . . arts. 17–18, p. 162.

[8] Court to Amarillas, 1755, *ibid.*, art. 15, p. 64; Croix, *Instrucción que* . . . . *dejó*, AGI, 88–5–13; Palafox to his successor, 1642, *Documentos inéditos* . . . . *de Mexico*, VII, 56–57.

tribunal, which controlled the revenue from the sale of bulls of cruzada.[9] Whenever possible the viceroy was expected to attend religious services and festivities. In 1643 the king commanded the viceroy to be present at least for one day at the patrocinio of the Holy Virgin. Viceroy Liñan of Peru said that he always tried to aid prelates of the regular orders in their reforms, and attend their principal festivities. After the English left Cartagena in 1740, Viceroy Eslava of Nueva Granada hastened to attend a solemn mass in the cathedral. Amarillas of Mexico contributed to the fiesta of the patrocinio of the Virgin of Guadalupe.[10]

The vice-patron was required to provide for the wants of ecclesiastics in China and the Philippines. Enríquez said that the king had spent more on the islands of China than he got out of them, but if God would help them gain possession of that great kingdom, it could not be called a bad undertaking. In 1668 it was decided by the viceroy, with the advice of the junta general de hacienda, to aid the Jesuits in the Ladrones or Marianas Islands by sending them ten thousand pesos. At first the Council of the Indies did not approve of this measure, since it drew a considerable amount of money from the treasury without a special order. After investigating the matter, the king gave his consent in a decree of June 1, 1671, and ordered Mancèra to help the mission as liberally as possible. Also in 1669 a cédula authorized the same viceroy to assist a Franciscan mission in China. The aid sent to the clergy of the Philippines was generally included in the regular subsidies. Mancera stated that the supplies which went to those islands were not so much for temporal matters as for the propagation of religion and to keep out foreigners.[11]

9 Palafox to his successor, 1642, *Documentos inéditos . . . . de Mexico*, VII, 30, 59, 67; *Recopilación*, ley 43, tit. 14, lib. 1; *Documentos inéditos . . . . de Indias*, XIX, 102–112.

10 *Recopilación*, ley 24, tit. 1, lib. 1; Liñan to Palata, 1681, *Memorias de los vireyes . . . .* I, 271; Groot, II, 34; Rivera Cambas, I, 380. For other cases see Gómez, Diario, *Documentos para la historia de México*, serie 2, pt. VII, 241, 286, 375, 388, 409.

11 Enríquez to Coruña, 1580, *Instrucciones que los vireyes . . . .* art. 10, p. 247; Mancera to Veraguas, 1673, *ibid.*, 287, 267.

3. BUILDING OF CHURCHES AND CONVENTS

The building and overseeing of churches and convents were important duties of the early vice-patrons. With the help of members from the religious orders of San Francisco and San Agustín, the zealous Mendoza drew up plans for monasteries in New Spain. He advised his successor to do the same thing for the Dominicans.[12] At first the consent of the viceroy, governor, or audiencia was sufficient for establishing convents, cathedrals and parochial churches, but on June 1, 1574, the king declared that no church, monastery or other sacred edifice was to be built without his special permission or that of his authorized representative.[13] The vice-patrons continued to employ this right for some years, until it was discovered that they too readily gave consent for the building of convents. Therefore a cédula of March 19, 1593, ordered that they should not give license for founding such buildings without first having the king's permission; a royal decree of June 14, 1616, to Viceroy Esquilache of Peru, and many laws of the Indies reaffirmed this. Sometimes viceroys were reprimanded severely for having disregarded these decrees.[14]

Viceroys were empowered to demolish all religious structures built without proper license. In 1608 Viceroy Montesclaros of Peru was ordered to destroy the convent of the Mercedarios, which the Count of Monterey had permitted to be established. A cédula of December 2 of the next year commanded him to report the number of convents already founded.[15] Mancera had the construction of a convent in Guanajuato suspended because the Count of Baños granted unsanctioned permission for its erection; he also gave orders that a convent in Celaya, which

12 King to Mendoza, 1535, *Documentos inéditos . . . . de Mexico*, XXIII, 426–427; Mendoza to Velasco, *Instrucciones que los vireyes . . . .* 239.

13 King to Mendoza, 1538, *Documentos inéditos . . . . de Mexico*, XV, 60–61, 187; Montesclaros to his successor, 1615, *Documentos inéditos . . . . de Indias*, VI, 194.

14 Solórzano, II, lib. 4, cap. 23, arts. 16–19, p. 196.

15 *Recopilación*, ley 1, tit. 3, lib. 1; Solórzano, II, lib. 4, cap. 23, arts. 20–21, p. 196.

Viceroy Alburquerque had allowed to be built by the society of San Juan de Dios, be torn down. The college of San Gerónimo in the city of Guatemala, organized by the order of Mercy without the king's consent, was the occasion for the royal decree of June 26, 1765, to the viceroys of Peru, New Spain, Nueva Granada, and to the presidents of audiencias, enjoining them to see that the laws concerning establishment of convents were kept, or account would be taken in their residencias.[16]

When he received the right of the patronato real, the king assumed the obligation of assisting in all expenses connected with the building of churches. According to canonical law the diezmos which the sovereign obtained were to be used for this purpose; therefore a third of the cost was paid from the royal treasury and the other two-thirds were furnished by the encomenderos and Indians. In Indian towns a fourth of the tribute could be set aside for erecting churches, and viceroys were to see that it was not wasted.[17]

Viceroys and prelates were expected to give necessary orders for finishing churches and cathedrals already begun and report to the Council of the Indies concerning the measures taken. Mancera decided to hasten the work on the cathedral of Mexico City because foreign nations ridiculed the slowness with which it was being built. As a result of his efforts the high altar and the sagrario were dedicated on August 15, 1678, a century after the temple was begun.[18]

---

16 Rivera Cambas, I, 215, 222; *Memorias de los vireyes* .... III, 5.

17 Ribadeneyra, 174–175; King to the viceroy, 1550, *Documentos inéditos* .... *de Mexico*, XV, 105; *Recopilación*, leyes 3–5, tit. 2, lib. 1. In fact the Indians really bore the entire burden for the construction of churches, since they provided the manual labor, and, by working on the encomiendas, enabled the encomenderos to pay their share. They paid tributes to the king from which the portion donated by the royal treasury was taken. Revillagigedo to Amarillas, 1754, *Instrucciones que los vireyes* .... arts. 150–151, p. 31.

18 *Leyes de Indias*, MS, ley 15, tit. 6; *Recopilación*, ley 15, tit. 2, lib. 1; King to the viceroy, 1550, *Documentos inéditos* .... *de Mexico*, XV, 104–105; Mancera to Veraguas, 1673, *Instrucciones que los vireyes* .... 288. The cathedral was started in 1573 during the rule of Viceroy Enríquez and had been formally dedicated in 1667. Most of the viceroys of the colonial

Whenever a church needed repairs its members might appeal to the viceroy. Sometimes Indians of the doctrinas, no doubt influenced by their priests, asked viceroys to remit the tribute of two or three years for the repair of churches injured by heavy rains and lightning. Mancera told his successor that he always investigated such matters by asking information of the justices of the partidos, and if the need was considered urgent a reasonable quantity of money was set aside for it. Palata thought that all the churches in his extensive viceroyalty of Peru were continually asking for repairs and ornaments. In the time of Croix, when petitions concerning the repairing of cathedral or Indian parochial churches of Mexico were proposed, they were examined by the fiscal. If the requests were agreed to conditionally, they were then submitted to the real acuerdo, which decided the amount of money that ought to be contributed from the royal treasury.[19]

Monasteries were to be located in places most convenient for the conversion and instruction of the Indians. Therefore the king ordered viceroys and prelates to confer, not only concerning the building of these edifices, but also to determine their sites. Without this precaution discords were apt to arise among the different religious orders on account of the buildings being too near to one another.[20] The royal cédula of March 4, 1561, stated that all monasteries had to be at least six leagues apart, and according to the bull of Urban VIII in 1622, the viceroy was not to permit the multiplying of small convents which did not have twelve monks.[21]

epoch had to oversee the building of some part of the cathedral, since it was not completed until 1813. The cost of the structure was about two million pesos. Rivera Cambas, I, 48–49.

[19] Revillagigedo to Amarillas, 1754, *Instrucciones que los vireyes* .... art. 151, p. 31; Mancera to Veraguas, 1673, *ibid.*, 288; Palata to Monclova, 1689, *Memorias de los vireyes* .... II, 10; Croix, *Instrucción, que* .... dejó, AGI, 88–5–13.

[20] *Documentos inéditos* .... *de Mexico*, XV, 59–61; *Documentos inéditos* .... *de Indias*, XXIII, 493, 522–523.

[21] *Recopilación*, ley 3, tit. 3, lib. 1; King to Mendoza, 1538, *Documentos inéditos* .... *de Mexico*, XV, 57; King to the viceroy, 1561, *ibid.*, 143–144; Palafox to his successor, 1642, *ibid.*, VII, 63.

Churches or convents founded by individuals with their own funds were always brought under the royal patronage. An interesting illustration is found in the convent of Jesús María of Mexico City, established January 21, 1578, by Pedro de Denia. The act of taking possession on October 2, 1588, by the vice-patron was a very solemn occasion. Villamanrique presented himself at the convent, received the patronage of the building in the name of the king, and made a brief address. Then the abbess reverently kissed the hand of the viceroy, and all the sisters did the same.[22]

4. LICENSES OF ECCLESIASTICS

All members of the clergy had to have licenses from the king to come to the New World. Under no condition could the viceroy grant them such permission, for this was one of the limitations upon his power. Their names, ages, places of birth, and the provinces or monasteries from which they came were recorded by the Council of the Indies and also by the Casa de Contratación. Expenses of transportation were paid by the royal treasury; therefore ecclesiastics were expected to go to the place or province indicated in their licenses, and viceroys had to see that they did so.[23] Sometimes religious who were sent to the Indies at great expense to the treasury did not go to the towns for which they were appointed, but remained in the larger convents. Amarillas was informed that they often asked to be sent to a mission as a pretext for coming to America to be with their friends, and the king requested him to try to prevent this abuse. The clergy sent to New Spain for the Philippines had a little more freedom than other ecclesiastics, since the viceroy might allow them to go to Japan.[24]

---

[22] González Obregón, *México viejo*, 156–160.

[23] Court to Amarillas, 1755, *Instrucciones que los vireyes* . . . . arts. 16, 18, p. 65; *Recopilación*, ley 19, tit. 14, lib. 1; *Documentos inéditos* . . . . *de Indias*, XI, 63–64.

[24] *Instrucciones que los vireyes* . . . . art. 19, p. 65–66; *Recopilación*, leyes. 27, 32, tit. 14, lib. 1.

The viceroys were to be sure that religious brought licenses with them, and if they came without, to send them back to Spain. Sometimes foreigners came to America to ask alms. During Liñan's administration in Peru two men from Spain and a priest, Juan Bautista Got, arrived from Rome for this purpose. In such cases the government was expected to see whether they had the proper authorization of the Council of the Indies. Before assuming the duties of their dioceses prelates had to show the viceroy the patent of their election and evidence of having taken the regular oaths of fealty to the crown.[25]

Over the question of showing licenses to preach and confess, an altercation occurred in 1647 between the Jesuits and Palafox. The Company claimed that Pope Gregory XIII, Gregory XIV, and Paul V had granted it full authority to preach without licenses, but Palafox prohibited the members from using their powers until they complied with the law. In 1754 there was a similar case in Peru, when Francisco Javier Soto of the order of Mercy refused to present to the audiencia the guarantee of his election. Five years later Estévan Aponte, a resident of Santiago, who had been a provincial of the Franciscans, objected to showing the patent of his election. The next morning the city was put under arms and the ecclesiastic deposed. After the case was reviewed in the real acuerdo, the provincial finally showed his papers to Viceroy Superunda.[26]

When once in the New World members of the clergy could not resign their office on a slight pretext and return to Spain. If they wished to return home they were obliged to ask permission first of the prelate of the diocese and then of the king. Viceroys were not allowed to grant license even for a parish priest to return to Spain. They might ask the king to give his consent for this, as

25 *Recopilación*, ley 8, tit. 7, lib. 1; ley 64, tit. 14, lib. 1; Liñan to Palata, 1681, *Memorias de los vireyes* . . . . I, 281.

26 Rivera Cambas, I, 144; Mancera to Veraguas, 1673, *Instrucciones que los vireyes* . . . . 285–286; Amat to his successor, 1773, *Memorias de los vireyes* . . . . IV, 406, 397–398.

the second Revillagigedo did in the case of Friar Joseph Falcón of the college of Zacatecas, who desired to go to Rome for the canonization of Antonio Margil. Testimonials concerning the character of Falcón were sent with the viceroy's recommendation.[27]

5. RELATION TO THE SECULAR CLERGY

Although the archbishop and dignitaries of the secular clergy had a great deal of power in ecclesiastical matters, they were subject to the vice-patron. Several cédulas and laws of the Indies required archbishops and bishops to swear solemnly before entering their offices not to violate at any time the rights of the royal patronage. However, secular authorities were not able to enforce those laws rigidly. As early as 1568, Francisco de Toledo had been commanded by the king to restore the patronage in Peru. This order was carried out in spite of the opposition of the archbishop and other prelates, who had usurped those powers.[28]

The vice-patron was enjoined repeatedly to encourage the study of Indian languages among the clergy. A law of March 17, 1619, required parish priests to know the dialects of the natives whom they were appointed to serve. Some later laws of 1634 and 1636 ordered that they should teach Spanish to the Indians, and the viceroy was expected to be informed whether this injunction was fulfilled.[29] Another of his duties was to see that prelates kept the rules of the establishment of their churches and did not change them.[30]

---

[27] King to the bishops of the Indies, 1563, *Documentos inéditos . . . . de Indias*, XI, 153; Court to Amarillas, 1755, *Instrucciones que los vireyes . . . .* art. 18, p. 65; *Recopilación*, ley 36, tit. 7, lib. 1; leyes 16, 18, tit. 12, lib. 2; Revillagigedo to Porlier, April 26, 1790, AGI, 89–6–13.

[28] *Recopilación*, ley 1, tit. 8, lib. 1; Solórzano, II, lib. 4, cap. 6, arts. 30–34, p. 38; Ribadeneyra, 209–213; Account concerning Toledo, *Documentos inéditos . . . . de Indias*, VIII, 237–239; Order of the king to the audiencia of Lima, *ibid.*, XIX, 102–103.

[29] *Leyes de Indias*, MS. ley 6, tit. 14; *Recopilación*, leyes 4–5, tit. 8, lib. 1; Court to Amarillas, 1755, *Instrucciones que los vireyes . . . .* art. 7, p. 60–61.

[30] *Recopilación*, ley 13, tit. 3, lib. 1; Croix, *Instrucción que . . . . dejó*, AGI, 88–5–13.

Sometimes certain individuals or encomenderos wished to act as vice-patrons and make appointments when they had built parish churches at their own expense and paid the salaries of the priests, but a cédula of November 3, 1567, and another in 1569, clearly declared that the rights of royal patronage extended to all parishes. If it was necessary to divide, unite, or suppress parishes, bishops or archbishops could not do it without consulting the viceroy.[31] Viceroy Góngora supervised the fixing of the boundaries of new bishoprics in Nueva Granada, and on December 19, 1793, the archbishop of Peru consulted Viceroy Lemos about the division of the parish of Chacallan, the dismemberment of Tapu and the erection of a third parish with the name of Yanaguanca. When the executive saw the maps, he permitted the plans to be carried out. Viceroys were held responsible for the punishment of all Spaniards who drove priests out of Indian towns or mistreated them.[32]

Ecclesiastics had to obey the summons whenever the vice-patron or audiencia wished to confer with them. In 1658 the first Alburquerque invited all the prelates of the religious orders to a conference in his palace so that he might give them special instructions. He commanded that priests should not go out on the streets alone at late hours of the night, whereupon the dignitaries obeyed the request of the viceroy by sending messages to all the priests ordering them not to go out alone, or in the company of seculars, after ten o'clock in the evening, and not to enter gambling houses.[33]

On the other hand, members of the clergy always had the protection of the chief executive, who allowed them to dispose of their estates as they saw fit and executed their wills. In 1788

---

[31] Solórzano, II, lib. 5, cap. 15, art. 12, p. 124; *Recopilación*, leyes 1, 43, 40, tit. 6, lib. 1; *Leyes de Indias*, MS, ley 68, tit. 2; Superunda to his successor, 1761, *Memorias de los vireyes* . . . . IV, 30.

[32] Groot, II, 199–201, 314–316; Lemos to Vallenari, 1796, *Memorias de los vireyes* . . . . VI, 18; *Documentos inéditos* . . . . *de Indias*, XXIII, 523–524.

[33] *Recopilación*, ley 22, tit. 11, lib. 2; Zamacois, V, 377.

the bishop of Concepción on the way to Valdivia was robbed of his baggage. As soon as Viceroy Croix was informed of the event by the comandante of the frontier, Ambrosio O'Higgins, action was taken to prevent another such crime and to restore the lost articles to the bishop. Such stringent measures were employed against the Indians that the road from Concepción to Valdivia remained quiet for some time after this.[34]

There was not a sufficiently large number of members of the secular clergy to fill all the positions in the doctrinas or Indian congregations during the early colonial period, so friars were employed. The far-seeing eye of the vice-patron extended even to the doctrinas, as the Indians were his special charge. He was ordered to prevent them from being oppressed by making offerings for masses, and not to permit the priests to have prisons or other means of torture. Doctrineros were to keep records of baptisms and burials, and send the certificates every year to the viceroys and governors.[35]

The vice-patron had power to make all appointments in the doctrinas according to the rules of the patronage, but it seems that many irregularities prevailed. Friars were installed and removed at the will of their superiors without consulting the viceroy.[36] Other abuses, like the accumulation of wealth by the doctrineros and neglect of religious instruction, were found; therefore Viceroy Palafox determined to correct them. In a short time he established thirty-six new curacies. Tithes were then imposed without any difficulty, thereby producing a strong incentive to the government for further secular occupation.[37]

---

[34] *Recopilación*, ley 6, tit. 11, lib, 2; *Documentos inéditos . . . . de Mexico*, XV, 231–232; Croix to Lemos, 1790, *Memorias de los vireyes . . . .* V, 84–85.

[35] Enríquez to Coruña, 1580, *Instrucciones que los vireyes . . . .* art. 4, p. 245; *Recopilación*, leyes 5, 6, tit. 15, lib. 1; leyes 4, 7, 6, 9, 25, tit. 13, lib. 1.

[36] *Ibid.*, leyes 1, 3, tit. 14, lib. 1; Memorial of Toledo, 1596, *Documentos inéditos . . . . de Indias*, VI, 517; Letter of Revillagigedo to Amarillas, Oct. 8, 1755, *Instrucciones que los vireyes . . . .* 42; Palafox to his successor, 1642, *Documentos inéditos . . . . de Mexico*, VII, 60–61.

[37] Rivera Cambas, I, 136.

The peace-loving Ferdinand VI decided that seculars should be appointed for all the doctrinas and parishes of the Indies, and the first act for their secularization was passed on October 4, 1749. It was the duty of the vice-patron to put the measure into effect, but this could not be done very quickly, as secular priests versed in the Indian languages could not be found[38] The elder Revillagigedo said that the friars had only been serving ad interim and it was the king's intention to secularize the parishes long before 1749, but the religious orders had become quite powerful and were aided by the judges of the audiencias, who would have prevented the change.

The order for secularization in Mexico was sent secretly to the viceroy, who instructed the governors concerning the manner in which to enforce it without disturbances. Revillagigedo and the archbishop agreed that the viceroy should order the regulars to be removed from all the parishes which they possessed in violation of the right of appointment, and that the archbishop should provide secular priests for them. The first step was taken in the doctrinas which the Augustinians had vacated; the change was then extended to all parishes where deaths of priests had occurred. In 1753 this measure was applied to all the bishoprics of the Indies. It was not difficult to accomplish the work of secularization because the Indians of many parishes were on bad terms with the friars. In order to hasten the process, Arriaga, minister of the Indies, thought it would be fitting to have the Indian languages taught in the University of Mexico and compel theological students to learn them within a definite time.[39]

During the administration of Viceroy Croix the task of secularization was still being continued. At this time the monks who were in small convents which did not have a guardian with a right to vote and eight friars, were obliged to go to live in the

---

[38] Revillagigedo to Amarillas, 1754, *Instrucciones que los vireyes* . . . . art. 147, p. 30.

[39] Revillagigedo to Amarillas, 1755, *ibid.*, 41–44; Arriaga to Amarillas, 1755, *ibid.*, art. 10, pp. 98–99.

houses that their superiors chose for them, leaving those which they departed from for the parish priests. In 1771 the same measure was being put into effect in Peru.[40] On August 9, 1834, Governor Figueroa of California issued a bando for secularization of the missions; it was to be put into effect gradually in order to maintain the good will of the missionaries and to prevent all the possible evils. In sixteen missions the friars were deprived of temporal management, but at first they were permitted to become curates. The final secularization came in 1845, when steps were taken for the sale of the missions.[41]

Archbishops had power to excommunicate viceroys, governors, and individual oidores. They also had complete authority to grant absolution. Mendoza and the members of the audiencia were excommunicated by Las Casas for having given sentence to cut off the hands of a clergyman in Oaxaca, but this penalty did not have any serious results.[42]

The most notable example of the excommunication of a viceroy was that of Gelves. In this case in many respects the dispositions of the viceroy and Archbishop Serna were alike. Both were energetic, inflexible, intolerant, and lacking in prudence. Hostility began very soon after the viceroy's arrival, the prelate joining the enemies of Gelves. The quarrel which led to the excommunication of the executive grew out of the question of the right of sanctuary. Melchor Pérez de Várez, alcalde of Metepec, was arrested for profiteering by order of the viceroy, and sought sanctuary in the convent of Santo Domingo. The secular judges, however, paid no attention to this, because the alcalde had broken

---

[40] Croix, *Instrucción que . . . . dejó*, AGI, 88–5–13. This procedure had first been applied to the Franciscan order in the kingdom of New Granada, but a royal cédula of Feb. 6, 1703, commanded that it should be kept in all the religious orders of the Indies. Castel-Fuerte to Villagarcía, 1736, *Memorias de los vireyes . . . .* III, 71–72; Croix to Lemos, 1790, *ibid.*, V, 6.

[41] For the details concerning secularization in California *see* Bancroft. *History of California* (San Francisco, 1882–87), III, 342 *et seq; ibid.*, IV, 546 *et seq.* Engelhardt, Zephyrin, *The Missions and Missionaries of California* (San Francisco, 1908–1916), III, 501 *et seq.*

[42] Ribadeneyra, 205; Cavo, lib. 3, art. 33, pp. 98–99.

jail and was not entitled to immunity. They therefore sentenced him to pay a fine of sixty thousand pesos and to perpetual banishment from the Indies, guarding the prison, lest he try to escape. The ecclesiastical judge ordered the guards to be removed within two days, but the demand was not obeyed. The archbishop then excommunicated the judges, the guards, and almost everyone connected with the case. Appeal went to the audiencia, and the sentence was suspended. Finally the viceroy was excommunicated for allowing such proceedings by that body. Although Gelves retaliated by condemning the archbishop to a fine of ten thousand ducats, confiscation of his property, and banishment, Serna refused to revoke the sentence even when commanded to do so by the papal delegate at Puebla. By sanction of the viceroy an attempt was made to take the rebellious prelate to San Juan de Ulúa, but this caused so much excitement that the oidores commanded that he be brought back to Mexico City. The executive, who had taken no part in this action of the judges, refused to permit it to be put into effect. On January 15, 1624, the archbishop issued a new decree of excommunication for the viceroy and put the capital under an interdict. A tumult resulted which became so dangerous that Gelves had to flee from the palace, and in a short time the king recalled him.[43]

6. THE VICEROY AND THE RELIGIOUS ORDERS

The religious orders always occupied a prominent place in the viceroyalties of the New World. Fifteen different societies were established in New Spain alone, and in relation to these the vice-patron had important duties.[44] Viceroys were to know the number of monks in their respective districts and send a report to the king every three years. On the basis of this information the monarch decided whether it was advisable or not to send

---

[43] Cavo, lib. 6, arts. 23–27, pp. 175–181; Riva Palacio, II, 570–582; Rivera Cambas, I, 114–118; Zamacois, V, 292–300.

[44] Rivera, *Principios críticos* . . . . I, 97–98.

visitors to reform the monasteries. Another obligation of the vice-patron was to compel ecclesiastics to live according to their monastic rules, and stay in their convents.[45] There were many religious in Peru belonging to orders that had not yet been established in the country; therefore on July 20, 1600, the king ordered Velasco to find out whether they had licenses for coming to America, to send all those without them back to Spain, and, after consulting with the prelates, to take necessary measures concerning other monks coming to the New World. Similar laws were passed in 1618, 1620, and 1646.[46] Whenever towns did not have a sufficient number of ecclesiastics, viceroys did not hesitate to ask the religious orders for friars. On September 3, 1591, Viceroy Velasco commanded the guardian of the Franciscans to send priests to the town of Los Valles, where the people had complained that there was no one to administer the sacred rites. The viceroy could stop the building of monasteries, as Mendoza did in 1541 in the town of Ocuituco, where the Augustinians were erecting a very expensive structure. The king furnished oil and wine for poor convents; accordingly it was another duty of the viceroys to be informed concerning the quantity of these articles used every year.[47]

General direction of missions was under the control of the vice-patron, who gave the necessary protection for those going out as missionaries, and provided for the payment of their salaries and expenses. He was also charged with the extension of missions to the frontiers and with being informed concerning their condition, but it was impossible for a viceroy to know all

---

[45] *Recopilación*, leyes 1–2, 42, 61, 83, tit. 14, lib. 1. An order of the king to the viceroy of Peru on May 21, 1747, required a report of this kind to be sent every year to the Council of the Indies. *Memorias de los vireyes* . . . . III, 34–35; Montesclaros to the king, 1607, *Instrucciones que los vireyes* . . . . 251.

[46] King to Velasco, *Documentos inéditos* . . . . *de Indias*, XIX, 123; *Recopilación*, ley 85, tit. 14, lib. 1.

[47] *Documentos inéditos* . . . . *de Mexico*, XV, 228–230, 83–86; Cañete to the emperor, 1556, *Documentos inéditos* . . . . *de Indias*, IV, 104; *Recopilación*, ley 7, tit. 3, lib. 1.

about them. A royal cédula of March 24, 1787, required him to
report to the king every two or three years concerning the spiritual progress of the missions, but the matter was sometimes
neglected.[48] The elder Revillagigedo thought that the Indians
would have been better disciplined under some other system and
prophesied the extinction of the missions. His celebrated son
opposed secularization because he thought that friars were able
to do more than secular priests.[49]

Croix had almost the same views when he said that "The
priests oppressed their parishioners by committing more excesses
than the monks on account of their . . . . differences of taste."
Villarroel thought that

> . . . . The religious, through their humility, poverty and weakness
> . . . . are better fitted for educating and governing the Indians than
> are secular ecclesiastics, because of the petulance, conceit and cupidity of
> the latter. The Indians look on the seculars with loathing and with
> horror, because they are accustomed to the kindly but respectful treat-
> ment of the regulars; this repugnance is enough to keep the Indians from
> making progress favorable to themselves and to society, while they are
> subordinate to the seculars.[50]

When aggrieved, the religious as well as seculars could appeal
to the viceroy. In 1541 the king informed the bishop and chapter
of the church in Mexico City that the religious could com-
municate with the viceroy if certain matters pertaining to services of the church were oppressive to them. The nuns of Puebla
appealed to Croix, denouncing the violence wherewith they were
confined to convents, and complaining that the rules of their
noviceship were entirely changed. The viceroy very tactfully
persuaded them to submit to the arrangement which their prel-

---

[48] *Recopilación*, ley 38, tit. 14, lib. 1; Revillagigedo, *Instrucción reservada*, art. 62.

[49] Revillagigedo to Amarillas, 1754, *Instrucciones que los vireyes* . . . .
arts. 152–155, pp. 31–32; Arriaga to Amarillas, 1755, *ibid.*, art. 9, pp. 97–98;
Letter of Revillagigedo to the court, Dec. 27, 1793, *Diccionario universal de
historia y de geografía* (Mexico, 1853–56), V, art. 420 *et seq.*, p. 469.

[50] Croix, *Instrucción que* . . . . *dejó*, AGI, 88–5–13; Villarroel, *Enfermedades políticas* . . . . MS, I, pt. I, p. 49.

ates had made.[51] Whenever there was any doubt concerning the rules of the establishment of their convents, ecclesiastics could appeal directly to the Council of the Indies, but if injury might result from delay, the viceroy could decide the matter temporarily. Appeal to the audiencia was permitted if the individual still felt aggrieved by the viceroy's decision.[52] During Marquina's administration in Mexico the Bethlehemites were especially troublesome with their recourses to the audiencia.[53]

The first Jesuits came to Mexico in 1572 during the government of Martín Enríquez and were given positions as secular priests in order that the Indians might receive instruction. The society soon became powerful in the New World and founded many colleges. Every year they submitted to the viceroys and audiencias lists of the religious in their convents and the priests employed in the doctrinas. As their authority increased, however, some of the communities refused to give account to secular officials.[54]

The question of the payment of tithes on their estates became a grave cause for contention. In Mexico and South America the Jesuits possessed many sugar mills, factories, warehouses, shops where cloth was sold, grocery stores, and taverns. In some parts of Peru they completely monopolized the trade in wheat, wine, brandies, tallow, sugar, glazed earthenware, glass, and other articles. The order alleged that it had pontifical privileges which exempted its members from paying tithes, although the kings of Spain had not granted this right. For many years lawsuits were carried on by the Company concerning this matter, and bishops tried to persuade the faithful not to transfer their property to the religious orders without reserving the right of the diezmos. Palafox became the champion of the bishops in

51 *Documentos inéditos* . . . . *de Indias*, XV, 81–82; Croix, *Instrucción que* . . . . *dejó*, AGI, 88–5–13.

52 Ribadeneyra, 204; *Recopilación*, leyes 34–35, tit. 15, lib. 2.

53 Marquina to Iturrigaray, 1803, *Instrucciones que los vireyes* . . . . arts. 62–63, p. 169.

54 Bancroft, *History of Mexico*, II, 708–709; Riva Palacio, II, 433–435.

their demand that the Jesuits pay tithes, thereby incurring the bitter hostility of the latter. The king decreed on June 16, 1736, that the payment of tithes should be enforced. Finding that they could not escape this order, the Jesuits decided to pay as little as possible; the settlement of the matter was delayed for over a century, almost to the eve of their expulsion.[55]

There were various reasons, which will not be discussed in this study, for the expulsion of the Jesuits from the European countries. Finally, on April 1, 1767, the command was carried out in Spain, and fifteen days before this it had started on its way to the colonies. Viceroys were granted the same powers that the king himself would have used to send the expelled Jesuits to Europe. In the sequestration of their wealth the viceroy was to exercise the greatest vigilance, and over all their missions in America and in the Philippines he was to appoint a governor ad interim. Viceroys could give all the necessary orders for putting the secular clergy into the positions vacated by the Jesuits. The greatest secrecy was observed in enforcing the royal orders and viceroys had to see that the Jesuits were well treated. Viceroy Amat of Peru was empowered to add details to these instructions so that the decree might be carried out successfully.[56]

Viceroy Croix received the order for the expulsion in New Spain on May 30, 1767, and fearing disorders among the people, was careful not to disclose it to any persons except to Visitor Gálvez and to his nephew, Teodoro de Croix. These three men arranged all the plans for putting the measure into effect. On the morning of June 25 and everywhere at the same hour, all the Jesuit establishments in the country were notified of the decree. The wealth of the society was immediately sequestrated. Troops

---

[55] Amat to his successor, 1773, *Memorias de los vireyes* . . . . IV, 411; García, *Don Juan de Palafox*, 145–149; Bancroft, *History of Mexico*, III, 134–135, 428–431.

[56] Riva Palacio, II, 834–835; Special instruction of Aranda, March 1, 1766, *ibid.*, 839–840; *Memorias de los vireyes* . . . . IV, 500–504. Sept. 3, 1759, they had been expelled from Portugal and on Feb. 22, 1764, from France.

were kept ready to put down any tumults in the larger towns, but the people were so much surprised that no disturbance occurred in Mexico City or Puebla. Most of the Jesuits conformed with the will of the king and were kindly treated. They remained at Vera Cruz until December 24, 1767, waiting for ships to take them to the port of Santa María and from there to the papal states.[57]

Revolts occurred in San Luis de la Paz, San Luis Potosí, Guanajuato, Valladolid, Pátzcuaro, and Uruapán.[58] Croix said that the rebellion in San Luis Potosí had previously been planned, and the expulsion of the Jesuits was only a pretext for the outbreak. The other disturbances were largely due to the renewal of orders against carrying arms, to the rigorous collection of tribute, and to the excises on regional beverages. On June 9, 1767, the viceroy sent Gálvez in person with five hundred men to quell these uprisings, which he did summarily and cruelly, sitting as military judge in his capacity as intendant of the army.[59]

The estates of the expelled Jesuits were very large, and on February 15, 1768, Croix found it necessary to appoint a board of directors to manage them. He declared that the profits from the estates during the four years under the new regulation exceeded those of the same number of years under Jesuit control.[60] By a decree of September 19, 1798, the temporalities of the ex-Jesuits were incorporated into the treasury, and the Pious Funds of the California missions were put under the charge of the treasury officials. The viceroy appointed a special

[57] Croix to the Marquis of Huechin, his brother, June 30, 1767, *Correspondance*, 207–208; *Varias cartas del marqués de Croix, XLV virey de la Nueva España* (Brussels, 1884), A. Núñez Ortega, ed.

[58] Among the officials sent to the provinces were members of the visitor's family. Gálvez, *Informe de el visitador,* p. 3a; Croix, *Correspondance,* 210; Riva Palacio, II, 842.

[59] Croix, *Instrucción que . . . . dejó,* AGI, 88-5-13; Priestley, *José de Gálvez,* 213–231; Gálvez, *Informe de el visitador,* 12a; Croix, *Correspondance,* 211.

[60] Riva Palacio, II, 843; Croix, *Instrucción que . . . . dejó,* AGI, 88-5-13.

administrator for this fund.[61] From the income of the property each ordained Jesuit exiled received a yearly pension of one hundred pesos, and each lay brother ninety, foreign-born members and those of bad conduct being excepted. That some of the Jesuits found their way back to the colonies before the society was reinstated in 1814, is evident from a royal order of March 25, 1801, commanding Marquina to transport to Spain all ex-Jesuits in the kingdom.[62]

In South America the Jesuits became very powerful, especially in Paraguay, where they caused the civil officials much annoyance. Shortly after Salvatierra entered into his administration in Peru he had to settle a serious struggle between the Jesuits of Paraguay and the bishop of Asunción over the patronage. The Jesuits declared that they did not have to present themselves to the bishop within thirty days for canonical instruction as specified by the order of March 27, 1647, since they were only missionaries. The quarrel almost assumed the nature of a civil war, during which the estates of the Society were confiscated. The viceroy had the religious restored to their doctrinas and finally they promised to obey the rules of the royal patronage.[63]

Again in 1750 an agitation occurred with the Jesuits when the boundary between Paraguay and Brazil was adjusted. In the treaty that was made, Colonia was given to Spain and seven Indian villages or reductions, founded by the Jesuits on the east of the Uruguay River, were ceded to Portugal. Naturally the Society opposed the treaty from the beginning, since it meant the destruction of their labors. The European enemies of the Jesuits at once imagined that they influenced the Indians to refuse to sur-

[61] Azanza, _Instrucción sobre las provincias de la Nueva España_, Sept. 19, 1800, MS, num. 17, pp. 95, 88; Flores to Revillagigedo, 1789, _Instrucciones que los vireyes_ .... art. 67, p. 126.

[62] Zamacois, V, 602; Marquina to Iturrigaray, 1803, _Instrucciones que los vireyes_ .... arts, 142–143, p. 182. The society was again expelled under a decree of the Cortés of 1820.

[63] Salvatierra to Alista, 1651, _in_ Polo, _Memorias de los vireyes_ .... 5–10.

render their villages, and accused them of building up a powerful state. The secular proprietors also were hostile to the Company, since its system seemed to be injurious to their opportunities.[64] The order for the expulsion from South America was first received by the governor of Panamá and then sent to Quito, Charcas, Chile, and Buenos Aires. The expulsion began in Buenos Aires at midnight of July 12, 1767, when the college of Saint Ignatius was entered by the soldiers of Governor Bucareli. Early in the morning of July 13 the edict was published throughout the city. During the latter half of the year the Jesuits from Paraguay and the outlying posts of Buenos Aires arrived in the city for transportation to Europe.[65]

Viceroy Amat received the order in Peru on August 20, 1767, at a little before ten o'clock in the morning. He confided concerning the measure only in his assessor, José de Salas, and his secretary, Antonio Elespuru, whom he required to take an oath to observe secrecy. Early next morning before the doors of the colleges were opened the decree was made known. The civil authorities then took charge of the archives, libraries, papers, writings of all kinds, and the keys. The guardians of the institutions were allowed to remain at least two months to answer questions about the estates, papers, and funds.[66] The expulsion in Chile took place August 26, and in Rio de la Plata on September 8, but it was not until the middle of May, 1768, that the Jesuits of the latter provinces reached the coast for transportation. The earlier date of August 1, 1767, had been set by Viceroy Cerda of New Granada for the expulsion in his viceroyalty, and the story reads like that of Mexico and Peru.[67]

64 Moses, Bernard, *Papers on the Southern Spanish Colonies of America* (Berkeley, 1911), 83 *et seq.*

65 *Memorias de los vireyes* . . . . IV, 505, 508. For more details *see* Moses, *Spain's Declining Power*, 107–122, and his *Papers on the Southern Spanish Colonies of America*, 103–126.

66 Amat to his successor, 1773, *Memorias de los vireyes* . . . . IV, 494–499, 506–507. The approximate number of Jesuits in Peru in 1752 was 31,349, Appendix 5.

67 Moses, *Spain's Declining Power*, 135, 129, 123, 143; Groot, II, 81 *et seq.*

The confiscated property in Lima amounted to almost one million pesos, large credits in gold and silver, and a body of five thousand two hundred slaves. In Chile the society had more than fifty haciendas. They were abundantly supplied with live stock and worked by many slaves.[68] A plan similar to the one employed by Viceroy Croix in Mexico was adopted for administering the estates. A special bureau was created at Lima in November, 1768, subject to a municipal junta established by a royal cédula of 1769. This board existed until June 7, 1785, when it was replaced by another body called the new administration. It attended to all business of the "temporalities." Viceroy Teodoro de Croix declared that the estates were administered well and with the greatest economy. In remote places the supervision was intrusted to the corregidores and a general director was appointed for the colleges and the collection of the "temporalities."[69]

7. CONTRIBUTIONS OF THE CHURCH TO THE STATE

The church in America was obliged to contribute liberally to the support of the government, but was still able to amass great wealth. As has been said above, the king had enjoyed the use of the tithes since 1501. Dos novenos or two-ninths, which were always deducted first from the diezmos, belonged especially to the royal patronage. Generally this amount was spent on churches, but the king had a right to use it for temporal matters if he wished. Treasury officials and not ecclesiastics had charge of leasing and collecting all the diezmos, but they could not spend any of the funds unless by command of the viceroy, president of the audiencia, or governor, and the consent of the prelate from whose diocese the money came.[70]

[68] Moses, *Spain's Declining Power*, 130–133.

[69] Avilés to Abascal, 1806, *Memoria del virey del Peru*, 87; Croix to Lemos, 1790, *Memorias de los vireyes* .... V, 347–354.

[70] *Recopilación*, leyes 24–25, 27, 31, tit. 16, lib. 1; Montesclaros to his successor, 1615, *Documentos inéditos* .... *de Indias*, VI, 256; Solórzano, II, lib. 6, cap. 7, art. 8, p. 459; *ibid.*, I, lib. 2, cap. 22, art. 48, p. 178.

One of the duties of the viceroy was to see that no person required to pay tithes escaped. It seems that the military orders of Santiago, Calatrava, and Alcántara tried to claim exemption from this obligation, but a royal order of 1539, reiterated by other laws of 1559, 1623, and 1628, very emphatically commanded the viceroy to compel them to pay the diezmos. In the religious orders, especially that of the Jesuits, the viceroy met the most stubborn resistance against the payment of tithes.[71]

The church also helped to pay the expenses of the state through the mesadas and ecclesiastical half annates, or salary taxes, which were granted to the king by Pope Urban VIII on December 23, 1625, and began to be collected in New Spain in 1638 by Viceroy Cadereyta. The sale of bulls of the Santa Cruzada was another means to raise revenue through the church. Viceroys were to restrict the asking of alms, which could not be solicited for any special religious order, in Indian towns or on vessels in the ports, without special permission, but they might be permitted for the sacred places in Jerusalem in order to inspire devotion.[72]

Whenever prelates died in the Indies the treasury officials were ordered to collect a fourth part of the rents from their offices for the crown. From these vacancies (vacantes) the king granted funds to churches and to dignitaries who applied for aid in their traveling expenses. Ecclesiastical subsidies were sometimes donated to the Spanish sovereigns by the popes. Two briefs of March 8, 1721, and January 8, 1741, gave the kings 4,000,000 ducats, but this amount was reduced in all parts of America to 2,000,000 through the great piety of the monarchs. A cédula of November 4, 1776, requested Viceroy Guirior of Peru to inform the king concerning the amount that had entered

[71] King to Mendoza, 1539, *Documentos inéditos . . . . de Mexico,* XV, 73; *Recopilación,* leyes 17, 15, 12, tit. 16, lib. 1. For the details of the tithe quarrels in Mexico *see* Bancroft, *History of Mexico,* III, 134–135, 428–431.

[72] Revillagigedo to Amarillas, 1754, *Instrucciones que los vireyes . . . .* arts. 148–149, p. 31; Riva Palacio, II, 695; *Recopilación,* leyes 1–2, 6, 9, tit. 21, lib. 1.

the treasury from these briefs, and it was found that only 30,000 pesos had been paid. When Viceroy Lemos came into office, he was commanded to collect this subsidy. From 1792 to 1795 in the archbishopric of Lima 80,000 pesos were collected and orders were given to the bishops to help obtain the remainder. Finally a total of 210,168 pesos was added to the treasury.[73]

8. PUNISHING IRREGULARITIES AND SETTLING RELIGIOUS DIFFERENCES

Punishing irregularities and settling religious differences among the clergy were difficult and annoying tasks for the vice-patron. Plenty of evidence could always be found that ecclesiastics engaged in trade in spite of the prohibitions against it. It is said that even the devout Zumárraga conducted a regular trade with the Indians through his majordomo, Aranguren, advancing money on future crops at good interest. Viceroys were to cause prelates to punish priests who violated the laws concerning trade, but only too often bishops failed to do so, since they themselves took from the poor to enrich their own families.[74] In 1596 Viceroy Toledo said that many priests and friars came to Peru on every fleet only to gain wealth and then return to Spain. Mancera stated that it was only a few months after the order of 1670, regulating trade, was passed until the disorders prevailed again and with greater force than ever, the religious forgetting their profession and enjoying the profits from business with the freedom of seculars.[75]

Preachers were not to utter in the pulpits scandalous words pertaining to the public administration, or to any officials. A

[73] Esquilache to Guadalcázar, 1621, *Memorias de los vireyes* . . . . I, 139; Lemos to Vallenari, 1796, *ibid.*, VI, 63–65.

[74] King to Mendoza, 1538, *Documentos inéditos* . . . . *de Mexico*, XV, 56; Bancroft, *History of Mexico*, II, 558; *Recopilación*, leyes 5, 8, tit. 11, lib. 2; Villarroel, *Enfermedades políticas* . . . . MS, I, pt. ı, p. 24.

[75] Memorial of Toledo, *Documentos inéditos* . . . . *de Indias*, VI, 517; Mancera to Veraguas, 1673, *Instrucciones que los vireyes* . . . . 269, 272.

Franciscan friar by the name of Rivera was very much angered because he was not permitted to speak with Enríquez at the viceregal palace. With the viceroy present in the cathedral he delivered a sermon about the negligence of the executive; therefore Enríquez, with the advice of the audiencia, ordered the priest to be sent to Spain, but he resisted the command and tried to raise a tumult by comparing his march to Vera Cruz with the exile of Israel from Egypt. To prevent popular excitement he was summoned back to Mexico City, but after the viceroy gave account of his conduct to the king, the friar was recalled to Spain. In the time of Palafox the laws pertaining to public utterances were again violated by ecclesiastics. Dr. Jacinto de Escobar tried to disgrace the alcalde mayor of Puebla by his severe criticisms. A Franciscan used improper language in the cathedral of Puebla against the visitor, and in the capital members of the same order preached seditiously against the viceroy. When the king learned of these abuses, he commanded Escalona not to permit such irregularities in the pulpit.[76]

Other sins of ecclesiastics are mentioned by Linares, who was a most severe critic of the clergy. He declared that both regulars and seculars embarrassed the administration of justice with their scandalous conduct, violated the vows of chastity, frequented gambling houses, kept places for the manufacture of prohibited drinks, and neglected the instruction of the Indians. In 1604 Velasco wrote to his successor, the Marquis of Monterey, saying that he would have a perpetual warfare in Peru concerning the royal patronage.[77] Palafox showed that the rules of patronage were very lax among the religious orders, who refused to present to the viceroy three names for appointments until the administration of Cerralvo. They also dispensed with the exam-

---

[76] *Recopilación*, ley 19, tit. 11, lib. 2; Cavo, lib. 5, art. 9, p. 137; Rivera Cambas, I, 139–140.

[77] Linares to Valero, 1716, *Instrucciones que los vireyes* .... 308–309; Mancera to his successor, 1648, *in* Polo, *Memorias de los vireyes* .... art. 17, p. 7; *Documentos inéditos* .... *de Indias*, IV, 426; *Recopilación*, ley 36, tit. 1, lib. 6.

ination of candidates by the bishops of the diocese, and as a result inefficient ecclesiastics were appointed. In 1673 Mancera said that prelates, instead of proposing three candidates for every vacancy, submitted to him twelve names for six parishes and sometimes fifteen for seven or ten for six, because of the lack of virtuous or experienced men.[78] Priests were removed according to the will of the prelates without consulting the vice-patron, and sometimes high prices were asked for performing the rites of the church.[79]

That the Indians were often oppressed by the religious is evident from many royal cédulas. In 1607 Montesclaros observed that each town employed more Indians in the service of the convent than in all other public employments, and twenty natives did not contribute as much to the king as did one to the doctrinero. Friars who came to the kingdom as commissioners or visitors also violated the rules of their order by collecting money for themselves and neglecting their tasks.[80] Irregularities prevailed among the higher officials just as with the priests and friars. Mancera explained how the commissioner-generals of the orders of Mercy and San Francisco tried to extend their powers, to the injury of the civil jurisdiction in Peru.[81]

If any priest committed a misdemeanor which was likely to cause scandal, the viceroy could write to the prelate of the diocese or summon him to a conference, in order that the guilty ecclesiastic might be punished justly.[82] On October 21, 1559, the king wrote to Mendoza requesting him to speak to the provincial of the

[78] Palafox to his successor, 1642, *Documentos inéditos* . . . . *de Mexico,* VII, 60–63; Mancera to Veraguas, 1673, *Instrucciones que los vireyes* . . . . 269.

[79] Montesclaros to his successor, 1615, *Documentos ineditos*. . . . *de Indias,* VI, 203; Queen to Mendoza, *Documents inéditos* . . . . *de Mexico,* XV, 44–45.

[80] Montesclaros to the king, *Instrucciones que los vireyes* . . . . 251–252; *Documentos inéditos* . . . . *de Indias,* XI, 65.

[81] Mancera to Veraguas, 1673, *Instrucciones que los vireyes* . . . . 273; Polo, *Memorias de los vireyes* . . . . art. 6, p. 3.

[82] *Recopilación,* ley 49, tit. 3, lib. 3; ley 70, tit. 14, lib. 1; Court to Amarillas, 1755, *Instrucciones que los vireyes* . . . . art. 15, p. 64; Croix, *Instrucción que* . . . . *dejó,* AGI, 88–5–13.

Franciscans concerning the chastisement of certain religious who mistreated a priest by the name of Juan de Ayllón. The viceroy was likewise ordered to compel the provincial of the Dominicans to punish some members of his order for creating a tumult and preaching publicly that excommunications were of no effect. This had occurred at the funeral of a certain Cristóbal de Chávez who died intestate in Antequera. The monks took his body forcibly to their monastery, although Chávez had a right to be buried in the cathedral church. During the turbulent days of the revolution, on August 12, 1811, Viceroy Venegas commanded the guardian of San Fernando to employ more severe discipline in his convent in order to prevent the spread of ideas concerning rebellion. Whenever bishops and superiors caused offense or became negligent in their manner of living, it was the duty of the viceroy to take effective measures to compel them to obey.[83] When it was necessary to reprimand an ecclesiastic, it was to be done secretly, for publicity would have bad influence upon the inhabitants.[84]

In the outlying towns and villages of Peru viceroys depended upon the corregidores to inform them concerning the conduct of priests. These officials were empowered to punish rebellious priests, but they had to report all cases of disobedience and the measures taken. Although the bishops of Truxillo disapproved of this method of correction, the other prelates favored it as the only available remedy for abuses. Viceroy Palata thought that it was not easy to control the clergy, for very often the dignitaries of the church were too lazy or indifferent to take action against existing evils.[85]

The viceroy was kept busy settling disputes and quarrels among the clergy. In 1536 the queen entreated Mendoza to com-

[83] *Documentos inéditos* . . . . *de Mexico*, XV, 126–231; *ibid.*, IX, 233–238; Palafox to his successor, 1642, *ibid.*, VII, 59.

[84] Mendoza to Velasco, *Instrucciones que los vireyes* . . . . art. 3, p. 227; *Recopilación*, ley 49, tit. 3, lib. 3.

[85] Castel-Fuerte to Villagarcía, 1736, *Memorias de los vireyes* . . . . III, 65, 68–69; Palata to Monclova, 1689, *ibid.*, II, 15–16.

pose all discords as quickly as possible, as they caused scandals among the Indians and contempt for Christianity.[86] The regular and secular clergy sometimes intermeddled in one another's affairs, thereby causing much disturbance. In 1569 the Franciscans from the parish of San José in Mexico were making a procession to the church of Santa María la Redonda, when a band of seculars ordered them to return to their convent. They refused to do this and a tumult resulted, whereupon Viceroy Enríquez had to send out the troops to quiet them.[87] On May 3, 1576, the king ordered the same viceroy to prevent the Franciscans, Dominicans, and Augustinians from entering towns under the secular clergy and persuading the Indians not to obey them.[88]

Differences arising during elections of the clergy greatly annoyed the viceroys. Elections were apt to be noisy among the religious orders and the chapters, hence it was the duty of the viceroy to see that they were conducted peacefully. He could appoint a judge to keep order among the voters and give him the aid of the troops if needed.[89] On December 16, 1672, a scandal occurred among the Carmelites in the election of a prior. The candidate was also rector of the college of his order. One of his followers, who was superior of the convent in Mexico City, threatened to throw out of the building all the friars hostile to the rector. The offended monks expelled the superior and his friends from the convent and took possession. The rector sent a band of forty armed men, among them friars and students, who forced open the doors, fell upon the other religious, took them prisoners, and wounded some of them. In Peru there were often serious conflicts over elections which were taken into the streets,

---

[86] Queen to Mendoza, *Documentos inéditos . . . . de Indias*, XXIII, 458.
[87] Cavo, lib. 4, art. 31, p. 126; Riva Palacio, II, 399.
[88] King to Enríquez, *Documentos inéditos . . . . de Mexico*, XV, 196–197.
[89] Revillagigedo to Amarillas, 1754, *Instrucciones que los vireyes . . . .* art. 167, p. 33; Croix, *Instrucción que . . . . dejó*, AGI, 88–5–13.

and the civil authorities had to restore peace. In Lima many
viceroys intervened in elections by sending out judges of the
audiencia to keep order.[90]

On July 9, 1790, a serious riot occurred in the convent of
San Francisco in Mexico City, caused by the seizure of the
guardian, Friar Mateo Jiménez, a gachupín. The two parties
came to blows and it required a military force to release Jiménez
after his captors twice refused to obey the orders of Viceroy
Mayorga.[91]

Sometimes noisy quarrels arose between the creole members
of the clergy and those who came from Spain. The plan adopted
was to alternate every two or four years in appointing prelates
of the religious orders from the creole and European parties.
This rule was first employed in Peru by Viceroy Castellar, but
it was not very effective because of the repugnance of the two
parties for one another. In Lima and Cuzco during Liñan's
administration many disturbances which led to violence arose
over attempts at such alternation. Whenever the European
faction foresaw that it was about to be beaten by its rival, it sent
to Europe for recruits, promising to put them into the missions
under their control. Villarroel says,

.... Without a doubt, many of those who leave Europe full of fervor
and the desire of conquering souls for Heaven, in a short time become
disillusioned and know that their coming has been for no other purpose
than that of augmenting the party, in order to divide the prelacies, the
priories, the guardianships, and other offices.[92]

Nuns as well as friars caused contentions which needed the
intervention of the viceroys. In Peru the sisters tried to get rid
of control over them by provincials and free themselves from

90 Riva Palacio, II, 709–710; *Mémorias de los vireyes* . . . . I, 216–279;
Solórzano, II, lib. 4, cap. 26, art. 14, p. 230.

91 Gómez, Diario, *Documentos para la historia de Mexico*, serie 2, pt. VII,
pp. 89, 91–92.

92 Court to Amarillas, 1755, *Instrucciones que ios vireyes* . . . . art. 20,
p. 66; Liñan to Palata, 1681, *Memorias de los vireyes* . . . . I, 271–275;
Villarroel, *Enfermedades políticas* . . . . MS, I, pt. I, p. 32.

their superiors. The nuns of Santa Catalina de Sena of Quito left their convent and caused the city to be divided into two hostile factions during their election. The convent of Encarnación in Lima was one of the centers of disorder. The majority of the inmates wanted to reëlect their abbess, Doña María de las Nievas. The others voted for Doña Rosa de la Cueva. Viceroy Marcillo, who was also archbishop, refused to approve the reëlection because it violated a law of the convent; accordingly he ordered the nuns to obey the candidate of the minority. The result was a schism among the nuns, and troops were sent to prevent violence between the partisans of the two abbesses in the streets. The conflict spread when Madre Nievas was removed to another convent.[93]

In 1743 Viceroy Villagarcía wisely intervened in a quarrel in the convent of Santa Clara, restored the abbess who had been suspended by archbishop Zeballos, and cut short the struggle. In 1780 another dissension, which was not settled until 1794, arose over the election of Concepción de Neyra and María de Tránsito in the convent of Santa Catalina at Quito. A royal decree finally prohibited the nuns from running for office during the administration of Lemos. This viceroy said that nuns caused much disturbance and a great void in the population because they did not marry.[94]

In New Spain the viceroy was confronted with the same kind of contentions between nuns. The convent of Santa Clara was conspicuous among the restless female communities, and it even went so far as to claim exemption from the payment of tithes. Under the administration of Monterey the nuns separated from the convent of Regina and founded the nunnery of San Bernardo, in spite of all the efforts of the viceroy to adjust their disagreements. When Mateo Heredia, provincial of the Franciscans,

---

[93] Liñan to Palata, 1681, *Memorias de los vireyes* . . . . I, 277–280; Castel-Fuerte to Villagarcía, 1736, *ibid.*, III, 74.

[94] Villagarcia to Superunda, 1745, *ibid.*, III, 386–387; Lemos to Vallenari, 1796, *ibid.*, VI, 35–38.

tried to remedy the abuses which he saw among the nuns of Mexico City, they appealed to the audiencia. The audiencia favored the nuns, but the viceroy upheld the ecclesiastical commissioner in his reforms. It was only through the activity of Mancera that a long and serious controversy was prevented.[95] Bucareli thought that the nuns of Puebla who were always in agitation gave a viceroy enough to do. The elder Revillagigedo did not have any difficulties with them, but commended them for their gentleness and willingness to obey the prelates; in 1771 Croix expressed the same opinion.[96]

Certain royal orders gave viceroys absolute power to expel rebellious ecclesiastics from their viceroyalties. In 1538 the king told the bishops of Mexico, Guatemala, and Antequera that the viceroy could cast wayward members of the clergy out of the country, and on May 1, 1543, Mendoza was commanded to expel all priests who had ceased to wear the religious garb and refused to obey their prelates. A law of 1568 added that after taking the ordinary judicial proceedings, viceroys could banish persons from the kingdom, but the causes for this action had to be submitted to the king.[97] In 1573 the king granted Viceroy Toledo complete power to expel ungovernable religious from Peru. A letter of March 17, 1619, to Esquilache said that when disturbances resulted from elections of the clergy and no other remedy availed to quiet them, the persons who caused the trouble should be embarked for Spain, but the viceroy must proceed with great circumspection.[98]

Several cases of actual expulsion of friars by viceroys have been found. Superunda sent to Spain a priest who had threatened the life of a prelate, but in a short time he was absolved

[95] *Ordenes de la corona*, MS, IV, pp. 15, 140–145; Riva Palacio, II, 710.

[96] Correspondence of Bucareli, Sept. 26, 1773, AGI, 146–4–2; Revillagigedo to Amarillas, 1754, *Instrucciones que los vireyes . . . .* art. 168, p. 34; Croix, *Instrucción que . . . . dejó*, AGI, 88–5–13.

[97] *Documentos inéditos . . . . de Mexico*, XV, 49, 94; *Recopilación*, leyes 84, 70, tit. 14, lib. 1; ley 61, tit. 3, lib. 3.

[98] Solórzano, II, lib. 4, cap. 27, arts. 17, 19–20, 23, pp. 245–246.

from all guilt and returned to Peru. Viceroy Teodoro de Croix also expelled Frier José de Azero from Peru, since he was implicated in the case of the imposter Manuel Figueroa.[99]

9. APPOINTMENTS IN THE CHURCH

Ecclesiastics virtually controlled the right of appointment in the church, although certain formalities belonged to the vicepatron. When a vacancy occurred edicts were posted in all the cities and towns so that candidates might present themselves for examination. The prelates of the diocese or persons of their designation carefully examined the competitors and chose three among the most worthy individuals. These names were then submitted to the viceroy and it was expected that the candidate best qualified to fill the position would be placed first on the list, but experience proved that this was not always done.[100]

Viceroys were to prevent positions from being vacant for a long time, reporting all vacancies to the king, who considered four months as the greatest length of time that ought to be allowed for them except in unusual cases; but with special permission a longer period might be granted.[101] On February 24, 1540, the viceroy was ordered to make new appointments when ecclesiastics were absent from their positions for more than a year, and in 1574 eight months only were permitted for absence in case of a legitimate cause.[102]

The religious orders and the secular clergy could hold their elections wherever they wished, but if it was necessary to change

[99] Superunda to his successor, 1761, *Memorias de los vireyes* . . . . IV, 41–42; Croix to Lemos, 1790, *ibid.*, V, 122.

[100] *Recopilación*, leyes 7, 15, tit. 6, lib. 1; Solórzano, II, lib. 5, cap. 14, art. 27, p. 117; Montesclaros to his successor, 1615, *Documentos inéditos* . . . . de *Indias*, VI, 198; Court to Amarillas, 1755, *Instrucciones que los vireyes* . . . . art. 4, p. 59.

[101] Velasco to Philip II, June 6, 1591, AGI, 58–3–11; *Recopilación*, ley 35, tit. 6, lib. 1; Court to Amarillas, 1755, *Instrucciones que los vireyes* . . . . art. 4, p. 59; Montesclaros to his successor, 1615, *Memorias de los vireyes* . . . . I, 14.

[102] *Documentos inéditos* . . . . de *Mexico*, XV, 74–75, 187.

the place they must notify the viceroy. The only control that the vice-patron had over elections was the power to appoint a royal assistant to attend examinations of competitors, but he did not have a vote. During the administration of the elder Revillagigedo a Jesuit held this position.[103] In Lima the asistente was always a theologian or a jurist. Occasionally both a theologian and a jurist were appointed for the same event.[104]

Sometimes the viceroy was present in person when the contestants delivered their theses before the ecclesiastical cabildo. In 1762 when two judges of the audiencia of Lima appointed by the viceroy failed to quiet the disturbance during an election of the Augustinians, it was decided that the viceroy should be present at the election, thereby following the example of many of his predecessors.[105]

When the three names decided upon by the prelates or chapter were submitted to the viceroy, he exercised the functions of the royal patron by choosing one. A decree of 1574 had stated that persons appointed by the king were always preferred to those presented by the viceroys. A law of April 4, 1609, however, gave the power of appointment in parishes and doctrinas entirely to the viceroys, but in regard to the higher offices a law of the same year said that viceroys should send the names of the candidates to the king in order that he might make the appointment.[106] The king appointed all chaplains for the armadas and fleets in the ports of the Indies.[107]

The laws enjoined viceroys always to prefer the most worthy and learned candidates, if possible men born of Spanish parents

---

[103] *Recopilación*, ley 59, tit. 14, lib. 1; ley 37, tit. 6, lib. 1; Revillagigedo to Amarillas, 1754, *Instrucciones que los vireyes* . . . . art, 146, p. 30; Marquina to Iturrigaray, 1803, *ibid.*, art, 18, p. 162; Croix, *Instrucción que* . . . . *dejó*, AGI, 88–5–13; Ribadeneyra, 185, 275–276.

[104] Amat to his successor, 1773, *Memorias de los vireyes* . . . . IV, 355, 357.

[105] Montesclaros to his successor, 1615, *Documentos inéditos* . . . . *de Indias*, VI, 195; Amat to his successor, 1773, *Memorias de los vireyes* . . . . IV, 428–429.

[106] Solórzano, II, lib. 5, cap. 15, arts. 9–10, p. 123; *Recopilación*, leyes 24, 7, tit. 6, lib. 1.

[107] Ribadeneyra, 278.

in the provinces, in order that the process of converting and instructing the Indians might be hastened.[108] Foreigners were not to be considered under any condition, or persons already holding office unless they resigned them.[109] Although the viceroy might choose freely any candidate on the list, it was customary to take the first one. Palafox and Liñan said that they could select the one who came last if he was judged most fit, but it was dangerous to do this. A royal cédula of August 10, 1801, implied that the second name might only be taken in cases of urgency.[110]

If none of the candidates were considered capable the prelates might be asked to submit a new list. Viceroy Palata said that he never required other nominees, but chose those less worthy. In 1762 Amat returned the names which had been given him to the ecclesiastical cabildo, ordering a new examination to be made. As a result more suitable candidates were obtained. Again in 1768 the king heard that the bishop of Truxillo was selecting certain of his followers and dependents for priests and doctrineros; therefore he commanded the viceroy to send back all of the fifteen names to the dignitary and ask for others, and the request was obeyed.[111] When there was but one competitor his name had to be presented to the viceroy just the same, in order that he could be certain that there was no other claimant for the vacancy. The viceroy was not to permit ecclesiastics to leave their parishes or monasteries to ask for appointments.[112]

---

108 Ribadeneyra, 265–266; *Recopilación*, ley 29, tit. 6, lib. 1; Montesclaros to his successor, 1615, *Documentos inéditos* . . . . *de Indias*, VI, 195–198; Court to Amarillas, 1755, *Instrucciones que los vireyes* . . . . art. 21, p. 66; *Documentos inéditos* . . . . *de Mexico*, XV, 187–189, 192.

109 *Ibid.*, XV, 193; Ribadeneyra, 271.

110 Revillagigedo to Amarillas, 1754, *Instrucciones que los vireyes* . . . . art. 144, p. 30; Ribadeneyra, 267; Croix, *Instrucción que* . . . . *dejó*, AGI, 88–5–13; Palafox to his successor, 1642, *Documentos inéditos* . . . . *de Mexico*, VII, 58; Liñan to Palata, 1681, *Memorias de los vireyes* . . . . I, 262; Avilés to Abascal, 1806, *Memoria del virey del Peru*, 6.

111 Court to Amarillas, 1755, *Instrucciones que los vireyes* . . . . 60; *Recopilación*, ley 28, tit. 6, lib. 1; Palata to Monclova, 1689, *Memorias de los vireyes* . . . . II, 11; Amat to his successor, 1733, *ibid.*, IV, 364–367.

112 Ribadeneyra, 268; *Recopilación*, ley 25, tit. 6, lib. 1; *Documentos inéditos* . . . . *de Mexico*, XV, 191–193; Palafox to his successor, 1642, *ibid.*, VII, 58.

The act of conferring the office and giving the canonical instructions was left to the prelates, who were expected to do this within ten days.[113] On the other hand, if the person appointed did not present himself within the fixed period he could not receive the position. Viceroy Liñan of Peru ordered corregidores and synods not to pay such ecclesiastics their salaries.[114]

In 1725, Membela, bishop of Truxillo, refused to confer an office. The Marquis of Castel-Fuerte had appointed Francisco Domonte, whose name appeared first on the list, to fill the doctrina of Varú. The viceroy requested the bishop to give a reason for his action and after some resistance, he sent a letter showing sufficient cause, so a reappointment was made for the town. Another notable incident of this kind arose in the bishopric of Guamanga. The viceroy chose Xavier Gallegos, who was not first on the list, for the curacy of Lauricocha and the bishop would not accept him. The priest was taken from his pulpit and imprisoned. He appealed to the viceroy who, with the advice of the real acuerdo, ordered the neighboring bishop of Cuzco to confer the office. The quarrel became so violent that it was necessary to threaten to take away the temporalities before Gallegos was installed in his office.[115]

Prelates and superiors could not remove ecclesiastics from office without first informing the viceroy of their reasons for so doing. When it was found best to make a removal, the viceroy did it without allowing appeal to the audiencia. The causes for all removals had to be sent to the king in order that he might know whether just measures had been taken.[116]

---

[113] *Recopilación*, leyes 24, 36, tit. 6, lib. 1; Solórzano, II, lib. 5, cap. 3, art. 26, p. 17; Montesclaros to his successor, 1615, *Documentos inéditos* . . . . *de Indias*, VI, 196; Court to Amarillas, 1755, *Instrucciones que los vireyes* . . . . 60.

[114] Order of the king, June 1, 1574, *Documentos inéditos* . . . . *de Mexico*, XV, 193; Liñan to Palata, 1681, *Memories de los vireyes* . . . . I, 264.

[115] Castel-Fuerte to Villagarcía, 1736, *ibid.*, III, 107–110; Solórzano, II, lib. 5, cap. 15, art. 10, p. 123.

[116] Court to Amarillas, 1755, *Instrucciones que los vireyes* . . . . art. 5, p. 60; *Recopilación*, ley 38, tit. 6, lib. 1; Ribadeneyra, 203, 196; Amat to his successor, 1773, *Memorias de los vireyes* . . . . IV, 370.

Viceroy Amat removed Victorio Cuenca, a Jesuit, who expressed his opinions in unbecoming language against the expedition of Matogroso ordered by the viceroy. He declared that without doubt commerce and illicit negotiations were to be carried on with the president of La Plata. In the viceroyalty of Buenos Aires, José Acosta, a Franciscan friar, censured from the pulpit the public amusements of the theatre patronized by Viceroy Vertíz, declaring that those who attended them would incur eternal damnation. The viceroy commanded him to be expelled from his monastery and requested that another religious should repudiate his utterances. Teodoro de Croix of Peru removed Gaspar de Ugarte from the province of Jauja, José de Hoya from Tarma, and Pedro de Escobar from the district of Guarochiri. This was done because they had tyrannized over their Indian parishioners and did not instruct them properly.[117] Resignations were to be made before the bishop of the diocese, who was required to report them to the viceroy and inform him whether there were sufficient reasons for allowing them.[118]

10. CHURCH COUNCILS

Provincial church councils could, according to the papal brief of December 6, 1610, be held in the Indies every twelve years, but only four actually took place in New Spain, the first one being in 1555 and the others in 1565, 1585, and 1771.[119] Six councils were held in Lima and three in the city of Santa Fé.[120] The

[117] Amat to his successor, 1773, *Memorias de los vireyes* . . . . IV, 426; Croix to Lemos, 1790, *ibid.*, V, 55; Coroleu, III, 51.

[118] Court to Amarillas, 1755, *Instrucciones que los vireyes* . . . . art. 6, p. 60; *Recopilación*, ley 51, tit. 6, lib. 1; Superunda to his successor, 1761, *Memorias de los vireyes* . . . . IV, 29.

[119] *Recopilación*, ley 1, tit. 8, lib. 1; Riva Palacio, II, 367, 377, 437; Bancroft, *History of Mexico*, III, 375. For the details of these councils consult the *Diccionario universal de historia y de geografía*, II, 480–485.

[120] The councils of Lima occurred in 1552, 1567, 1585, 1591, 1601 and 1775. Gómez Zamora, Matias, *Regio patronato español y indiano* (Madrid, 1897), 404; Groot, I, 181, II, 149; Moses, *The Spanish Dependencies* . . . . II, 86.

vice-patron was to attend these meetings in person, as the representative of the king, in order to see that the rights of the patronage were not violated, but only the bishops had a vote. Much attention was paid to ceremony at these gatherings. The viceroy was allowed to sit on the throne under a canopy, and he sometimes delivered an address.[121]

The matters discussed at these assemblies usually pertained to the morality and good conduct of the clergy, enforcement of the decrees of the Council of Trent, and the good treatment or instruction of the Indians. The measures of the provincial councils were sent to the Council of the Indies and if approved by that body they were forwarded to the pope, who might order them published in the province where the meeting had taken place.[122]

Synodical councils were to be held in the colonies every year. Whatever was done in these gatherings had to be submitted to the vice-patron so that he might know whether any action was contrary to the royal patronage. He could overrule the measures of the synods, but it was still possible to send them to the Council of the Indies for approval.[123]

11. QUESTIONS BETWEEN CHURCH AND STATE

Although the questions between church and state in America were not serious, there were several points of friction. The papal nuncios at Madrid caused many of these difficulties. They tried to interfere in religious matters in the Indies, sometimes creating a division among the clergy. A notable case of a nuncio exceeding his authority arose from the proclamation of a jubilee by Clement X, on his accession to the pontifical power. The brief which the pope issued on this occasion was sent by the

---

[121] *Recopilación*, ley 2, tit. 8, lib. 1; *Leyes de Indias*, MS, ley 1, tit. 7; Croix, *Instrucción que* . . . . *dejó*, AGI, 88–5–13.

[122] *Ibid.*, AGI, 88–5–13; Riva Palacio, II, 366–367, 377, 437.

[123] *Recopilación*, leyes 3, 6, tit. 8, lib. 1; ley 147, tit. 15, lib. 2.

nuncio at Madrid, without securing the approval of the Council
of the Indies, to a certain prelate in New Spain, who immediately
published it by posting the document in the churches, but without the knowledge of the political administration. This act was
condemned by a royal cédula of June 10, 1642, showing that the
crown was opposed to the direct correspondence between authorities of the church in Europe and America.[124]

Papal bulls and briefs unsanctioned by the Council of the
Indies entered the colonies in many mysterious ways. Some of
them were sent for the purpose of recovering estates left by
deceased prelates or dues from vacant ecclesiastical seats. Others
went directly to the religious orders, which were only too willing
to usurp, in many cases, the jurisdiction of the bishops. On
many occasions viceroys were commanded to collect all original
papal bulls and briefs which had not passed the Council of the
Indies and send them to Spain on the first fleet. The Council
might keep those documents if it saw fit and make supplica-
tion to the pope to withdraw them, but not many bulls were
retained.[125]

Archbishop Vizarrón published two papal briefs in Mexico
without the consent of the Council of the Indies. One granted
permission to eat meat, and the other fixed the days of fiesta on
which the faithful might work after hearing mass, but the viceroy stopped their circulation. Shortly before the arrival of Viceroy Fuenclara in 1741 the famous Italian, Lorenzo Boturini, had
received a bull from the pope to collect alms in order to provide
the image of Guadalupe with a crown of gold and precious stones.
He neglected, however, to obtain the proper sanction for putting
the document into effect. Fuenclara took rather severe measures
against Boturini, imprisoning him and confiscating all his papers

---

[124] Mancera to Veraguas, 1673, *Instrucciones que los vireyes* . . . . 270.

[125] *Documentos inéditos* . . . . *de Indias*, XIX, 122; *ibid.*, XVIII, 413;
Recopilación, leyes 2–8, tit. 9, lib. 1; King to the viceroy and audiencia,
1571, *Documentos inéditos* . . . . *de Mexico*, XV, 179–180. According to
Ribadeneyra there were only six cases in which bulls were retained by the
Council of the Indies. *Op. cit.*, 226–229.

pertaining to a history of America. The Italian was then sent to Spain where he was pardoned and pensioned for his loss.[126] Prelates in Rome sometimes addressed patentes or letters to ecclesiastics in America in which they made certain requests or gave permission for measures to be taken concerning religious matters. Teodoro de Croix and some other viceroys of Peru declared all patentes void.[127] Later in 1777 it was commanded that, even if papal bulls were approved by the Council of the Indies, they were not to be circulated without the consent of the vice-patron.[128]

Many royal cédulas requested viceroys and archbishops to avoid contentions, but they were both jealous of their power, each one believing himself to be the first person in the colony, and as a result many quarrels occurred.[129] Some of these disputes were based on most trivial matters. In the procession of Corpus Christi a ridiculous contention concerning their pages took place between the first Alburquerque and the haughty archbishop Buguerio, and it was finally decided that neither the pages of the viceroy nor those of the prelate should attend. The Count of Baños tried to have the route of the same procession changed so that it would pass the viceregal palace, but he met with energetic opposition from Archbishop Osorio, who forbade any deviation from the rule. This incident led to more serious misunderstandings with the viceroy, who caused letters addressed to Osorio to be destroyed. Among these there were six dispatches making the archbishop viceroy of Mexico.[130]

Archbishop Liñan of Lima contended that he had a right to have six mules to draw his carriage, but Viceroy Palata declared that he alone ought to enjoy this dignified privilege. In 1752

126 Rivera Cambas, I, 371, 355–357; Zamacois, V, 564–566.

127 Croix to Lemos, 1790, *Memorias de los vireyes* . . . . V; 16; Avilés to Abascal, 1806, *Memoria del virey del Peru*, 11–12.

128 *Leyes de Indias*, MS, ley 15, tit. 3; *Ordenes de la corona*, MS, I, 201–202.

129 King to the archbishop, 1576, *Documentos inéditos* . . . . *de Mexico*, XV, 198–199; Palafox to his successor, 1642, *ibid.*, VII, 29.

130 Bancroft, *History of Mexico*, III, 148; Riva Palacio, II, 624–626; Zamacois, V, 389–394.

on the last day of the Novena de la Concepción, Superunda commanded Barroeta, the archbishop of Lima, not to use a parasol
in the procession. The prelate insisted upon this right and
appealed to the Council of the Indies. The king permitted him
to have the parasol temporarily until other measures could be
taken.[131] Another point of dispute was whether dignitaries of
the church might enter the viceroy's apartment with their train-
bearers. The king finally decided the matter by ordering that
they must drop their trains at the door, but when accompanying
the viceroy at some public function their trains might be carried
by pages.[132]

On matters of ceremony the laws of the Indies were very
explicit. When coming to church the viceroy was to be saluted
with the courtesy due him. The deans and chapters were to meet
him at the door, and accompany him to the threshold of the building when leaving. Upon entering a church, college, or monastery
for the first time or after a long absence, the chapter received
him with the raised cross. At the door the viceroy knelt on a
cushion and kissed the cross in the hand of the bishop, then
the chapter made a procession, carrying the symbol of the faith
to the high altar.[133] In processions he always went with the
oidores, the ranking oidor walking by his side, and the prelates
following, but when the viceroy passed through the city with
the archbishop he always walked on the right. In some of the
rites of worship ecclesiastics were served first, as when the holy
water was given and on the day of the Purification, when the
clergy received the candles before the viceroy and the audiencia.[134] This was to show the preëminence of the church over
the state in strictly spiritual matters.

131 Palata to Monclova, 1689, *Memorias de los vireyes* . . . . II, 75;
Superunda to his successor, 1761, *ibid.*, IV, 8–9.
132 *Documentos inéditos* . . . . *de Indias*, XIX, 88; *Recopilación*, ley 39,
tit. 15, lib. 3.
133 *Ibid.*, leyes 6–7, 10, tit. 15, lib. 3.
134 *Ibid.*, leyes 1, 25, 55, 36, 9.

Occasionally viceroys had to settle ceremonial controversies which arose between ecclesiastics. In the city of Truxillo the cabildo and justices got into a dispute with the bishop, who thought that those officials should accompany him whenever he went out of his house until he returned, just as on pontifical occasions. The cabildo wrote its objections to Castel-Fuerte, who with the advice of the real acuerdo, decided that the ceremony did not have to be performed for the prelate, and the king approved the action taken by the viceroy in a cédula of June 7, 1729.[135]

Numerous other matters besides ceremonies caused quarrels between the viceroy and the highest dignitary of the church in the Indies. Guadalcázar had serious dissension with Gonzalo de Ocampo, fourth archbishop of Lima. This viceroy defended the prerogatives of the crown with great firmness, but so great was the arrogance and influence of the ecclesiastic that evil would have befallen the executive, if he had not died when he did.[136] In New Spain Montesclaros had trouble with the archbishop, Santa María Mendoza, and in 1635 there was a dispute between Manso de Zúñiga and Viceroy Cerralvo.[137]

The disagreement between Escalona and Palafox, who was also visitor, was probably the worst quarrel between a viceroy and the archbishop, excepting that of Gelves and Serna. The source of the difficulty seems to have been the viceroy's love of pleasure and amusement. The ill-will of the viceroy was shown when Palafox refused to pardon a certain prisoner. The duke retaliated by vexing the prelate and his friends, and forbade him to supervise the dispatch of the fleet to the Philippines, though Palafox had royal instructions to do so. Palafox took his revenge by keeping his appointment to the office of viceroy secret and making Escalona leave the palace hurriedly. There was a misunderstanding between Mancera and Archbishop Rivera

---

[135] Castel-Fuerte to Villagarcía, 1736, *Memorias de los vireyes* . . . . III, 80–81.

[136] Coroleu, II, 107.   [137] Riva Palacio, II, 711.

in the same viceroyalty, because the latter declared the day of San Benito a fiesta without informing the viceroy.[138] Another serious conflict occurred between Viceroy Palata and the archbishop of Lima. Liñan resented the intervention of the viceroy in the affairs of the church and expressed his anger by opposing Palata's administration. He bitterly denounced the conduct of the viceroy in his sermons, describing it as anti-Catholic. While the prelate remained hostile Palata requested the members of the audiencia and other officials not to go to the cathedral. In 1687 the prelate and cabildo refused to coöperate with the government in rebuilding churches destroyed by earthquake. They contended that the expenses should be borne by the royal treasury.[139]

During the eighteenth century struggles of this kind were not serious. In Nueva Granada Viceroy Guirior said that ecclesiastics still desired to extend their power to the detriment of the royal jurisdiction.[140] In New Spain Marfil said: "The functions of the vice-patron, which are among the most extensive privileges conceded by the sovereign to his viceroys, were entirely accepted and in use." He also commended the zeal of the archbishop and bishops of the kingdom and their desire for coöperation with the government.[141]

12. THE VICEROY AND THE INQUISITION

The first tribunal of the Inquisition was established at Lima in 1569 by Viceroy Toledo. Others were soon founded in Mexico in 1571, and at Cartagena in 1610. Sunday, November 4, 1571, was a very solemn occasion when the inquisitor Moya de Contreras met in the cathedral of Mexico with the viceroy and audiencia, and the order of Philip II concerning the establishment

[138] Riva Palacio, II, 598–600; García, *Don Juan de Palafox*, 104; Rivera Cambas, I, 141, 234.
[139] Palata to Monclova, 1689, *Memorias de los vireyes* . . . . II, 49–51.
[140] Groot, II, 147.
[141] Marfil to Cagigal, 1760, *Instrucciones que los vireyes* . . . . 109.

of the tribunal was read. The inquisitor's oath promising to perform his duties faithfully, which he had already taken on October 26 before the licenciado Bonilla, was read also. Then Viceroy Enríquez swore:

As a good and faithful Christian to be now and always in favor, aid and defense of our Holy Catholic Faith and the Holy Inquisition, the officials and judges of it . . . . guard its privileges and immunities, and not to conceal heretics and the enemies [of the tribunal] . . . .

After the viceroy had finished, the oidores and regidores took the same oath.[142] The Inquisition in the colonies had the same object as in Spain. Its jurisdiction extended over all the people in the New World except the Indians.[143] Viceroys were instructed to aid the inquisitors as much as possible. On the other hand they were to uphold the dignity of the viceroy, and give him the chief place at autos de fé. On May 8, 1589, the inquisitors were reprimanded severely because they tried to precede.the Count of Villar in a procession during an auto de fé. The king ruled that the inquisitors ought not to go before the viceroy, who represented the royal person.[144] As soon as a new viceroy arrived, he was expected to send his greetings and offer his services to the tribunal. Then the inquisitors did likewise, but the viceroy took the first step. In 1636 the tribunal complained to the king that Montañez failed to offer his courtesies to it.[145]

Viceroys were to keep account of the fines and confiscations made by the tribunal. Every year the treasurer of the Holy Office was to submit an account of the money in his possession to

142 Riva Palacio, II, 401–404; Medina, José Toribio, *Historia del tribunal del santo oficio de la Inquisición en México* (Santiago de Chile, 1905), 27. For the officials of the tribunal *see Documentos inéditos . . . . de Indias*, VIII, 233.

143 Solórzano, II, lib. 4, cap. 24, arts. 17–18, 30, pp. 207, 209; *Leyes de Indias*, MS, ley 10, tit. 11.

144 Palafox to his successor, 1642, *Documentos inéditos . . . . de Mexico*, VII, 86; Court to Amarillas, 1755, *Instrucciones que los vireyes . . . .* art. 17, p. 65; *Recopilación*, ley 1, tit. 19, lib. 1; Solórzano, II, lib. 4, cap. 24, arts. 12, 29, pp. 204, 209.

145 *Documentos inéditos . . . . de Mexico*, V, 141–143, 181–182.

the treasury officials. The secular arm of the government collected the fines imposed by the tribunal, and viceroys saw that all foreigners who had been condemned were embarked for Spain. Inquisitors might not intermeddle in matters that did not belong to cases of faith or proceed against the viceroy in any rivalry of jurisdiction, nor were they to engage in trade or take anything against the will of the owners.[146]

Frequently the inquisitors tried to extend their power to the detriment of the prerogatives and patronage of the king. Both Philip II and Philip III in decrees of March 10, 1533, February 7, 1569, and May 22, 1610, called the concordia, reprimanded the judges of the Holy Office who exceeded their authority. Palafox advised that, when the tribunal usurped the rights of the secular jurisdiction, the viceroy should try to settle the matter amicably. Mancera stated that viceroys and audiencias did not endeavor to check the tribunal without urgent necessity, because its power was so absolute. If the tribunal should interfere with the royal jurisdiction, Croix's plan was first to discuss the matter peaceably with the oldest member, but when it could not be settled the question might be brought up in the proper legal form and be decided by the viceroy.[147]

Minor cases of conflict between the tribunal and the secular courts usually were adjusted in a conference of the senior oidor and the ranking inquisitor. When these two men could not agree three ecclesiastical dignitaries might be appointed, one by the viceroy and the other two by the inquisitors, to determine the case; if they did not reach any conclusion the viceroy reviewed the case and made the final decision. In more serious disputes between viceroys and inquisitors, concerning jurisdiction, two members of the general council of the Inquisition and another two from the Council of the Indies considered the matter.[148]

---

146 *Recopilación,* leyes 11–12, 18–19, 21, 29, tit. 19, lib. 1.
147 Palafox to his successor, 1642, *Documentos inéditos . . . . de Mexico,* VII, 86; Mancera to Veraguas, 1673, *Instrucciones que los vireyes . . . .* 270–271; Croix, *Instrucción que . . . . dejó,* AGI, 88-5-13.
148 Solórzano, II, lib. 4, cap. 24, arts. 44–45, p. 214; *Recopilación,* leyes 29–30, tit. 19, lib. 1.

During the administration of Castellar, a slight misunderstanding over the imprisonment of a certain criminal occurred with the Holy Office in Peru. As soon as the fiscal learned of the case, plans were made for the sala del crimen to take cognizance of the matter, but when further investigations were made it was found that the claim of the tribunal was just and the culprit was at once handed over to it. Castel-Fuerte, aided by a royal order of September 3, 1729, judiciously settled a struggle between the cruzada and the Inquisition over their respective powers. At this time the shrewd Philip V decided to check the powers of the Holy Office by definitely declaring the number of attendants that it could have and by defining its privileges.[149]

On one occasion Superunda adjusted a case which was pending from his predecessor's administration. There had been some trouble between the consulado and the Inquisition over the possessions of the deceased Felix de Vargas. Upon the recommendation of his council, Villagarcía ordered a special sala of the audiencia to be formed to decide the matter, but the inquisitors opposed this measure and nothing was done until Superunda arrived. After many private conferences with the ecclesiastics and much persuasion by the new viceroy, the sala was convened, but the disagreement was not adjusted at once, for a foolish bickering over ceremony and style of dress occupied the attention of the members of the chamber.[150]

A contest occurred in the viceroyalty of Nueva Granada between the civil officials and the Holy Office over the royal cédula of March 19, 1754, which declared that the crime of polygamy was of mixed fuero, and that the civil as well as the ecclesiastical authorities should have cognizance of it. The great opposition of the tribunal, no doubt, was the occasion for the decree of September 8, 1766, revoking the former measure and

---

[149] Castellar to his successor, 1681, *Memorias de los vireyes* . . . . I, 160; Castel-Fuerte to Villagarcía, 1736, *ibid.*, III, 86–90; Rivera Cambas, I, 332.

[150] Superunda to his successor, 1761, *Memorias de los vireyes* . . . . IV, 69–73.

leaving to the royal justices only the power to make a summary investigation or to arrest a criminal within five leagues from the location of the office of the Inquisition, when the crime was well known.[151]

The reforms of Charles III gave the viceroy the final word in all matters of disputed jurisdiction with the Inquisition. A further check was imposed when it was ordered that the viceroy must be notified before any edict of the Holy Office could be published.[152]

The desire to keep the colonies loyal to the Catholic faith led to prohibition of importation of numerous classes of books, but in spite of this forbidden writings entered the Indies. Sometimes they were received with papers from Spain. Mancera said that ordinarily they went to idle persons, who congregated in ecclesiastical houses to discuss and praise them, and in a short time their slanderous ideas spread throughout the city. It was the duty of viceroys to arrange for such works to be examined by the Inquisition, which had a number of persons called qualifiers who inspected all printed matter and images to find whether there was anything about them offensive to the church. At the same time opinions on new publications were reported to the tribunal.[153] After 1575 only the monastery of San Lorenzo had the right to print books of divine service for Spain and the New World, hence viceroys were to prevent all other prayer books from entering their viceroyalties.[154]

The Inquisition later placed the more modern philosophical works under the band. A royal order of August 10, 1785, commanded viceroys to collect and burn all copies of the works of Montesquieu, Raynal, Machiavelli, Legros, Linquet, Belisario de

---

[151] Amat to his successor, 1773, *Memorias de los vireyes* . . . . IV, 491.

[152] Croix, *Instrucción que* . . . . *dejó*, AGI, 88–5–13; Revillagigedo, *Instrucción reservada*, arts. 93, 97.

[153] Mancera to his successor, 1673, *Instrucciones que los vireyes* . . . . 272; *Recopilación*, ley 7, tit. 24, lib. 1; Moses, *South America on the Eve of Emancipation*, 16–17.

[154] *Recopilación*, leyes 1, 8, 13, tit. 24, lib. 1.

Marmontelo, and the Encyclopedia.   Teodoro de Croix tried to
enforce this decree very rigidly in Peru by organizing a commission to examine public libraries.[155]   In 1803 the curate of
Axuchitlan, Juan Antonio Olavarrieta, became the victim of an
auto de fé in Mexico for writing a book entitled ''Man and
Beast,'' having for its frontispiece a caricature of a tyrant king.
The author was tried with great solemnity and sent to Spain, but
he escaped during the voyage.[156]

The Holy Office had power to reprimand a viceroy, but it
seems that the inquisitors got along with him better than did the
archbishops; therefore this authority was seldom used.   The
Marquis of Croix had been denounced for some reason by the
tribunal and was summoned to appear before it.   Wishing to
fulfil the law, he went to the inquisitor's palace accompanied by
many troops; he asked them to break open the doors if he did
not appear within half an hour.   When the viceroy entered the
room where the inquisitors were seated, he took out his watch
and told them to hurry and explain their accusation against him,
for they had scarcely twenty-five minutes until his troops would
join him with fixed bayonets.   Then the inquisitors stammered
and asked him to withdraw.[157]

On one occasion the viceroy of Peru made use of the tribunal
to bring about the removal of Francisco de Aguirre, governor
of Tucumán.   Hitherto, the administrators of this province had
been chosen either by the governors of Chile or by the viceroys of
Peru, but Tucumán lay within the jurisdiction of the audiencia
of Lima and the viceroy was desirous of assuming the sole power
of appointment.   In 1569 Aguirre was accused of heretical and
scandalous remarks.   His trial lasted for almost five years, at
the end of which time he was absolved from any excommunication
or censure he might have incurred.[158]

---

[155] Croix to Lemos, 1790, *Memorias de los vireyes* . . . . V, 85–86.

[156] Cavo, art. 21, p. 671.

[157] Croix, *Correspondance*, 248–249.

[158] Accusation of Aguirre, 1569, *Documentos inéditos* . . . . *de Indias*,
XXV, 362–384; Moses, *The Spanish Dependencies* . . . . II, 35–58.

The Inquisition was not extreme in America. The first auto de fé in Mexico was held in 1574 and from this time until the tribunal was abolished only forty-one persons were put to death as unreconciled heretics. A year earlier the first auto occurred in Lima, and during the history of the Holy Office in Peru there were twenty-nine autos de fé, a number surpassed in a single day in Spain under the fanatical Philip II.[159]

An auto de fé was made the occasion for a great celebration which lasted many days and was attended by people from far and near. The viceroy, vicereina, audiencia, high ecclesiastics, members of the cabildos of the city and of the university took seats of honor prepared for them at the place of execution. The edict inviting all the faithful in the city and outside of it to attend the auto was published in all the towns of the viceroyalty. In 1601 Viceroy Monterey was present at one of these gatherings and occupied the seat of honor in the principal chapel of the cathedral of Mexico. The proceedings began March 18th and lasted until the 26th. On the day when the heretics, three men and a woman, were executed, the viceroy and his household rose at three o'clock in the morning to hear mass. Next day the viceroy entered into the general rejoicing by coming out of his palace and driving about the city, thereby expressing his happiness that the faith had triumphed.[160] Other notable cases in 1596, 1688, and 1696 of Mexican viceroys viewing the tortures of condemned heretics might be described.[161]

---

[159] Bourne, 224, 313; Moses, *South America on the Eve of Emancipation*, 14.

[160] Rivera Cambas, I, 172–173; Riva Palacio, II, 713–720.

[161] Diario de Don Antonio Rivera, *Documentos para la historia de Mexico*, serie 2, pt. VI, pp. 32, 94; Priestley, *The Mexican Nation*, 112.

13. THE TRIBUNAL OF THE CRUZADA

The powers of the vice-patron extended also to the tribunal of the cruzada. The income from bulls of cruzada or indulgences had been granted by Pope Pius V to the Spanish monarchs to use against the Turks and infidels. Like the other rights of patronage, it was applied to the colonies; the first bull being published in New Spain in 1533.[162] The commissioner-general resided in Spain, but at Lima, Mexico City, Santa Fé, Cartagena, Guatemala, Santo Domingo, and Manila, there was a sub-delegate who took charge of the sale of the bulls and appointed treasurers to keep the funds collected until they could be sent to Spain. In the beginning indulgences were published annually, but in 1578 it was ordered that this should be done in Mexico every two years. Later a cédula of March 6, 1618, to Viceroy Esquilache of Peru, showed that it was impossible to issue them every year in the vast provinces of South America.[163]

Tribunals of cruzada were to be established in each district of an audiencia. The subdelegate-general was to review, sentence, and decide within his jurisdiction all cases pertaining to the administration or collection of money from the sale of indulgences. The principal officials of these tribunals consisted of the sub-delegate, the senior oidor of the audiencia, and a civil fiscal or assessor, who was also the treasurer.[164] If difficulties arose between the sub-delegate and the other ecclesiastical or secular courts, a cédula of June 20, 1609, ordered the viceroy to settle them. In 1636 it was commanded that a secular or ecclesiastical judge should meet with the sub-delegate to determine the disputed matter, but when they could not agree, the viceroy might

162 Cédula for Toledo, 1573, *Documentos inéditos* . . . . *de Indias*, XVIII, 398; Bancroft, *History of Mexico*, III, 665.

163 Solórzano, II, lib. 4, cap. 25, arts. 10, 12, 30, pp. 219–220, 223.

164 *Recopilación*, ley 1, tit. 20, lib. 1; Mancera to Veraguas, 1673, *Instrucciones que los vireyes* . . . . 271; Croix, *Instrucción que* . . . . *dejó*, AGI, 88–5–13.

decide the case. Viceroys and audiencias were to influence the people to receive bulls with all reverence, and aid their publication and distribution.[165]

The collection of money from the sale of indulgences was a duty of the treasury officials and the funds were not united with the branches of the temporal treasury.[166] In the time of Croix, the viceroy appointed the treasurer-general of the cruzada in Mexico City. He had to see that the tribunal did not take unjust action against anyone, and he prevented it from collecting any part of the estates of deceased persons who died intestate.[167]

The viceroy was superintendent-general of the branch of the cruzada, since he was at the head of the treasury. The presidents of the audiencias and governors of Buenos Aires, Tucumán and Paraguay were also given this title, but they were subordinate to the viceroy of Peru and did not have power to dispose of the funds of the tribunal. The viceroy had authority to change the rules of this division of finance as it seemed good to him. Superunda discovered a way to promote harmony with the cruzada. He wisely formed an acuerdo having the chief commissioner as a member, and this man became the first one to obey the viceroy's orders. The idea did not originate with Superunda, since a cédula of November 27, 1624, provided for a junta, consisting of the viceroy or president of the audiencia, an oidor, and the commissioner, to be formed in each audiencia district where there was a tribunal of cruzada, to decide matters of jurisdiction.[168]

Sometimes the tribunal overreached its jurisdiction and engaged in trade. However, it seems to have been easier for

---

[165] Solórzano, II, lib. 4, cap. 25, art. 19, p. 222; *Recopilación*, leyes 15, 5–6, tit. 20, lib. 1.

[166] Mancera to Veraguas, 1673, *Instrucciones que los vireyes* . . . . 271–272; Revillagigedo to Amarillas, 1754, *ibid.*, art. 95, p. 23.

[167] Croix, *Instrucción que* . . . . *dejó*, AGI, 88–5–13; *Recopilación*, leyes 24, 18, tit. 20, lib. 1; Solórzano, II, lib. 4, cap. 25, art. 58, p. 225.

[168] Superunda to his successor, 1761, *Memorias de los vireyes* . . . . IV, 259–261; Liñan to Palata, 1681, *ibid.*, I, 270.

viceroys to control than the Inquisition.   In 1609 some doubts arose over ceremonies, but a royal cédula declared that in processions, the sub-delegate should be preceded only by the viceroy. When the executive was absent the commissioner could go before all the other oidores.[169]

When the tribunal was abolished in Mexico in 1751 Viceroy Amarillas had a notable lawsuit to settle with the Count of Santiago and the Countess of Miravalles.   Their families had the privilege of appointing the chancillor and alguacil mayor of the cruzada; therefore indemnity was sought and allowed.   The government paid 139,109 pesos to the count and 269,699 pesos to the countess.[170]

---

169 Palafox to his successor, 1642, *Documentos inéditos* .... *de Mexico,* VII, 86–87; Solórzano, II, lib. 4, cap. 25, art. 20, p. 222; *Recopilación,* ley 7, tit. 20, lib. 1.

170 Riva Palacio, II, 811.

CHAPTER VI

THE VICE-PATRON: EDUCATION, HOSPITALS, AND CHARITY

1. EDUCATION

Education, hospitals, and institutions of charity were important divisions of the patronato real. The viceroy was vice-patron of the principal schools and colleges in his kingdom, since they were largely under the control of the church. A viceroy might devote as much of his energy to education as he liked. The Duke of Linares said that the colleges of Mexico gave the administration little to do, except the college of Santos which, pretending to be greater than other halls of learning, caused rivalry with the university.[1]

The vice-patron conferred fellowships and professorships in the colleges under the royal patronage. At the beginning of the nineteenth century the most important of these institutions in New Spain were San Ildefonso, San Juan de Letrán, San Gregorio, the Royal and Pontifical University in Mexico City, El Carolino in Puebla, and the Royal University in Guadalajara.[2] In fact, all secular colleges and seminaries, and later those which had belonged to the expelled Jesuits, were under the royal patronage. During the administration of the second Revillagigedo forty-two fellowships and twenty professorships were provided for by the viceroy.[3]

---

[1] Linares to Valero, 1716, *Instrucciones que los vireyes* . . . . 310.

[2] Marquina to Iturrigaray, 1803, *ibid.*, art. 18–19, p. 162.

[3] Croix, *Instrucción que* . . . . *dejó*, AGI, 88–5–13. San Pedro and San Pablo of Mexico, incorporated in 1618 with San Ildefonso, belonged to the patronage while under Jesuit control. *Recopilación*, ley 13, tit. 23, lib. 1; Revillagigedo, *Instrución reservada*, art. 37.

Not many serious educational reforms were undertaken, since many of the viceroys were military men or priests. Viceroys were not to hinder the universities in the election of rectors and professors, but always allow them to choose the men they wished and to confer degrees according to their statutes. A law of 1618 gave the viceroy power to appoint some one to investigate elections and punish all misdeeds, and a later one in 1642 ordered that, when it was convenient, some of the oidores of the audiencia should be present when voting for professorships occurred.[4]

Vice-patrons were to take special care to favor, aid, and advise colleges, but leave the administration entirely to the prelates. Sometimes the monarch or the Council of the Indies made special requests to the viceroy for certain kinds of information. This was his chance to influence educational policies and a wise executive usually took advantage of it.[5] Viceroys had to see that the statutes of colleges were kept; only when there was a legitimate cause could they change them and give account of their action to the king.[6] Because of the multiplicity and confusion of the statutes of the University of Mexico, Marquina decided to simplify them somewhat, and his measure found favor with the king.[7] Whenever disputes arose over jurisdiction or ceremonies the viceroy had to decide them. A royal cédula of 1579 empowered Enríquez to settle all disagreements between the Jesuits and the University of Mexico concerning courses of study and conferring of degrees. It was arranged that the Jesuit schools were to be considered as seminaries of the University.[8]

---

[4] *Recopilación*, leyes 5, 45, 41, tit. 22, lib. 1.

[5] Court to Amarillas, 1755, *Instrucciones que los vireyes* . . . . arts. 12–13, pp. 63–64; Enríquez to Coruña, 1580, *ibid.*, art. 14, p. 248; Marquina to Iturrigaray, 1803, *ibid.*, art. 104, p. 178; *Recopilación*, ley 1, tit. 23, lib. 1; ley 4, tit. 14, lib. 3; ley 6, tit. 22, lib. 1.

[6] *Ibid.*, leyes 3, 14, tit. 22, lib. 1; Revillagigedo to Amarillas, 1754, *Instrucciones que los vireyes* . . . . art. 160, p. 33.

[7] Marquina to Iturrigaray, 1803, *ibid.*, art. 124, pp. 179, 286; Croix, *Instrucción que* . . . . *dejó*, AGI, 88–5–13.

[8] Riva Palacio, II, 523.

Private schools which did not come under the rules of the patronage were also permitted. The ayuntamiento of Mexico City founded various elementary schools for children and certain professors opened them in their homes, as Gonzalo de Valverde did in 1536 and Diego Díaz in 1550. Dr. Francisco de Salazar likewise devoted himself to this profession. Pedro de Gante, a relative of the great Charles V, established a school in the Indian quarter of the capital, which was well attended. The instruction consisted of elementary and higher branches, including both the mechanical and fine arts.[9]

The education of needy mestizo children in New Spain was provided for by Mendoza, who in 1553 founded a college which existed for more than three centuries. Other children soon found a place in this school, called San Juan de Letrán. Reading, writing, arithmetic, and subjects relating to good morals were taught. The viceroy was to supply everything needed for this school; accordingly he assigned to it the funds derived from the sale of stray cattle, and informed himself how the money was spent.[10] In 1755 the king ordered Amarillas to examine the mestizo children and find out whether anything was lacking in their education. Every year the viceroy or an oidor had to visit the school.[11] Francisco de Toledo opened similar schools in Cuzco and Lima for the instruction of the children of caciques. Many laws of the Indies ordered viceroys to aid such schools in Peru and Mexico, and see that the proper persons were chosen to teach the pupils in the Christian faith.[12]

Schools for Indian children were also established in Mexico and Peru, perhaps the most noted one being the College of Santiago in New Spain. The king ordered Mendoza to see that

---

[9] Riva Palacio, II, 520; García Icazbalceta, Joaquín, *Obras* (Mexico, 1905), Tomo I, 175–176.

[10] King to the viceroy, 1550, *Documentos inéditos . . . . de Indias*, XXIII, 525–526; Mendoza to Velasco, *Instrucciones que los vireyes . . . .* art. 12, pp. 228–229; Riva Palacio, II, 519–520; Priestley, *The Mexican Nation*, 118.

[11] Court to Amarillas, 1755, *Instrucciones que los vireyes . . . .* arts. 12–13, p. 64.

[12] Memorial of Toledo, 1596, *Documentos inéditos . . . . de Indias*, VI, 521; *Recopilación*, ley 11, tit. 23, lib. 1.

the building was repaired and provide what was necessary. Likewise the queen, who was much interested in this institution, asked the viceroy to give his opinions to her concerning the ability of the natives to learn the sciences and arts. When the same viceroy was serving in Peru, on December 25, 1551, the king commanded him to build a school for Indian children at the expense of Francisco de Chávez, a captain of Pizarro's army, who had killed six hundred native children to avenge the death of his master.[13] In 1797 Branciforte was grieved at the ignorance of the Indians, who did not even know the Spanish language; therefore he founded in Mexico schools for natives, and expressed the hope that his successor would care for those institutions.[14]

Mendoza also established a school for destitute girls. Besides being instructed in religion, the pupils learned sewing and embroidering. When they reached the proper age marriages were arranged for them. At the same time Mendoza created a school for abandoned children of both sexes in the province of Michoacan.[15]

In 1539 the establishment of the University of Mexico was seriously thought of because of the large number of children who were sent to Spain to take courses in the schools. Mendoza submitted the suggestion to the king and on September 25, 1551, he ordered the viceroy to found a university. The oidor Rodríguez de Quesada was chosen the first rector. The government of the university was of course medieval, and was under the control of the students, professors, and alumni, who elected the rector annually. The fees for matriculation were moderate; as a result nearly thirty thousand bachelor's degrees, many master's degrees, and about one thousand doctoral degrees were conferred between 1553 and 1775.[16]

[13] *Documentos inéditos . . . . de Mexico*, XV, 62, 71–72; *Documentos inéditos . . . . de Indias*, XVIII, 481.

[14] To Azanza, *Instrucciones que los vireyes . . . .* art. 92, p. 141.

[15] Mendoza to Velasco, *ibid.*, art. 12, p. 229 Riva Palacio, II, 520; *Recopilación*, leyes 17–19, tit. 3, lib. 1; Zamacois, IV, 618.

[16] Riva Palacio, II, 520–521; Priestley, *The Mexican Nation*, 77, 152, 153.

In Peru the most noted institutions for higher learning under
the royal patronage were the colleges of San Felipe, San Martín,
Santo Toribio, the University of San Marcos in Lima, and the
University of Córdova. The first of these colleges was immediately dependent upon the vice-patron, since the funds for its
establishment came from the royal treasury. He provided twelve
fellowships with the advice of the rector and the steward. In
San Martín, built in 1582 during the administration of Martín
Enríquez, the king always reserved twelve fellowships which the
viceroy filled. The third college was established by the archbishop of the same name. In the University of San Marcos of
Cuzco the viceroy gave the fellowships to the sons of the noble
inhabitants of the viceroyalty. San Martín of the same city was
under the management of the Jesuits, but there were two fellowships reserved for the viceroy's appointment.[17]

The vice-patron, perhaps, had more duties to perform in the
larger universities of South America. Viceroy Castellar was
commanded to form a junta, composed of the rector, the maestre-
escuela, a doctor and three oidores of the audiencia whom he
chose, to examine everything pertaining to the University of
Lima. The junta was held on September 26, 1676, and some
changes were proposed in regard to the voting for professors by
the students. A royal cédula of September 24, 1754, enjoined
Viceroy Superunda himself to investigate the course of study in
this university. In order to fulfil a royal decree of 1768, Viceroy
Amat ordered that all graduates, professors, and masters of the
universities in Peru should take an oath to observe and teach the
doctrine according to the Council of Constance.[18] At first the
University of Cordova was under the administration of the
Jesuits, but after their expulsion the chief authority was vested

---

[17] Amat to his successor, 1773, *Memorias de los vireyes* . . . . IV, 482–
485; Liñan to Palata, 1681, *ibid.*, I, 296–297; Superunda to his successor,
1761, *ibid.*, IV, 68–69.

[18] Castellar to Liñan, 1681, *ibid.*, I, 172–173; Superunda to his successor,
1761, *ibid.*, IV, 67; Amat to his successor, 1773, *ibid.*, IV, 481–482.

in the governor of Buenos Aires and later in the viceroy, who appointed the rector and the professors.

A number of viceroys became enthusiastic patrons of education and culture long before any attempts were made to establish schools in the neighboring English and French colonies. Already we have seen how the first viceroy of New Spain tried to dispel ignorance. The elder Velasco followed his splendid example; one of his first acts when assuming office was to summon the teachers of the schools and colleges, in order to urge them to be careful concerning the education of the young. Enríquez tried to aid education as much as possible, and made its needs known to the king.[19] The Count of Galve was interested in promoting the use of the Spanish language, and created schools for this purpose. ''The instruction of youth and the promotion of science and art is one of the fundamental principles of good government . . . .'' said the culture-loving Viceroy Guirior of Nueva Granada, who always tried to encourage education within his jurisdiction. It was he who established a public library in Santa Fé.[20]

Matías de Gálvez of Mexico patronized the Academy of Fine Arts, named San Carlos, where painting, sculpture, and architecture were taught. He influenced the king to endow the institution with nine thousand pesos annually. Gálvez also granted exclusive privilege to Manuel Valdés to publish the *Gaceta* of the viceroyalty, and the concession was approved by the king on February 4, 1785, at which time it was requested that some attention be given to geographical subjects and natural history. The cultured Espeleta established elementary schools in the capital of Nueva Granada, and soon had them extended to all the other towns. The second Revillagigedo took measures to

---

[19] Cavo, lib. 4, art. 10, p. 107; Rivera Cambas, I, 35; Enríquez to Coruna, 1580, *Instrucciones que los vireyes . . . .* art. 14, p. 248.

[20] Rivera Cambas, I, 272; Coroleu, I, 337–338.

found schools in many towns of his viceroyalty where efficient teachers were to be employed.[21]

Mexico has the honor of having the first printing press in the New World one hundred years before her English neighbor to the north. Viceroy Mendoza brought it with him from Europe, and in 1536 the first work, entitled *La escala espiritual* by San Juan Clímaco was published.[22] This book was followed by grammars, dictionaries, and the writings of missionaries in the native languages. The elder Revillagigedo established the first public library in New Spain, which began with the collection of books left for this purpose by Juan Gómez de Parada, the bishop of Guadalajara.[23]

During the rule of Espeleta in Nueva Granada the first periodical appeared, the viceroy being its protector. The first number of this publication was sent to a literary society in Lima with the viceroy's recommendation. Thus through his patronage, Espeleta encouraged the spread of those liberal ideas which were to weaken the Spanish rule in America. In Peru Viceroy Lemos approved the creation of a periodical presenting articles relating to the progress of the kingdom, and offered material from the archives for publication. In this way, under the protection of the viceroy the *Mercurio Peruano* came into existence. Later in 1793, Lemos made arrangement for the printing of the *Gaceta de Lima*. The viceroy considered that it was essential for the people to have the proper means to receive correct news.[24]

The study of science was promoted by the viceroys, hence scientific thought soon became as advanced in the colonies, especially in New Spain and Nueva Granada, as in Europe. The collection of botanical specimens had been desired by the kings

[21] Rivera Cambas, I, 450; Coroleu, I, 342; Revillagigedo, *Instrucción reservada*, arts. 335–336.

[22] González Obregón, *México viejo*, 593. For further details consult García Icazbalceta, *Obras*, Tomo I, pp. 1, *et seq.*

[23] Zamacois, IV, 596; Rivera Cambas, I, 378.

[24] Coroleu, I, 341–342; Lemos to Vallenari, 1796, *Memorias de los vireyes* . . . . VI, 97.

from an early date, and perhaps the greatest advance made in the sciences in Mexico City was the Botanical Garden. The organization in 1777 of a botanical expedition to Ecuador and Chile influenced Viceroy Góngora of Nueva Granada to establish researches in botany in his viceroyalty. He chose José Celestino Mutis, a man whose name was well known in Europe and who had more than twenty years of experience in collecting specimens, as director of the bureau which was created. The principal result of the scientific activities was the discovery of many oils, gums, rosins, precious woods, and the tea of Bogotá.[25]

Medical science was not neglected. In 1785 the king ordered that a room should be set aside in the royal hospital of San Andrés in Lima for the study of anatomy under professors of medicine. This course was intended to teach how to preserve the public health in the city. With the assistance of Viceroy Lemos three thousand eight hundred and thirty pesos were collected for the building of an ampitheater for dissecting and operating. Another five hundred pesos were gathered for establishing a chair of anatomy and purchasing instruments.[26] Viceroy Góngora of Nueva Granada also founded a chair for instruction in medical science in the College of Rosario and contemplated the formation of a public clinic for the care of the poor.[27] All cases of leprosy were sent to the hospital of San Lázaro in Lima, and Viceroy Avilés commanded that discoveries made by Doctor Baltazar Villalobos for curing this disease should be tried there. On June 19, 1804, the physician began his experiment with twelve cases. In a few months the patients were examined by the members of the medical board. One was pronounced entirely cured and the others showed good results.[28]

During the epidemic of 1779 in Mexico Viceroy Mayorga assigned a room in the hospital of San Hipólito for the vaccina-

---

[25] Revillagigedo, *Instrucción reservada*, art. 47; Coroleu, I, 340–341.

[26] Lemos to Vallenari, 1796, *Memorias de los vireyes . . . .* VI, 97–98.

[27] Moses, *Spain's Declining Power*, 226.

[28] Avilés to Abascal, 1806, *Memoria del virey del Peru*, 22–23.

tion of anyone who wished it. Finally in 1801 the value of
Jenner's discovery was recognized by the Spanish government
and the professor of medicine, Alejandro Arboleya, was commissioned to introduce vaccination into America. His method of
preserving vaccine was defective, so Iturrigaray had some of
the fluid imported from Havana. The viceroy permitted his little
son to be vaccinated as an example for others. From New Spain
the vaccine was taken to Manila, New Granada, Buenos Aires,
Peru, and Guatemala.[29]

2. HOSPITALS

From the very early days of the conquest governors had been
requested to set aside in every town a house to be used as a
hospital for the poor. When a new town was established it was
customary to build a hospital near the church or in a cloister of it,
whereupon the royal patronage was extended to the institution.[30]

The royal hospital for Indians of Mexico City, founded during
the rule of Mendoza in 1540, was under the care of the viceroy.
A superintendent was in charge of the hospital, but the viceroy
was expected to visit it on frequent occasions. Sometimes he
delegated the power of inspection to the oidores of the audiencia.[31]

The hospital of San Andrés in the same city was controlled
by the archbishop, and other similar establishments in the
country were intrusted to the orders of San Juan de Dios, San
Hipólito, and the Bethlehemites, but the viceroy had a right to
inspect their financial condition. At any time he could order
the accountants of the treasury to show the condition of their

---

[29] Cavo, arts. 42, 19–20, pp. 332, 670–671; Zamacois, V, 628.

[30] *Recopilación*, leyes 1–2, tit. 4, lib. 1.

[31] Revillagigedo to Amarillas, 1754, *Instrucciones que los vireyes* .... art.
157, p. 32; Court to Amarillas, 1755, *ibid.*, art. 14, p. 64; Marfil to Cagigal,
1760, *ibid.*, 106–107; Cagigal to Cruillas, *ibid.*, 116; Marquina to Iturrigaray,
1803, *ibid.*, art. 20, p. 162; Revillagigedo, *Instrucción reservada*, art 50;
Recopilación, ley 3, tit. 4, lib. 1. The daily number of patients in this
hospital was 220 and at times 300. In 1776 the number increased to 3287.
During the epidemic of 1736 the sick cared for were 8361 daily. González
Obregón, *México viejo*, 80.

books.[32] By 1736 there were nine government controlled hospitals, besides several private ones, in Mexico City. In 1774 another hospital for the insane was added. The father superior of the order of San Hipólito laid the matter of the insane before Bucareli, who applied to the consulado for the necessary funds to begin the work. Six thousand pesos were furnished from the avería, and the consulado financed the construction of the building. On the birthday of Charles III, January 20, all the demented inmates of the other institutions were with the aid of the viceroy transferred to the new establishment.[33]

There were four hospitals in Lima in 1604. The Indian Hospital of Santa Ana belonged to the royal patronage. For the support of this institution and others in their towns, the Indians of Peru contributed a tomín to the corregidores and alcaldes mayores when they paid their tributes. Under Castel-Fuerte the annual funds of this hospital were five thousand pesos, and in 1732 five hundred cases were treated there in one month.[34]

There was also the hospital of San Andrés for poor Spaniards, which Viceroy Velasco put under the control of a board of twenty-four persons of ability. The hospital of San Diego for convalescents was under the same board of directors as San Andrés. The hospital of Espíritu Santo for mariners was supported by alms taken from their salaries. There was a hospital for the aged at Lima in which the second Cañete was much interested. He even sent food from his own table for the inmates.[35]

The hospital of La Caridad for women, San Bartolomé for Negroes and mulattoes of both sexes, and San Lázaro for lepers

[32] Court to Amarillas, 1755, *Instrucciones que los vireyes* . . . . art. 13, p. 92; Marquina to Iturrigaray, 1803, *ibid.*, art. 21, p. 162; *Recopilación, leyes* 12–13, tit. 4, lib. 1.

[33] Cavo, lib. 2, arts. 4, 6, pp. 271–272; *Suplemento* de Bustamante, *ibid.*, art. 26, pp. 318–319.

[34] Velasco to Monterey, 1604, *Documentos inéditos* . . . . *de Indias*, IV, 430–431; *Recopilación, leyes* 7–8, tit. 4, lib. 1; Castel-Fuerte to Villagarcía, 1736, *Memorias de los vireyes* . . . . III, 123–124.

[35] Velasco to Monterey, 1604, *Documentos inéditos* . . . . *de Indias*, IV, 430–432; Account concerning Cañete, *ibid.*, VIII, 363–364.

were later added to hospitals under the royal patronage in Lima. Abascal founded a great hospital in the same city and united it with the school of medicine. There were other hospitals in Lima which were not under the direct control of the vice-patron, as San Pedro for priests and Nuestra Señora de Atocha for foundling children, but they were considered worthy of assistance by the government.[36]

Permission for founding hospitals had to be obtained from the king, but sometimes viceroys might agree temporarily to the establishment of hospitals, while waiting for the royal cédula. When Doña Josefa Cordeo, an inhabitant of the city of Ica, wished to establish a hospital and a home for neglected children, Viceroy Teodoro de Croix gave his consent for the work until the king's approval could be received.[37]

3. CHARITY

Public charity, as at the present time in Latin-American countries, was largely under the control of the church and can be considered a branch of the royal patronage. The Indians were always objects of charity, and there were plenty of other needy people in the larger cities. Viceroy Velasco built schools in Lima for poor children, paid the teachers who instructed them, and set aside money obtained from the tribute for their maintenance. Private charity was always welcomed. For four or five years a good man of Lima gathered together and trained needy Spanish children. Viceroy Flórez of Nueva Granada was interested in the poor and orphans, and he caused houses, where they could find shelter, to be erected for them.[38]

There was a hermitage of charity in Lima which the viceroy cared for in an indirect way. Here many poor people, widows,

36 Superunda to his successor, 1761, *Memorias de los vireyes* . . . . IV, 63–64; Liñan to Palata, 1681, *ibid.*, I, 285; Coroleu, II, 167.

37 Croix to Lemos, 1790, *Memorias de los vireyes* . . . . V, 31–32.

38 Velasco to Monterey, 1604, *Documentos inéditos* . . . . *de Indias*, IV, 433–434; Coroleu, I, 338.

girls and sick persons were collected. It is said that forty or fifty marriages were planned every year for the doncellas, who were each given a dowry of four hundred pesos. Velasco established in Lima a house of refuge for women of bad reputation. The patroness of the hospital of San Diego donated a house, which the viceroy aided financially for this purpose.[39] In the same city, Viceroy Lemos founded a house of correction named ''Las Amparadas de la Purísima Concepción.'' The institution was under the patronage, and later Viceroy Liñan asked the king for three thousand pesos annually for its support.[40]

There were other establishments of a similar nature in the capital of Peru. The first Cañete provided a home where poor girls, the descendants of the conquistadores, could find refuge.[41] In 1690 Viceroy Monclova gathered all scandalous women into such a house, which was maintained entirely from alms. Viceroys were required to be informed concerning the number of women and girls educated there. At the beginning of the nineteenth century Avilés learned that the women were free to enter and go out of this house whenever they liked. He therefore commanded the porter to close the doors at eight o'clock at night and only open them after that hour in cases of great urgency.[42]

Occasionally viceroys took much pleasure in the distribution of charity. The second Cañete made contributions from the tributes to deserving old men in Lima. In 1685 Viceroy Laguna gave one thousand pesos of alms for the virgin of Los Remedios in Mexico.[43] In 1761 when Viceroy Solís of Nueva Granada entered a convent, he gave thirty thousand pesos to the hospital of San Juan de Dios and the remainder of his possessions to the poor. The charity of Teodoro de Croix, reputed to be the poorest

[39] *Documentos inéditos . . . . de Indias*, IV, 432.

[40] Liñan to Palata, 1681, *Memorias de los vireyes . . . .* I, 285–286.

[41] Cañete to the Emperor, 1556, *Documentos inéditos . . . . de Indias*, IV, 105.

[42] Avilés to Abascal, 1806, *Memoria del virey del Peru*, 14–16.

[43] Account concerning Cañete, *Documentos inéditos . . . . de Indias*, VIII, 372–373; Diario de Don Juan Antonio Rivera, *Documentos para la historia de Mexico*, serie 2, pt. VI, p. 32.

man in Lima, was inexhaustible. He generously assisted hospitals, beggars, prisoners, mendicant friars, and the sick. When he left Peru the admiral of the fleet was obliged to advance to him money for the expense of his passage. At the port a poor woman was awaiting him to ask alms for the maintenance of her children. The viceroy, finding his pockets empty, exclaimed: "It shall not be that the last poor woman who asks for aid before my departure shall go away with empty hands." Taking his sword he broke off the point which was of silver and gave it to the poor woman. At his own expense and that of his wife, Avilés built the hospital of refuge for women in Lima.[44]

Poorhouses were likewise under the royal patronage. Bucareli caused one of these institutions to be opened in New Spain on February 2, 1774, where two hundred and fifty destitute persons of both sexes found refuge. It was managed by an administrative junta, which had at its disposal annually nineteen thousand pesos from alms, without mentioning the funds from other pious works.[45] Workshops were established in the buildings, where occupation was given to the needy of both sexes according to their intelligence and strength. The articles made by the inmates were sold and the money was used to help keep up the institution. Sometimes wealthy citizens left funds for poorhouses, as did Francisco de Zúñiga in Mexico and Diego de Guevara in Lima.[46] In 1757 the latter gentleman offered his wealth to Superunda for this work and the king gave his permission on November 24, 1759. The royal order was not carried out until 1765, a fact which shows how long viceroys could withhold the king's decrees. Later Viceroy O'Higgins formed a society entitled "Beneficencia Pública" to establish factories for spinning where the poor might be employed.[47]

[44] Coroleu, I, 336; *ibid.*, II, 167; Croix, *Correspondance*, 250.

[45] *Suplemento de Bustamante,* to Cavo, art. 25, p. 318.

[46] Marquina to Iturrigaray, 1803, *Instrucciones que los vireyes . . . .* art. 104 *et seq.*, p. 177.

[47] Avilés to Abascal, 1806, *Memoria del virey del Peru,* 40.

The monte de piedad or pawnshop in Mexico City, founded by
the Count of Regla with a capital of three hundred thousand
pesos, was under the royal patronage. This institution was
established for the purpose of aiding the public by loaning money
on jewels and other articles. The second Revillagigedo spoke of
having appointed the officials of the establishment.[48] He also
suggested to the royal court that a pawnshop for the very poor
be created with funds from the lottery. The monte de piedad of
the Count of Regla refused to make loans of less than three pesos;
as a matter of fact the capital was seething with beggars and
needy persons who did not possess personal effects to this amount.
In a royal cédula of July 15, 1797, the king thanked the viceroy
for his solicitude and authorized him to apply money from the
lottery for the work.[49] There was a monte de ánimas in Lima
under the immediate protection of the viceroy and the archbishop. Its constitution, approved by royal decree of October 20,
1792, was modeled upon that of the pawnshop in Mexico.[50]

The care of widows and orphans was a special charge of the
viceroys. In 1765 the montepío militar was introduced into New
Spain as a kind of charitable institution to maintain widows and
orphans of military officers. On July 31, 1779, the king designated a third of the income of vacant religious offices to be
applied for this purpose, but the bulk of the fund came from a
monthly payment which every officer gave and a tax of one-half
per cent of his pay. His widow or children received annually
one-fourth of the salary he was receiving at the time of his death.
This device for making the military service more attractive had,
by the year 1793, brought into the royal treasury, which adminis-

---

[48] Croix, *Instrucción que . . . . dejó*, AGI, 88–5–13; Revillagigedo,
Instrucción reservada, arts. 1407–1408.

[49] *Suplemento de Bustamante*, to Cavo, arts. 148–149, p. 389.

[50] The officials were a director, a treasurer, a contador, a fiscal and over
all a judge of the audiencia presided with the title of judge protector.
Avilés to Abascal, *Memoria del virey del Peru*, 18. The monte de piedad
in Mexico had a judge of auction and an inspector besides the first four
officials named, but no judge protector. Revillagigedo, *Instrucción reservada*,
art. 1407.

tered its funds, over 360,000 pesos, and left, after all expenses had been paid, a surplus of over 280,000 pesos.[51]

In the foregoing two chapters we have learned that the royal patronage in America was granted by the pope to the Spanish sovereigns because of their services against the infidels. This authority in religious matters was jealously guarded by the king, who intrusted it to no one but his highest representatives in the New World. As vice-patron the viceroy had a certain prestige though his influence depended largely upon his personality. He aided the clergy in their missionary enterprises, supervised the building of churches and convents, saw that they were located on desirable sites, and attended to their repair. However, in order to establish a new church, mission, college or hospital, all the reasons therefor had to be sent to the Council of the Indies and the consent of the king obtained. The vice-patron saw that all ecclesiastics coming to America had licenses, and he inspected their papers granting them the right to preach.

The archbishop and dignitaries of the secular clergy were subject to the legal control of the vice-patron, but at the same time he protected them and their representatives on the long journeys to the frontiers. The secularization of parishes and finding capable priests to replace the religious occupied the attention of a number of viceroys. The vice-patron was expected to inform himself concerning the number of persons who had taken vows under the various religious orders in his viceroyalty and see that they lived according to their monastic rules. He had charge of the general direction of missions and their extension to the more distant frontiers; he was made responsible for all measures incident to the epoch-making expulsion of the Jesuits and the later administration of their estates; and he supervised the collection of the contributions of the church to the state.

The principal annoyance pertaining to discharge of the vice-patron's functions was the settling of endless religious differences

---

[51] *Ordenanza . . . . de intendentes . . . .* art. 208; Revillagigedo, *Instrucción reservada,* arts. 734–735, 738, 1390–1391.

and misdemeanors. Appointments in the church were virtually under the control of the clergy, but certain formalities, like the choosing of one of the three names submitted to him, belonged to the vice-patron. He had a slight control over elections by his designation of a royal assistant to attend the examination of the competitors for office, and prelates might not remove ecclesiastics from their positions without first informing the viceroy concerning the cause for taking such action.

The viceroy had the right to attend the provincial church councils, and whatever action was taken in the annual synodical councils had to be submitted for his approval. The chief questions between church and state in America arose from the occasional interference of the papal nuncio of Spain in colonial affairs and the sending of papal bulls to ecclesiastics in the viceroyalties without the sanction of the Council of the Indies. It was the duty of the viceroy to collect all such bulls and send them back to Spain before there was time for publication. Many quarrels, usually over questions concerning their respective powers or matters of precedence and ceremonies, occurred between viceroys and archbishops. The vice-patron settled all the differences of the tribunal of the Inquisition with the other courts, tried to prevent it from exceeding its jurisdiction, and attended autos de fé. He also exercised the same power over the tribunal of the cruzada and saw that the money made from the sale of indulgences was collected for the royal treasury.

The viceroy was likewise vice-patron over institutions of learning. He conferred fellowships and professorships in the colleges under the royal patronage, but left their administration entirely to the prelates. Some of the viceroys were enthusiastic patrons of education, culture, and science long before their English and French neighbors made any attempts to found schools. The rules of the patronage applied to hospitals and institutions of charity, as well as to schools; therefore the viceroy acted as superintendent 'over them. Although the vice-patron did not originate many important ecclesiastical measures, the people always looked to him in times of crises. On such occasions he acted temporarily and gave account to the king later. An executive might devote a great deal of time to the duties of vice-patron, or he could very easily shun them. They gave the widest opportunity to encourage all the beneficent and gracious influences of colonial life. The vice-patron was the chief responsible agent of Spain in her long task of transmitting to America the best of her culture and spirit. Most of the viceroys, even if they did not envisage the task in full appreciation of its deep historical significance, discharged their duties capably, with the interests of the subjects of the king at heart.

CHAPTER VII

THE VICEROY AS CAPTAIN-GENERAL

The rank of captain-general was the highest military title conferred by the king, either in Spain or America. It was, perhaps, the most essential office in the New World, since it kept the native population in subjection, preserved order among the Spaniards, and defended the colonies from foreign enemies. From the very beginning the military aspect of events was predominant in the Spanish-American possessions, and it increased with the dangers of foreign wars, so that the captaincy-general became the dominant aspect of government under the later viceroys. The duties of the captain-general included putting down internal revolts and piracy, participation in foreign wars for colonial defense, and exploration and extension of the frontiers. The viceroy's relations with the home government and his activities in discharge of his military functions are now to be discussed.

That the mother country regarded these functions as most important, may be understood from the fact that military men were usually chosen for viceroys. This was true especially on the eve of Spanish-American independence, when it seems that the military side of the administration was emphasized at the expense of the civil. The second Revillagigedo clearly expressed his ideas concerning the captain-general by saying that his tasks were of a higher and more extensive nature than those of the governor, vice-patron, or superintendent of the treasury. He thought that better results would have been obtained if the same powers had been extended to all branches of government.[1]

---

[1] *Instrucción reservada*, arts. 512, 514.

1. INITIATIVE IN MILITARY MATTERS

The viceroy acted more on his own initiative as captain-general than in any other office. In cases of emergency for which he had no instructions, he did as he thought best and informed the king later. Strategical measures during a sudden attack by an enemy could not be arranged for beforehand in Spain; therefore the highest military chieftain had absolute freedom. If there was plenty of time he might confer with the junta de guerra, but ordinarily that body could not be summoned quickly enough for consultation. In 1793, when the news of the war with France reached Peru, Viceroy Lemos took defensive measures to avoid any surprises. The entire coast was divided into three comandancias generales, each one hundred leagues in extent. The central one, including Lima, was under the control of the captain-general himself, and the other two under commanders whom he appointed. Watches were established at different points, and the viceroy gave instructions to the comandantes in the north and south concerning various matters of defense. This scheme was not approved by the king until the next year.[2] During the war with England, Marquina in New Spain adopted strategic methods whereby Vera Cruz might be defended and communication with the interior of the kingdom be kept open.[3]

Mendoza was authorized to act on his own responsibility and provide what was necessary in the building of fortifications, whenever he saw that harm would result from delay of royal measures. In 1559 the Count of Nieva was granted extraordinary power to be used only in case of rebellion in Peru. After consulting with the audiencia or two of the treasury officials, he could draw from the treasury the amount that he thought

---

[2] Lemos to Vallenari, 1796, *Memorias de los vireyes* . . . . VI, 314–317.

[3] To Iturrigaray, 1803, *Instrucciones que los vireyes* . . . . art. 208, pp. 189–190.

sufficient for the pacification of the province. Later, viceroys of New Spain also enjoyed this right.[4]

The captain-general might declare war against the Indians. Having conferred with the most trustworthy residents in Cuzco and with the cabildo, after reviewing all persons capable of bearing arms and inspecting the munitions, Viceroy Toledo declared war upon the rebellious Inca of that region. The viceroy likewise made treaties of peace with native tribes, as Velasco the younger of Mexico did with the Chichimecs in 1591.[5]

The first Alburquerque was given unusual authority for the reoccupation of Jamaica. At the request of the governor of the island, he arranged to send aid before receiving the royal order to do so. Another notable instance of viceroyal initiative in military matters was the case of Colonia, on the border of Brazil and Paraguay. By the treaty of 1701 the town had been ceded to Portugal, but in the War of the Spanish Succession this nation went against Spain; accordingly Viceroy Monclova of Peru assumed that he was not bound by the treaty and commanded the governor of Rio de la Plata to take possession of the post, which was done on October 17, 1704. At the end of the war, however upon the insistence of England, Colonia was again returned to Portugal.[6]

Sometimes the king permitted the captain-general to vary royal measures. Fuenclara was empowered to change them to suit the circumstances with respect to the defense of Vera Cruz. Bucareli assumed authority to postpone for a year an exploring voyage to the northwest ordered by the king, so that he might send a supply ship to California, lest Spain lose that important possession.[7]

4 King to Mendoza, 1535, *Documentos inéditos . . . . de Indias*, XXIII, 440, 444; Instruction of the princess to Nieva, 1559, *ibid.*, XXV, 52–53; Rivera Cambas, I, 199.

5 Account concerning Toledo, *Documentos inéditos . . . . de Indias*, VIII, 271; Cavo, lib. 5, art. 23, p. 146.

6 Rivera Cambas, I, 199; Moses, *Spain's Declining Power*, 27–28.

7 Fuenclara, *Instrucción reservada*, April 23, 1742, AGI, 90–2–17, art. 5; Chapman, C. E., *A History of California, The Spanish Period* (New York, 1921), 284–286.

The captain-general drew up military instructions for the viceroyalty. On August 25, 1790, the second Revillagigedo formed regulations for guarding the coasts of Vera Cruz, and the next year they were approved by the king. Teodoro de Croix sent instructions for defense to the intendants of each province in Peru and inserted a copy of the royal order charging him to defend the viceroyalty from attacks by the English, who were at war with Spain. Again in 1796, when war was declared between England and Spain, Branciforte published bandos ordering the governors, military leaders, and intendants of Mexico to take all necessary protective measures.[8]

A new viceroy usually examined the fortifications of the port where he landed, and occasionally made trips of inspection to the coast during his administration. Mancera decided to make one of these journeys to Vera Cruz to provide for its defense.[9] When Spain joined France and the United States in the war against England, Viceroy Mayorga did the same thing. Before Revillagigedo made his regulations for guarding the coasts, Charles IV had ordered him to inspect the ports of his kingdom and examine the artillery and munitions.[10] In 1801 Marquina marched to Vera Cruz to examine the fort of San Juan de Ulúa and to provide what was needed for it.[11] During the early days the viceroy personally reviewed the troops, but later the task was performed by the subinspector-general. Marquina wished to revive this duty, and his successor is said to have actually performed it to arouse the military spirit among the Mexicans.[12]

When subordinate officers committed misdeeds, the viceroy as the highest military authority reprimanded them. Marquina reproached the governor of Vera Cruz for lack of precaution

---

[8] Revillagigedo, *Instrucción reservada*, art. 899; Croix to Lemos, 1790, *Memorias de los vireyes* .... V, 240; Rivera Cambas, I, 492–493.

[9] *Recopilación*, ley 13, tit. 3, lib. 3; Rivera Cambas, I, 231.

[10] Riva Palacio, II, 761, 856; Rivera Cambas, I, 477.

[11] *Suplemento de Bustamante*, to Cavo, art. 211, p. 659.

[12] Marquina to Iturrigaray, 1803, *Instrucciones que los vireyes* .... art, 226, pp. 192–193; *Suplemento de Bustamante*, to Cavo, art. 28, p. 674.

when enemy vessels were reported to him and for slowness in obeying the viceroy's measures. Iturrigaray severely censured the comandante-general of California for having permitted the Russian, Resanov, to disembark at San Francisco for a conference and to obtain provisions.[13]

2. MILITARY ASSISTANTS OF THE VICEROY

The junta de guerra, a council of military men, assisted the viceroy as commander-in-chief of the army in time of war. Croix says,

. . . . A vicéroy has much to do in the line of warfare and cannot attend to everything [himself], therefore it is necessary for him to make use of advice and . . . . apply it. This influenced the Count of Revillagigedo in the time of his viceroyship to propose, divide, and delimit districts and to appoint officials [over them] who should command under the orders of the viceroy, giving account of everything to him.[14]

The viceroy mentioned by Croix thought that checking Indian hostilities and deciding military cases were sufficient to occupy him, when there was no danger from foreign invasions. The laws of the Indies enjoined captains-general to avoid Indian wars as much as possible, but they often could not be prevented or the viceroy be relieved from the burdens which they caused.[15]

The junta de guerra as an advisory body was not always a great success. Palata of Peru said that in order to avoid complaints from those who believed that military matters could not be managed without their opinion, he held juntas with the principal leaders of the army, but the viceroy was criticized frequently because he did not heed all their ideas. Later, Teodoro de Croix summoned juntas in the same country to discuss certain financial matters relating to army, military discipline, the reform

---

[13] Marquina to Iturrigaray, 1803, *Instrucciones que los vireyes* . . . . art. 209, p. 190; Rivera Cambas, I, 529.

[14] Croix, *Instrucción que* . . . . *dejó*, AGI, 88–5–13.

[15] Revillagigedo to Amarillas, 1754, *Instrucciones que los vireyes* . . . . art. 126, p. 27; *Recopilación*, leyes 8–9, tit. 4, lib. 3.

of some battalions, and the regulation of the price of transportation of soldiers from Peru to Spain. The visitor as well as the viceroy was present at those gatherings.[16] Sometimes the superior military chief went to Vera Cruz to attend councils of war, only to accomplish nothing because of hostile opinions.[17] Thus we see that the junta might act as a limitation upon the military powers of the viceroy. There was no regularly organized general staff, though several officials might be called upon for advice. The auditor de guerra, a kind of special counsel, dispatched matters pertaining to the junta de guerra. Viceroy Castel-Fuerte thought that this office ought always to be given to a judge of the audiencia, since it was so important.[18] Even so, the viceroy might ignore his auditor de guerra, as Croix did in New Spain, and seek the advice of an assessor of his own choosing.[19] There were to be eight military engineers at the disposal of the viceroy of Mexico, but Marquina complained in 1803 that only four were available.[20]

The subinspector-general, appointed by the king, was next in rank to the captain-general. In 1764 Juan de Villalba first held this office in New Spain, whither he was sent to organize an army. Dissension soon arose between him and Viceroy Cruíllas over their respective powers. The viceroy won in this contention and Villalba was replaced in 1768 by the Marquis of Rubí.[21] He submitted to the viceroy a plan for improving the condition of the presidios of the Provincias Internas, which he had inspected. Subinspector Francisco Crespo prepared a complete scheme for reorganizing the military forces in Mexico, which with some slight modifications was approved by the king on October 20,

---

[16] Palata to Monclova, 1689, *Memorias de los vireyes* . . . . II, 276–278; Croix to Lemos, 1790, *ibid.*, V, 222–225.

[17] Marquina to Iturrigaray, 1803, *Instrucciones que los vireyes* . . . . art. 207, p. 189.

[18] To Villagarcía, 1736, *Memorias de los vireyes* . . . . III, 267.

[19] Croix, *Instrucción que* . . . . *dejó*, AGI, 88–5–13; *Correspondance*, 284.

[20] To Iturrigaray, 1803, *Instrucciones que los vireyes* . . . . art. 158, p. 184.

[21] Riva Palacio, II, 820; Bancroft, *History of Mexico*, III, 404–405.

1788. Revillagigedo the younger thought that this office ought to be given to one of the generals in the service of the viceroyalty, for the sake of economy. The request seems to have been granted, since in 1803 we find Marquina asking for the reëstablishment of the inspector-general.[22]

3. PRESERVATION OF PEACE IN THE COLONIES

Preservation of peace was one of the chief duties of the captáin-general. After Pedro de Alvarado had been killed during the Mixtón War, Mendoza collected a force of about six hundred Spaniards and many Indian allies, and in October, 1541, marched to the scene of disturbance. The savages were dealt with summarily and cruelly, but the province was pacified and the city of Valladolid (now Morelia) founded as a defensive measure.[23] In 1570 Enríquez led some troops against the Chichimecs; the revolt was put down and a line of presidios established. We also hear of the Marquis of Guadalcázar going out to restore order in the province of La Plata.[24] Most captains-general were willing to intrust campaigning entirely to their subordinates.

Negroes, as well as Indians, proved to be a source of danger which caused the early viceroys much anxiety, while the white population was still small. In 1537 the Negroes of New Spain, realizing the weakness of the colony, conspired to rise against the Spaniards and elect a king of their own. As soon as Mendoza received an inkling of the plot he took prompt action, dispatching letters to all towns and mines where Negroes were employed. The plot was checked, but the viceroy requested the king not to send any more Negroes. Serious consequences might have resulted from this event, for the Indians knew of the scheme

---

[22] Revillagigedo, *Instrucción reservada*, art. 515; Marquina to Iturrigaray, *Instrucciones que los vireyes* . . . . arts. 285–287, p. 200.

[23] Herrera, IV, decada 7, lib. 2, cap. 12, p. 54; Rivera Cambas, I, 31; Riva Palacio, II, 271–272.

[24] Cavo, lib. 4, art. 32, p. 127; Mancera to his successor, 1648, *in* Polo, *Memorias de los vireyes* . . . . art. 67, p. 23.

and only four hundred and fifty horsemen prepared for warfare
could be found in Mexico City.   In 1546 another Negro rebellion
in the region of Tenocha and Tlatelulco had for its aim the death
of all Spaniards.[25]   Several Negro uprisings occurred at Córdoba,
the most serious one being in 1609.   The rumor came to the ears
of the younger Velasco that the Negroes intended to kill the
whites and elect a slave, Yanga by name, as their king.   At first
he did not believe it, but when he found that there was some
foundation for the report, an expedition was sent to quell the
disturbance.   As late as 1735 a Negro insurrection in the same
district was suppressed by Viceroy Vizarrón.[26]   There were not so
many Negro revolts in South America as in Mexico, but the most
famous case was in Brazil, where the Negro Republic of Palmares,
which lasted for almost half a century, was established.[27]

There were often restless spirits among the whites who disturbed the peace.   In 1549 during the administration of the first
viceroy of New Spain an uprising against the Spanish governors
was instigated by Juan Román, a certain Juan Venegas, and an
unnamed Italian.   Peru abounded in adventurous whites who
were only too ready to create tumults.   The king permitted the
first Cañete to expel the more dangerous characters from the
country, except under certain conditions.[28]   This viceroy tried to
get rid of the riffraff by sending them on expeditions of discovery
and conquest.   The marquis found it necessary to fortify the
house in which he dwelt with ten pieces of artillery, and put it
under the charge of a general from Spain.   Fifty sharpshooters
were stationed in the patio.   His apartment was guarded by day
and night, and twelve halberdiers always accompanied him to the

25 Mendoza to the emperor, 1537, *Documentos inéditos* . . . . *de Indias*, II,
198–200; Cavo, lib. 3, art. 33, p. 98.

26 Riva Palacio, II, 548–550; Zamacois, V, 268–271; Rivera Cambas, I;
93–96, 107–108.

27 For the details *see* Chapman, C. E., ''Palmares: the Negro Numantia,''
in *Journal of Negro History*, III, 1918, pp. 29–32.

28 Cavo, lib. 4, art. 5, p. 103; King to Cañete, 1555, *Documentos inéditos*
. . . . . *de Indias*, XXIII, 548 *et seq.*

sala of the audiencia.[29] The mining region of Potosí was noted for disorders, and when gold was discovered in the province of Paucarolla they were repeated there. In the latter place on June 24, 1665, there was a bloody conflict between the partisans of the wealthiest mine owners, José and Gaspar Salcedo, and the smaller proprietors. By 1688 the affairs of the mines became so critical that Chinchón had to take severe measures to restore order.[30]

Viceroys coöperated with one another and with presidents of audiencias in putting down dangerous revolts. Mendoza made plans to help Pedro de la Gasca restore peace in Peru after the first viceroy, Blasco Núñez Vela, had been killed. In 1547 he enlisted six hundred men under his son Francisco, with Cristóbal de Oñate as maestre de campo. Many persons of high rank in New Spain joined the expedition, but when it was about to embark, news came that the rebellion in Peru had been quelled.[31]

In 1765 when the insurgents of Quito assumed the airs of a victorious party and tried to direct the affairs of the audiencia, the viceroy of Peru aided Cerda of Nueva Granada to place a strong garrison in the city. During the serious war with Tupac Amarú in 1780, Vertíz of Buenos Aires sent three detachments of soldiers to assist the viceroy of Peru in subduing the rebels. When Buenos Aires was captured by the British in 1806, the Peruvians, under the leadership of Viceroy Abascal, sent money, munitions and supplies to that city.[32]

There was often coöperation in the matter of freeing the seas from pirates. In 1587 the viceroy of Peru sent word to New Spain that three enemy ships were off the coast of Chile. This gave the viceroy of Mexico time to strengthen the garrison at Acapulco, and send a vessel to warn the treasure fleet coming

---

[29] Letter of Cañete to the emperor, May 25, 1556, *Documentos inéditos . . . . de Indias*, IV, 90–91, 95.

[30] Moses, *The Spanish Dependencies . . . .* II, 176–177.

[31] Cavo, lib. 4, art. 1, p. 101; Torquemada, I, 611; Riva Palacio, II, 353–354.

[32] Moses, *Spain's Declining Power*, 101–102, 186, 349–350.

from the Philippines. On July 18, 1594, the viceroy of Peru wrote to Velasco informing him that Hawkins had captured Valparaiso and after passing Lima had sailed for New Spain. Sentinels were immediately placed on the coasts of Mexico, fifty men were added to the force at Acapulco, and Alonso de Arellano was sent to warn the Manila galleon.[33]

The problem of restraining bandits on the highways was ever present for the captain-general. Travel was rendered unsafe by the Chichimecs, Otomis, Pimas, Apaches, and in Chile by the fierce Araucanos, who though often defeated were not entirely suppressed until a very late date. Organized bands of brigands lay in wait for the treasure from the mines, and for travelers. No distinction was made between rich and poor; frontier settlers often became victims of horrible atrocities. The first Velasco tried to deal with the situation in Mexico by the establishment of the Santa Hermandad. In Chile a more effective force was needed for the terrible Araucanos. Only the troops could accomplish any permanent results. In 1792 it was necessary for a picket of the garrison from Valdivia to unite with the veteran bodies and the militia of Quinchilca to punish the Indians.[34]

Linares was ordered to establish secret police or a spy system in New Spain, since theft, assassination, and intrigues had not yet abated at the beginning of the eighteenth century. He did little to put this request into effect, for he thought it would show the weakness of the monarchy and might corrupt society by offering the employment of espionage to men already skilled in calumny. During the early struggle for independence Venegas relied upon such a police service as the only means of keeping order in the larger cities.[35]

[33] Villamanrique to Philip II, Oct. 28, 1587, AGI, 58–3–10; Velasco to the king, Oct. 24, 1594, AGI, 58–3–12.

[34] Cavo mentions the hermandad as early as 1554, lib. 4, arts, 13–14, 16, pp. 110–111, 113; Lemos to Vallenari, 1796, *Memorias de los vireyes* . . . . VI, 148–149.

[35] Riva Palacio, II, 767; Letter of Venegas to the cabildo of Mexico, Aug. 18, 1811, *Documentos inéditos* . . . . *de Mexico*, IX, 240–242.

4. EXTERNAL DEFENSE OF THE VICEROYALTIES

As the Spanish colonies were always exposed to the attack of foreign enemies, the viceroy had to be continually on the alert to resist them. To do this he might call upon the encomenderos for money and men. If they refused he was to take away their Indians and give them to more worthy persons. Wealthy residents, the ayuntamiento, and rich merchants could be asked for aid to keep up the necessary armament.[36] The viceroyalties were intended to be self-supporting in all minor military matters, although in case of war financial help was expected from Spain.

Erection of fortifications, especially on the coasts, was under the care of the captains-general, and audiencias might not intermeddle with their duty of providing them. Two treasury officials were to be present during the construction of the works, keeping account of expenses and paying for materials and wages. When they were once established, the viceroy had to see that fortresses were supplied with plenty of munitions and men.[37] The first viceroy took measures, not only to fortify the capital of Mexico, but also the chief seaport.

Vera Cruz was always regarded as the key to the kingdom and the possible entrance for foreign invasion, therefore most viceroys of New Spain made an effort to protect it. At an early date the fortress of San Juan de Ulúa was erected. It must have existed before 1567, since Cavo speaks of Viceroy Peralta withdrawing to the fort after the arrival of the pesquisidores Muñoz and Carillo.[38] The office of castellano of San Juan was one of the most important military positions in New Spain. A law of 1606 declared him to be directly subordinate to the generals of the fleets and not dependent upon the alcalde mayor of the city, appointed by the viceroy. The captain-general was not to pro-

---

[36] Solórzano, II, lib. 5, cap. 13, arts. 28–29, p. 381; *ibid.*, I, lib. 3, cap. 25, art. 36, p. 373; Rivera Cambas, I, 500.

[37] *Recopilación*, leyes 7–8, tit. 6, lib. 3; ley 3, tit. 7, lib. 3.

[38] Bancroft, *History of Mexico*, III, 214; Cavo, lib. 4, cap. 28, p. 124.

ceed against him except in urgent cases, and then the junta de guerra of the Council of the Indies must be informed concerning what had happened and the reason for the action.[39]

Frequent repairs were made on the stronghold by several viceroys. Whenever a war broke out in Europe and there was danger that it might extend to America, the captain-general was enjoined to defend the harbor and strengthen the garrison in the port. When the War of the Spanish Succession occurred, Viceroy Montañez put the fortress in a condition of security, raised companies on the coasts to aid Vera Cruz and Tampico, and hurriedly constructed new ships in Campeche to reinforce the armada of the Windward Islands.[40] In 1742 Fuenclara was notified concerning the activities of the English in the West Indies, ordered to defend Vera Cruz diligently, and requested to see that the governor of San Juan de Ulúa fulfilled his measures. Later, Viceroy Croix supervised the construction of batteries on the promontory of Moncelbo, facing the island of Sacrificios, on the horns of San Rico, and in the port of Alvarado.[41]

The stronghold of Perote, on the route from Vera Cruz to Mexico City, served as a rallying place in case the former town was captured. It was built under the supervision of Viceroy Croix in 1767 and 1768, as a depository for military supplies and a rendezvous for troops. Its climate, being more healthful than that of the immediate seacoast, caused it to be a good place for the cantonment of soldiers.[42]

On the Pacific side of the viceroyalty of New Spain, foreign attacks were not very much feared. It was thought that few enemies would venture to make the long journey around Cape Horn to reach Acapulco. Mancera made some repairs on the fortifications of Acapulco, but the second Alburquerque was the

---

[39] *Recopilación*, leyes 11, 25, tit. 8, lib. 3.

[40] Mancera to Veraguas, 1673, *Instrucciones que los vireyes* . . . . 277; Riva Palacio, II, 754.

[41] Fuenclara, *Instrucción reservada*, April 23, 1742, AGI, 90–2–17, art. 3; Croix, *Instrucción que* . . . . *dejó*, AGI, 88–5–13.

[42] *Ibid.*, AGI, 88–5–13; Marquina to Iturrigaray, 1803, *Instrucciones que los vireyes* . . . . art. 173, pp. 185–186.

first viceroy who began active measures to protect the town. At this time the French had begun to carry on commerce with Peru and were entering the South Sea by the strait of Magellan. The English had also come to the Pacific and had sacked the port of Guayaquil.[43] After Anson had been seen off the coast of Acapulco in February, 1742, the port was again put in a state of defense, and signal stations were erected to warn the galleons, but this did not prevent the Englishman from capturing the treasure ship from the Philippines. The fort was built at the beginning of the seventeenth century; it was in this that Viceroy Croix later collected eighty-one cannons and four hundred and fifty guns with bayonets and some other weapons.[44]

The province of Yucatan was open to repeated foreign attacks. Troops were provided for its defense as early as 1645; in 1672 the king ordered that forts should be built and garrisons placed in them. Although the province was under a governor who acted as captain-general, the viceroy of New Spain was expected to help in its defense as much as possible. During the administration of the Count of Galve the wall around Campeche and its fortresses were begun. The armament of this stronghold was increased from time to time, when danger from pirates and other enemies became threatening. It was also the special duty of the viceroy of Mexico to defend the Philippines, but of course, with the coöperation of the governor of the islands. After the Dutch became menacing by their occupation of the island of Formosa, the king commanded Viceroy Salvatierra to act promptly. He authorized him to collect vagabonds and refugees who wished to enter the military service, and to reward those enlisting voluntarily with habits of the military orders of Santiago, Calatrava, and Alcántara.[45]

43 Mancera to Veraguas, 1673, *Instrucciones que los vireyes* . . . . 278; Riva Palacio, II, 759.

44 Revillagigedo to Amarillas, 1754, *Instrucciones que los vireyes* . . . . art. 137, pp. 28–29; Croix, *Instrucción que* . . . . *dejó*, AGI, 88–5–13.

45 Bancroft, *History of Mexico*, III, 419; Riva Palacio, II, 614.

The coasts of Peru and Chile were so long that it was impossible to fortify all the ports; therefore the method of defense adopted was for the people of the small towns to withdraw inland with all their movable possessions whenever they saw an enemy appear. The port of Callao was an exception. There were numerous attempts to establish a permanent presidio in this seaport, but more dependence was placed upon the Spanish men-of-war stationed in that region.[46] As early as 1604 the king kept four ships of the armada in the harbor to protect the transportation of precious metals from the mines. Occasionally the number of ships dwindled down to three, and perhaps even to a smaller number when the others were being repaired.[47]

Mancera, because of the hostilities of Holland and Portugal, built a wall around Callao and erected several batteries. His preparations for safeguarding the viceroyalty had been so extensive that in 1643 he was able to send against the Dutch who had captured Valdivia an expedition of twelve ships, under the command of his son.[48] Callao was strengthened repeatedly with men and munitions by many executives. A commissioner of war resided in this city, and according to the opinion of Teodoro de Croix the office was considered necessary, for in 1788 he advised the king that it ought to be continued.[49]

Other points of defense for which the viceroy of Peru had to provide were Buenos Aires, Valdivia, Panamá, and the island of Chiloé. The proximity of the Portuguese to Buenos Aires made it imperative to establish a presidio there. During the administration of Salvatierra its garrison consisted of one hundred soldiers.[50]

---

[46] Montesclaros to his successor, 1615, *Documentos inéditos* . . . . *de Indias*, VI, 269–270.

[47] Velasco to Monterey, 1604, *ibid.*, IV, 429–430; Castel-Fuerte to Villagarcía, 1736, *Memorias de los vireyes* . . . . III, 216.

[48] Mancera to his successor, 1648, *in* Polo, *Memorias de los vireyes* . . . . 44–48; Moses, *The Spanish Dependencies* . . . . II, 78.

[49] Croix to Lemos, 1790, *Memorias de los vireyes* . . . . V, 209–210.

[50] Salvatierra to Aliste, 1651, *in* Polo, *Memorias de los vireyes* . . . . art. 84, pp. 71–72.

In Chile during the seventeenth century there was much danger of Dutch invasions. In 1635 Chinchón was ordered to form a settlement in Valdivia and fortify it without burdening the treasury, but he did nothing except draw up plans. Mancera wanted to put this cédula into effect, so he appointed a Portuguese, Francisco Quirós, to examine the harbor. The report of Quirós was unfavorable and showed the difficulty of fortifying the port, hence the project was suspended. After Valdivia was entered by the Dutch in 1643, the armada sent by Mancera established three posts in this town and left six hundred men with supplies and munitions to last two years. The same viceroy took measures to protect Cartagena and Panamá.[51] Viceroy Lemos realized the possibility that the island of Chiloé might serve as a stepping-stone for foreign occupation on the mainland and took up with the comandante of the province the matter of fortifying it.[52]

The pirates of the sixteenth and seventeenth centuries made the task of defense difficult. No sooner had one part of the colonial empire been freed from their raids, than they appeared in another. Enríquez, when he first arrived in New Spain, encountered some English corsair ships under the famous Hawkins anchored at the island of Sacrificios. The viceroy immediately sent three ships of his fleet in pursuit of the invaders, and they were obliged to withdraw. When coming from the West Indies to Vera Cruz, Escalona saw three pirate vessels, so he gave orders for the coasts to be cleared of them.[53]

The laws of the Indies were very rigid concerning matters of piracy. Viceroys had power at any time to dispatch captains against corsairs and call upon justices to aid them. They could administer justice upon captured freebooters without consulting the king, and were to see that the monarch obtained a fifth of

51 Mancera to his successor, 1648, *in* Polo, *Memorias de los vireyes* . . . . arts. 131–133, 122–123, pp. 53–55, 51.

52 Lemos to Vallenari, 1796, *Memorias de los vireyes* . . . . 190–193.

53 Cavo, lib. 4, art. 30, p. 126; García, *Don Juan de Palafox*, 63–65.

all prizes taken. No one in the Indies was to trade with corsairs or foreigners on pain of death and loss of possessions. Governors who were near the pearl fisheries were to keep sentinels always on the lookout for pirates and inform the viceroy of their approach.[54]

After 1567, the year in which the bold Hawkins entered the harbor of Vera Cruz and almost lost his life in making his escape, although the Spanish officials had promised him protection, a seaman's feud arose between the English and Spanish that continued for two centuries, in time of peace as well as war. Drake and his daring followers took their revenge upon the Spanish colonies only too often. By 1578 Drake made his way to Lima, attacked that city, and later committed many depredations along the Pacific Coast. In 1587 on the coast of New Spain Cavendish captured the *Santa Ana* laden with rich goods from China. Other famous pirates soon followed in the wake of Drake, among them Frenchmen like Pié de Palo and Dutchmen who paralyzed Spanish commerce.[55]

Whenever the corsairs became too troublesome, the captain-general was forced to send expeditions to check their raids and protect the treasure fleets. Mancera, having been reproached by the king for not taking more prompt action, dispatched a frigate and three small boats to dislodge some English pirates from the island of Santa Ana, whence they went out to rob three Indian towns, imprisoning the natives, who refused to furnish maize without barter. The enemy vessel was run aground and burned. Another voyage was made to Campeche to drive out the logwood cutters, but nothing was accomplished except the capture of some small crafts and supplies.[56] In 1681 Viceroy Liñan of Peru gave orders for an armed ship to examine the coast of Chile, the island of Juan Fernández and other neighboring shores in search of marauders. Even the king became alarmed, and in

[54] *Recopilación,* leyes 2–4, 8, 11, tit. 13, lib. 3.

[55] Moses, *The Spanish Dependencies* . . . . I, 198; Zamacois, V, 190–192.

[56] Mancera to Veraguas, 1673, *Instrucciones que los vireyes* . . . . 284–285.

a cédula of December 7, 1682, ordered that no boat of any kind should set sail without being well armed and manned.[57]

Vera Cruz was sacked in 1683, in spite of all preventive measures, whereupon the viceroys of Mexico and Peru began to take energetic action for defense. The Marquis of Laguna summoned to the port all the residents of Mexico City capable of bearing arms. A force of about two thousand men was raised. Even the viceroy marched to the coast, but assistance came too late.[58] In Lima a wall was immediately built around the city. Palata asked the cabildo, the university, and the religious orders to contribute to this work; the king permitted the rent from the monopoly of paper to be used for the project.[59]

In 1684 Tampico suffered the fate of Vera Cruz and many of its inhabitants were made prisoners by the corsairs. In the same year the South Sea was again invaded by three enemy ships. Viceroy Palata sent the armada to pursue them, although the king had requested it to be used only for commerce. Campeche was raided in 1685, and the people left destitute, but the viceroy of Mexico sent three hundred thousand pesos to the unfortunate citizens. The king now decided to take a drastic measure, ordering on September 26, 1686, that all pirate captains made prisoner should be put to death and their crews sent to Spain.[60]

We next hear of the coasts of Yucatan being laid waste by corsairs. Viceroy Galve raised an ill-fated expedition against them and put it under the command of Martín Rivas who was mortally wounded in the encounter. In 1718 an undertaking against Laguna de Términos caused the English to take refuge in Jamaica. The pirates returned in a short time from the West Indies and drove out the Spaniards.[61] In a few years the English

[57] Liñan to his successor, 1681, *Memorias de los vireyes* . . . . I, 334–339; Palata to Monclova, 1689, *ibid.*, II, 345.

[58] Rivera Cambas, I, 254–257; Riva Palacio, II, 640.

[59] Palata to Monclova, 1689, *Memorias de los vireyes* . . . . II, 366–370.

[60] Riva Palacio, II, 641–642; Palata to Monclova, 1689, *Memorias de los vireyes* . . . . II, 289–295, 341.

[61] Riva Palacio, II, 651, 769.

pirate, John Clipperton, entered the Pacific by way of Cape Horn, captured a Spanish vessel, and did considerable damage on the western coast of South America. Although Viceroy Morcillo of Peru sent a number of armed vessels in pursuit of him, they returned to Callao without accomplishing their object.[62] Viceroy Superunda in 1745 dispatched a vessel to be on the lookout for the English who were on their way to the South Sea with four ships under Captain Barnet. Governors all along the coasts were commanded to watch for the foreign sails and report to the viceroy.[63]

During the latter half of the eighteenth century French vessels, and boats from the small republic of the United States, many of them of piratical character, appeared in Spanish waters. Coast guard ships never succeeded in entirely freeing the colonies from their pillagings. A law of the Indies, dated 1627, commanded viceroys to keep vessels running from January to July along the coasts of Chile and north as far as Panamá.[64]

Enemies frequently tried to gain a foothold in the Spanish colonial possessions. While Philip II was fighting the Netherlands, the intrepid Dutch sailors made piratical voyages and explorations to the New World. They continually defied the commercial regulations of Spain, swarming to "the various islands and ports on the coast of the mainland and finding them unprovided with cloth .... they sold it .... cheap."[65] In 1615 they routed the armada of Peru, whereupon the viceroy consulted all persons in the kingdom experienced in warfare. The result was that Esquilache increased the navy to seven war vessels and two small boats, strengthened the presidio at Callao, and set up twelve pieces of large artillery there.[66] The object

[62] Moses, *The Spanish Dependencies* .... II, 278–279.

[63] Superunda to his successor, 1761, *Memorias de los vireyes* .... IV, 263–266.

[64] Bucareli, *Personal and Official Correspondence*, 1777–80, AGI, 146–4–1; *Recopilación*, ley 28, tit. 10, lib. 3.

[65] Wätjen, Hermann, *Das hollandische Kolonialreich in Brazilien* (The Hague, 1921), 28.

[66] To Guadalcázar, 1621, *Memorias de los vireyes* .... I, 108–109.

of the Dutch West India Company, created in 1621, was "to obtain rich booty and to distract the attention of the Spaniard from the Dutch theater of war." The first attempt of Holland to gain a stronghold on the mainland was at Bahía in May 1624. In the same year a powerful Dutch squadron suddenly appeared at Acapulco. After a few days it withdrew, then the viceroy took measures to reinforce the fortress. Next year the Dutch returned, but with no hostile intentions. The governor of Acapulco permitted them to obtain supplies and they sailed peacefully away.[67] In 1628 Piet Hein captured the first Spanish treasure fleet for the Dutch. Two years later, on March 3, Pernambuco was entered, without the viceroy of Peru, under whose control Brazil was at that time, being able to send any assistance because of the great distance. As late as 1747 a Dutch ship appeared at the port of Matanchel or Jalisco in New Spain. Pedro de Vaquera, the alcalde mayor, invited the captain and crew on shore to dinner. Some of the Dutchmen accepted only too eagerly. When they were at the banquet, armed men imprisoned the guests, while those on shipboard made good their escape. The prisoners were conducted to Mexico City, treated very well, and sent by the first Revillagigedo to Spain.[68]

The Portuguese in Brazil were not strong enough to cause the viceroy of Peru much anxiety. There were some border feuds and slave-hunting expeditions into Spanish territory, but the greatest problem was that of illicit trading between the two nations. During the uprising in Portugal to shake off the Spanish yoke, the Brazilians became objects of suspicion, but even this did not occasion great defensive measures on the part of the executive of Peru. Mancera asked the audiencia of La Plata to send a company of infantry into the provinces of Charcas and Buenos Aires to prevent the Portuguese from cross-

[67]Wätjen, 30, 40–41. The Dutch held their position at Bahía until April 28, 1625. Riva Palacio, II, 583–584.

[68] Wätjen, 43–50; Riva Palacio, II, 795–796.

ing the border, and to disarm those who had already settled in Spanish territory. In 1642 the same viceroy put a stop to the raids of the Mamelucos, who carried off Indians to serve as slaves on their haciendas. In 1676, the Portuguese again plundered four Indian towns and captured four thousand natives. Viceroy Liñan sent aid to Paraguay and asked the audiencia of La Plata to defend Buenos Aires. Spain soon found a chance on August 7, 1680, to retaliate for the seizure of the slaves by taking possession of a Portuguese garrison and some valuable papers.[69]

The English were the foreigners most dreaded. Since the defeat of the Spanish Armada in 1588, England had continued to grow in sea power, hence it was against her that the greatest defensive precautions were taken. Upon the arrival of Viceroy Castellar in 1674, Lima was in great commotion over information received from Chile that the English were colonizing the strait of Magellan. The viceroy sent vessels to examine the region as far south as 52°, but no enemy settlements were discovered.[70] The enthusiastic, but unwise attempt of the Scotchman, William Paterson, to found a colony at Darien was no illusion, even if the small colony of 1698 could not endure the fatal tropical climate and disappeared entirely by the year 1700. Again, about 1703, an English colony, consisting of pirates, logwood cutters, and merchants of dyewood, was founded by Peter Wallace in Yucatan. In spite of the efforts of the governors of that province and the armada of the Windward Islands to dislodge them, they kept their grip upon that coast.[71]

The increase of the contraband trade under the guise of the Asiento Treaty of 1713 soon led to the War of Jenkins' Ear. The waters surrounding the West Indies were covered with enemy ships and in 1740 the new viceroy, Figueroa, on his way

---

[69] Mancera to his successor, 1648, *in* Polo, *Memorias de los vireyes* . . . . arts, 54–57, pp. 18–19; Liñan to Palata, 1681, *Memorias de los vireyes* . . . . I, 347–351.

[70] Moses, *The Spanish Dependencies* . . . . II, 182–183.

[71] Bancroft, *History of Central America*, II, 570–579; Riva Palacio, II, 756–757.

to New Spain, barely escaped being captured by the English.[72] Anson arrived off the coast of Acapulco two years later on his voyage around the world, revealing the Spanish secrets of the Pacific to England. Acts of aggression against the Spanish colonies continued because of British ambition to possess the greatest empire and the richest commerce. The capture of Manila and Havana during the Seven Years' War showed the danger of leaving the colonies without adequate defense. Viceroys of New Spain were fearful whenever England sent forces to her North American colonies, lest she might decide to use them to wrest possessions from her neighbor. In 1769 the viceroy considered it necessary to increase the Spanish forces and to take more careful defensive measures on account of the restlessness of England's American colonies.[73]

Meanwhile the English activities continued. In 1770 the captain-general of Buenos Aires expelled some Englishmen from the Falkland Islands, but by the treaty of the next year Spain had to recognize England's claim to part of those islands.[74] The viceroy of Mexico was able to strike the enemy a severe blow during the American Revolution by sending an expedition to Campeche and imprisoning all the English inhabitants.[75] In the northern Pacific, Biron, Wallis, Carteret and Cook pressed forward on their famous voyages, and Alexander McKenzie reached the western coast of America at British Columbia in 1793.

The Nootka affair of 1790 and 1794 was almost a duplicate of the Falkland Island incident. After this event informal hostilities continued. Branciforte in a letter to his successor, dated May 28, 1798, spoke of being informed by Manuel Godoy concerning an expedition that the British were fitting out against

[72] Zamacois, V, 562–563.

[73] Esquilache, Bucareli, Gálvez, Correspondence, 1769–74, AGI, 146–4–1.

[74] Chapman, Charles E., *A History of Spain* (New York, 1918), 388–389.

[75] Bucareli, Correspondence, 1777–80, AGI, 146–4–1.

Mexico, in which Miranda was to be one of the chief actors.[76] During the administration of Marquina armed vessels arrived frequently at the ports of California. They pretended to be fishing for whales, and often sailed under the flag of the United States. Marquina said that it was difficult for Spanish officials to distinguish between the English and the Americans either by their appearance or language. The proximity of the English, and the defenselessness of the coasts of California caused him much anxiety.[77] The expedition of the English against Buenos Aires in 1806 showed clearly that Great Britain had designs upon the Spanish possessions.

French achievements in the Gulf region necessitated defensive measures on the part of the viceroy of Mexico. When word was received that La Salle had established himself there, the Marquis of Laguna sent out an expedition from Havana, in 1686, under Juan Enríquez Barroso to discover the French settlement. After exploring the Gulf from Cape Lodo to Apalache, Barroso returned to Vera Cruz without finding the enemy. The new viceroy, Monclova, summoned a junta to decide what to do about the French. As a result, on March 7, 1687, two ships were dispatched from Tampico, but the only trace of the French which they saw was a stranded vessel. The next year a frigate of the armada of the Windward Islands went out in March for the same purpose, since an English prisoner had reported a mysterious colony. The vessel proceeded to Mobile Bay but in May returned to Vera Cruz unsuccessful.[78]

Viceroy Galve persisted in the search; accordingly in 1689 Alonso León, governor of Coahuila, who led an expedition by land, found the remains of an abandoned settlement and some

---

[76] *Instrucciones que los vireyes* . . . . 149–150.

[77] Rivera Cambas, I, 503; Marquina to Iturrigaray, 1803, *Instrucciones que los vireyes* . . . . 159; *ibid.*, arts. 134–137, 194, pp. 181, 187.

[78] Riva Palacio, II, 641–644; Dunn, Wm. E., *Spanish and French Rivalries in the Gulf Region of the United States,* 1678–1702 (Austin, Texas, 1917), 75–85.

skeletons of Frenchmen killed by the Indians. This was the establishment of La Salle. Next year the same party was sent out again and the mission of San Francisco de Texas was founded. As a further protection for the coast of Florida, Galve sent Andrés de Pez to select a proper place for a fortress. They arrived on April 8, 1693, at the bay which they named Santa María de Galve, where five years later the stronghold of San Carlos de Panzacola was erected.[79]

French traders from Louisiana were a menace to the Spanish frontiers. When the first Revillagigedo reported to the king that some Frenchmen from New Orleans had entered New Mexico and Texas, a royal decree of June 26, 1751, provided that they should be considered as deserters and not be permitted to return to their province. It was decided at a junta summoned by the viceroy in 1753 that no trade should be allowed with the French, and the governor of Texas was to prevent the Indians within his jurisdiction from carrying on friendly intercourse with them. Since the boundaries between the Spanish and French possessions had never been definitely settled, Amarillas was ordered to send the engineer, Agustín de Cámarasaltas to make an exact map of the northern frontier of New Spain. The executive was to take special notice of the distance of the French from the royal mines and of the opportunities offered by land and water to usurp trade.[80]

Rumors of Russian settlements on the distant northwestern coast of America began to reach the ears of the viceroys of Mexico in the eighteenth century. Viceroy Croix heard that they were moving southward from the Alaskan coast and that three hundred Russians had been killed in a skirmish with the Indians. He therefore sent word to Visitor Gálvez in 1768 to try to

---

[79] Riva Palacio, II, 648–650; Rivera Cambas, I, 265, 269; Dunn, *Spanish and French Rivalries* . . . . 101–109, 120–123, 158 *et seq.;* Lerdo de Tejada, *pt.* v, p. 291.

[80] Arriaga to Amarillas, 1755, *Instrucciones que los vireyes* . . . . art. 8, pp. 96–97.

protect California from the encroachments of this nation.[81] The
next year Gálvez himself went to Lower California, and the
missions of San Diego and Monterey were founded in Alta California as defenses for Spain. Bucareli was informed of Russian
activities in 1773, but did not become alarmed. Although a number of Russian voyages were directed toward North America after
the fearless Vitus Bering sighted the mainland above 58° on
July 16, 1741, no attempt to establish a fur-trading colony on
the coast of Alaska was made until 1783. The next year the
first Russian post in America was established on the island
of Kadiak. Sitka on the mainland of Alaska was founded in
1799, and by 1812 Russian settlements extended as far south
as the Farallón Islands, outside of San Francisco Harbor. This
was sufficient to cause various examinations of the coasts by order
of the viceroys for the purpose of checking the Russians.[82]

The United States, like other foreign nations, was regarded
with suspicion. In 1788 an American vessel from Boston with
Grey and Kendrick on board landed at the island of Juan
Fernández; the Spanish governor, González, permitted repairs
to be made and supplies to be taken on board. Teodoro de
Croix deposed the governor for having furnished aid to the dis-
tressed vessel, and ordered the intendants and sub-delegates of
the provinces to be on the lookout for foreign ships by placing
sentinels on the coasts.[83] During the war between Spain and
England in 1796, danger was feared from the United States,
since it was believed that the Americans would be eager to find a
pretext to invade Florida and Louisiana. A few years later, in
1801, Philip Nolan made an entry into Mexico as far south as
Nueva Santander with a view to purchasing horses and erecting
small forts. Marquina sent a force against the American and

---

[81] Grimaldi to Bucareli, Feb. 23, 1774, AGI, 146–4–2; Letter of Croix to
Gálvez, May 20, 1768, AGI, 104–3–2.

[82] Chapman, *A History of California*, 272–273, 259–260; Flores to
Revillagigedo, 1789, *Instrucciones que los vireyes* . . . . art. 61, p. 125.

[83] Croix to Lemos, 1790, *Memorias de los vireyes* . . . . V, 254–260.

his followers.   In the skirmish which followed Nolan was killed and his partisans dispersed or imprisoned.[84]   Aaron Burr was the next foreigner to attempt a similar incursion.   Spanish authorities opposed Americans, not merely because they would overthrow the old trade regulations, but they might also propagate political ideas which would injure the Spanish colonial system.

The organization of the Provincias Internas or interior provinces was the principal measure adopted for the defense of the frontiers against foreigners.   This change in the viceroyalty of Mexico was effected by a royal order of August 22, 1776, whereby the provinces of Nueva Vizcaya, Coahuila, Texas, New Mexico, Sinaloa, Sonora and the Californias were established under a new government.[85]   Later Nuevo León and Nuevo Santander were added.   These provinces were ruled by a comandante-general, a military chieftain, whose first duty was to protect the extensive frontier.   They were practically independent of the viceroy for he was too far distant and too busy to make his orders felt in the remote provinces.   The comandante recognized the superiority of the viceroy by keeping him informed concerning all his measures and by asking help from him in cases of urgency or danger.   Two years after the first commander, Teodoro de Croix, became viceroy of Peru in 1783, the former authority of the viceroy over the Provincias Internas was partially restored. Viceroy Bernardo de Gálvez was thoroughly acquainted with the conditions of the frontiers, since he had been governor of Louisiana, but at his death in 1786 the comandancia general again became independent of the viceroy.[86]

In 1788 Flórez exercised the same powers as did Gálvez over the Provincias Internas.   The four provinces of the east and

---

[84] Marquina to Iturrigaray, 1803, *Instrucciones que los vireyes . . . .* arts. 46–47, p. 166.

[85] Beleña, Eusebio Bentura, *Recopilación sumaria de todos de los autos acordados de la real audiencia y sala del crimen de esta Nueva España* (Mexico, 1787), I, pt. III, 290–291.

[86] Bolton, H. E., *Guide to Materials for the History of the United States in the Principal Archives of Mexico* (Washington, 1913), 75–76.

west were put under men dependent upon him and the office of comandante was suppressed. Marquina still continued to control Nuevo León and Nuevo Santander because of Indian hostilities in that part. The two Californias also were kept subject to the viceroys. Marquina gives the impression that all the viceroys were opposed to the independence of the border provinces, but this is hardly true because their establishment relieved the captain-general of some of his many responsibilities.[87]

Although Yucatan was not one of the Provincias Internas, it was ruled by a governor and captain-general exempt from the jurisdiction of the viceroy. This was a defensive measure, permitting the governor to take immediate action against corsairs. Nevertheless, viceroys of Mexico continually sent military and financial aid to this province, just as they did to all the Provincias Internas.[88]

5. THE ARMY

The army was almost a negative quantity during the early days of the viceroyalties. It consisted of adventurers led by captains having commissions from the king. In cases of sudden danger the encomenderos and all available persons were called upon by the viceroy to go on military expeditions or furnish substitutes. Some executives with a military bent made attempts at the organization of forces. In 1555 the first Cañete of Peru formed some cavalry companies called lancers and archers, also other infantry bodies named halberdiers. These troops were obliged to defend the kingdom and guard the viceroy when occasion arose. A royal decree of September, 1560, ordered Viceroy Nieva to reduce this body to only thirty cavalrymen and twenty foot soldiers, but the count did not obey the cédula.

---

[87] Flores to Revillagigedo, 1789, *Instrucciones que los vireyes* . . . . arts. 57–58, p. 125; Marquina to Iturrigaray, 1803, *ibid.*, arts. 204, 290, pp. 189, 201.

[88] Mancera to Veraguas, 1673, *Instrucciones que los vireyes* . . . . 278; Croix, *Instrucción que* . . . . *dejó*, AGI, 88–5–13.

Francisco de Toledo was permitted in 1568 to have one hundred
lancers, fifty archers, and fifty halberdiers, but at the same time
Enríquez of New Spain could only have twenty soldiers for a
guard.[89] The king never tried to maintain habitually a standing
army in the colonies. At this early period there was not so much
danger from foreigners, and a real army was not needed to cope
with the Indians.

In New Spain there seem to have been no regular troops until
1642, when Portuguese sympathizers were feared because of the
uprising of the Duke of Braganza against Spain. At this time
twelve companies of infantry were formed. Later several short-
lived companies were created, but it was not until the time of
Cruíllas that anything like an army was established. The
capture of Havana by the English in 1762 greatly alarmed the
viceroy; therefore elaborate plans for defense were made, and
seven regiments and a few private companies were organized.[90]

The new system had in 1764 been put under the charge of
Juan de Villalba, who was appointed comandante-general and
inspector of the troops in New Spain. Five field marshals,
fourteen or fifteen other officials, and seventy soldiers accompanied him from Spain. The government furnished the arms of
those new forces, but the localities from which they came paid
for uniforms and other equipment.[91]

The soldiers, because of their military privileges, felt superior
to the townspeople, hence there were continual quarrels with
them and sometimes injuries and deaths occurred. Beside his
many other duties, the captain-general had to settle these contentions. The military body was not held to very strict discipline.
In 1615 Montesclaros lamented that soldiers in Peru led scandalous lives, almost like vagabonds, and were embarrassing to good
government. They went among the natives, whom they treated

---

[89] Solórzano, I, lib. 3, cap. 33, arts, 2–5, 11, pp. 434–435.
[90] Cavo, lib. 7, p. 194; *ibid.*, lib. 12, p. 296; Rivera Cambas, I, 143;
Riva Palacio, II, 819.
[91] *Ibid.*, II, 820.

with insolence; accordingly the viceroy vainly tried to prohibit them from living in Indian towns. Viceroy Palata said that it was almost impossible to subject men to the routine work of soldiers and to severe discipline.[92] Villarroel stated that the same condition prevailed in New Spain. Many soldiers coming to America became corrupted, and if they returned later to Spain they were no longer of any value. He declared that the officers indulged in gambling, in love-making, and in every amusement. The soldiers, following the example of the officers, did the same. They dressed extravagantly and wore two watches. They loathed the regular uniform and could not be kept in barracks.[93] The people were not kindly inclined toward service in the army, so desertions were frequent. Marquina was forced to pardon many deserters, but was unable to check the escape from military service in Vera Cruz. He corrected as much as possibe the abuse of forcing deserters into the domestic employ of army officials.[94]

The army was composed largely of creoles and mestizos. Most of the officials and the veteran troops were European. However, some of the minor officers were taken from the castes.[95] Several of the laws of the Indies ordered that Negroes, mulattoes, or

[92] Croix, *Instrucción que* . . . . *dejó*, AGI, 88–5–13; Rivera Cambas, I, 405; Montesclaros to his successor, 1615, *Documentos inéditos* . . . . *de Indias*, VI, 229–230; Palata to Monclova, 1689, *Memorias de los vireyes* . . . . II, 267.

[93] *Enfermedades políticas* . . . . MS, I, pt. I, p. 5; *ibid.*, III, pt. v, pp. 145–147.

[94] Marquina to Iturrigaray, 1803, *Instrucciones que los vireyes* . . . . arts. 240, 263, pp. 194, 197.

[95] Alamán, *Historia de Méjico* . . . . I, 81. One of the greatest mistakes in the Spanish army was the superfluous number of officials. In the early part of the seventeenth century Palafox spoke of twelve or sixteen captains being appointed for the Philippines, but only a few of them ever went to those islands. To his successor, 1642, *Documento inéditos* . . . . *de Mexico*, VII, 55–56. Villarroel declared that the king had more officers than soldiers in the provinces, and that commissions were given to men who had never handled a firearm. Some were entirely ignorant of the military art and did not know how to give commands or serve. *Enfermedades políticas* . . . . MS, III, pt. v, pp. 159–160. In 1797, however, Branciforte commended the officials for their zeal and activity. To Azanza, 1797, *Instrucciones que los vireyes* . . . . art. 49, p. 135.

mestizos were not to become soldiers.[96] These rules were not observed, since mestizos entered the white companies. There were whole companies of ''pardos.'' Negroes often became officers on the frontiers. Forces of free blacks were employed in the unhealthy coast regions. The total strength of the army at any definite period is difficult to determine. Authorities do not agree concerning the number of men actually under the royal service. The troops were increased spasmodically whenever urgent danger appeared, and disbanded as soon as it was over. In Mexico after the reforms of Villalba, according to Rivera Cambas, Bucareli found 10,000 infantrymen and 6000 cavalrymen, without counting the regiment of La Corona and the urban bodies of Mexico City, Puebla, and Vera Cruz.[97]

Riva Palacio considered 40,000 a fair estimate of the soldiers in all the military organizations, the veteran troops consisting of 10,000 men, the provincial militias of 22,000, the coast guard of 7200, and the companies of merchants from the capital and Puebla of 2000.[98] This number may be somewhat exaggerated, but in May, 1798, Branciforte, who decided to reëstablish the bodies of provincial militia disorganized by Revillagigedo, left a document wherein the total armed force was set at 31,594, as many as 25,502 men being in the field army.[99] In 1807 Pinkerton gave 43,191 men as the total for the viceroyalty; summing up the figures quoted by Alamán for the next year, however, we fall short of this number.[100]

There is just as much variation concerning military statistics in Peru. In 1796 Viceroy Lemos mentioned 56,696 soldiers, yet this number is probably too large, for the same viceroy also recorded 45,437. In 1802 Avilés gave 52,413 men as the military

96 *Recopilación*, ley 12, tit. 10, lib. 3.
97 *Los gobernantes de México*, I, 424.
98 *México á través de los siglos*, III, 23.
99 Branciforte to Azanza, *Instrucciones que los vireyes* . . . . 148.
100 Pinkerton, *Modern Geography*, III, 165; Alamán, *Historia de Méjico*, I, 78–80.

force in his viceroyalty.[101]   The wide variation in these figures indicates faulty enumeration or exaggeration, but they may be taken as an approximate estimate.

Before the close of the eighteenth century the whole viceroyalty of Mexico was divided into ten military divisions, over which a comandante de brigada or brigadier was placed. Each brigadier acted as inspector-general within his district.[102]   The different divisions did not have the same number of soldiers, neither did the men carry the same kind of weapons. The uniforms in the companies and even in the squadrons were of different colors.[103]

Some antiquated divisions were kept until the nineteenth century. These were the companies of pardos and morenos, nonwhite soldiers, which were stationed on the hot coastal plains. Branciforte said they were useful for defense in time of war, and in peace they could prevent strife, seize deserters, conduct galley slaves to their destination, and perform garrison duties. There were usually two of these companies at Vera Cruz, and two for the remainder of the Gulf.[104]   There were five divisions on the west coast consisting largely of companies of pardos, and on the northern coast four divisions of free whites and pardos. Altogether thirty-five companies of non-whites remained after the militia had been reduced by the second Revillagigedo.[105]

Besides the other regular troops there were lancers. They too, performed very useful service in Vera Cruz.[106]   In Peru this

[101] Lemos to Vallenari, 1796, *Memorias de los vireyes* . . . . VI, 309–311, Appendix 33; Avilés to Abascal, *Memoria del virey del Peru, Appendix* XI.

[102] Marquina to Iturrigaray, 1803, *Instrucciones que los vireyes* . . . . 169, 257, pp. 185, 197.

[103] Pinkerton mentions the colors of the uniforms of each division in his *Modern Geography*, III, 162–165.

[104] Branciforte to Azanza, 1797, *Instrucciones que los vireyes* . . . . art. 55, p. 136. In 1803 the number of pardos was 1010 and in 1808 it was 3400. Marquina to Iturrigaray, *ibid.*, art. 162, p. 184; Alamán, *Historia de Méjico*, I, 80.

[105] Revillagigedo, *Instrucción reservada*, arts. 617–618; Marquina to Iturrigaray, 1803, *Instrucciones que los vireyes* . . . . art. 166, p. 184.

[106] Croix, *Instrucción que* . . . . *dejó*, AGI, 88–5–13.

organization was esteemed by gentlemen of rank. From it viceroys and governors filled official positions in the army and civil government. The gentlemen lancers enjoyed special privileges. Viceroy Toledo provided that they could not be imprisoned for debts, nor pay them by selling their arms and other equipment.[107] In New Spain Azanza increased the lancers to one thousand men, but the king ordered Marquina to reduce it. The latter viceroy made a strong plea to the monarch for the company but he was compelled to disband all but one hundred men.[108]

Commercial regiments were formed in Mexico City, Puebla, and Vera Cruz. They were recruited from the merchants and various gilds, and came under the designation of urban militias. In Mexico City the famous Regimiento de Comercio, dating from the seventeenth century, composed of bakers, butchers, tanners, and silversmiths, went out to guard the public buildings whenever danger arose. Croix said that these companies were of much assistance during the expulsion of the Jesuits and were proud of the military privileges which he gave them.[109] In 1790 this regiment was reviewed by the subinspector-general, who reported to the viceroy in the following year that it had 608 men distributed among two companies of grenadiers and eight companies of fusiliers. In 1793 the force was increased to 1018 men.[110] On July 7, 1802, the king commanded that the commercial regiment should be subject to the first brigadier of militia, but the consulado could still fill all vacancies. A similar

[107] Account concerning Cañete, *Documentos inéditos* . . . . *de Indias*, VIII, 405–418.

[108] Marquina to Iturrigaray, 1803, *Instrucciones que los vireyes* . . . . arts. 237–238, p. 194.

[109] Revillagigedo to Amarillas, 1754, *ibid.*, art. 133, p. 28; Croix, *Instrucción que* . . . . *dejó*, AGI, 88–5–13; Revillagigedo, *Instrucción reservada*, arts. 585, 587.

[110] *Ibid.*, arts. 610, 613. Villarroel said that the majority of the soldiers serving under the consulado were mercenaries who afterwards became vagabonds. When they committed crimes, they refused to come before the tribunal of the consulado, alleging their military privilege. *Enfermedades políticas* . . . . MS, III, pt. v, pp. 160–162.

commercial regiment was established in 1742 at Puebla. The horses were furnished by the gilds and their equipment by the government.[111]

There were always some veteran troops from Spain in the viceroyalties. They formed the viceroy's bodyguard and other palace forces. Up to 1642, according to Palafox, the viceroys had two or three of these companies to keep the populace in check, but the king gave orders for them to be discontinued to save expense.[112] They must have been reëstablished, for in 1716 Linares spoke of the two companies of the palace being his only comfort, since they could be used for night patrols, for giving warning in case of fires, and in apprehending criminals.[113] The veteran soldiers were employed in the garrisons of Mexico City, Puebla, Perote, Vera Cruz, and San Juan de Ulúa.[114] Most of the Spanish soldiers brought to New Spain for the organization of the army under Villalba returned to Europe in 1772, but it was always considered necessary to keep some European troops in the colonies.

The usefulness of the provincial militia was questioned by some viceroys, while others recognized its value. Viceroy Croix of Mexico said that, although Villalba had tried to make progress in the establishment of the militia, until his own arrival it had merely existed on paper. He thought that the militia could be depended upon. He refuted the chief arguments of its opponents who said that the king lost tribute on account of it, by showing that only the Indians and mulattoes paid tribute at this time, that natives did not enter the militia, and that the mulattoes were in other companies. There could be no objection to the

---

[111] Marquina to Iturrigaray, 1803, *Instrucciones que los vireyes* . . . . arts. 246–250, pp. 195–196; Revillagigedo, *Instrucción reservada,* arts. 614, 626.

[112] Palafox to his successor, *Documentos inéditos* . . . . *de Mexico,* VII, 33.

[113] Linares to Valero, *Instrucciones que los vireyes* . . . . 315. In 1754 there were more than 700 men in these troops. Revillagigedo to Amarillas, *ibid.,* arts. 131–132, p. 28.

[114] Branciforte to Azanza, 1797, *ibid.,* arts. 40, 42, p. 134.

militia on the ground of expense to the treasury, since the troops were clothed and equipped by the inhabitants of the regions whence they came. Special taxes were levied by the larger cities to meet these expenditures. The second Revillagigedo held the militia in slight esteem, but this was not surprising, since he was a military man himself, trained in the Spanish army. He believed that in times of war the veteran troops would have to be depended upon.[115]

Flying companies of militia, composed of mixed divisions of infantry and cavalry with little discipline and no uniforms, were used for guarding the coasts, presidios, and frontiers. In 1794 there was one flying company in Nuevo León, consisting of one hundred men, three in Nuevo Santander with seventy-five men in each division, and five in California, the number of men ranging from thirty-eight to sixty-one. As late as 1808 the same number of companies existed in these provinces. There were twelve lookout stations scattered among the different groups of militia, which notified the flying companies whenever a hurried expedition was to be made against an enemy.[116]

The enlistment of men for the army and armadas was another rather laborious task of the captain-general. There was no regular system of conscription. In case of peril the viceroy usually called upon all able-bodied men to enlist. Francisco de Toledo did this when the hostile Chiriguanaes threatened some of the cities in Peru.[117] In 1624, upon the arrival of a powerful Dutch armada at Lima, Viceroy Guadalcázar summoned all the inhabitants to come to the defense of the city, no matter what privileges of nobility they had enjoyed.[118] Again in 1637 even students and ecclesiastics were enlisted in the same city to safeguard it against

---

[115] Croix, *Instrucción que* . . . . *dejó*, AGI, 88–5–13; Revillagigedo, *Instrucción reservada*, art. 663.

[116] Revillagigedo, *ibid.*, arts. 727, 623; Alamán, *Historia de Méjico*, I, 80.

[117] Memorial of Toledo, 1596, *Documentos inéditos* . . . . *de Indias*, VI, 527–528.

[118] Solórzano, I, lib. 3, cap. 25, art. 20, p. 371.

the Dutch fleet under Jacob Heremita Clark.[119] Viceroy Castellar raised more than eight thousand four hundred men for an armada to be sent to the strait of Magellan to search for enemy sails.[120] After Havana was captured by the English in 1762, Viceroy Cruíllas worked hard to enlist soldiers, and as a result many volunteer companies of merchants were formed. The second Revillagigedo recruited men for the flying companies of militia by having lists drawn up of all persons within his jurisdiction qualified to serve, according to the ratio of one soldier for every fifteen families of pure blood.[121]

It was not easy to obtain a sufficient number of men for the army. On one occasion the citizens of Nuevo León protested against serving in Texas, alleging that they had endured the burdens of wars for years and were continually giving assistance in the conquest of new colonies.[122]

Bancroft says,

As late as 1775, a committee appointed by the government to aid in developing the military defenses, declared both the old Spaniards and their descendants unreliable; for at the least rumor of war they would disappear.[123]

Many enlisted voluntarily, but only too frequently the viceroy had to order levies to be made on all the idle, vagabonds, and deserters in the towns and cities.[124] Branciforte did not favor a general military conscription since the treasury could not bear the expense.[125]

Supplying arms and ammunition for the enlisted men was the next problem of the captain-general. There was a notorious scarcity of these from the days of the first colonial viceroy, who wrote to the king on December 10, 1537, saying that, since arms

119 Moses, *The Spanish Dependencies* . . . . II, 73.

120 Castellar to Liñan, 1681, *Memorias de los vireyes* . . . . I, 247.

121 Riva Palacio, II, 819; Revillagigedo, *Instrucción reservada*, art. 628.

122 *Testimo. de los autos sobre el asalto y attaque* . . . . *en el presidio de San Luis de las Amarillas* . . . . AGI, 92–6–22, pp. 246–274.

123 *History of Mexico*, III, f. 404.

124 Croix to Lemos, 1790, *Memorias de los vireyes* . . . . V, 231.

125 To Azanza, 1797, *Instrucciones que los vireyes* . . . . arts. 36–37, p. 133.

had to be sent to Peru, almost none were left in New Spain.[126] Seldom did a viceroy receive the number of weapons asked for from Spain. Usually he could expect about half of them. Sometimes he had to collect old arms in order to meet an emergency.[127] After repeated attempts to obtain weapons from Spain, Mancera tried to meet the difficulty by arranging for Baltasar de Resusta, a resident of Mexico City, to bring them into Vera Cruz at his own expense. At first the king seemed to approve of this measure, but later he reversed his policy. In 1703 the second Alburquerque advised the king to have more care concerning the supply of munitions in the ports of New Spain, since conditions in Europe were so critical.[128] So hard pressed was Branciforte for firearms and sidearms, that he had to give orders for them to be constructed temporarily from old ones in the royal magazines. There was a sala de armas in Mexico City on which the viceroy had to direct his attention occasionally, although it had a keeper.[129]

Arms might not be taken to the Indies without royal permission, under penalty of losing them. Teodoro de Croix decided to retain all prohibited weapons in the custom-house of Peru until the owners could send them back to Spain. Viceroys were ordered to see that irresponsible persons like mulattoes, zambos, and Indians did not carry weapons, and mestizos might bear them only under a special permit. Powder was manufactured in Mexico City in the first part of the seventeenth century and somewhat later in Lima. From these centers the captain-general had it sent to the more distant parts of the viceroyalties.[130]

---

[126] *Documentos inéditos . . . . de Indias*, II, 200; Puga, Cedulario, I, foja 109, p. 376.

[127] Enríquez to Coruña, 1580, *Instrucciones que los vireyes . . . .* art. 16, p. 248; Palafox to his successor, 1642, *Documentos inéditos . . . . de Mexico*, VII, 34.

[128] Mancera to Veraguas, 1673, *Instrucciones que los vireyes . . . .* 275; Alburquerque to Philip V, March 31, 1703, AGI, 61–1–23.

[129] Branciforte to Azanza, 1797, *Instrucciones que los vireyes . . . .* art. 47, pp. 134–135; Council of the Indies to Amarillas, 1755, *ibid.*, art. 12, p. 92.

[130] Croix to Lemos, 1790, *Memorias de los vireyes . . . .* V, 78–80; *Recopilación*, leyes 12, 14, 8, tit. 5, lib. 3; ley 31, tit. 1, lib. 6.

It was also the duty of the viceroy to have plenty of supplies and other necessary equipment, not including arms, provided for the troops. He was expected to enforce rules of military discipline, but not much attention was paid to the maneuvers of troops. Branciforte said that he tried to see that the cantoned militias were instructed in military evolutions and discipline.[131]

Barracks had to be furnished for the troops by the captain-general. This, however, applied only to the veteran forces, as there was no attempt to obtain quarters for the militia. In 1762 the king commanded that barracks should be established at Vera Cruz and appropriated ten thousand pesos annually for the enterprise. Although the work began the next year, nothing much was done for twenty-one years. The permanent cantonment at Jalapa was not finished until the beginning of the nineteenth century.[132] At this time the soldiers of Mexico City were still being lodged in rented houses and inns. Marquina made plans to improve the situation, but the treasury was not in a condition to bear the expense.[133] In Lima during the administration of Teodoro de Croix, ten barracks were built at a cost of forty thousand pesos. The viceroy was forced to take this action, for sickness had occurred among the troops, due to exposure in their lodgings at the hospital of the Bethlehemites and in the College of San Felipe.[134]

Military hospitals likewise had to be secured. The prevalence of diseases in the unhealthful coast regions caused much desertion from the army and increased the difficulty of obtaining recruits. In 1601 we find Monterey asking the king for alms to establish a hospital at Vera Cruz, so that sick sailors coming on the fleets might be properly cared for.[135] Finally the hospital of San

---

[131] Letter of Branciforte to Azanza, May 30, 1798, *Instrucciones que los vireyes . . . .* 149.

[132] Revillagigedo, *Instrucción reservada*, art. 676; Riva Palacio, III, 36.

[133] Marquina to Iturrigaray, 1803, *Instrucciones que los vireyes . . . .* arts. 282–284, p. 200.

[134] Croix to Lemos, 1790, *Memorias de los vireyes . . . .* V, 228–229.

[135] Branciforte to Azanza, 1797, *ibid.*, art. 66, p. 137; Monterey to the king, May 20, 1601, AGI, 53–3–13.

Carlos was founded at Vera Cruz, the expense being met by the royal treasury. Marquina did not consider this institution or the other hospitals of that port very good. He said that to enter them in the summer was sufficient to run the risk of contracting a serious illness. Through his influence an expediente was drawn up for the erection of a more spacious building, but no further action was taken.[136]

A small hospital for the care of soldiers and sailors was built at Acapulco. It was administered by a prior and a corps from the order of San Hipólito; but the viceroy had to oversee it in a general way. As the amount of money assigned to the hospital did not cover expenditures, the viceroy, with the consent of the king, deducted 2 per cent from salaries of the members of the various crews landing in the port.[137] Because of the lack of military hospitals in the capital of New Spain, sick soldiers were cared for at San Andrés, a hospital under the archbishop's charge. This arrangement was not very satisfactory, since there were constant disputes between the soldiers and the hospital staff. In May, 1790, Revillagigedo made arrangements to establish a military hospital at Chihuahua.[138] At Callao there was a similar institution, having one hundred beds, controlled by the comandante de marina, who was subordinate to the viceroy, of Peru.[139]

Many military appointments seem to have been made by the viceroys before the reforms of Villalba. Francisco de Toledo appointed Rodrigo de Quiroga captain-general of Chile, and Lorenzo Bernal maestre de campo of the same province. A royal cédula of June 7, 1595, gave Velasco, as captain-general of Peru, the right to appoint, remove, and make reappointments in military positions.[140] There was a curious arrangement for presidios

---

[136] Revillagigedo, *Instrucción reservada*, art. 683; Marquina to Iturrigaray, 1803, *Instrucciones que los vireyes* . . . . arts. 215–217, p. 191.

[137] *Vireyes de Mexico* . . . . MS, serie 1, art. 2, pp. 4–5, 15.

[138] Revillagigedo, *Instrucción reservada*, arts. 682, 684.

[139] Lemos to Vallénari, 1796, *Memorias de los vireyes* . . . . VI, 41.

[140] *Documentos inéditos* . . . . *de Indias,* XXV, 535; *ibid.,* XVIII, 256–257.

similar to the method of supplying vacancies in the church. The captain-general could make ad interim appointments, but he had to submit to the king three names accompanied by a statement of the services and qualifications of each man for the position, so that the sovereign could choose one for permanent appointment.[141] Officers' commissions in the militia were given by the viceroy subject to confirmation by the crown.[142]

Viceroy Castellar said that he always tried to furnish good captains and governors in Peru, accordingly he appointed Francisco de Delso sargento mayor of Callao, Diego de Martos maestre de campo, Antonio de Vea and Pascual de Iriarte captains.[143] At any moment the king might change his mind and decide to make his own appointments, as he did in a cédula of December 19, 1680. At this time the sovereign reserved the right to appoint the governor, the veedor and contador of the fortress of Valdivia, but still permitted the viceroy to select the other officials. By another decree of 1688 the king suppressed the position of general of Callao, which was usually filled by a relative of the viceroy, and selected two chiefs in his place, one for matters pertaining to the land and the other for the sea.[144] In the next century however, we find Superunda making this appointment again. Early viceroys were permitted to give twelve of their relatives places in their bodyguard, but they could not hold other military positions. Palata objected to this rule, since many of the followers of a viceroy were trained military men and would make good officers.[145]

In 1754 the first Revillagigedo said that the captain-general filled military vacancies even among the officials of royal designa-

---

[141] *Recopilación,* ley 3, tit. 3, lib. 3; ley 1, tit. 10, lib. 3; Palata to Monclova, 1689, *Memorias de los vireyes* . . . . II, 417.

[142] *Recopilación,* ley 2, tit. 10, lib. 3; Bancroft, *History of Mexico,* III, 407.

[143] To Liñan, 1681, *Memorias de los vireyes* . . . . I, 238, 244.

[144] Liñan to Palata, 1681, *ibid.,* I, 315; Palata to Monclova, 1689, *ibid.,* II, 274–275.

[145] Superunda to his successor, 1761, *Memorias de los vireyes* . . . . IV, 334–336; Palata to Monclova, 1689, *ibid.,* II, 121–122, 128, 130, 132.

tion, and all others which pertained to his right.[146]   After the reforms of Villalba, according to Riva Palacio and Bancroft, the viceroy appointed colonels and lieutenant-colonels of the army, but the subinspector-general chose the other officers with the consent of the viceroy.[147]   The captain-general could recommend but not make promotions in the army.   Marquina advised the monarch not to advance men two ranks at one time, since better service would be performed if it were done gradually.[148] The viceroy provided for the salaries and pensions of soldiers. He tried to prevent employees in the army from being oppressed on account of debts, and to prohibit salaries being paid in merchandise.[149]   He had to see that the pay of deserters or absent soldiers went to the treasury, and that the treasury officials kept a list of all the soldiers and the amount each received.[150]   The viceroy supervised the system of pensions for widows and orphans of soldiers and sailors through his powers of vice-patron over the montepío militar.[151]

The founding of presidios was an important duty of the earlier viceroys.   This was the means taken to secure the routes of travel, protect communication with rich mines, and stop the invasions of hostile Indians.   Sometimes the places where they were situated consisted of scarcely more inhabitants than the soldiers themselves and their families.   They had their farms or small haciendas near by.[152]   Occasionally viceroys sent out visitors to the presidios.   Between 1724 and 1728 Viceroy Casafuerte had them inspected by Pedro de Rivera.   He regulated the number

[146] To Amarillas, *Instrucciones que los vireyes* . . . . art. 123, p. 27.

[147] Riva Palacio, II, 821; Bancroft, *History of Mexico*, III, 403–404.

[148] Marquina to Iturrigaray, 1803, *Instrucciones que los vireyes* . . . . arts. 253–254, p. 196.

[149] *Recopilación*, leyes 1, 3, tit. 12, lib. 3.   In spite of this prohibition, the law was not always enforced.   We hear of captains of the presidios paying their soldiers in all kinds of useless merchandise.   Linares to Valero, 1716, *Instrucciones que los vireyes* . . . . 313; Croix, *Instrucción que* . . . . *dejó*, AGI, 88–5–13.

[150] *Recopilación*, leyes 6, 19, tit. 12, lib. 3.

[151] Croix to Lemos, 1790, *Memorias de los vireyes* . . . . V, 213.

[152] Linares to Valero, 1716, *Instrucciones que los vireyes* . . . . 313.

of soldiers which each one ought to have and the salaries to be received. A collection of rules, or reglamento, was drawn up which was approved by the king; through it many abuses, especially with respect to the payment of soldiers, were abolished.[153] At this time there were twenty presidios in New Spain, the most distant one being in New Mexico.[154]

Later viceroys added more presidios to the list. In 1754 the elder Revillagigedo established one in the province of Sonora to check the raids of the Apache tribes, and one at Panzacola to oppose the French. By the middle of the eighteenth century there were others in Lower California, and one on the island of Cármen to keep the dyewood cutters in check.[155] In 1757 Viceroy Amarillas established the presidio of San Sabá in Texas with one hundred deported criminals.[156] After 1769 the viceroys of Mexico had to attend to the construction of presidios in Upper California. By 1772 the presidios for the defense of the northern frontier were reduced to fifteen upon recommendation by the Marquis of Rubí, who inspected them in 1765.[157]

In South America there was never any need for the establishment of a line of presidios to protect a frontier, as in New Spain. Although less numerous, the presidios were much larger than in Mexico. Viceroy Palata spoke of the presidio of Buenos Aires having nine hundred soldiers. The garrison of the presidio of Lima consisted of five hundred men, when it was first erected, and in 1746 that of Callao had four hundred and twenty-one men.[158]

---

153 Fuenclara, *Instrucción reservada*, April 23, 1742, AGI, 90–2–17, art. 9.

154 Bancroft, *History of Mexico*, III, 410. The number of men in these establishments varied. The presidio of New Mexico had 77 soldiers and it seemed to be one of the largest, since some of the others had less than 50 defenders. The total strength of the presidios in 1742 was only 846 men.

155 Revillagigedo to Amarillas, 1754, *Instrucciones que los vireyes* . . . . arts. 138–141, p. 29.

156 Dunn, Wm. E., ''Apache Mission,'' *Southwestern Historical Quarterly*, XVII, 389–390, Croix, *Instrucción que* . . . . *dejó*, AGI, 88–5–13.

157 *Ibid.*, AGI, 88–5–13; Bolton, *Texas* . . . . 108, 379–380.

158 Palata to Monclova, 1689, *Memorias de los vireyes* . . . . II, 417; Superunda to his successor, 1761, *ibid.*, IV, 262, 271.

The sending of subsidies to the presidios was one of the principal cares of the captain-general. The presidios reported to the viceroy what they needed in the way of provisions and munitions, and the treasury officials saw that the proper purchases were made. Powder, arms, and supplies were the articles asked for most frequently. The Philippine Islands were entirely dependent upon the viceroys of New Spain for supplies, ammunitions, and in case of danger, soldiers. These articles were dispatched annually on the galleons.[159] Aid was sent to the West Indies by the viceroys from an early date. The money and supplies were transported to Vera Cruz, whence the armada of the Windward Islands or merchant ships took them to Havana to be distributed among the presidios of the other islands. The subsidies for Florida also went first to Havana. Linares thought that the viceroy ought to have the power to inspect the garrisons in the Windward Islands, if he continued to send supplies to them. They were not under the direct control of the viceroy, yet he had to suffer from complaints made to Spain concerning them.[160] In case of great danger the viceroys were asked to provide them men. After the corsair, Drake, had taken possession of Santo Domingo in 1586, Villamanrique sent to Havana three hundred and fifty-two soldiers who had been enlisted for the Philippines and eighty-five additional men from Vera Cruz.[161] On July 27, 1672, Mancera dispatched to the West Indies two vessels containing one hundred and seventeen men, besides the usual supplies. A little later in 1690, Viceroy Galve sent an expedition of two thousand six hundred soldiers to Santo Domingo, to complete the Spanish possession of the northern part of that island.[162]

[159] *Recopilación*, ley 10, tit. 9, lib. 3; ley 13, tit. 4, lib. 3; Mancera to Veraguas, 1673, *Instrucciones que los vireyes* . . . . 276; Linares to Valero, 1716, *ibid.*, 313.

[160] Palafox to his successor, 1642, *Documentos inéditos* . . . . *de Mexico*, VII, 50–53; Linares to Valero, 1716, *Instrucciones que los vireyes* . . . . 312–313.

[161] Villamanrique to Philip II, March 23, 1586, *Cartas de Indias*, 352–353.

[162] Mancera to Veraguas, 1673, *Instrucciones que los vireyes* . . . . 281; Cavo, lib. 9, art. 15, p. 232.

The subsidies for Florida were sometimes considered rather large and even burdensome. The amount sent to that province during Mancera's administrations was 732,652 pesos, besides one hundred and twenty-two soldiers. At the beginning of the War of the Spanish Succession the governor of Havana dispatched six hundred men to Florida and frantically called upon Viceroy Alburquerque to send troops for the garrison at Havana.[163] Linares thought that the presidio of Panzacola was useless and said that he did not furnish a peso for it which did not cause him grief, but the king wished it, therefore the money was paid.[164] The providing of supplies for California during the famine of 1774 was one of the grave problems which Bucareli had to meet, but he surmounted the many obstacles, sent a supply ship, and saved the province.[165]

The viceroy of Peru was held responsible for conveying the subsidies to Panamá, Cartagena, Santa Marta, Chile, Valdivia and Buenos Aires. Huge sums of money, indeed, went to those presidios. The amount raised in the ten years preceding 1734 was 3,800,000 pesos, and Viceroy Castel-Fuerte transmitted 380,000 pesos of subsidy to them annually. Under Superunda the yearly supplies for Valdivia were valued at 50,692 pesos, besides the 10,000 pesos contributed from the treasury of Santiago de Chile.[166] In July, 1788, Viceroy Teodoro de Croix sent 300,000 pesos to Panama and four months later he added 385,674 pesos to this sum.[167] The second Revillagigedo appropriated the enormous fund of 3,400,000 pesos for subsidies and only 1,500,000 pesos were set aside for the cost of maintaining the government.[168]

---

163 Mancera to Veraguas, 1673, *Instrucciones que los vireyes* . . . . 279; Alburquerque to Philip V, March 31, 1703, AGI, 61–1–23.

164 Linares to Valero, 1716, *Instrucciones que los vireyes* . . . . 313.

165 Chapman, *A History of California,* 283–284.

166 Castel-Fuerte to Villagarcía, 1736, *Memorias de los vireyes* . . . . III, 201–206; Superunda to his successor, 1761, *ibid.,* IV, 276.

167 Croix to Lemos, 1790, *ibid.,* V, 313–314.

168 Revillagigedo, *Instrucción reservada,* art. 744.

6. THE NAVY

The armadas were under the direct control of admirals appointed by the king. They received their instructions from Spain, yet the captain-general had special duties with respect to them. While in the New World the admirals and generals of the fleets were subject to the orders of viceroys and audiencias, unless there was a provision to the contrary in their instructions.[169] Viceroys were to see that admirals did not allow their men to commit misdemeanors in port, and they were to permit their generals to search for deserters. Justices were ordered to aid admirals in their inspection of the fortresses in the ports.[170]

The viceroys of Peru exercised much authority over the armadas of the South Sea because of the great distance from the mother country. They supervised the building of ships for those waters, and were required to inspect the officials of the armada every year. According to a law of the Indies of 1527, reiterated by others in 1572, 1587, and 1608, there was to be a pilot on each ship of the fleet and two on the captain's and admiral's vessel.[171] In the last quarter of the eighteenth century Viceroy Guirior made a rule that no ships were to sail from Peru without a pilot, and he required large vessels to have two. A royal order of February 18, 1784, favored this plan, and in 1786 Croix commanded that a pilot who had passed the proper examination must go with every boat. When returning from a voyage the pilots were to show their diaries to the civil authorities so that they might know how the expedition had been directed.[172]

It was the duty of the captain-general to provide supplies for the armada in the port of Callao. In case of extraordinary expenditures for the fleet, the viceroy was to summon an acuerdo

---

169 *Recopilación*, leyes 60, 79, tit. 15; lib. 9; Rivera Cambas, I, 218.

170 *Recopilación*, leyes 63, 69, 80, 86, tit. 15, lib. 9.

171 *Ibid.*, leyes 1, 18, tit. 44, lib. 8; ley 35, tit. 23, lib. 9.

172 Croix to Lemos, 1790, *Memorias de los vireyes* . . . . V, 242–245; *Recopilación*, ley 11, tit. 44, lib. 8.

of oidores and treasury officials who were to help him decide the matter.[173]

The dispatching of fleets was a special right of the viceroy as captain-general. All navigation to the Philippines was under the control of the viceroy of New Spain, and he appointed officers of the ships. Supplies were furnished by his orders and he decided the date of departure.[174] The king fixed certain periods within which the armada ought to sail, but the viceroy could use his own judgment as to the exact time. According to Palafox, the galleon usually left Acapulco in December or January, but sometimes not until February or March.[175] The return vessels had to leave Manila before the end of June in order to avoid the storms.

The last of April was supposed to be the latest date for the dispatch of fleets from Mexico to Spain. Nevertheless, Mancera said that it was not until the latter part of May that the supplies for exportation could be collected and the ships set sail.[176] The dispatch and safe arrival of the armadas were considered so important that thanks were given every year in the principal churches and convents of New Spain. This custom was still continued in the eighteenth century, the viceroy himself often taking part in the services.[177]

In 1728 a new plan was tried for dispatching the fleets of Peru. A royal cédula of December 2 ordered that juntas be formed, composed of the viceroy as presiding official, the fiscal, the contador of the tribunal of accounts whom the viceroy chose, the prior and four deputies of the consulado, to supervise the dispatch of armadas. Account of the action taken was to be given to the king. At this date the fleets of Peru were dispatched three times a year.[178]

---

[173] Esquilache to Guadalcázar, 1621, *Memorias de los vireyes* . . . . I, 143–144.
[174] Velasco to Philip II, Dec. 22, 1590, AGI, 58–3–11.
[175] To his successor, 1642, *Documentos inéditos . . . . de Mexico*, VII, 55.
[176] To Veraguas, 1673, *Instrucciones que los vireyes* . . . . 268, 282–283.
[177] Cavo, lib. 9, art. 24, p. 239; Rivera Cambas, I, 120, 333–334, 391.
[178] Castel-Fuerte to Villagarcía, 1736, *Memorias de los vireyes* . . . . III, 231, 242.

The most famous armada was that of the Windward Islands. It was formed for the purpose of protecting the Gulf of Mexico and the West Indies from the ravages of pirates. The Marquis of Cadereyta received orders from the king to raise money for it. All the islands and the mainland from Panamá northward to Mexico were to contribute to it, and a sum was also appropriated from the royal treasury. The total amount to be collected was 600,000 pesos, Mexico's share being 200,000. The viceroy of New Spain had to make an estimate concerning what each part of his viceroyalty should pay and then confer with the cabildo and treasury officials of Mexico City as to the best way to raise the money. He wrote to the governor of Yucatan and the president of the audiencia of Guatemala so that they might pay promptly their contribution of 40,000 pesos each. When built, the ships had to be manned. Palafox thought that young gentlemen or sons of officials in New Spain ought to serve on the fleet at least two years, so that they might obtain experience and training for further promotion in the army.[179]

The first armada of the Windward Islands was to consist of twelve galleons and two smaller vessels, but it usually had about half this number. During the administration of Escalona there were six vessels. Occasionally the viceroy appointed the general and admiral of the fleet.[180] In 1665 Mancera found an armada of five ships, to which he added two, and during the administration of Viceroy Galve, it acquired the rather large number of fourteen vessels. By 1696, however, it decreased again to six, and Viceroy Moctezuma was obliged to have two additional ships constructed.[181] The armada of the South Sea, stationed at Callao, was usually composed of four men-of-war, but in case of necessity this number was raised. In 1796 Viceroy Lemos of Peru said

---

[179] Palafox to his successor, 1642, *Documentos inéditos . . . . de Mexico*, VII, 41–50.

[180] Riva Palacio, II, 598.

[181] Mancera to Veraguas, 1673, *Instrucciones que los vireyes . . . .* 283; Rivera Cambas, I, 286, 289.

that a squadron of fifteen vessels could be gathered if occasion demanded.[182]

The naval department of San Blas was established in 1769 in order to aid the military expeditions to Sonora and as a base of operations for occupying the Californias. A dry-dock was constructed in that port at the expense of the consulado. The second Revillagigedo considered it "a point of the greatest importance for maintaining us in the rightful possession of these distant and valuable lands which belong to his Majesty in that region."[183]

It was found that the port was very unhealthy. The climate was so hot that provisions for the Californias could not be kept there very long; accordingly it was proposed to transfer the dockyards and magazines of the whole marine department to Acapulco, but this change never took place.[184] In 1776 there were five boats attached to the port of San Blas which Bucareli was able to use for exploring purposes and furnishing supplies to California. Toward the end of the century, however, the naval force had decreased to three frigates and some smaller boats.[185]

Sometimes the viceroy was much annoyed by the difficulty of obtaining supplies for the department of San Blas. In 1775 tools, iron, and rigging being needed, Bucareli immediately sent to Spain for them, but the tools and iron arrived at San Blas a year after the request had been made. Having repeatedly tried in vain to obtain the other articles from Europe, finally at the end of two years Bucareli asked the viceroy of Peru to send them.[186] Another problem confronting the viceroy was to secure men for service at San Blas. This was no easy matter, for the dangerous journeys to Upper California were dreaded by all men. Recruits for those voyages almost had to be seized and placed on the ships by force.

[182] Lemos to Vallenari, *Memorias de los vireyes* . . . . VI, 307.

[183] Croix, *Instrucción que* . . . . *dejó*, AGI, 88–5–13; Revillagigedo, *Instrucción reservada*, art. 703.

[184] *Ibid.*, art. 797; Humboldt, II, 183.

[185] Chapman, *A History of California*, 285; Revillagigedo, *Instrucción reservada*, art. 705.

[186] Chapman, *A History of California*, 286.

7. EXPLORATION AND CONQUESTS

Exploration, conquests, and the extension of the frontiers came under the powers of the viceroy as captain-general, since they almost always involved the raising of military forces. The ordinances of 1563 concerning new discoveries enjoined viceroys to be informed whether there were any lands to be explored and pacified within the boundaries of their viceroyalties. If so, they could make arrangements with the proper persons to undertake a conquest. The king, however, had to be consulted first by the viceroy and his special permission obtained before a captain or adelantado could set out on a journey of discovery.[187] Explorations were not to be made at the expense of the royal treasury. We find that when Oñate made his expedition into New Mexico, he equipped, paid the salaries of his men, and provided everything necessary for the expedition. One of the reasons, no doubt, why he was chosen by Velasco, was because he was rich.[188] Nevertheless when religious wished to make discoveries for the spread of the Gospel, Philip II ordered that they be provided with sufficient funds from the treasury. No viceroy was to take part in discoveries by land or sea, on account of the inconveniences which would result from his absence in the capital; but he had authority over all captains who went out to conquer lands, and could punish them if they should exceed their powers.[189]

The first viceroy of New Spain might be called an expansionist. When news of the seven cities of Cíbola reached the capital, it is said by some historians that Mendoza wished to lead an expedition in person to that region. He was persuaded not to engage in such an adventure, and Francisco de Coronado was

---

[187] *Documentos inéditos . . . . de Indias*, VIII, 486–487; Ordinance of 1573, *ibid.*, XVI, 143–144; *Recopilación*, ley 28, tit. 3, lib. 3; ley 4, tit. 1, lib. 4.

[188] *Ibid.*, ley 17, tit. 1, lib. 4; Monterey to the king, May 8, 1598, 58–3–13; *Documentos inéditos . . . . de Indias*, XVI, 188–189.

[189] *Recopilación*, ley 3, tit. 4, lib. 4; Ordinances of 1571, *Documentos inéditos . . . . de Indias*, XVI, art. 40, p. 394; *ibid.*, XXIII, 502.

appointed to find the cities. The result of this journey of 1540 to 1542, which started with more than two hundred Spaniards and one thousand Indian allies, was the conquest of the Zuñi villages, the reaching of the Colorado River and Lower California, and a disappointing march into eastern Kansas.[190] The viceroy did not seem to be discouraged by the failure of the Coronado expedition, for in June, 1542, he sent to the north two vessels under the command of Juan Rodríguez Cabrillo. This exploring party reached 44° north latitude. Mendoza was also intent upon trading with the East Indies. He therefore fitted out two more of Alvarado's ships and put them under the leadership of Ruy López Villalobos. The expedition was lost, Villalobos died, and only a few of the sailors returned to tell the tale. It was at this time that the Philippines were named.[191]

The first Velasco followed in the footsteps of Mendoza as an expansionist. His first achievement was the sending out of Francisco Ibarra in 1554 to discover rich mines in Zacatecas.[192] The king was eager for the conquest of Florida, since a treasure fleet had been lost on its reefs in 1553 and the land was reported to be rich in precious metals. In 1559 the viceroy hesitatingly dispatched Tristán de Luna y Arellano with a force of five hundred soldiers and one thousand Indian allies for the conquest and colonization of the country. Velasco himself accompanied the ill-fated expedition as far as Vera Cruz. After the failure of Luna the viceroy sent Angel Villafañe on a second undertaking which had no better success.[193] Velasco next turned his

---

[190] Riva Palacio, II, 260; Bolton, H. E., *The Spanish Borderlands* (New Haven, 1921), 79–105.

[191] Herrerra, IV, decada 7, lib. 5, cap. 3, p. 113; *ibid.*, caps. 5–8, pp. 115–121. For details of the loss of the expedition *see* the letter of Friar Jerónimo Santiesteban to Mendoza, also the report of García Descalante Alvarado, *Documentos inéditos . . . . de Indias*, XIV, 151 *et seq.; ibid.*, V, 117 *et seq.*

[192] Herrera, IV, decada 8, lib. 10, pp. 335 *et seq.*

[193] Cavo, lib. 4, arts. 16–17, pp. 113–114. For the effect of these expeditions upon Cuba refer to Wright, I. A., *The Early History of Cuba 1492--1586* (New York, 1916), 225.

attention to the Philippines. He fitted out a fleet of four vessels headed by Miguel Gómez de Legaspi. Due to the viceroy's death, Legaspi was sent to those islands in 1564 by the audiencia. The voyage was prosperous and a rapid conquest of territory soon took place.[194]

In Mexico nothing much with respect to coastal exploration was accomplished until the rule of the second Velasco, although Villamanrique had given orders for two frigates to go out to examine the coasts, ports, rivers, and mountains of the northern part of New Spain, so that a good landing place might be found for the Manila galleon.[195] This Velasco was a promoter of expansion on the northern frontier. It was he who signed the contract for Oñate to make discoveries and settlements in New Mexico.[196] He was anxious to secure a port on the California coast for vessels from the Philippines; therefore he entered into a contract with Sebastián Vizcaíno to explore and occupy California. After some hesitation, in 1602 Velasco's successor, Monterey, permitted Vizcaíno to go on his voyage. Cape Mendocino was reached the next year, but on the whole the expedition was futile. During his second administration Velasco sent Vizcaíno, in 1611, to discover the fabulous islands called Rica de Oro and Rica de Plata. Japan was visited and some friendly correspondence took place with the emperor, but the results were not successful.[197]

Up to the time of Croix, numerous viceroys of New Spain undertook conquests and a few added new territories. The first Alburquerque's attempt to recapture Jamaica from the English in 1656 failed absolutely. Laguna had the same fortune when he tried to reconquer New Mexico, which had revolted against the Spaniards. Finally in 1692 Viceroy Galve was able to win back

---

[194] Zamacois, V, 59–64.

[195] Villamanrique to the king, May 10, 1586, AGI, 58–3–9.

[196] Twitchell, Ralph Emerson, *The Leading Facts of New Mexican History* (Cedar Rapids, Iowa, 1911–12), I, 304–305.

[197] Velasco to Monterey, 1595, AGI, 58–3–13; *Documentos inéditos . . . . de Indias*, VIII, 539–542; Riva Palacio, II, 550–557.

this province. He tried to make some further pacification of Texas, but in October, 1693, it had to be abandoned because of Indian insurrections.[198] On February 6, 1697, Viceroy Moctezuma gave Fathers Kino and Salvatierra permission to explore Lower California at their own expense. By 1701 Kino became convinced that California was a peninsula. Valero conquered the province of Nayarit, which had always defied the attempts of former viceroys to reduce it, and he made some gains at the expense of his French neighbors in the north by reoccupying the bay of Espíritu Santo. The first Revillagigedo had the satisfaction of seeing Tamaulipas pacified by José de Escandón.[199]

When Croix became viceroy, vigorous plans were made for expansion in the northwest. The visitor, José de Gálvez, was sent into Sonora to pacify that province and from there two expeditions to California were planned, one by sea and the other by land. In 1769 the ports of San Diego and Monterey were safely entered and taken possession of in the name of the king. The viceroy then decided to send help to those posts; therefore provisions were taken and the permanent existence of the new establishments guaranteed.[200]

Bucareli put into effect further measures to hold California. In 1773 he authorized Colonel Austin Crame to explore the isthmus of Tehuantepec to find a road for transportation of artillery and military supplies. This expedition accomplished its purpose, though the route was never used by the Spaniards. Next year the viceroy sent Captain Anza to open a trail by land to Upper California and the journey proved successful. On January 24, 1774, Juan Pérez set out from San Blas for the reconnaissance of the northwest coast. He got almost as far north as 55°, but had to turn back because of bad weather. No foreign

---

[198] Riva Palacio, II, 619, 637, 647, 649.

[199] *Ibid.*, II, 658–659, 769, 771, 768, 797–799.

[200] Croix, *Instrucción que* . . . . *dejó*, AGI, 88–5–13; *Correspondance*, 221–222.

settlements were found and only slight information concerning the coasts was brought back. Bucareli then turned his attention to the development of California as a barrier to foreign occupation in the northwest and tried to encourage emigration to that province.[201]

In 1790 Viceroy Revillagigedo sent Francisco Eliza to Nootka to establish a colony. Eliza began to construct some buildings and sent several of the other officers to explore and take possession of the neighboring coasts. Not much was accomplished by the expedition, which returned to San Blas in October. It was only a few years later that the lands to the north of the Spanish settlements were opened to the entry of England. For this reason Branciforte asked the king to send families from the Canary Islands to hasten the occupation of California, and advised that a company of volunteers composed of married men should go there with their families.[202]

The viceroys of Peru were lured on by the fascinating tales of El Dorado to make discoveries in South America. The first Cañete eagerly fitted out an expedition under the governors, Gómez Arias and Juan de Salinas. As a result many men were lost, but extensive regions hitherto unknown and undreamed of were explored, and a new town was established.[203] As late as 1782 the story of the city of the Caesars had an attraction for the royal court; accordingly Manuel de Orejuela was commissioned to undertake its discovery. The president of the audiencia of Chile was a man of sound judgment, and he advised the king to give up such an uncertain adventure. Many voyages of discovery, which opened vast territories to human knowledge, were made in order to find traces of foreign establishments. Even the bleak shores of Patagonia were carefully examined in 1793

---

[201] Chapman, *A History of California*, 273–291; Coroleu, I, 368.

[202] Riva Palacio, II, 879; Branciforte to Azanza, 1797, *Instrucciones que los vireyes* . . . . arts. 78, 81, p. 139.

[203] Report of all that happened in the province of El Dorado by Pedro de Orsua, *Documentos inéditos* . . . . *de Indias*, IV, 215 *et seq.*

and 1794.[204]   The interesting story of expansion in South America reads much like that of New Spain; therefore no attempt will be made to relate it.

The viceroy as captain-general was supreme military chieftain in the New World. Military leaders always have occupied a prominent place in countries newly discovered or exposed to foreign aggressions; for this reason many of the viceroys were chosen from among men experienced in the arts of war. As captain-general the viceroy acted on his own initiative more than under any of his other titles, since there were many cases of emergency to meet and strategic measures to be employed in Indian wars and in foreign attacks. In time of war he was assisted by the junta de guerra, but there was no regularly organized general staff. His chief assistant was the auditor de guerra, a kind of special adviser.

The preservation of peace in the country was one of the chief duties of the viceroy. There were restless spirits and outlaw adventurers who threatened the security of the colonies. In putting down dangerous revolts and freeing the seas from pirates, viceroys often coöperated with one another. However the greatest task of the captain-general was the external defense of the viceroyalty, which involved the building and repairs of fortifications. During European wars there was always the possibility of the enemy gaining a foothold in the Spanish colonial possessions. At times the Dutch, Portuguese, English, French, Russians, and even the new republic of the United States were a menace to the viceroyalties.

The captain-general was the commander-in-chief of the army and supervised it in a general way. One of his chief duties was the enlisting of men for the army and the armadas—not an easy task by any means, since men did not wish to serve in the unhealthful coast regions and go on hazardous voyages. The

---

[204] Croix to Lemos, 1790, *Memorias de los vireyes* . . . . V, 181–182, 246–252; Lemos to Vallenari, *ibid.*, IV, 176–177.

supplying of arms and munitions for the enlisted men was another problem of the captain-general, because there was always a great scarcity of these articles in the viceroyalty. Barracks and military hospitals had to be provided for the soldiers. The early viceroys made a number of military appointments, but this power seems to have decreased later, especially after the arrival of Villalba in New Spain. The founding of presidios was a defensive measure adopted by the viceroys, and they had to be furnished continually with supplies and ammunitions.

While in the New World, admirals of armadas were subject to the orders of the viceroy, and he supervised the building of ships in American waters. The captain-general provided supplies for armadas and dispatched them to the places of their destination. He was always interested in the famous armada of the Windward Islands, which protected the coasts and the treasure fleets from pirates and foreign enemies. It was not until 1769 that the naval department of San Blas was created for the expeditions to the northwest. Exploration, conquests, and the extension of the frontiers pertained to the powers of the captains-general, many of whom were real expansionists.

CHAPTER VIII

THE VICEROY AND THE PEOPLE

The classes of society in the viceroyalties were far from homogeneous. The conquistadores, first settlers, and the later arrivals, European-born Spaniards, constituting the rank and file of those who held public offices, were the most important. Next came the creoles, descendants of the discoverers and Europeans, but who owned America as their birthplace. Below these were the mestizos and various castes, the Negroes, and the native Indians, who greatly outnumbered all the other people. Then there were the foreigners who made their entrance into the viceroyalties whenever a good opportunity arose. Over this mixture of races governed the viceroy, the chief representative of the king. It was he who tried to prevent their vices, to raise the standard of public morality, and to regulate their amusements.

1. THE WHITES AND THE CASTES

The first immigrants coming to the New World were for the most part adventurers recruited from the nobility and the army— men who had taken part in the Moslem wars. After those conflicts had ceased, they endeavored to find employment in America, where there was a chance to replenish their resources. The clergy eagerly undertook the hazardous voyage to the distant dependencies in order to save the souls of the Indians. When the fervor of the discoveries had subsided somewhat the common people went to the Indies.

Spain adopted a restrictive policy of colonization from the beginning, the effort of the government being to limit the privilege of forming settlements to Spaniards of old Christian families, so that heretics might not corrupt the natives; but this regulation could not be strictly enforced. At the time of his second voyage, such throngs of people entreated Columbus to take them with him, that the rule was adopted to permit no one to go to the Indies without a special license.[1] The viceroy was to take great care that every person coming to the colonies had the proper licenses. As soon as they arrived arrangements were to be made to inspect their papers. When they came without these the executive was to send them back to Spain immediately, making no exception.[2] Generals of armadas daring to bring license-evaders to America were in danger of incurring the penalty of loss of their office and cargo. Even viceroys, judges of the audiencia, and governors might not take their wives with them to the Indies without the royal permission.[3]

The same restriction was imposed upon people wishing to return to Spain. It seems that sometimes the early viceroys gave their consent for individuals to go back to the home country, but later the king had to be advised before this could be done.[4] It was not desired that ecclesiastics and colonial officials should return to Madrid to attend court because their long absence would be injurious to the good government of the viceroyalties.[5]

It is difficult to give any correct statistics for the population of the Spanish dependencies during the early colonial period, since the Indians were hard to enumerate on account of their migratory habits. In 1794 Revillagigedo the younger estimated the population of New Spain at 3,500,000 persons. At the end of the eighteenth or the beginning of the nineteenth century, Riva Palacio declared it was 8,000,000, only 1,000,000 of this number

[1] Herrera, I, decada 1, lib. 3, cap. 2, p. 83.

[2] Cédulas and provisiones of 1568, *Documentos inéditos . . . . de Indias*, XVIII, 121–122; Court to Amarillas, 1755, *Instrucciones que los vireyes . . . .* art. 25, pp. 67–68; *Recopilación*, leyes 59, 64, tit. 26, lib. 8.

[3] *Ibid.*, leyes 2, 28.

[4] *Ibid.*, ley 65; Cédulas and provisiones for the audiencia of La Plata, 1565, *Documentos inéditos . . . . de Indias*, XVIII, 55–56.

[5] *Recopilación*, ley 56, tit. 2, lib. 2.

belonging to the white race. There were about 20,000 European-born inhabitants.[6] In 1796 Viceroy Lemos stated that the population of Peru was about 1,500,000 people, and if Buenos Aires and the presidency of Quito were included, it was 3,500,000.[7]

The conquistadores and their descendants were the most favored people. They had been granted the choice encomiendas in the colonies and were preferred to others in the appointments to the corregimientos.[8] Viceroy Enríquez was much disturbed by their demanding the right to hold the chief offices in the vice-royalty. If this claim was not heeded, they carried on noisy lawsuits or went to Spain to make their complaints. The viceroy reported to the king that many of those born in the Indies were not fit to serve in public positions. The sovereign replied that Enríquez should not be annoyed by their murmurings, but should honor really worthy conquistadores. Montesclaros was requested to keep the descendants of the conquerors satisfied by giving them offices; however, he too advised the monarch that merit ought to be considered above everything else.[9] Many individuals received public positions in America, just because they had taken part in the conquest. Indeed, some of them were almost incorrigible at home, and had been sent to the New World to sow their wild oats. Experience soon proved that these reprobate adventurers did not make good administrators.

Europeans went to America for various motives. Some came for the purpose of serving the king, others were so poor that they performed the menial duties of servants to pay for their passage, some were polizones or license-evaders hoping to win fortunes for themselves, still others were deserters from ships and refugees from justice.[10] Although the Europeans married into colonial

[6] Revillagigedo, *Instrucción reservada,* art. 143; Riva Palacio, II, 913; *ibid.,* III, 19.

[7] Lemos to Vallenari, 1796, *Memorias de los vireyes* . . . . VI, 76.

[8] King to Mendoza, 1535, *Documentos inéditos* . . . . *de Indias,* XXIII, 433; Code of laws for the Indies, 1571, *ibid.,* art. 47, p. 399.

[9] Enríquez to Coruña, 1580, *Instrucciones que los vireyes* . . . . art. 18, p. 249; Montesclaros to the king, 1607, *ibid.,* 254–255.

[10] Villarroel, *Enfermedades políticas* . . . . MS, III, pt. v, pp. 149–150.

society and became wealthy, the remembrance of their former miserable condition was a sore spot concerning which their enemies made much sport.[11]   In Mexico they were called gachupines as a term of derision because of their pointed shoes, and in South America they were nicknamed chapetones.[12]   The Europeans were always determined to maintain a dominant position and for this reason much hostility arose against them.   This became one of the reasons why the lower classes desired to win independence from Spanish rule.

There were many nobles among the Spaniards who tried to please the viceroy because they were dependent upon him for favors.[13]   Palafox thought that the executive ought to respect the nobility so that they would not lose their reverence for him, but that he ought not to make too great a demonstration of politeness, since his position was higher than theirs.[14]   Villarroel said that

. . . . Those who are considered men of rank, the attendants of the palace, have no other aim than to charm the viceroy, flatter him, and discover his tastes and amusements in order to cater to them, although it might be detrimental to the public, and to the weight of their authority and reputation.   All affect a humbleness, a servile respect in his presence, and are the first on leaving to censure his attitude and his acts.   Yet no one will tell him what is complained of or said in public of his government and personal conduct.[15]

On the whole this class was loyal to the king and easy for the viceroy to control, if it were treated with kindness.[16]

The merchants, who constituted rather a small class of society were Europeans.   Vera Cruz is said to have had two hundred Spanish families, all of whom were merchants and shopkeepers.[17]

---

[11] Juan and Ulloa, *Noticias secretas de America*, 417 et seq.

[12] Alamán, *Historia de Méjico*, I, 7; Bourne, 226.

[13] Montesclaros to his successor, 1615, *Documentos inéditos* . . . . *de Indias*, VI, 226.

[14] To his successor, 1642, *Documentos inéditos* . . . . *de Mexico*, VII, 28.

[15] *Enfermedades políticas* . . . . MS, II, pt. III, pp. 48–49.

[16] Mancera to Veraguas, 1673, *Instrucciones que los vireyes* . . . . 258; Croix, *Instrucción que* . . . . *dejó*, AGI, 88–5–13.

[17] Keller, A. G., *Colonization* (Boston, New York, 1908), 226.

The first Cañete of Peru regarded these men with some suspicion, since they were always eager for wars in order to sell their merchandise and to promote their own interests.[18] Later viceroys frequently obtained financial assistance from them when important public projects were to be undertaken. Sometimes money was loaned without interest to the viceroy.[19] The merchants closely resembled the nobility, whom they imitated and with whom they intermarried. In New Spain this class, like the nobility, was peaceful, but in Peru there were differences between the Andalusian and Biscayan merchants which greatly annoyed the viceroy.[20] The first Revillagigedo also made complaints against those Spanish merchants who penetrated to the interior of the country and intimidated the people by the changing and lowering of prices, thereby causing injury to the Mexican merchants.[21]

The polizones and vagabonds coming from Spain caused the executive much trouble by committing crimes and corrupting society. The second Revillagigedo took measures for license-evaders to be apprehended as soon as they landed, but he was unable to stop their coming.[22] They frequently lived among the Indians where they caused much injury, and viceroys were enjoined repeatedly to prevent this evil.[23] The problem of freeing the country from the vices of the idle and all kinds of vagabonds was a serious one, indeed, for the executive.[24] Most viceroys considered that indolence was only one step removed from

---

[18] Cañete to the emperor, 1556, *Documentos inéditos* . . . . *de Indias*, IV, 96–97.

[19] Montesclaros to his successor, 1615, *ibid.*, VI, 228; Croix, *Instrucción que* . . . . *dejó*, AGI, 88–5–13.

[20] Mancera to Veraguas, 1673, *Instrucciones que los vireyes* . . . . 258–259.

[21] Revillagigedo to Amarillas, 1754, *ibid.*, art. 56, p. 16.

[22] *Instrucción reservada*, art. 152.

[23] King to the viceroy of Mexico, 1550, *Documentos inéditos* . . . . *de Indias*, XXIII, 545–546; *Recopilación*, ley 1, tit. 4, lib. 7.

[24] Martín Cortés to Philip II, 1563, *Documentos inéditos* . . . . *de Indias*, IV, 458; Council of the Indies to Amarillas, 1755, *Instrucciones que los vireyes* . . . . art. 15, p. 92; Croix, *Instrucción que* . . . . *dejó* AGI, 88–5–13.

crime, therefore they made every effort to overcome the bad habit. On May 2, 1702, Viceroy Montañez visited the prison of Mexico City and found it full of lazy people amusing themselves by listening to the trials. He commanded that the doors should be closed and imprisoned the spectators for some hours, then set them free, recommending that thereafter they ought to spend their time on their own affairs.[25]

Cases of idleness had to be reported to the viceroys in order that they might compel all able-bodied men either to seek work for themselves, or assign them to public tasks. Viceroy Valero sent vagabonds to the presidios of Florida and Croix ordered the governor of Vera Cruz to make all those who came from Spain without licenses serve in the troops. The latter viceroy caused a proclamation to be published commanding all the idle to find work or they would be assigned to some occupation.[26] If any gypsies came to the Indies, the viceroys were to see that they and their families were sent back to Spain on the first returning vessels.[27]

The creoles or American-born Spaniards began to regard themselves as a separate class because of their exclusion from public offices and the discrimination made in regard to them by Europeans. The most ignorant Spaniard thought himself superior to the whites born in the colonies, and as the result a hatred arose between the creoles and gachupines. After 1789 the creoles began to call themselves Americans.[28] Enríquez was not afraid to make use of creoles in public offices in Mexico, but most of the other viceroys held that this class was not fit for gubernatorial responsibilities. Mancera considered them a bitter race which always had a repugnance for subordination and a

---

[25] Zamacois, V, 512.

[26] *Recopilación*, leyes 2–4, tit. 4, lib. 7; Rivera Cambas, I, 318, 412; Croix, *Instrucción que . . . . dejó*, AGI, 88–5–13.

[27] *Recopilación*, ley 5, tit. 4, lib. 7; Cédulas and provisiones for the audiencia of Charcas, 1581, *Documentos inéditos . . . . de Indias*, XVIII, 138–139.

[28] Humboldt, I, 204–205.

craving for authority.[29] The pride of the creole would not permit him to engage in manual labor, but he often sought to practice law, since this was one of the few vocations without stigma.[30] There was the same objection to creoles serving in the church. The Augustinians admitted only creoles into their order and excluded Spaniards; therefore Mancera, acting upon a royal decree of November 28, 1667, commanded them to receive Europeans. They promised to do this, but only on one occasion did Spaniards attempt to enter the organization. On the other hand, the barefoot Carmelites were opposed to having creoles as members of their society. The policy of alternation of creoles and Spaniards in elections of priors of the orders was adopted finally to eliminate bitter rivalries within them. This arrangement did not put an end to the quarrels.[31] It is a well-known fact that very few creoles ever held high positions in the church or in the state.

The mestizos, who had Spanish and Indian blood, were despised by the Spaniards still more than the creoles. Certain laws of the Indies specifically excluded them from some kinds of public offices, such as treasurers (receptores) and protectors of the Indians, but by a law of 1588 they were granted the right to enter the church if their lives and habits were good and they were of legitimate birth.[32] Nevertheless, a royal cédula of December 13, 1577, directed to the bishop of Cuzco, commanded that mestizos should be excluded from offices in the church until further provisions were made. In spite of the later laws of 1697, 1725, and 1774 permitting this class of people to enter the sacred

---

[29] Priestley, *The Mexican Nation*, 88; Mancera to Veraguas, 1673, *Instrucciones que los vireyes* . . . . 259.

[30] Leroy-Beaulieu, Paul, *De la colonisation chez les peuples modernes* (ed. 4, Paris, 1891), 9. Among the 166 viceroys and 588 captains-general, governors, and presidents of audiencias in the colonies only eighteen were creoles. Nevertheless creole lawyers served satisfactorily in the audiencia of Mexico during the Gálvez visitation. Priestley, *José de Gálvez*, 52.

[31] Mancera to Veraguas, 1673, *Instrucciones que los vireyes* . . . . 272–274.

[32] *Recopilación*, ley 1, tit. 27, lib. 2; ley 7, tit. 6, lib. 6; ley 7, tit. 7, lib. 1.

calling, custom prevented them from doing so.[33] It was thought that the mestizos who lived among the natives caused disturbances and aided the Indians in their litigation against the Spaniards; accordingly many of the viceregal measures aimed to prevent them from dwelling in native towns.[34]

The castes were so numerous that it would be difficult to find names enough for all of them. The Spaniards were always very careful to differentiate blood mixture, and any persons having a slight strain of white blood were distinguished by the term "gente de razón" or people possessed of reasoning power. This element thought itself superior to the lower group of society generally known as the "pardos y demas castas" which included all of dark complexion who were not pure Indians or Negroes. Sometimes mulattoes and persons with dark skins succeeded in being declared white by a court decision.[35]

The poor in the larger cities represented the castes at their worst. They lived on a very low level of civilization. Viceroy Enríquez said that he did not believe it a sin to suspect them of any evil. As late as 1765 when Viceroy Croix arrived, it was a common occurrence to find murdered persons lying in the streets of Mexico City every morning.[36] One famous highwayman and robber was the companion of a very religious man and lived on his estate with him. Another rang the bells in the cathedral during the day, and when Prójimo, the most noted of them all, was hung the people pitied him. The ease with which food might be obtained from charitable organizations only encouraged beggary, and if these provisions did not suffice, the poor supported themselves by all kinds of petty thefts.[37] The

---

[33] Solórzano, II, lib. 4, cap. 20, art. 5, p. 171; Robertson, II, Appendix, pp. 506–507.

[34] Enríquez to Coruña, 1580, *Instrucciones que los vireyes* . . . . art. 3, p. 244; Montesclaros to his successor, 1615, *Documentos inéditos* . . . . *de Indias*, VI, 224–225.

[35] Humboldt, I, 246–247.

[36] Enríquez to Coruña, 1580, *Instrucciones que los vireyes* . . . . art. 15, p. 248; Croix, *Instrucción que* . . . . *dejó*, AGI, 88–5–13.

[37] Linares to Valero, 1716, *Instrucciones que los vireyes* . . . . 307.

plebians were noted for their drunkenness, gambling, and lewdness, the checking of which proved to be a very serious problem for the viceroy. They used knives called belduques and stones with which they wounded their enemies. When crimes were committed these criminals sought the right of sanctuary in the churches, but finally in 1764 this privilege was taken away from them by royal order.[38] The first Revillagigedo said that, although the common people were worthless and vicious, they were also cowardly, and a few soldiers among great masses of them were able to check their disorders and excesses.[39]

2. THE INDIANS AND NEGROES

From the first Spain adopted a very humanitarian policy toward the Indians, who were to be free vassals of the king. Viceroys were repeatedly enjoined to guarantee freedom to the natives, but this was not always easy to do when the exploiters of colonial wealth desired to enslave their Indian laborers.[40] A royal cédula of May 26, 1608, permitted the Spaniards to make slaves of Indians waging open war in Chile, but two years later this measure was suspended, due to the entreaties of the Jesuits.[41] In New Spain the first viceroy enslaved many Indians after the Mixton Wars, but his successor, Velasco the "Emancipator," devoted himself to freeing them. The natives were at liberty to marry whom they wished, but according to the rites of the church. Unions between Spaniards and Indians also were permitted as a means of furthering the spread of European civilization in the colonies.[42]

---

[38] Croix, *Instrucción que* . . . . *dejó*, AGI, 88–5–13.

[39] To Amarillas, 1754, *Instrucciones que los vireyes* . . . . art. 4, p. 6.

[40] *Recopilación*, leyes 1–3, 9, tit. 2, lib. 6; King to Mendoza, 1535, *Documentos inéditos* . . . . *de Indias*, XXIII, 440–441; Montesclaros to his successor, 1615, *ibid.*, VI, 211.

[41] Solórzano, I, lib. 2, cap. 1, art. 28, p. 63.

[42] *Recopilación*, ley 2, tit. 1, lib. 6. When the king permitted this right to the Indians, he recognized them as rational beings and in 1531 Pope Paul III officially declared that they had reasoning powers. Zamacois, IV, 637.

The conversion of the Indians was one of the chief motives for the Spanish conquest of America. The conversion and instruction of the natives were to take place through the instrumentality of the church, but viceroys had to see that it was done in the proper way, and they were to aid the prelates as much as possible. The first measure to be adopted by the viceroy was to give orders for all idols, altars and temples to be destroyed. The stones might be used for building churches and monasteries, but if any articles of value were found, the viceroy could spend the profits from their sale for construction and ornamentation of Christian sanctuaries.[43] When the Indians persisted in keeping idols in their homes, the viceroy was to see that they were punished. Priests who taught idolatry were to be sent to convents to be instructed in the Christian faith.[44] The viceroy was to provide that at a certain hour each day the Indians of the towns went to church to hear religious teachings. He was to inform himself whether the natives working in cloth factories and sugar mills received proper instruction in the Gospel.[45] At first thousands of Indians were baptized by the wholesale without knowing the significance of the act, therefore the king commanded the viceroy to cause them to learn at least the fundamentals of the faith before being baptized. This ideal program for converting the natives also included secular learning and the teaching of Spanish. Monterey said that he had furnished Spanish teachers for the Indians of Mexico before he received the royal order to do so.[46]

The entire policy of governing the Indians was intrusted to the viceroys, not to the audiencias. The chief source of vexation

---

[43] *Recopilación*, leyes 7, 5, tit. 1, lib. 1; King to Mendoza, 1538, *Documentos inéditos . . . . de Mexico*, XV, 65–66, 47–48.

[44] King to Mendoza, 1540, *ibid.*, XV, 76; *Recopilación*, ley 9, tit. 1, lib. 1.

[45] *Ibid.*, leyes 11–12, tit. 1, lib. 1; King to the viceroy of Peru, 1540, *Documentos inéditos . . . . de Indias*, XXIII, 500; Court to Amarillas, 1755, *Instrucciones que los vireyes . . . .* art. 2, pp. 58–59.

[46] Memorial of Toledo, 1596, *Documentos inéditos . . . . de Indias*, VI, 521; Cédulas and provisiones for the viceroy of Peru, 1550, *ibid.*, XVIII, 472–473; Monterey to the king, April 25, 1598, AGI, 58–3–13, p. 41.

for the natives came from the alcaldes mayores and priests because of their demands for services, excessive taxes, and dues. The viceroy had to investigate thoroughly the charges made by the natives against those officials and priests, since they were not always true, and the Indians were easily influenced by the enemies of those men.[47] In order to defend the Indians in their many litigations, protectors were appointed in the audiencias to try their lawsuits so that they did not have to leave their homes. The cases were to be dispatched briefly and without expense to the litigants.[48] Palafox thought that the natives could be protected better if the viceroy had a good assessor who was acquainted with the trifles concerning which they complained.[49] It was said that a Spaniard seldom received the death penalty when he was guilty of a grave offense against the natives, but in a royal decree of December 29, 1593, the king ordered the viceroys not to make any distinction between Spaniards and other people in this matter.[50]

The whole policy of dealing with the Indians was very paternalistic. This was especially true under the mission system, but it is a question whether any better methods of Christianizing and governing the natives could have been found. At any rate, they surpassed the English plan of non-interference, which left the Indians to struggle alone as best they could against a higher civilization. The viceroy was expected to attend to the many details concerning the natives, just as a father provided for his children. He was to prevent their health from being injured by prohibiting them to be taken from one province to another, and they were not to carry heavy burdens.[51] He was to aid them

---

[47] Croix, *Instrucción que . . . . dejó*, AGI, 88–5–13; Court to Amarillas, 1755, *Instrucciones que los vireyes . . . .* arts. 8–9, pp. 61–62; Palafox to his successor, 1642, *Documentos inéditos . . . . de Mexico*, VII, 68, 72–73.

[48] Memorial of Toledo, 1596, *Documentos inéditos . . . . de Indias*, VI, 539.

[49] To his successor, 1642, *Documentos inéditos . . . . de Mexico*, VII, 70.

[50] Cédulas and provisiones for the audiencia of Charcas, *Documentos inéditos . . . . de Indias*, XVIII, 554–555.

[51] King to the viceroy of Peru, 1540, *ibid.*, XXIII, 495–497; Cédulas and provisiones, 1543, *ibid.*, XVIII, 468–469.

in farming and see that they were instructed in the cultivation of grains and vegetables, also in the handicrafts. It was the duty of the viceroy to try to decrease idleness among the natives by assigning them some profitable labor. They were not to become merchants, but all the more menial occupations were open to them.[52] The executive was to have the Indian tribute-payers counted every five years in order to see whether they had diminished or increased.[53]

The general supervision of the encomiendas was another task of the viceroy. In theory the encomienda system was ideal. Under it the Indians were to be fed, clothed, and Christianized in return for their labor. The humanitarian designs of the king, however, could not be reconciled with the economic greed for wealth, and the status of the natives soon changed from serfdom to actual slavery. Viceroys, judges of the audiencia, governors, other public officials, ecclesiastics, women, and foreigners might not have encomiendas. Nevertheless, Viceroy Guadalcázar of Peru was granted six thousand ducats in rents from an encomienda when he married María de la Riere, and after her death he was allowed to keep this income for the education of his children.[54] The viceroy had to see that one third of the dues from vacant encomiendas was paid to the treasury, and that the former owners had fulfilled all their financial obligations, before a successor could take charge of the estate.[55]

Whenever a person who had an encomienda died, within six months his successor had to go in person or send his lawyer to the viceroy in order to present his claims for the inheritance and to receive a new title to possess the grant for the second genera-

---

[52] Mendoza to Valero, *Instrucciones que los vireyes* . . . . 236; *Documentos inéditos* . . . . *de Mexico*, XV, 51; King to the viceroy of Mexico, 1550, *ibid.*, XXIII, 530–531.

[53] Court to Amarillas, 1755, *Instrucciones que los vireyes* . . . . 81–82.

[54] *Recopilación*, leyes 12–14, tit. 8, lib. 6; Solórzano, I, lib. 3, cap. 16, arts. 10–13, p. 316.

[55] *Recopilación*, leyes 131, 34, tit. 15, lib. 2; ley 66, tit. 3, lib. 3; leyes 7–8, tit. 8, lib. 6; Solórzano, II, lib. 5, cap. 13, art. 13, p. 378; *ibid.*, I, lib. 3, cap. 28, arts. 4, 8, 10, 14, pp. 394–395.

tion. If this was not done the rents were to go to the crown.[56] Encomenderos could not absent themselves from their possessions without the permission of the viceroy or the governor of the province in which they resided. The penalty for absence without obtaining the viceroy's consent was to have the Indians taken away from the encomendero and placed under the protection of the crown.[57] It was also the duty of the viceroy to be informed whether the encomenderos instructed the Indians on their estates in the Christian faith and whether they treated them well. He was to order the owners of the encomiendas to marry within three or four years, since it was found that unmarried men were negligent in the performance of their duties and that they caused injuries to the natives.[58]

In the province of Charcas the large estates were called charcaras, and the Indians assigned to them were known as yanaconas. Viceroy Toledo commanded the natives to live on those farms permanently, and the owners were to provide them with lands for their crops, pay their tributes, and give them Christian instruction, in return for their services. Many Indians came to the charcaras of their own free will in order to escape from the mita, and at the invitation of the proprietors. There they were treated better and had less work than under the mita system. Royal orders declared that these laborers were to be considered free and could leave whenever they wished, but they were not enforced for fear of losing the Indian workers. Viceroy Velasco tried to have the Indians placed again under the mita, except those assigned to the estates by Toledo, but he was not successful.[59]

---

[56] Royal cédula of Dec. 19, 1568, *Documentos inéditos* . . . . *de Indias,* XIX, 101.

[57] Solórzano, I, lib. 3, cap. 27, art. 26, p. 389; *ibid.,* arts. 12, 16, p. 388; Code of laws for the government of the Indies, 1571, *Documentos inéditos* . . . . *de Indias,* XVI, art. 48, p. 400; Cédulas and provisiones for the audiencia of Charcas, 1589, *ibid.,* XVIII, 202–203.

[58] King to Mendoza, 1538, *ibid.,* XXIII, 494; *ibid.,* XVIII, 17.

[59] Velasco to Monterey, 1604, *Documentos inéditos* . . . . *de Indias,* IV, 420–423; Montesclaros to his successor, 1615, *ibid.,* VI, 221–224.

It was under the mita system that the Indians suffered the most hardships. It consisted of a kind of forced labor or corveé usually applied to the mines, but it could be used for labor on the large estates, in sugar mills, cloth mills, in cutting wood on the mountains, in the service of messengers and in many other occupations. During the early days in the mines of Peru the abuses of this system were terrible. As a result, the viceroys made stricter regulations to be applied to the mita. Indians no longer were permitted to be so used in pearl fishing, in vineyards, olive orchards, sugar mills, or in cutting wood on the mountains.[60] Finally in a cédula of April 5, 1720, it was ordered that the forced work of the mita in Peru should cease, and the Indians might only labor of their own free will or for wages.[61] In Peru there were some Indians called mingados who were not under the mita. They worked voluntarily for wages, and the owners of the mines used them when in need of laborers.[62]

The reduction of Indians to towns occupied the attention of the early viceroys. If the natives were assembled in one place, they could be instructed more easily in the Christian faith. Then, too, they would not be able to escape from paying tribute and their lands could be given to the Spaniards.[63] The Indian villages were to be separated from the Spanish towns or confined to the suburbs of the larger cities. Neither whites, Negroes, nor mulattoes were to reside in the native towns, and merchants might remain there only three days.[64]

In New Spain the early reductions were not very successful. When the second Velasco sent commissioners to compel the

---

[60] *Ibid.*, VI, 217–220; Montesclaros to his successor, 1615, *Memorias de los vireyes* . . . . I, 26–27.

[61] Castel-Fuerte to Villagarcía, 1736, *ibid.*, III, 151–152. In Peru seven per cent of the population was subjected to the service of the mita, but in Mexico only four per cent worked under this institution.

[62] Montesclaros to his successor, 1615, *Documentos inéditos* . . . . *de Indias*, VI, 238–239.

[63] Solórzano, I, lib. 2, cap. 24, arts. 12–16, p. 185; *ibid.*, arts. 35, 39, pp. 187–188; King to Mendoza, 1538, *Documentos inéditos* . . . . *de Mexico*, XV, 64; *Recopilación*, ley 1, tit. 3, lib. 6.

[64] *Ibid.*, leyes 21–22, 24.

nomadic northern Indians to leave their old homes and live in
towns, their distress was very great. Some of them fled to the
wilderness and others committed suicide rather than abandon
their old haunts. Learning of this, Velasco wisely suspended the
measure and explained to the king the injuries that it caused.[65]
His successor, however, undertook the problem of the reductions
in earnest, appointing one hundred commissioners and two hundred clerks to find the best sites for the new towns. It required
almost a year to fulfil this part of the work. Monterey discovered
that some of the commissioners had not selected the proper places
for the reductions; therefore he appointed an entirely new set of
officials. The measure was just as unfortunate as that under
Velasco, the Indians being forcibly and cruelly removed from
their dwellings. In 1605 the king granted the natives the right
to return to their former homes, after many of them had died and
others had fled to the mountains.[66]

The reductions in South America were more prosperous than
those in Mexico. The plan of Viceroy Toledo was to form Indian
villages of four or five hundred persons, having a priest to
instruct them in religion, a church, a hospital and a prison. This
viceroy established six reductions in Peru. In the first town to
be founded all the Indian carpenters were settled, and in the
second one, called Santiago, all the silversmiths were located.
A Spanish inspector of silver was hired by the government to
instruct the residents of the latter town in their occupation.[67]

The chief official of the Indian towns was the cacique or chief,
who received his position sometimes by inheritance and other
times by election. Mendoza permitted the natives to choose the
cacique according to their ancient customs, but if it was found
that he was not fit, the viceroy removed him and ordered that

[65] Zamacois, V, 203–204.

[66] Riva Palacio, II, 452–454, 540; Zamacois, V, 254; Rivera Cambas, I,
72.

[67] Account concerning Toledo, *Documentos inéditos* . . . . *de Indias,*
VIII, 290.

another man be elected.[68]   In Peru when the inheritance to this
office went to a child, the corregidor of the district presented
three names to the viceroy, who selected one.   While the arrangements were being made for a successor, the oldest Indian official
served ad interim.   The corregidor might not arrest a cacique
except for a serious crime.   The viceroy had to see that caciques
did not exact more tributes and personal services from their
people than was necessary.[69]

The Spanish crown claimed a share of all Indian treasures.
Viceroys were commanded to search diligently for hidden wealth
in the temples and tombs of the natives.   Half was to go to the
king and the remainder to the lucky finder.[70]   In 1540 the viceroy
of Peru was enjoined to see that the king received a sixth of all
gold, silver, precious stones, and pearls taken during an Indian
war, and the other parts were to be divided among the conquistadores, after the fifth (quinto) was taken out for the
sovereign.   When a cacique was killed in battle half of his wealth
went to the king, and when an Indian chieftain made peace he
was to pay a sum of gold and silver to the victors from which
the crown obtained one-third.[71]

Indians had to pay a moderate tribute to the state and tithes
to the church.   This decision was made in 1529 at a meeting in
Barcelona.[72]   At first the tribute was paid in kind, in the grains,
the produce of the lands, and blankets, but sometimes it could be
commuted into money.[73]   Indians from eighteen to fifty years of

---

[68] Mendoza to Velasco, *Instrucciones que los vireyes* . . . . 234; Solórzano,
I, lib. 2, cap. 27, arts. 14, 16–17, pp. 202–203.

[69] Montesclaros to his successor, 1615, *Documentos inéditos* . . . . *de
Indias*, VI, 209–210; King to Mendoza, 1535, *ibid.*, XXIII, 435; Mendoza
to Valero, *Instrucciones que los vireyes* . . . . 235.

[70] King to Mendoza, 1535, *Documentos inéditos* . . . . *de Indias*, XXIII,
435; Solórzano, II, lib. 6, cap. 5, arts. 9, 12, 15–17, pp. 447–449.

[71] *Documentos inéditos* . . . . *de Indias*, XXIII, 485–488.

[72] Solórzano, I, lib. 2, cap. 22, art. 16, p. 174.

[73] *Documentos inéditos* . . . . *de Mexico*, XV, 48–49 Montesclaros to his
successor, 1615, *Documentos inéditos* . . . . *de Indias*, VI, 213; King to
Mendoza, 1535, *ibid.*, XXIII, 428; Velasco to Monterey, 1604; *ibid.*, IV,
419.

age were subject to the tribute,[74] the amount of which varied from time to time. A cédula of November 1, 1591, fixed it at four reales a year, and at the beginning of the seventeenth century the Indians paid one peso of eight reales annually.[75]

The viceroy was to protect the natives in the paying of tribute. Viceroy Toledo of Peru was urged to keep the tribute reasonably low and uniform in all parts of the country, and lower than it had been before the conquest. He was likewise to prevent excessive tithes from being imposed upon the Indians by the church.[76] Sometimes in case of serious epidemics the viceroys exempted the natives from the obligation of paying tribute, as Enríquez did in 1576, when the terrible scourage of matlazáhuatl caused almost two million deaths in Mexico.[77]

Enforcement of the rules concerning personal service by the Indians was one of the chief difficulties of the viceroy. From the time of the conquest the natives were so hostile to labor that, in order to found a new régime, it was necessary to force them to work. At first it was impossible to put into effect the New Laws of 1542 and 1543, which provided for the abolition of all personal service, and they had to be repealed. The viceroys, however, gradually tried to better the condition of the Indians and to fulfil the royal measures relating to them. As has been mentioned, they had roads and bridges constructed so that the Indians might be relieved from carrying burdens, and in the provinces where the carriers still remained minute regulations were made concerning them. They could only do this kind of work voluntarily and for sufficient wages. They were not permitted to go from the cold regions to the warm climates because of injuring their health.[78] The viceroy had to see that proper wages were

---

[74] Lemos to Vallenari, 1796, *Memorias de los vireyes* . . . . VI, 216.

[75] Riva Palacio, II, 689. By a cédula of April 27, 1575, Negroes and mulattoes were to pay two pesos of tribute each year.

[76] Solórzano, I, lib. 2, cap. 19, art. 30, p. 157; Cédulas and provisions for the viceroys of Peru, 1551, *Documentos inéditos* . . . . *de Indias*, XVIII, 476–477; Velasco to Monterey, 1604, *ibid.*, IV, 424.

[77] Solórzano, I, lib. 2, cap. 20, arts. 32–35, p. 164.

[78] *Documentos inéditos* . . . . *de Indias*, XLI, 149–157.

paid for the services of Indians. Viceroy Toledo of Peru ordered that the natives should not serve Spaniards against their will, and he fixed the wage to be paid them according to the kind of work done. A law of 1608 commanded that Indians working in the mines should be paid every Saturday afternoon. They were not to perform personal service for the payment of tributes.[79]

It was in the obrages, cloth or woolen mills, that the condition of the Indians was intolerable. They were brought into these establishments under the system of the mita, or were kidnapped. Many died from exhaustion and the cruel treatment which they received. Finally a law of the Indies of 1595, reaffirmed by another in 1601, prohibited the natives from laboring in workshops of cloth, wool, silk, cotton, and sugar mills. Negroes were to be employed instead. Indian boys might serve voluntarily in woolen mills, in order to learn a trade.[80] On March 2, 1596, a royal decree sent to the viceroy of Peru ordered that Indians should not spend their time making cloth for corregidores, justices, priests, or any public official.[81] In spite of these laws, the natives were still serving in the sugar mills of New Spain in 1771, for Croix said that sometimes they were locked in the refineries for whole years without being allowed to go out on the street, and were punished cruelly. Therefore this viceroy made regulations to be observed in the sugar mills, and had them posted conspicuously in the building.[82]

Negroes were imported into the colonies when Indian slaves no longer could be employed and personal service of the natives was forbidden. Negro slavery never played such a great part, either in Mexico or in the South American dependencies, as in

---

[79] Memorial of Toledo, 1596, *ibid.*, VI, 541–544; *Recopilación*, ley 9, tit. 15, lib. 6; Solórzano, I, lib. 2, cap. 8, art. 6, p. 96.

[80] Cédulas for Velasco, 1601, *Documentos inéditos . . . . de Indias*, XIX, 153–155; Monterey to the king, Oct. 4, 1599; AGI, 58–3–13; *Recopilación*, leyes 8, 10, tit. 13, lib. 6.

[81] *Documentos inéditos . . . . de Indias*, XIX, 86–87.

[82] *Instrucción que . . . . dejó*, AGI, 88–5–13.

Brazil, the West Indies, and the United States. Only in Lima was the use of slaves predominant as a form of luxury. From the census report of 1793 there were only six thousand Negro slaves in all New Spain, and most of these were found in the coastal regions. The total number of slaves for the Spanish-American possessions including the West Indies, did not exceed three-quarters of a million. In the sixteenth century, however, the slaves outnumbered the whites in many localities, and slave rebellions were sometimes a menace. In the next century Mancera said that the importation of slaves into New Spain would never be a cause for anxiety, since the number was not large and they were very docile and servile. Emancipations were frequent. Slaves could contract marriages, buy their freedom, their wives and children, and when treated cruelly could appeal to the audiencia, which could declare them free.[83]

The viceroys were to see that no Barbary slaves or Moslems entered the colonies because of the bad influence that their faith would have upon the converted Indians. They were ordered to take measures to prevent Negroes or mulattoes from living among the Indians, since their pernicious habits would set a bad example.[84] The viceroy was to make Negroes and mulattoes pay tribute to the king, and he commanded all slave owners to send their Negroes regularly to the church or monastery to receive religious instruction. They were not to work on Sundays and on religious holidays.[85]

---

[83] Humboldt, I, 236 *et seq.*; Leroy-Beaulieu, 17; Navarro y Lamarca, II, 361; Mancera to Veraguas, 1673, *Instrucciones que los vireyes* . . . . 260; King to Cañete, 1593, *Documentos inéditos* . . . . *de Indias*, XIX, 68. For the rules concerning the treatment of Negro slaves see *ibid.*, XI, 82–88. The chief Spanish authority on Negro slavery is Saco, José Antonio, *Historia de la esclavitud* (Barcelona, 1875–79).

[84] Cédulas and provisiones of 1542, 1580, *Documentos inéditos* . . . . *de Indias*, XVIII, 12, 136; *ibid.*, XI, 49–50; *Recopilación*, ley 29, tit. 5, lib. 7.

[85] *Ibid.*, leyes 1–2, tit. 5, lib. 7; leyes 13, 17, tit. 1, lib. 1.

3. FOREIGNERS

Spain's intolerant policy toward foreigners did not keep them out of America. As early as 1503 there were fifteen foreigners in the island of La Española. Shortly after the year 1550, Visitor Valderrama reported to the king that New Spain was full of them. The discovery of precious metals at Potosí caused them to rush there, often without license.[86] They usually pretended to be sailors, artillerymen, and officers on the ships in which they set sail.[87]

The Portuguese constituted, perhaps, the most numerous foreign element in the Spanish-American possessions. The Spanish government did not hesitate to bring Portuguese settlers from the Canary Islands, and many of them became the most hardy pioneers in the Spanish dependencies. Again whenever Spain and Portugal were on friendly terms, special concessions were granted to these people, as in the case of Pedro Reiner, who obtained the right (asiento) to bring a certain number of slaves into the viceroyalty of Peru by way of Buenos Aires. Under this asiento Reiner introduced some Portuguese ecclesiastics and laymen into the country. Viceroy Velasco informed the king that they were restless, seditious, and showed a difference of faith; therefore he was ordered to cast them out of Peru.[88]

During the union of the two Iberian countries under one crown, from 1580 to 1640, many Portuguese entered the viceroyalties and assimilated with the inhabitants; hence in 1641 at the time when the Duke of Braganza rose to cast off the Spanish yoke, the colonial officials had to be more vigilant than usual to exclude them from the Spanish-American domains.[89] The people

---

[86] Becker, 110; Letter of Valderrama to Philip II, *Documentos inéditos . . . . de Indias*, IV, 359.

[87] Court to Amarillas, 1755, *Instrucciones que los vireyes . . . .* art. 26, p. 68.

[88] Velasco to Monterey, 1604, *Documentos inéditos . . . . de Indias*, IV, 428–429.

[89] Royal cédula to the governor of Nueva Granada, Jan. 7, 1641, *Documentos inéditos . . . . de Indias*, VI, 567–570; Palafox to his successor, 1642, *Documentos inéditos . . . . de Mexico*, VII, 33.

of Mexico were alarmed because Viceroy Escalona was a near relative of the Duke of Braganza, and showed sympathy with the Portuguese. This became one of the causes for his recall. The real danger from the Portuguese was along the Brazilian frontiers, where at the beginning of the seventeenth century many of them entered the Spanish colonies by way of the province of Rio de la Plata. Mancera, viceroy of Peru in 1641, commanded the audiencia of La Plata to send a company of infantry into Charcas and Buenos Aires to prevent disorders and disarm the foreign inhabitants. Many Portuguese had married with the residents of Lima and Callao, but the vigilance of the viceroy prevented any disturbances.[90]

In 1528 the Germans of the Welser family were granted by Charles V the right of exploration in Venezuela, but no extensive colonization was made by them. Their chief purpose was trade, of which they had a monopoly. No merchant of any other nationality might trade there without the consent of the Welser Company. The principal complaint against them was that they charged high prices and tried to avoid paying duty on their merchandise.[91] During the administration of Viceroy Mendoza in New Spain, the king gave two Germans, Mizer Enríque and Alberto Guon, an asiento for the production of saffron and colors for drawing (pastel). The viceroy was ordered to favor them, since their undertaking might be a means of increasing the funds of the treasury.[92] German miners were likewise sent to the viceroyalties to instruct the Spaniards in the latest European methods of mining.[93]

---

[90] Order of the king to Velasco, April 16, 1601, *Documentos inéditos . . . . de Indias*, XIX, 185–186; Mancera to his successor, 1648, *in* Polo, *Memorias de los vireyes . . . .* arts. 54–57, pp. 18–19.

[91] Letter of the treasury officials of Venezuela to the king, July 30, 1530, *Documentos inéditos . . . . de Indias*, XLI, 315–317; Haring, *Trade and Navigation . . . .* 99–101.

[92] King to Mendoza, 1535, *Documentos inéditos . . . . de Indias*, XXIII, 444.

[93] Revillagigedo, *Instrucción reservada*, art. 481 *et seq.;* Lemos to Vallenari, 1796, *Memorias de los vireyes . . . .* VI, 156–157; Avilés to Abascal, 1806, *Memoria del virey del Peru*, 73.

The French gained entrance to the Spanish colonies as traders in the sixteenth century. Whenever France and Spain were hostile to each other, the indirect system of trading was evolved—namely, using a Spanish merchant's name in order to ship goods to America on the flotas and galleons. In this way a large amount of French merchandise was brought to Cartagena, Porto Bello, and Vera Cruz. This commerce did not cease during the later centuries, and many Frenchmen made their homes in Spanish America. In 1701 the French Guinea Company obtained a contract to import 42,000 Negroes into the Indies in ten years. Between the years 1707 and 1717 the ports of Chile were crowded with French vessels and many of their passengers settled in that southern province. In 1713 and 1714 the bold merchants of Saint Malo made celebrated expeditions to the port of Callao.[94] There were a few French residents in Buenos Aires in the seventeenth century, and Jacques Liniers, the brave defender of that port against the English in 1806 and 1807, was a Frenchman. Viceroy Croix of Mexico and Teodoro de Croix of Peru were Flemings.

Contact between the Spanish and French in the Gulf region caused some assimilation between the two nations. Sometimes Frenchmen held responsible positions in their new homes, as did Juan de La Conte in the presidio of Florida. He was called the prince of surgeons, physicians, and barbers, and in 1602, when he asked permission to return to Europe it was realized that his services could not be spared, and the governor recommended that his salary be raised.[95] When the French Revolution broke out a large number of French ecclesiastics sought refuge in Spain,

---

[94] For a comprehensive discussion of French trade with the Spanish possessions *see* Sinclair, Marguerite Craig, *French Commercial Relations with the Spanish-American Colonies* (M. A. thesis, Berkeley, 1922); Altamira, IV, 304–305; Watson, Robert G., *Spanish and Portuguese South America during the Colonial Period* (London, 1884), II, 163; Antúnez y Acevedo, Rafael, *Memorias históricas sobre la legislación, y gobierno del comercio de los Españoles con sus colonias en las Indias Occidentales* (Madrid, 1797), 277.

[95] Letter of the governor of Florida to the king, May 22, 1601, AGI, 54–5–9.

and, no doubt, some of them found their way to America. Repeated royal orders commanding the viceroys to take action against the French during the Revolution and the Napoleonic Wars show that many of the inhabitants were of French nationality. Both Branciforte and Marquina took action against the French in New Spain, and when the English became involved in the European wars in 1796 they suffered the same fate in Spanish America as did the French.[96]

English traders in the Spanish dependencies were never numerous. Now and then Englishmen were tried by the Inquisition, but most of them were captured pirates or smugglers, not permanent residents. From the earliest days Jews gained entrance to the Indies, many of them came with the Portuguese. They finally became powerful enough in Peru to control the commerce of Lima. It was they who most frequently fell under the ban of the Inquisition in America.[97]   A law of October 6, 1571, referred to the Genoese in the Indies, and in the following century Mancera of Mexico spoke of a contract which two Genoese had obtained to introduce Negro slaves.[98]   There were also some Dutch residents on Spanish-American soil by 1608. They had a settlement, with a Protestant church, near Puerto Cabello where they monopolized the trade in cacao and tobacco.[99]   The Manila galleons brought with them, both Chinese and Malays, who added to the race problem. A colony of Greek laborers existed near Puebla; how they came there, no one seems to know.[100]

Spain's plan of excluding foreigners was adopted to save the Indians from heretical beliefs, and preserve absolute control of all her possessions. According to the mercantile theory foreigners

[96] Branciforte to Azanza, 1798, *Instrucciones que los vireyes* . . . . arts. 11–15, pp. 130–131; Marquina to Iturrigaray, 1803, *ibid.*, art. 66 *et seq.*, p. 170; *ibid.*, arts. 44, 47, p. 166.

[97] Moses, *The Spanish Dependencies* . . . . I, 376; Riva Palacio, II, 712.

[98] Antúnez y Acevedo, 272; Mancera to Veraguas, 1673, *Instrucciones que los vireyes* . . . . 267–268.

[99] Antúnez y Acevedo, 272; Haring, *Trade and Navigation* . . . . 119.

[100] Humboldt, I, 130; Riva Palacio, II, 472, 478.

would take the gold out of the country, and thereby upset the balance of trade in favor of their nations. The severe Spanish regulations stand out in sharp contrast to England's indifference as to what kind of people went to her dependencies. In the early days commerce with foreigners was prohibited under the penalty of death, but it was soon found that this trade was needed, as Spain was not always able to supply the commercial wants of her American possessions. As a result special permission was granted for foreigners to come to the Indies. This right was called ''composición'' and at first foreigners might not leave the port where they sold their merchandise.[101] A later law of 1615 permitted them to dwell in the colonies and trade in the provinces of their residence. In 1618 and 1619 they were allowed to live where they wished and carry on their occupations.[102] A royal cédula of 1621 ordered the executive to protect foreign mechanics, if they did not engage in commerce. The viceroys were always to keep account of the number of foreigners within their jurisdictions and see that property was not willed to them.[103] Mancera published a proclamation in all the large cities of New Spain commanding all foreigners to show their licenses within four days to a special commission of judges whom he had appointed or be subject to banishment.[104] In Peru Viceroy Lemos ordered the police to find out how many Europeans had come to America since 1790, keep a record of their names and countries, and examine their passports.[105]

Viceroys frequently confiscated the property of foreigners during European wars. Cadereyta was ordered to confiscate and sell all French estates in Mexico; he appointed a commission to fulfil the royal decree, which was to be kept secret. The French residents, however, escaped the worst part of the confiscation by

101 *Recopilación*, leyes 7, 4, tit. 27, lib. 9.
102 Riva Palacio, II, 679.
103 *Recopilación*, leyes 10, 13, tit. 27, lib. 9; ley 44, tit. 32, lib. 2.
104 Rivera Cambas, I, 236.
105 Lemos to Vallenari, 1796, *Memorias de los vireyes* . . . . VI, 90–91.

sending their movable possessions to Europe with the aid of the French merchants of Spain. Again in 1689, Viceroy Galve was authorized to confiscate the property of all the French and banish them from the country.[106] In 1767 a royal cédula enjoined Amat of Peru to expel all foreigners from Callao and sell their goods. Proceedings were taken against two Frenchmen and two Genoese registered under the names of Spaniards. Their possessions were confiscated and the Spaniards who permitted them to use their names were punished.[107]

4. REGULATING THE MORALS OF THE PEOPLE

The correction of the many public sins of the people was another important duty of the viceroy.[108] The chief vices were gambling, drunkenness, falsehood, jealousy, quarreling and robbery. Stolen articles were taken in Mexico to a shop called the baratillo, where they were sold cheap to the poor. Many vagabonds and criminals assembled at this store, and caused the viceroy much annoyance. Several attempts were made to abolish it, but without success.[109] Assassinations were frequent. Viceroy Croix estimated that from eight hundred to one thousand murders were committed annually in Mexico City. The dissolute Philip IV ordered the viceroys and public officials to punish severely persons who used profane language.[110]

The viceroy tried to regulate the dress of the people and to make the lower classes wear clothes. Montesclaros ordered that women of Lima should not appear on the streets closely veiled and asked their husbands to prevent this custom. Liñan pub-

---

106 Riva Palacio, II, 593; Bancroft, *History of Mexico*, III, 223–224.
107 King to the viceroy of Peru, 1767, *Memorias de los vireyes* . . . . III, 49–52.
108 Queen to Mendoza, 1536, *Documentos inéditos* . . . . *de Indias*, XXIII, 459.
109 Linares to Valero, 1716, *Instrucciones que los vireyes* . . . . 302–304, 306; Villarroel, *Enfermedades políticas* . . . . MS, II, pt. III, pp. 195 *et seq.*
110 Croix, *Correspondance*, 206; *Recopilación*, ley 25, tit. 1, lib. 1.

lished proclamations requiring mulatto women of the same city to dress more modestly. The second Revillagigedo allowed four months for the employees of the tobacco factory and the mint of Mexico City to obtain clothes, and made it known publicly that if at the end of this time they were not properly clad they would not be admitted to the establishments.[111] The viceroys were likewise to prohibit the people from carrying weapons.[112]

Sometimes it was necessary for the viceroy to take action in regard to the family life of his people. He was to see that married men returned to Spain when their licenses had expired, and he could not permit them to remain longer in the colonies.[113] When husbands and wives made complaint about each other's conduct the viceroy investigated the facts in the case before making a final decision. If a difference concerned the common people, Croix of Mexico submitted the matter to a justice. In serious offenses between husbands and wives the viceroy had power to banish the husband and confine the wife to a convent.[114] A matrimonial dispute between a captain of the provincial militia and his wife was brought before Marquina late one night. The señora fled from the town of Tacuba in Mexico, where her husband had tried to shoot her, and came to the viceregal palace. Her father was summoned immediately by the viceroy and she was placed under the custody of her uncle, who was an administrator of the mint. Marquina tried to unite the couple, but was not successful. He then permitted the preliminary proceedings for a separation to begin and reported the matter to the king.[115] The viceroys

[111] Montesclaros to his successor, 1615, *Documentos inéditos . . . . de Indias*, VI, 230; Liñan to Palata, 1681, *Memorias de los vireyes . . . .* I, 295; Revillagigedo, *Instrucción reservada*, arts. 248, 250–251.

[112] Cédulas and provisiones for the audiencia of Charcas, 1564, *Documentos inéditos . . . . de Indias*, XVIII, 50–52.

[113] Memorial of Diego Robles, 1570, *ibid.*, XI, 14; Cédulas and provisiones for the audiencia of Charcas, 1592, *ibid.*, XVIII, 221–222; Court to Amarillas, 1755, *Instrucciones que los vireyes . . . .* art. 27, p. 68; *Recopilación*, leyes 1–2, tit. 3, lib. 7.

[114] Croix, *Instrucción que . . . . dejó*, AGI, 88–5–13; Revillagigedo to Amarillas, 1754, *Instrucciones que los vireyes . . . .* art. 72, p. 19.

[115] Marquina to Iturrigaray, 1803, *ibid.*, 222–223.

encouraged the marriage of Spanish girls and aided them as much as possible.[116]

The executive also acted as the protector of children who were punished too severely by their parents. Fathers often presented their unruly sons to the service of the king, at whose expense they were sent to the presidios without any examination of the case being made. The first Revillagigedo thought this was unjust unless the circumstances could be investigated; therefore he refused to banish ill-behaved sons.[117] Viceroy Croix was likewise annoyed by these cases and ordered the justices to inquire into the conduct of both the parents and the sons, so that innocent boys might not be sent to distant presidios.[118]

The question of regulating intoxicating beverages was another vital matter for the attention of the viceroy. Pulque was the principal intoxicant of the Indians in Mexico, but it was used by all classes as well. In 1663 the king requested the audiencia to find out whether this drink injured the health of the Indians or hindered the commerce in Spanish wines. The report of 1664 favored the continuance of the use of pulque, and the imposts placed upon it since the days of the conquest were legalized. The viceroys were to see that only thirty-six pulque shops, twenty-four for men and twelve for women, were permitted in the capital. In the food riots of 1692, Viceroy Galve prohibited the sale of pulque, but it was permitted again in 1697 by a royal cédula.[119] The first Revillagigedo ordered taverns in which Spanish wines were sold to be closed at nine o'clock, and he appointed a commission to punish the manufacturers of chinguirito or brandy made from sugar cane. These judges were also to inspect pulque shops frequently and prevent all disorders in them.[120]

---

[116] Mendoza to Velasco, *Instrucciones que los vireyes* . . . . 235.

[117] To Amarillas, 1754, *ibid.*, art. 71, p. 19.

[118] Croix, *Instrucción que* . . . . *dejó*, AGI, 88–5–13.

[119] *Recopilación*, ley 37, tit. 1, lib. 6; Riva Palacio, II, 702.

[120] Revillagigedo to Amarillas, 1754, *Instrucciones que los vireyes* . . . . art. 21, p. 9. The manufacture of chinguirito was prohibited because its sale was thought to injure the commerce of Spanish wines.

The viceroy likewise exercised control over public amusements. Mendoza was empowered to make ordinances concerning the amusements of the people. The king was informed that much gambling existed in Peru; therefore the viceroy was ordered to fine the players and use the money to aid poor girls in making good marriages.[121] The viceroys were to punish crimes committed in gambling houses, and could reprove even the oidores for frequenting such haunts.[122] Gambling was difficult to regulate, since it was carried on in private homes and in the houses of priests. The judges of the audiencia did not stop these evils because they did not wish to get into quarrels with ecclesiastics, officials, or influential families.[123]

Cockfighting was another popular amusement. In 1762 Viceroy Amat gave his consent for the construction of a building in Lima for this sport, when Juan Garial agreed to pay five hundred pesos annually to the hospital of San Andrés and one thousand pesos into the treasury for the privilege of managing the amusement.[124] Of course the bullfight was the favorite amusement of the people and was attended by all classes of people. The populace and even the highest functionaries took pleasure in public festivals to celebrate the birthday of the sovereign or the colonial executive, the canonization of saints, the dedication of churches, the entrance into the country of viceroys or archbishops, the appointment of professors in the universities, and on religious holidays. On these occasions companies of men from the gilds, the organization of the city, and noble gentlemen masqueraded to represent historical, mythological or biblical characters.[125] Sacred dramas were presented in the convents and comedies were

---

[121] Mendoza to Velasco, *ibid.*, 231–232; King to the viceroy of Peru, 1540, *Documentos inéditos . . . . de Indias*, XXIII, 498–499.

[122] *Recopilación*, leyes 2–3, tit. 2, lib. 7.

[123] Revillagigedo to Amarillas, 1754, *Instrucciones que los vireyes . . . .* arts. 23–24, p. 10; Villarroel, *Enfermedades políticas . . . .* MS, II, pt. III, pp. 178 *et seq.*

[124] Lemos to Vallenari, 1796, *Memorias de los vireyes . . . .* VI, 283.

[125] González Obregón, *México viejo*, 250–251; Pinkerton, *Modern Geography*, III, 203–204.

played at the viceregal palace. Plays were given at the Hospital Real for Indians in Mexico City, and after this building was burned in 1722, a new theater was erected.[126] According to Villarroel, all disputes arising in the theater were submitted to the viceroy, although there was a special judge of the theater appointed.[127]

The viceroy was also expected to supervise the reading of the people. He was to see that they did not have books of romance and of profane writers in their homes.[128] The chief assistant of the executive in this matter was the Inquisition, but in spite of strict regulations, during the French Revolution liberal ideas gained entrance into the viceroyalties. In Lima the young creoles assembled at the home of Antonio Nariño to read French philosophy. Nariño obtained a copy of the "Declaration of the Rights of Man" in 1794, had it printed at his residence and sent out to his friends. The viceroy gave orders for the original copy to be burned. The property of Nariño was confiscated and he was sentenced to serve in Africa for ten years, but he escaped to France.[129] After this incident Viceroy Lemos caused the secret police force to be more vigilant in preventing the propagation of liberal ideas. In New Spain the younger Revillagigedo commanded that the post office of the capital should give him notice of all foreigners who received letters and where they lived, and if necessary he would apply the same care to the other cities.[130]

The tasks of a viceroy were intricate and thankless. All the people looked to the executive for the promotion of their interests and the redress of their grievances, and were only too ready to criticize him if he failed. He was expected to be a father of the people, the patron of the monasteries, education, and hospitals, and the protector of the downtrodden. The great Mendoza

---

[126] Priestley, *The Mexican Nation*, 160–161.

[127] *Enfermedades políticas* . . . . MS, II, pt. III, p. 83.

[128] Queen to Mendoza, 1536, *Documentos inéditos* . . . . *de Indias*, XXIII, 457.

[129] Navarro y Lamarca, II, 547–548; Groot, II, 304–306.

[130] Revillagigedo to Valdes, Jan. 14, 1790, AGI, num. 111.

declared that Indian affairs alone were enough to drive a viceroy mad, and that many people were ready to offer advice and suggest corrections, but there were few who really aided him. He added that the one who governed stood alone and had to protect himself. To avoid mistakes it was necessary to act slowly and do little.[131] Enríquez said that many people in Spain thought that the viceroy's work was easy, but experience proved that this was not true, since everything had to pass through his hands in America, while a viceroy of Spain was aided in the performance of his duties by many persons.[132] Montesclaros also found it hard to govern the Indians because of their limited understanding.[133]

The viceroy's duties were rendered more burdensome when his subordinates did not consider the seriousness of their service, but merely esteemed their offices for the emoluments to be obtained from them.[134] The routine work alone, which sometimes required from four to six hours daily, made the task of administration difficult. It is said that the celebrated Revillagigedo worked during the day and part of the night, sleeping only three or four hours. Marquina stated that important matters could not be intrusted to assistants; therefore a viceroy had to work long hours without any rest.[135] Palafox laid down a safe rule to be followed by all viceroys, and later Croix suggested it to his successor saying:

It is fitting for the viceroy not to undertake [too] many reforms at one time, although he may consider them necessary for the service of the king and the public, especially in matters that may be unpopular. [He must not allow such measures] to follow each other too rapidly.[136]

---

[131] Mendoza to Velasco, *Instrucciones que los vireyes* . . . . 238.

[132] Enríquez to Coruña, 1580, *ibid.*, art. 2, p. 243.

[133] To his successor, 1615, *Documentos inéditos* . . . . *de Indias*, VI, 208.

[134] Linares to Valero, 1716, *Instrucciones que los vireyes* . . . . 316.

[135] Rivera Cambas, I, 486; Marquina to Iturrigaray, 1803, *Instrucciones que los vireyes* . . . . art. 6, p. 160.

[136] Croix, *Instrucción que* . . . . *dejó*, AGI, 88–5–13; Palafox to his successor, 1642, *Documentos inéditos* . . . . *de Mexico*, VII, 34.

The people considered the viceroy a great ruler indeed. To the populace and the Indians he seemed even higher than the monarch himself whom they had never seen and could hardly imagine. Pomp and splendor had a great attraction for the people, and many executives emphasized it in order to inspire awe and reverence. The early colonial period was an age when great personages towered far above the common people; therefore it was natural that the viceroy should be the greatest figure in colonial society—one worthy to represent the king. At the beginning of the nineteenth century this worshipful respect for the viceroy still existed in the more distant parts of the vice-royalties. When Iturrigaray visited the mines of Guanajuato the people of that region had never seen a viceroy before and their tributes to him were beyond all bounds. To them the handsome and splendidly arrayed viceroy was nothing less than a king.[137]

The viceroy governed people of many races and varying shades of complexion. The restrictive policy of emigration to the New World helped to prevent Spanish America from becoming entirely a white man's country. The whites came to be classified as Europeans and creoles or American-born Spaniards, and the greatest hostility soon arose among those two divisions because the former considered themselves superior to their American kinsmen.

The mestizos or those with Spanish and Indian blood constituted a considerable portion of the population, since unions between Spaniards and natives were encouraged from the beginning. Below the mestizos were the castes, too numerous to describe and of many different hues. Their vagabondage and crimes became a serious problem for the executive to solve. Since all the power for governing the natives was intrusted to the viceroy, he attended to their wants as a father, saw that they were converted and instructed in matters of faith, also in the elements

---

[137] *Suplemento de Bustamante,* to Cavo, art. II, pp. 668–669.

of secular learning, and tried to prevent their ill treatment under the encomienda and mita systems. He established reductions or towns where the Indians could be better instructed and taxed. He provided for the collection of tributes from the natives, endeavored to enforce the laws of personal service, and undertook to better their condition. Negroes were imported into the colonies when the natives no longer could be used as slaves, and the viceroy protected them also. Foreigners gained entrance into the Spanish possessions, in spite of the intolerant policy toward them. The Portuguese were foremost in number, then there were Germans, French, English, Italians, and Jews; in New Spain, Chinese and Malays came on the Manila galleons.

The viceroy had to regulate the morals of his people and correct their sins. He sometimes intervened in affairs relating to family life; he controlled the use of intoxicating beverages and all kinds of public amusement, and he even tried to supervise the reading of his people. His task was far from easy, for the people depended upon him to promote all their interests and to redress their grievances. On the other hand, he was compensated for the difficulties of his position by the reverence shown to him by the populace, to whom he was supreme, and in most instances he was not without the later preferences which demonstrated the gratitude of kings.

CONCLUSION

The viceroy, the direct representative of the king, was without a peer in America. He was endowed with almost royal prestige and had extensive powers, being able to do and order all that the king would provide if he were present in person. It was intended that the viceroys should be great personages; therefore some grandees, many nobles, archbishops, and military leaders were chosen to fill the high position. The viceroy was an imperial functionary far removed from all the turmoils of the conquest— an impartial umpire for all classes of people. In the name of the sovereign from whom he received his authority the viceroy acted as he thought best in cases of emergency.

As the chief administrator in the colony, the viceroy put the royal orders into effect, withheld them, or even modified them according to his own interpretation for the public welfare. He issued proclamations and ordinances concerning almost every subject, gave instructions to the governors and all minor officials in the country when the king did not do so, tried to see that only worthy persons obtained public offices, and promoted harmony among those functionaries. His power to make appointments depended on the will of the monarch. He had to inform himself concerning the conduct of all public officials whether of his own choice or of royal designation. He was empowered to rebuke them for misdeeds and suspend them temporarily from office. It was he who distributed lands as a reward for services, granted legal titles for them, and sold the public domain when the treasury needed funds. He encouraged colonization in the more distant parts of his viceroyalty to insure security against all foreign aggressions. He supervised the building of all new towns, and caused the census to be taken. Great public works, even of local nature, were under his care.

The viceroy was expected to attend to the wants of his people and redress their grievances. At all times he heard their complaints. The Spaniards hoped to win rewards and favors from him, while the populace looked to him for bread. The Indians were his special charge—his wards—to be converted, instructed, and cared for as children. The viceroy regulated amusements, corrected vices, and raised the standards of public morality, but these ends were very difficult to attain among such a diversity of races and castes.

The executives promoted such industries as had not been especially prohibited. Not many of them made great industrial reforms, however, as they were too much restricted by the narrow economic theories of their era. In every respect the industries of the viceroyalties were medieval, even up to the beginning of the nineteenth century, and the gilds flourished in all the larger towns. The chief attention of the viceroy was directed to mining and its improvement, because the royal fifths brought large amounts of wealth into the treasury.

Commerce was just as much limited as industry. It was carried on by means of the consulado, an organization of Spanish merchants, over which the viceroy exercised the right of supervision and the power to adjust all dissensions. The viceroy of New Spain had entire control of the commerce with the Philippines. All of the early colonial executives were to take severe measures against coastwise trade, but the problem of dealing with smuggling became too difficult to solve.

As superintendent of the treasury the viceroy was the head of the whole financial system in the colony. He had to keep a constant vigilance over functionaries who handled public funds in order that they might not misappropriate or misspend them. The same careful surveillance had to be exercised over the government monopolies, and over the numerous divisions of finance. When sufficient revenue to meet extraordinary expenditures did not enter the treasury by ordinary channels, the viceroy had to resort to forced loans, gifts, and other unpopular methods of raising money. A number of the more serious minded executives bent their energies upon reform of the treasury which they found empty, but others simply took temporary measures to relieve a critical situation. The protection of the riches coming from the mines and the dispatch of the treasure to the mother country were important duties of the executive. The viceroy was the president of the council of finance wherein all serious problems of the treasury were considered, and the officials of the mint were subject to him.

In theory, the viceroy in his capacity of president of the audiencia represented the king as the fountain of justice. As presiding officer he kept order among the judges, saw that their attendance was regular, settled their disputes, and determined the days for sessions. He corresponded with the other audiencias in his viceroyalty and sent instructions to them. The viceroy could decide what affairs belonged to the domain of civil administration and what might come under the jurisdiction of the audiencia. He divided the audiencia into salas and assigned the judges to serve in them. The viceroy's real judicial function, however, consisted in the power to take cognizance of Indian cases in first instance, and he was also the supreme military judge for all persons enjoying the military privileges. Over the various tribunals the executive exercised a general control through his power to adjust misunderstandings among them.

The ecclesiastical patronage—one of the king's most cherished prerogatives—was intrusted to the colonial executives. As vice-patron the viceroy aided the clergy in reforms, promoted their friendships, supervised the building and repairing of all religious establishments, and informed himself whether ecclesiastics brought licenses to come to the Indies. The viceroys directed missions in a general way, and put into effect the royal measures for the secularization of parishes and the expulsion of the Jesuits. They saw that the people paid tithes to the church; they settled religious quarrels, and caused any misdemeanors of the clergy to be punished. The vice-patron's power of making appointments in the church consisted of choosing for the office one of the three names submitted to him by the prelates. The viceroy had the right to preside at the great church councils or send a substitute. He had to take care that no papal bulls and briefs which had not been sanctioned by the Council of the Indies were circulated in his viceroyalty. He was to work in harmony with the Inquisition and the tribunal of the cruzada, but at the same time he had to prevent them from exceeding their jurisdiction. The powers of the vice-patronage likewise extended to institutions of learning. The viceroy conferred fellowships and professorships in the colleges under the royal patronage, and occasionally introduced educational reforms. Hospitals and institutions of charity were also under the vice-patron.

As captain-general the viceroy was the highest military authority in the country. It was in this office, perhaps, that he exercised most initiative. On his own responsibility the viceroy raised military forces, declared war against hostile Indians, and planned strategic methods to be applied against a sudden attack of pirates or foreign enemies. The captain-general drew up military ordinances for his viceroyalty, inspected fortifications, and reproved subordinates for their misdeeds. The task of preserving peace and order within his jurisdiction consisted of putting down Indian revolts, Negro uprisings, calming the adventurous spirits among the whites, and restraining highwaymen; but by far the greatest problem was the defense of the colony against pirates and foreign attacks. The viceroy had to keep the presidios, which served for the purpose of defense, constantly supplied with men, munitions, and provisions. The captain-general was commander-in-chief of the army and provided for all its needs. The early executives made many military appointments, but the later ones were more restricted in this respect. When armadas were in American waters, their officials were subject to the direct orders of the viceroy. It was under the powers of the captain-general that vast regions of both North and South America were explored and many conquests made.

The viceroy was aided in civil administration by his secretaries, his council, the audiencia, and the cabildos. It was in the secretariat that the numerous details so burdensome to the Spanish system of government were worked out. The viceregal council advised and also assisted the viceroy in gubernatorial affairs. The executive assigned some duties of a civil nature to the judges of the audiencia, and to the municipal councils, but the latter bodies needed continual watching because they were apt to become negligent. In matters of justice the viceroy was assisted by his assessor, who was a lawyer. It was by means of him that the viceroy was able to take cognizance of Indian and military cases. Ecclesiastics, both regulars and seculars, were the chief agents who carried out the wishes of the vice-patron. They undertook for him the tremendous work of converting and civilizing the Indians. The Inquisition aided the viceroy in preserving the purity of the faith, and in detecting and destroying prohibited writings. The junta de real hacienda was the council on which the viceroy relied most to solve difficult financial problems, but he was also aided by the tribunal of accounts. In military matters the captain-general was assisted and advised by the council of war, and the chief official of this military board, the auditor de guerra, became one of his principal legal advisers.

Many limitations were imposed upon the viceroys in order to keep them under royal control. They did not have power to originate legislation, and there was no law-making in the colonies except by bandos and special ordinances. Then too, the almost endless reports concerning every imaginable subject which the viceroy was required to send to the king left no opportunity for him to do anything that the monarch did not know about. The audiencia was always a check upon the viceroy's authority, for the judges were permitted to correspond directly with the sovereign, and at any time they might give him information against the viceroy. The very necessity of consulting his council had a slight restraining influence upon the executive, even if he seldom took its advice. Among the people whom he governed there were always some who were influential enough to gain a hearing at the royal court; accordingly it became necessary for the viceroy to be careful about his conduct. Custom itself came to serve as a limitation upon the power of later viceroys. In financial matters viceroys were checked by not being permitted to draw funds from the treasury without a royal order except under extraordinary circumstances. The dread of the visitation tended to curb the actions of many viceroys and keep them in the path of duty. The establishment of the office of regent in 1776 and of the intendancies by 1786, while they were created to relieve the work of the viceroy, at the same time decreased his powers. When the other means employed to restrain a viceroy failed, the fear of the residencia was, as a rule, effective in keeping him faithful to his duties.

The chief weakness of some of the viceroys was due to the fact that they were trained only for military service. They were often incapable of performing well civil and other gubernatorial duties. On the other hand, viceroys who were ecclesiastics were naturally more interested in religious matters. Generally an archbishop viceroy was a better civil administrator than a military chieftain. Grandees were not any better than the other viceroys. One of the great defects of the Spanish colonial system was that the very detailed nature of the laws and instructions of the viceroy did not leave room for him to develop his abilities to the highest point. Only a great man or a favorite of the king could rise above the petty regulations. There was a total lack of democratic development— that great redeeming but perturbing feature of any colonial system.

Strong traces of viceregal administration still exist in the Spanish-American countries. The military tradition of the captain-general is much alive. It may be seen in the numerous military dictatorships of the Latin-American republics. The functions of the captain-general seemed to appeal most to the popular imagination; therefore the military spirit naturally lived on, although independence was won. Another bad effect of the viceregal system arose from its paternalism which was always injurious to the development of the self-reliance of the people. Everything was mapped out for the American subjects by the most minute regulations and there was no need for them to think for themselves. When the controlling power of Spain and the viceroy was removed the people were as children without a guide. The narrow economic restrictions of the early days caused commercial and industrial backwardness, and as a result, some of the smaller republics are still struggling with financial problems and have had to submit to foreign intervention in the matter of settling debts. Remains of the encomienda system may be seen in the peonage of the large estates in Mexico, and in the disdain for manual labor on the part of the upper classes. The exclusion of the creoles from public offices deprived the Americans of valuable training in public administration, the effects of which are still being experienced.

And yet the viceregal system was a great success in many respects. The very fact that under it the vast colonial empire was spread and maintained for a span of almost three centuries is its best recommendation. In the colonial era the highly centralized form of administration was better than any other. It was able to ward off foreign enemies at a time when Europe was seething with wars and intrigues. It controlled the various admixture of races and castes with a strong hand and at the same time assimilated them, leaving them united in religion, language, culture, and traditions. The heritage of Spain in the New World is the fruit of long lines of able administrators at the head of four princely kingdoms, through whose official intervention in every detail of life the transmission of European culture was superintended.

THE VICEROYS OF MEXICO

1535–1550. Antonio de Mendoza, count of Tendilla.

1550–1564. Luis de Velasco (died in office).

July 31, 1564–Sept. 1566. Audiencia.

1566–1568. Gastón de Peralta, marquis of Falces.

March 1568–Nov. 5, 1568. Audiencia.

1568–1580. Martín Enríquez de Almansa.

1580–1583. Lorenzo Suárez de Mendoza, count of Coruña (died in office).

June 19, 1583–Sept. 25, 1584. Audiencia.

1584–1585. Pedro Moya de Contreras, archbishop of Mexico.

1585–1590. Álvaro Manrique de Zúñiga, marquis of Villamanrique.

1590–1595. Luis de Velasco, marquis of Salinas (the younger).

1595–1603. Gaspár de Zúñiga y Acevedo, count of Monterey.

1603–1607. Juan de Mendoza y Luna, marquis of Montesclaros.

1607–1611. Luis de Velasco, marquis of Salinas.

1611–1612. Frey García Guerra, archbishop of Mexico (died in office).

Feb. 22, 1612–Oct. 18, 1612. Audiencia.

1612–1621. Diego Fernández de Córdoba, marquis of Guadalcázar.

March 14, 1621–Sept. 12, 1621. Audiencia.

1621–1624. Diego Carrillo de Mendoza y Pimentel, marquis of Gelves.

Feb. 15, 1624–Nov. 3, 1624. Audiencia.

1624–1635. Rodrigo Pacheco y Osorio, marquis of Cerralvo.

1635–1640. Lope Díaz de Armendáriz, marquis of Cadereyta.

1640–1642. Diego López Pacheco, duke of Escalona.

1642 (June to November). Juan de Palafox, archbishop of Mexico.

1642–1648. García Sarmiento de Sotomayor, count of Salvatierra.

1648–1649. Marcos de Torres y Rueda, bishop of Yucatan (died in office).

April 22, 1649–June 28, 1650. Audienca.

1650–1653. Luis Enríquez de Guzmán, count of Alba de Liste, marquis of Villaflor.

1653–1660. Francisco Fernández de la Cueva, duke of Alburquerque.

1660–1664. Juan de Leiva y de la Cerda, marquis of Leiva and count of Baños.

1664 (June to October). Diego Osorio de Escobar, bishop of Puebla.

1664–1673. Antonio Sebastián de Toledo, marquis of Mancera.

1673. Pedro Nuño Colón de Portugal, duke of Veragua (died in office).

1673–1680. Frey Payo Enríquez de Rivera, archbishop of Mexico.

1680–1686. Tomás Antonio de la Cerda y Aragón, count of Peredes, marquis of Laguna.

1686–1688. Melchor Portocárrero, count of Monclova.

1688–1696. Gaspar de la Cerda Sandoval, count of Galve.

Jan. 21, 1696–Feb. 27, 1696. Audiencia.

1696 (February to December), Juan Ortega y Montañez, bishop of Michoacán.

1696–1701. José Sarmiento Valladares, count of Moctezuma.

1701–1702. Juan Ortega y Montañez, archbishop of Mexico.

1702–1711. Francisco Fernández de la Cueva Enríquez, duke of Alburquerque.

1711–1716. Fernando de Alencastre, duke of Linares (died before leaving Mexico).

1716–1722. Baltasar de Zúñiga, marquis of Valero.

1722–1734. Juan de Acuña, marquis of Casafuerte (died in office).

1734–1740. Juan Antonio de Vizarrón y Eguiarreta, archbishop of Mexico.

1740–1741. Pedro de Castro y Figueroa, duke of la Conquista (died in office).

Aug. 22, 1741–Nov. 3, 1742. Audiencia.

1742–1746. Pedro Cebrián y Agustín, count of Fuenclara.

1746–1755. Juan Francisco de Güémes y Horcasitas, 1st count of Revillagigedo.

1755–1758. Agustín de Ahumada y Villalón, marquis of Amarillas (died in office).

1758–1760. Francisco Cagigal de la Vega (ad interim).

Feb. 5, 1760–April 28, 1760. Audiencia.

1760–1766. Joaquín de·Montserrat, marquis of Cruíllas.

1766–1771. Carlos Francisco de Croix, marquis of Croix.

1771–1779. Frey Antonio María de Bucareli y Ursúa (died in office).

April 9, 1779–Aug. 29, 1779. Audiencia.

1779–1783. Martín de Mayorga (ad interim).

1783–1784. Matías de Gálvez (died in office).

Nov. 3, 1784–June 17, 1785. Audiencia.

1785–1786. Bernardo de Gálvez (died in office).

Oct. 15, 1786–March 8, 1787. Audiencia (Regent Eusebio Ventura Beleña).

1787 (May to August). Alonso Núñez de Haro y Peralta, archbishop of Mexico (ad interim).

1787–1789. Manuél Antonio Flórez.

1789–1794. Juan Vicente de Güémes Pacheco de Padilla, count of Revillagigedo.

1794–1798. Miguel de la Grúa Talamanca y Branciforte, marquis of Branciforte.

1798–1800. Miguel José de Azanza.

1800–1803. Félix Berenguer de Marquina.
1803–1808. José de Iturrigaray.
1808–1809. Pedro de Garibay.
1809–1810. Francisco Xavier de Lizana y Beaumont, archbishop of Mexico.
May 8, 1810–Sept. 13, 1810. Audiencia.
1810–1813. Francisco Xavier de Venegas.
1813–1816. Felix María Calleja del Rey.
1816–1821. Juan Ruiz de Apodaca, count of Venadito.
1821.   Juan O'Donojú (died in office).

APPENDIX II

VICEROYS OF PERU

1544–1546. Blasco Núñez Vela (died in office).
1546–1551. The licenciado Pedro de la Gasco (president of the audiencia).
1551–1552. Antonio de Mendoza, ex-viceroy of Mexico (died in office).
1552–1555. Audiencia.
1555–1561. Andrés Hurtado de Mendoza, marquis of Cañete (died before Nieva came).
1561–1564. Diego de Acevedo y Zúñiga, count of Nieva (died in office).
1564–1569. The licenciado Lope García de Castro (entitled governor and captain-general).
1569–1581. Francisco de Toledo.
1581–1583. Martín Enríquez, ex-viceroy of Mexico (died in office).
1583–1585. Audiencia.
1585–1590. Fernando de Torres y Portugal, count of Villardompardo.
1590–1596. García Hurtado de Mendoza, marquis of Cañete.
1596–1604. Luis de Velasco, marquis of Salinas, ex-viceroy of Mexico.
1604–1605. Gaspar de Zúñiga y Acevedo, count of Monterey, ex-viceroy of Mexico (died before leaving Peru).
1605–1607. Audiencia.
1607–1615. Juan de Mendoza y Luna, marquis of Montesclaros, ex-viceroy of Mexico.
1615–1621. Francisco de Borja y Aragón, prince of Esquilache.
1621–1622. Audiencia.
1622–1629. Diego Fernández de Córdoba, marquis of Guadalcázar, ex-viceroy of Mexico (died in office).
1629–1639. Jerónimo Fernández de Cabrera, Bobadilla y Mendoza, count of Chinchón.
1639–1648. Pedro de Toledo y Leyva, marquis of Mancera.
1648–1655. García Sarmiento de Sotomayor, count of Salvatierra, ex-viceroy of Mexico.

1655–1661. Luis Enríquez de Guzmán, count of Alba de Liste, ex-viceroy of Mexico.

1661–1666. Diego de Benavides y de la Cueva, count of Santisteban (died in office).

1666–1667. Audiencia.

1667–1672. Pedro Fernández de Castro y Andrade, count of Lemos (died in office).

1672–1674. Audiencia.

1674–1678. Beltasar de la Cueva Enríquez y Saavedra, count of Castellar.

1678–1681. Melchor de Liñan y Cisneros, archbishop of Lima.

1681–1689. Melchor de Navarra y Rocafull, duke of Palata (died at Porto Bello).

1689–1705. Melchor Portocarrero, count of Monclova, ex-viceroy of Mexico (died in office).

1705–1707. Audiencia.

1707–1710. Manuel Oms de Santa Pau, marquis of Castelldosríus (died in office).

1710–1716. Diego Ladrón de Guevara, bishop of Quito.

1716–1720. Carmine Nicholás Caracciolo, prince of Santo Bono.

1720–1724. Frey Diego Morcello Rubio de Auñón, archbishop of la Plato.

1724–1736. José de Armendáriz, marquis of Castel-Fuerte.

1736–1745. Antonio José de Mendoza, marquis of Villagarcía.

1745–1761. José Antonio Manso de Velasco, count of Superunda, ex-captain-general of Chile.

1761–1776. Manuel de Amąt y Junyent, ex-captain-general of Chile.

1776–1780. Manuel de Guirior, ex-viceroy of Nueva Granada.

1780–1784. Agustín de Jáurequi, ex-captain-general of Chile.

1784–1790. Teodoro de Croix.

1790–1796. Fancisco Gil de Taboado y Lemos, ex-viceroy of Nueva Granada.

1796–1801. Ambrosio O'Higgins, marquis of Osorno, ex-captain-general of Chile.

1801–1806. Gabriel de Avilés y Fierro, marquis of Avilés, ex-captain-general of Chile and ex-viceroy of Buenos Aires (died before leaving Peru).

1806–1816. José Fernando de Abascal.

1817.   Joaquín de la Pezuela.

APPENDIX III

VICEROYS OF NUEVA GRANADA

1718–1719. Antonio de la Pedrosa y Guerrero.
1719–1724. Jorge Villalonga (office of viceroy suppressed).
1740–1749. Sebastián Eslava.
1749–1753. José Alfonso Pizarro, marquis of Villar.
1753–1761. José Solís Folch y Cardona.
1761–1773. Pedro Mejía de la Cerda.
1773–1775. Manuel Guirior.
1775–1776. Audiencia.
1776–1782. Manuel Antonio Flórez.
1782.   Juan Pimienta, ex-governor of Cartagena (died in 4 days).
1782–1788. Antonio Caballero y Góngora, archbishop of Santa Fé.
1788–1789. Audiencia.
1789 (January to July). Francisco Gil y Lemos.
1789–1797. José de Espeleta Galdeano Dicastillo y Prado, ex-captain-general of Cuba.
1797–1803. Pedro Mendinueta.
1803–1810. Antonio Amar y Borbón.

APPENDIX IV

VICEROYS OF RIO DE LA PLATA

1776–1778. Pedro Antonio de Caballos.
1778–1784. Juan José de Vertíz.
1784–1789. Nicolás del Campo, marquis of Loreto.
1789–1795. Nicolás de Arredondo.
1795–1797. Pedro Melo de Portugal.
1797–1799. Audiencia and Antonio Olaguer Feliu.
1799–1801. Gabriel de Avilés.
1801–1804. Joaquín de Pino y Rozas.
1804–1806. Rafael de Sobremonte.
1806–1809. Santiago Liniers.
1809–1810. Baltasar Hidalgo de Cisneros.

BIBLIOGRAPHY

I. LIST OF MANUSCRIPTS CITED

ALBURQUERQUE to Philip II, Mexico, March 31, 1703, AGI, 61–1–23. Consulta en vista del papel que hace acusación contra Alburquerque. Madrid, June 2, 1711, AGI, 60–5–2.

AZANZA. Instrucción sobre las provincias de la Nueva España; dada por el Exmo. Sr. D. José de Azanza á su sucesor. . . . á 29 de Abril de 1800.

BUCARELI. Personal and official correspondence of Bucareli and others. Havana and Madrid, 1777–80, AGI, 146–4–1. Private correspondence of Bucareli, Arriaga, Grimaldi, etc., AGI, 146–4–2.

CASAFUERTE to Patiño, Mexico, November 1, 1731, AGI, 90–2–17. Summary of events in the kingdom. Mexico, April 16, 1733, AGI, 61–2–14.

CROIX, CHARLES FRANÇOIS, marqués de Croix, Instrucción que dejó . . . . a su sucesor Don Antonio Bucarely y Ursua. Mexico, September 1, 1771, AGI, 88–5–13.

ENRÍQUEZ to Philip II, Mexico, December 13, 1577, AGI, 58–3–96.

FUENCLARA. Instrucción reservada que dió al conde de Fuenclara para el gobierno de Nueva España. Aranjuez, April 23, 1742, AGI, 90–2–17.

GÁLVEZ, JOSÉ DE. Instrucción reservada al visitador general Joseph Gálvez. Madrid, March 14, 20, 1765, AGI, 136–5–3.

GOVERNOR of Florida to the King, May 22, 1602, AGI, 54–5–9.

GRIMALDI to Bucareli, El Pardo, February 23, 1774, AGI, 146–4–2.

LEYES DE INDIAS (Código de . . . . with addenda and glosses to 1801).

MARQUINA to Urquijo, Mexico, October 27, 1800, AGI, Papeles de estado, leg. 9, num. 107.

MEDÉLLIN to the king, AGI, 141–5–8.

MONTEREY to the king, Mexico, April 25, 1598, AGI, 58–3–13. To the king, Mexico, May 8, 1598, AGI, 58–3–13. To the king, Mexico, October 4, 1599, AGI, 58–3–13. To the king, Mexico, May 20, 1601, AGI, 53–3–13.

MONTESCLAROS to the king, Mexico, January 15, 1604, AGI, 58–3–15.

ORDENES DE LA CORONA.

REVILLAGIGEDO to Porlier, Mexico, January 10, 1790, AGI, 89–6–13.

To Valdes, Mexico, January 14, 1790, AGI, num. 111.

To Valdes, Mexico, March 27, 1790, AGI, num. 388 (28).

To Porlier, Mexico, April 26, 1790, AGI, 89–6–13.

To Porlier, Mexico, April 30, 1790, AGI, 89–6–13.

To Valdes, Mexico, April 30, 1790, AGI, num. 115.

To Floridablanca, Mexico, October 30, 1790, AGI, leg. 1, num. 55.

Dictamen que en cumplimiento de reales ordenes de S. M. produce el virey de Nueva España conde de Revillagigedo, sobre la precisión de adicionar la ordenanza de yntendentes expedida en 4 de dizre de 1786, Mexico, May 5, 1791. Mexico, Archivo general y público, 54, num. 402.

September 1, 1791, Mexico, AGI, 24, num. 128.

Residencia de 1795.

Testimo. de los autos sobre el asalto y attaque que los Indios Cumanches hicieron en el presidio de San Luis de las Amarillas que esta a cargo del coronel Don Diego Ortiz Parrilla. AGI, 92–6–22.

VELASCO al consejo, Mexico, AGI, 58–3–11.

To the king, Mexico, October 8, 1590, AGI, 58–3–11.

To Philip II, Mexico, December 22, 1590, AGI, 58–3–11.

To Philip II, Mexico, June 6, 1591, AGI, 58–3–11.

To the king, Mexico, October 30, 1591, AGI, 58–3–11.

To Philip II, Mexico, March 6, 1592, AGI, 58–3–11.

To Philip II, Mexico, June 2, 1592, AGI, 58–3–11.

To the king, Mexico, February 2, 1593, AGI, 58–3–11.

To the king, Mexico, October 24, 1594, AGI, 58–3–12.

To Philip II, Mexico, October 25, 1594, AGI, 58–3–11.

Los advertimientos que el virey D. Luis Velasco dejó al conde de Monterey. Mexico, 1595, AGI, 58–3–13.

Los advertimientos que el virey Don Luis Velasco dejó al conde de Monterey para el gobierno de Nueva España. AGI, 58–3–11.

VILLAMANRIQUE. Memorial del marqués de Villamanrique, AGI, 58–3–11.

To the king, Mexico, May 10, 1586, AGI, 58–3–9.

To Philip II, Mexico, October 28, 1587, AGI, 58–3–10.

To Philip II, Mexico, January 17, 1589, AGI, 58–3–11.

VILLARROEL, HIPÓLITO.

Enfermedades políticas que padece la capital de esta Nueva España en casi todos los cuerpos de que se compone; y remedios, que se la deben aplicar para su curación si se quiere qué sea util al rey y al público. Tomos 4.

Justa repulsa del reglamento de intendencias de 4 de diciembre de 1786. Motivos en que se funda. Providencias que debieron tomarse con anticipación para que fuese menos dificil el establecimiento, y reglas

que se prescriben para que pueda ser util al rey y a los vasallos.
Sirve también de apendice a las Enfermedades políticas y remedios
para su curación, del mismo autor. Mexico, 1787; contemporary
copy in the Bancroft Library.
Vireyes de Mexico, instrucciones, residencias, ser. 1 and 2.

II. PRINTED DOCUMENTS AND LAWS

Archivo mexicano. Documentos para la historia de Mexico. 2 vols.
Mexico, 1852–1853.

Avilés, Gabriel de Avilés y del Fiero, marqués de.
Memoria del virey del Peru. Lima, 1901. Carlos Alberto Romero, ed.

Barrio Lorenzot, Francisco de.
Ordenanzas de gremios de la Nueva España. Mexico, 1920. Genaro
Estrada, ed.

Beleña, Eusebio Bentura.
Recopilación sumaria de todos los autos acordados de la real audiencia
y sala del crimen de esta Nueva España y providencias de su superior
govierno. 2 vols. Mexico, 1787.

Cartas de Indias. Madrid, 1877.

Colección de documentos para la historia de España. 113 vols. Madrid.
1842–1912.

Colección de documentos inéditos, relativos al descubrimiento, conquista y
organización de las antiguas posesiones españolas de América y
Oceanía. 42 vols. Madrid, 1864–1884. Many of the instructions of
the viceroys are found in this collection.

Colección de libros y documentos referentes a la historia del Peru. 15 vols.
in 8. Lima, 1916–1920.

Documentos inéditos ó muy raros para la historia de Mexico. 35 vols.
Mexico, 1905–1911.

Documentos para la historia de Mexico. 21 vols. in 17. 4 series, Mexico,
1853–1857.

Gálvez, José de.
Informe general que en virtud de real órden instruyó y entregó el Exmo.
Sr. marqués de Sonora, siendo visitador general de este reino, al
Exmo. Sr. virey frey D. Antonio Bucarely y Ursua con fecha de 31
de diciembre de 1771. Mexico, 1867.
Reglamento del gremio de panaderos de esta capital para su abasto y
erección de un pósito de trigos y harinas á beneficio de su común.
Mexico, 1771.

GARCÍA ICAZBALCETA, JOAQUÍN, ed.
Colección de documentos para la historia de México. 2 vols. Mexico, 1858–1866.
Nueva colección de documentos para la historia de Mexico. 5 vols. Mexico, 1886–1892.

HERNÁEZ, FRANCISCO JAVIER.
Colección de bulas, breves y otros documentos relativos á la iglesia de América y Felipinas. 2 vols. Bruselas, 1879.

INSTRUCCIONES que los vireyes de Nueva España dejaron a sus sucesores. Mexico, 1867. This volume contains ten of the instructions of the viceroys of Mexico to their successors, two royal instructions to the viceroys, and some of the correspondence of the viceroys.

MEMORIAS de los vireyes del Peru, Lima, 1896. José Toribio Polo, ed. This volume contains the instructions of Mancera and Salvatierra to their successors.

MEMORIAS de los vireyes que han gobernado el Peru. 6 vols. Lima, 1859. These volumes consist of the long and very detailed instructions of ten viceroys to their successors.

MONTEMAYOR Y CÓRDOVA DE CUENCA, JUAN FRANCISCO DE.
Sumarios de las cédulas, ordenes, y provisiones reales, que se han despachado por su Majestad, para la Nueva España. Mexico, 1678.

ORDENANZA del consulado de la universidad de mercaderes de esta Nueva España (1636). Mexico, 1772.

PÉREZ Y LÓPEZ, ANTONIO XAVIER.
Teatro de la legislación universal de España é Indias, por orden chronológico de sus cuerpos, y decisiones no recopiladas. 28 vols. Madrid, 1791–1798.

PUGA, VASCO DE.
Provisiones, cédulas, instrucciones de su Magestad . . . . para la administración y governación de esta Nueva España . . . . desde el año 1525 hasta . . . . 1563. 2 vols. Mexico (1563), 1878.

REAL ORDENANZA para el establecimiento é instrucción de intendentes de ejército y provincia en el reino de la Nueva España. Madrid, 1786.

REALES ORDENANZAS para la dirección, régimen y gobierno del importante cuerpo de la minería de Nueva España, y de su real tribunal general. Madrid, 1783.

RECOPILACIÓN de leyes de los reinos de las Indias. 3 vols. Ed. 4; Madrid, 1791.

REGLAMENTO y aranceles reales para el comercio libre de España e Indias de 12 de octubre de 1778. Madrid, 1778.

REVILLAGIGEDO, JUAN VICENTE GÜÉMEZ PACHECO DE PADILLA HORCASITAS Y
AGUAYO, conde de.

Instrucción reservada que el conde de Revilla Gigedo, dió a su sucesor
en el mando, marqués de Branciforte sobre el gobierno de este
continente en el tiempo que fue su virey. Mexico, 1831.

RODRÍGUEZ DE SAN MIGUEL, JUAN NEPOMUCENO.

Pandectas hispano-megicanos, ó sea código general comprensivo de las
leyes generales, utiles y vivas de las Siete partidas, Recopilación
novísima, la de Indias, Autos y providencias conocidas por de Montemayor y Beleña, y cédulas posteriores hasta el año de 1820. 3 vols.
Mexico, 1852.

SOLÓRZANO Y PEREYRA, JUAN DE.

Política indiana. 2 vols. Madrid (1629–1639), 1776. Francisco Ramiro
de Valenzuela, ed.

III. OTHER MATERIALS

AITON, ARTHUR.

Antonio de Mendoza, First Viceroy of New Spain. MS. (Ph.D. Thesis,
Dept. of History, University of California). Berkeley, 1923.

ALAMÁN, LUCAS.

*Disertaciones sobre la historia de la república megicana desde la época
de la conquista que los Españoles hicieron á fines del siglo XV y
principios del XVI de las islas y continente americano hasta la
independencia.* 3 vols. Mexico, 1844–1849.

*Historia de Méjico desde los primeros movimientos que prepararon su
independencia en el año de 1808 hasta la época presente.* 5 vols.
Mexico, 1849–1852.

ALCEDO, ANTONIO DE.

Diccionario geográfico-histórico de las Indias Occidentales ó America.
5 vols. Madrid, 1786–1789.

ALTAMIRA Y CREVEA, RAFAEL.

Historia de España y de la civilización española. 4 vols. Barcelona,
1913–1914.

ÁLVAREZ, IGNACIO.

Estudios sobre la historia general de México. 6 vols. Zacatecas,
1869–1877.

ANCONA, ELIGIO.

Historia de Yucatan desde la época más remota hasta nuestros días.
4 vols. Ed. 2; Barcelona, 1889.

ANTEQUERA, JOSÉ MARÍA.

Historia de la legislación española. Ed. 2; Madrid, 1884.

ANTÚNEZ Y ACEVEDO, RAFAEL.
    *Memorias históricas sobre la legislación y gobierno del comercio de los
    Españoles con sus colonias en las Indias Occidentales.* Madrid, 1797.
ARMSTRONG, EDWARD.
    The Emperor Charles V. 2 vols. London and New York, 1902. London, 1910.
BANCROFT, HUBERT HOWE.
    History of Arizona and New Mexico, 1530–1888. San Francisco, 1889.
    History of California. 7 vols. San Francisco, 1882–1887.
    History of Central America. 3 vols. San Francisco, 1882–1887.
    History of Mexico. 6 vols. San Francisco, 1883–1887.
    History of the North Mexican States and Texas. 2 vols. San Francisco, 1884–1889.
BECKER, JERÓNIMO.
    La política española en las Indias. Madrid, 1920.
BERISTAIN Y SOUZA, JOSÉ MARIANO.
    Biblioteca hispano americano setentrional. 4 vols. Amecameca and
    Santiago de Chile, 1883–1897. Adiciones y correcciones, Mexico, 1898.
Biographie universelle ancienne et moderne. 21 vols. Brussels, 1843–1847.
BLACKMAR, FRANK WILSON.
    Spanish Institutions of the Southwest. Baltimore, 1891.
BOLTON, HERBERT EUGENE.
    Athanase de Mézières and the Louisiana-Texas Frontier, 1768–1780.
    2 vols. Cleveland, 1914.
    *Guide to Materials for the History of the United States in the Principal
    Archives of Mexico.* Washington, 1913.
    The Spanish Borderlands, A Chronicle of Old Florida and the Southwest. New Haven, 1921.
    *Texas in the Middle Eighteenth Century. Studies in Spanish Colonial
    History and Administration.* Berkeley, 1915.
BOLTON H. E. and MARSHALL, T. M.
    The Colonization of North America, 1492–1783. New York, 1922.
BOURNE, EDWARD GAYLORD.
    Spain in America, 1450–1580. New York, 1904.
BURKE, EDMUND.
    An Account of the European Settlements in America. London, 1808.
CAVO, ANDRÉS.
    *Los tres siglos de Méjico durante el gobierno español hasta la entrada
    del ejército trigarante; obra escrita en Roma por el padre D. Andrés
    Cavo de la compañia de Jesús. Publicado con notos y suplemento
    en 1836 por el licenciado D. Carlos María de Bustamante.* Jalapa, 1870.

CHAPMAN, CHARLES EDWARD.

The Founding of Spanish California; the Northwestward Expansion of New Spain, 1687–1773. New York, 1916.

A History of California: The Spanish Period. New York, 1921.

A History of Spain. New York, 1918.

"Palmares: the Negro Numantia," *Journal of Negro History,* 1918, III, 29–32.

The Spanish Consulados of the Eighteenth Century. MS. (Master's Thesis, Dept. of History, University of California), Berkeley, 1909.

COLMEIRO, MANUEL.

Historia de la economía política en España. 2 vols. Madrid, 1863.

COROLEU É INGLADA, JOSÉ.

América, historia de su colonización, dominación é independencia. 3 vols. Barcelona, 1894–1895.

COXE, WILLIAM.

Memoirs of the Kings of Spain of the House of Bourbon. 5 vols. London, 1815.

CROIX, CHARLES FRANÇOIS, marqués de Croix.

Correspondance du marquis de Croix capitaine general des armees de S.M.C., vice-roi du Mexique. Nantes, 1891. Charles Marie Philippe de Croix, ed. Contains a translation of the Instrucción que.... dejó, listed in the manscript sources.

Varias cartas del marqués de Croix, XLV virey de la Nueva España. Brussels, 1884. A. Núñez Ortega, ed.

CUNNINGHAM, CHARLES HENRY.

The Audencia in the Spanish Colonies. Berkeley, 1919.

"The Institutional Background of Spanish-American History," *Hispanic American Review,* I, 24–39.

"The Residencia in the Spanish Colonies," *Southwestern Historical Quarterly,* XXI, 253–278.

DANVILA Y COLLADO, MANUEL.

El poder civil en España. 6 vols. Madrid, 1885–1886.

Historia del reinado de Carlos III. 6 vols. 1891–1896. *In* Real academia de la historia, Madrid, *Historia general de España.* 18 vols. Madrid, 1890–1898. Antonio Cánovas del Castillo, ed.

Significación que tuvieron en el gobierno de América la Casa de la Contratación de Sevilla y el Consejo Supremo de Indias. Madrid, 1892. *In* Ateneo científico, literario y artístico de Madrid, *el continente Americano; conferencias dadas con motivo del cuarto centenario del descubrimiento de América.* 'Tomo III. 3 vols. Madrid, 1894.

DESDEVISES DU DÉSÈRT, GASTÓN.
  L'Espagne de l' ancien régime: III. Les institutions. Paris, 1899.
  "La Louisiane á la fin due XVIIIᵉ siècle," *Revue de l'histoire des colonies françaises,* tŕoisième annèe, 235–260.
  "Vice-rois et capitaines gènèraux des Indes espagnoles a fin du XVIIIᵉ siècle," *Revue historique,* CXXV, 223–264; CXXVI, 14–60, 225–270.
  Diccionario universal de historia y de geografía. 10 vols. Mexico, 1853–1856.

DUNN, WILLIAM EDWARD.
  "Apache Mission," *Southwestern Historical Quarterly,* XVIII, 389–390.
  Spanish and French Rivalries in the Gulf Region of the United States, 1678–1702. Austin, Texas, 1917.

ENGELHARDT, FR. ZEPHYRIN.
  The Missions and Missionaries of California. 5 vols. San Francisco, 1908–1916,

ESCRICHE, JOAQUÍN.
  Diccionario razonado de lagislación y jurisprudencia. 3 vols. Madrid, 1847–1851.

FABIE, ANTONIO MARÍA.
  Ensayo histórico de la legislación española en sus estados ultramar. Madrid, 1896.

FERNÁNDEZ, DIEGO.
  Historia del Peru. 2 vols. Madrid, 1913–1914.

FEUDGE, SISTER MARGARET MARY.
  The Viceregal Administration of Luis de Velasco the Second. MS. (Master's Thesis, Dept. of History, University of California), Berkeley, 1920.

FONSECA, FABIÁN and CARLOS DE URRUTIA.
  Historia generai de real hacienda escrita por . . . . orden del virey, conde de Revillagigedo. 6 vols. Mexico, 1845–1853.

GALLO, EDUARDO L., ed.
  Hombres ilustres mexicanos. 3 vols. Mexico, 1873–1874.

GARCÍA, GENARO.
  El clero de Mexico durante la dominación española, segun el archivo archiepiscal metropolitano. Mexico, 1907.
  Don Juan de Palafox. Mexico, 1918.
  La Inquisición de Mexico, sus orígines, jurisdicción, competencia, procesos, autos de fé relaciones con los poderes públicas, ceremoniàs, etiquetas y otros hechos. Mexico, 1906.

GARCÍA ICAZBALCETA, JOAQUÍN.
  Obras. 2 vols. in 1. Mexico, 1905.

GACETAS DE MÉXICO.
    44 vols.   Mexico, 1784–1821.

GÓMEZ ZAMORA, MATÍAS.
    Regio patronato, español é indiano.   Madrid, 1897.

GONZÁLEZ OBREGÓN, LUIS.
    *México viejo; noticias históricas, tradiciones, leyendas y costumbres,
    1521–1821.*   Paris, Mexico, 1900.
    Los precursores de la independencia Mexicana en el siglo XVI.   Mexico,
    1906.

GRANADOS Y GÁLVEZ, FR. JOSEPH JOAQUÍN.
    *Tardes americanas; gobierno católico; breve y particular noticia de toda
    la historia indiana.*   Mexico, 1778.

GROOT, JOSÉ MANUEL.
    Historia eclesiástica y civil de Nueva Granada.   5 vols.   Ed. 2; Bogotá,
    1889–1893.

HANOTAUX, GABRIEL.
    *Origines d' institution des intendants des provinces d' après les docu-
    ments inedits.*   Paris, 1884.

HARING, CLARENCE HENRY.
    The Buccaneers in the West Indies in the XVII Century.   New York,
    1910.
    *Trade and Navigation between Spain and the Indies in the Time of the
    Hapsburgs.*   Cambridge, London, 1918.

HELPS, SIR ARTHUR.
    *The Spanish Conquest in America and its Relation to the History of
    Slavery and to the Government of Colonies.*   4 vols.   New York,
    1900–1904.   M. Oppenheim, ed.

HERRERA Y TORDESILLAS, ANTONIO DE.
    *Historia general de los hechos de los Castellanos en las islas i tierra
    firme.*   4 vols.   Madrid, 1601–1615.

HUGHES, CONSTANCE.
    Trade Gilds of New Spain.   MS. (Master's Thesis, Dept. of History,
    University of California), Berkeley, 1921.

HUMBOLDT, ALEXANDER.
    Political Essay on the Kingdom of New Spain.   4 vols.   London, 1814.

JAMES, HERMAN G. and MARTIN, PERCY A.
    *The Republics of Latin America, Their History, Governments and
    Economic Conditions.*   New York, London, 1923.

JONES, O. GARFIELD.
    ''Local Government in the Spanish Colonies as provided by the Re-
    copilación,'' *Southwestern Historical Quarterly,* XIX, 65–90.

JUAN, JORGE and ULLOA, ANTONIO DE.
   Noticias secretas de America. Madrid, 1826.
   ''A Voyage to South America,'' in Pinkerton, John, *A General Collection
   of the Best and Most Interesting Voyages and Travels in all Parts
   of the World,* XIV. London, 1813.

KELLER, ALBERT GALLOWAY.
   Colonization. Boston, New York, London (cop. 1908).

KLEIN, JULIUS.
   ''The Church in Spanish American History, *Catholic Historical Review,*
   III, October, 1917.

LAFUENTE, MODESTO.
   Historia general de España. 30 vols. Madrid, 1850-1867.

LANNOY, CHARLES DE, and HERMAN VANDER LINDEN.
   *Histoire de l' expansion coloniale des peuples Européens. Portugal et
   Espagne.* Brussels, 1907.

LAS CASAS, BARTOLOMÉ.
   Historia de las Indias . . . . *ahora por primera vez dada á luz por el
   marqués de la Fuensanta del Valle y Don José Sancho Rayon* . . . .
   5 vols. Ginesta, 1875-76.

LEA, HENRY CHARLES.
   The Inquisition in the Spanish Dependencies. New York, 1908.

LERDO DE TEJADA, MIGUEL.
   *Apuntes históricos de la heróica ciudad de Vera Cruz desde su funda-
   ción hasta nuestros días.* 5 parts. Mexico, 1850-1851.
   Comercio exterior de Mexico desde la conquista hasta hoy. Mexico, 1853.

LEROY, JAMES A.
   ''The Philippine 'situado' from the Treasury of New Spain,'' *The
   American Historical Review,* X, 929-932; XI, 722-723.

LEROY-BEAULIEU, PIERRE PAUL.
   De la colonisation chez les peuples modernes. Ed. 4; Paris, 1891.

Liceo Mexicano, el. 2 vols. Mexico, 1844.

LORENZANA, FRANCISCO ANTONIO.
   Historia de Nueva España. Mexico, 1770.

LOWERY, WOODBURY.
   The Spanish Settlements within the Present Limits of the United States.
   Florida, 1562-1574. New, York, 1911.

MARKHAM, SIR CLEMENTS ROBERT.
   A History of Peru. Chicago, 1892.

MARTÍNEZ ALCUBILLA, MARCELO.
   Diccionario de la administración española, peninsular, y ultramarina.
   12 vols. Madrid, 1868-1870.

MEDINA, JOSÉ TORIBIO.
   Historia del tribunal del santo oficio de la Inquisición en Mexico.
   Chile, 1905.

MENDIETA, GERÓNIMO DE.
   Historia eclesiástica indiana, obra escrita á fines del siglo XVI.
   Mexico, 1870.

MERRIMAN, ROGER BIGELOW.
   The Rise of the Spanish Empire in the Old World and in the New. 3 vols.
   New York, 1918–1925.

MOSES, BERNARD.
   The Establishment of Spanish Rule in America. New York, 1898.
   Papers on the Southern Spanish Colonies of America. Berkeley, 1911.
   South America on the Eve of Emancipation. New York, 1908.
   Spain's Declining Power in South America 1730–1806. Berkeley, 1919.
   The Spanish Dependencies in South America. 2 vols. London, 1914.

NAVARRO Y LAMARCA, CARLOS.
   Compendio de la historia general de America. 2 vols. Buenos Aires,
   1913.

NEWTON, ARTHUR PERCIVAL.
   *The Colonizing Activities of the English Puritans; the last Phase of
   the Elizabethan Struggle with Spain.* New Haven, 1914.

OROZCO, WISTANO LUIS.
   Legislación y jurisprudencia sobre terrenos baldíos. 2 vols. Mexico,
   1895.

PINKERTON, JOHN.
   *Modern Geography, A Description of the Empires, Kingdoms, States
   and Colonies, with the Oceans, Seas and Isles, in all Parts of the
   World.* 3 vols. London, 1807.

PRIESTLEY, HERBERT INGRAM.
   José de Gálvez, Berkeley, 1916.
   The Mexican Nation, A History. New York, 1923.
   ''Spanish Colonial Municipalities,'' *California Law Review,* September
   1919, and the *Louisiana Historical Society Quarterly,* April 1922
   (1923).

RIBADENEYRA, ANTONIO JOACHIN.
   Manual compendio de el regio patronato indiano. Madrid, 1755.

RICHMAN, IRVING BERDINE.
   California under Spain and Mexico, 1535–1847. Boston, 1911.

RIVA PALACIO, VICENTE, ed.
   México á través de los siglos. 5 vols. Barcelona, 1888–1889.

RIVERA, AGUSTÍN.
Principios críticos sobre el vireinato de la Nueva España i sobre la revolución de independencia. 3 vols. San Juan de los Lagos, 1884–1888.

RIVERA CAMBAS, MANUEL.
Los gobernantes de México. 2 vols. Mexico, 1872–1873.

ROBERTSON, WILLIAM.
The History of Amertca. Ed. 1; 2 vols. London, 1777.

ROSCHER, WILHELM GEORG FRIEDRICH.
The Spanish Colonial System. New York, 1904. E. G. Bourne, ed.

SACO, JOSÉ ANTONIO.
Historia de la esclavitud. 3 vols. Barcelona, 1875–1879.

SCELLE, GEORGES.
La traite négrière aux Indes de Castille. 2 vols. Paris, 1906.

SCHMIDT, GUSTAVUS.
The Civil Law of Spain and Mexico. New Orleans, 1851.

SCHURZ, WILLIAM LYTLE.
"The Manila Galleon and California," *Southwestern Historical Quarterly*, XXI, 107–126.
A Study in the Beginning of trans-Pacific Trade. MS. (Master's Thesis, Dept. of History, University of California), Berkeley, 1912.

SHEA, JOHN GILMARY.
The Catholic Church in Colonial Days. 4 vols. New York, 1886–1892.

SINCLAIR, MARGUERITE CRAIG.
French Commercial Relations with the Spanish American Colonies. MS. (Master's Thesis, Dept. of History, University of California), Berkeley, 1922.

SMITH, DONALD EUGENE.
The Viceroy of New Spain. Berkeley, 1913.

STEVENS, H. and LUCAS, F. W.
The New Laws of the Indies for the Good Treatment and Preservation of the Indians 1542–1543. London, 1893.

STEVENSON, W. B.
A Historical and Descriptive Narrative of Twenty Years' Residence in South America. 3 vols. London, 1825.

SUÁREZ DE FIGUEROA, CRISTOBAL.
Hechos de D. García Hurtado de Mendoza cuarto marqués de Cañete. *In* Markham, Sir Clement Robert, *The Hawkins' Voyages during the Reigns of Henry VIII, Queen Elizabeth, and James I.* Hakluyt Society, London, 1878.

360   *University of California Publications in History* [Vol. 15]

TORQUEMADA, JUAN DE.
   Primera [segunda, tercera] parte de los veinte i un libros rituales i monarchia indiana. 3 vols. Madrid, 1723.

TWITCHELL, RALPH EMERSON.
   The Leading Facts of New Mexican History. 2 vols. Cedar Rapids, 1911–1912.

VANDER LINDEN, HERMAN.
   ''L'expansion coloniale de l'Espagne jusqu'au début du XIXᵉ siècle,'' in C. de Lannoy and H. Vander Linden, *Histoire de l'expansion coloniale des peuples Europeens,* 241–436.

VETANCURT, AGUSTÍN DE.
   Teatro mexicano, descripción breve de los sucessos. 4 vols. Mexico, 1870–1871.

VILLA-SEÑOR Y SÁNCHEZ, JOSÉ ANTONIO DE.
   Teatro americano, descripción general de los reynos, y provincias de la Nueva-España, y sus jurisdicciones. 2 vols. Mexico, 1746–1748.

Voyages interessans dans different colonies. London, 1788.

WÄTJEN, HERMANN.
   Das Hollandische Kolonialreich in Brazilian. Haag, Gotha, 1921.

WATSON, ROBERT G.
   Spanish and Portuguese South America during the Colonial Period. 2 vols. London, 1884.

WRIGHT, IRENE A.
   The Early History of Cuba 1492–1586. New York, 1916.

ZAMACOIS, NICETO DE.
   Historia de Méjico desde sus tiempos más remotos hasta nuestros días. 18 vols. Mexico, 1877–1882.

ZAMORA Y CORONADO, JOSÉ MARÍA.
   Biblioteca de legislación ultramarina. 6 vols. Madrid, 1844–1846.

INDEX

Vizarrón, Juan Antonio de, viceroy of Mexico, charges against, 46; ordered to confiscate an estate, 55; aiding the sick, 78; archbishop, 169; stopping circulation of papal bulls, 220; putting down Negro revolt, 258.

Vizcaíno, Sebastián, 299.

Wallace, Peter, 270.

Wallis, English explorer in northern Pacific, 271.

War of Jenkin's Ear, 270.

War of the Spanish Succession, 253, 262, 292.

Warrants, on the treasury, 95–96, 98, 99.

Weapons, 280, 329.

Welser Company in Venezuela, 324.

West Indies, 126, 262, 265, 267, 270, 291, 295, 322.

Wheat, introduction of, 108.

Windward Islands, 126.

Wine shops, 80; industry of, 110; 330, 330 n. 120.

Women, audience with, 161; education of, 237; hospitals for, 243; 245, 247; might not have encomiendas, 315; 328, 329.

Wool industry, 111.

Workshops, 159, 246.

Writings, prohibited, 228–229, 332.

Yanaconas, 316.

Yanaguanca, parish in Peru, 192.

Yanga, Negro leader, 258.

Yubillaga, Joaquín, 166.

Yucatan, 109; open to commerce, 126; 263; laid waste by corsairs, 267; English colony of, 270; 276.

Zabala, Bruno de, 89.

Zacatecas, mines in Mexico, 57, 298.

Zambos, 285.

Zárate, Ortíz de, 23.

Zeballos, archbishop of Lima, 212.

Zumárraga, Fray Juan, 206.

Zumpango, lake in Mexico, 65.

Zuñi, villages in New Mexico, 298.

Zúñiga, Francisco de, 246.

Zúñiga, Manso de, archbishop of Mexico, 223.